D0929987

CLEARED FOR TAKEOFF

Airline Labor Relations Since Deregulation

E 70

Edited by Jean T. McKelvey

ILR PRESS
New York State School of Industrial and Labor Relations
Cornell University

Cover design by Kat Dalton

Library of Congress Cataloging-in-Publication Data

Cleared for takeoff : airline labor relations since deregulation /
    edited by Jean T. McKelvey
        p.   cm.
    Includes indexes.
    ISBN 0-87546-139-5.   ISBN 0-87546-140-9 (pbk.)
    1. Collective bargaining—Aeronautics—United States—Con-
gresses. 2. Aeronautics, Commercial—United States—Deregulation—Congresses.
    I. McKelvey, Jean T. (Jean Trepp) 1908–
HD6515.A427C56   1988
331.89′0413877′0—dc19   88-21578
                                                            CIP

*The chapters by Seth Rosen, Jalmer D. Johnson, and Captain Henry A.
Duffy are printed by permission of the Air Line Pilots Association, Washington, D.C.*

Copies may be ordered from
ILR Press
New York State School of
Industrial and Labor Relations
Cornell University
Ithaca, NY 14851–0952

Printed on acid-free paper in the United States of America
5   4   3   2   1

331.8904138
C623

Contents

Tables and Figures

Preface

On June 16–18, 1987, the New York State School of Industrial and Labor Relations at Cornell University, the National Mediation Board (NMB), and the Society of Professionals in Dispute Resolution (SPIDR) jointly sponsored a national conference on air transport labor relations, held in Washington, D.C. The program was developed by a twenty-two-member planning committee chaired, as was the conference, by Mark L. Kahn, then president of SPIDR. The committee also included Marcia Greenbaum, the immediate past president of SPIDR; Lamont Stallworth, then first vice president of SPIDR; three members of the NMB—Walter Wallace, Helen Witt, and Charles Woods; and Alice Grant and Jean T. McKelvey of the New York State School of Industrial and Labor Relations.[1]

This was the second national conference on labor relations in the airlines, the first having been held in 1969 at Southern Methodist

---

1. The other members of the planning committee were Meredith Buel, NMB; Michael H. Campbell, Ford & Harrison; Peter Cappelli, University of Pennsylvania; James E. Conway, NFL Management Council; Stephen Crable, Association of Flight Attendants; William J. Curtin, Morgan, Lewis & Bockius; Terry M. Erskine, Northwest Airlines; Robert H. Nichols, Cotton, Watt, Jones & King; Charles A. Pasciuto, American Airlines; Charles M. Rehmus, arbitrator; Seth D. Rosen, Air Line Pilots Association; William L. Scheri, International Association of Machinists; Charles W. Thomson, Flying Tiger Line; and Roland P. Wilder, Jr., Baptiste & Wilder.

University in Dallas.[2] In the interim, the Airline Deregulation Act had been enacted. The impact of this momentous legislation on airline labor relations was the theme of the 1987 conference.

From the outset, the planning committee was well aware of the then-current turbulent nature of airline labor relations, although it hardly anticipated how rapidly developments would take place both before and after the conference as new mergers and acquisitions swept the industry and many of the players on both the management and union teams lost their positions, moved to other airlines, or changed bargaining agents. The fears of a few skeptics that this turbulence would wreak havoc with the best-laid plans of the planning committee proved unfounded. Not only did all forty speakers who were asked to speak respond enthusiastically, but with only a few exceptions, they submitted their papers ahead of the deadline. The plenary session speakers included Robert L. Crandall, chief executive officer, American Airlines; Henry A. Duffy, president, Air Line Pilots Association; Carl Icahn, president, Trans World Airlines; William W. Winpisinger, president, International Association of Machinists; and Alfred E. Kahn, who, as chairman of the Civil Aeronautics Board in 1977–78, had acquired the title of "the father of deregulation."

Attendance at the conference was by invitation only. The three hundred guests included industrial relations staff from every major carrier; officials and staff from all major airline unions; NMB mediators; arbitrators with substantial experience in the airline industry; and economists who have done significant research in airline labor relations. As described by Helen Witt, this was "the first time that airline management and labor had had an opportunity to join ranks in a national forum to discuss the changing developments and critical problems that have affected the industry so dramatically since airline deregulation." Another participant labeled the conference as "the kind of family picnic the industry really needed at this time." Benjamin Aaron, professor emeritus of law at the University of California, Los Angeles, who accepted the unenviable task of summarizing the conference, closed the proceedings with these comments:

---

2. The papers and discussions from that conference were published in 35 J. Air Law & Commerce (Summer 1969).

In summary, all speakers agreed that deregulation has caused a great upheaval in the airline industry. Labor representatives stressed the hardships deregulation has caused airline employees and called for a limited amount of regulation, for example: statutory imposition of labor protective provisions; management representatives emphasized the opportunities created by deregulation for industry growth, higher employment, and greater benefits to both shareholders and consumers.

Everybody calls for more cooperation and less confrontation in labor-management relations; but if the views expressed by the union speakers and the management speakers reflect the prevailing attitudes in the industry, the new era of good feeling is not yet a realistic possibility except in a few individual cases.

The Conference itself, however, provided valuable opportunity for union and management protagonists to meet face to face and to explore their differences calmly and candidly. What effect, if any, it will have on day-to-day relationships in the industry remains to be seen.[3]

Except in a few instances, I have refrained in editing the volume from the temptation to update material written for the conference. I or the authors have noted significant changes, however, in areas such as administrative rulings or legislative policy. What is captured is a snapshot of changing labor relations in the airline industry at a moment in time.

Much of what has happened to airline labor relations as a consequence of deregulation has also occurred in other industries subject to deregulation, such as trucking and communications. Moreover, although the papers in this volume are confined to developments in a single industry, they deal with topics and problems that are significant in the larger universe of industrial relations in the United States today, such as two-tier wage systems, concession bargaining, alcohol and drug testing, employee assistance programs, employee stock ownership plans, the rise of nonunion competition, double-breasted operations, and takeovers, mergers, and acquisitions. As in many other industries, labor relations in the airlines are undergoing a transformation whose outcome cannot be predicted at this time.[4]

This volume should also provide the background necessary to understand emerging developments in the airline industry. Many of these issues are the subject of great interest and attention in the

---

3. Quoted in 11 SPIDR News (Aug.-Nov. 1987).

4. See T.A. Kochan, H. Katz, & R. McKersie, The Transformation of American Industrial Relations 121–27 (1986).

media, as well as in Congress and in such administrative agencies as the NMB, the Federal Aviation Administration, and the Department of Transportation.

Because of limitations of space and the need to avoid repetition and redundancy, not all of the excellent papers presented at the conference could be included in this volume. Those selected have also suffered cuts and excisions. In making these changes, I have been assisted by the authors, whose cooperation has been invaluable, and by four anonymous outside reviewers, whose painstaking appraisals and evaluations have been uniformly helpful. Unfortunately, because they remain anonymous, they cannot be thanked by name.

Throughout the process of preparing this volume for publication, the ILR Press rendered its usual superb assistance. In particular, I wish to acknowledge the encouragement, ideas, and technical editorial help I received from Erica Fox, who served as overall editor, and from Frances Benson, the director.

Finally, everyone involved in the conference owes enormous gratitude to Mark L. Kahn for his indomitable and unflagging efforts to recruit the speakers, design the program, and demand the high quality evident in the presentations.

I am also grateful for the enlightening introduction he has written for this volume. It was eminently fitting that at the October 1987 SPIDR annual conference Walter Wallace, a member of the National Mediation Board, presented outgoing President Mark Kahn with a Distinguished Service Award, only the second one conferred by the NMB in the first half-century of its existence. This award was given in recognition of his "Distinguished Service to the Airline Industry" in conceiving, planning, and executing the 1987 Air Transport Labor Relations Conference.

JEAN T. McKELVEY
December 1987

Introduction
Mark L. Kahn

With the enactment in October 1978 of the Airline Deregulation
Act, the airline industry was "cleared for takeoff" into a radically
changed market environment. Forty years of structural stability under rigorous but maternal economic regulation by the Civil Aeronautics Board (CAB) would now be replaced by reliance on open
competition. Except for some temporary restrictions, the airlines,
old and new, could now fly on any domestic routes they chose and
set whatever fares they elected to charge.

Widespread and bipartisan support for airline deregulation led to
its consideration by Congress in 1975 at the initiative of President
Gerald Ford. Subsequently, deregulation was strongly endorsed by
President Jimmy Carter and by the CAB. Alfred E. Kahn, President
Carter's 1977 appointee as CAB chairman, summarized the views
of those favoring deregulation:

> Understandably, in view of its mission to nurture and promote the
> growth of what was once a weak, infant industry, regulation has had a
> strong tendency to protect the established carriers against competition,
> both among themselves and from newer aspiring entrants seeking to
> offer the public new and more diversified choices in service quality and
> price....
> ... Air transportation shows all the signs of being, potentially, a nat-
> urally competitive industry. But for government restrictions, entry
> would be relatively easy. So would exit. This is one of the few industries
> in which the physical capital employed can itself move easily out of

1

crowded into empty markets. In these circumstances, it is extremely difficult to envisage competition becoming destructive.[1]

Unions in the airline industry did not share the sanguine expectations of the deregulation advocates, and five of them told Congress:

[T]his proposed experiment in free market economics would be of no measurable benefit to the traveling and shipping public but would cause irreparable harm to airline employees. Stronger carriers would seize this opportunity to abandon their public service responsibilities and to prey upon their weaker competitors in their profitable markets. Cutthroat price competition would undoubtedly ensue resulting in a bloodbath of financially-depressed airlines and a reorganization of the industry into an oligopolistic structure insensitive to the needs of consumers. To invite such consequences would be shortsighted and foolhardy.[2]

What now seems clear, in retrospect, is that the decision to deregulate air transportation, and the accompanying timetable, was adopted with virtually no analysis of its probable impact on labor relations institutions, job rights, and employment conditions. As Robert L. Crandall, chief executive officer of American Airlines, notes in his chapter of this volume:

Unfortunately, we have heard far too little about the most profound change of all: the impact of deregulation on the *people* who work for our nation's airlines and on whom the public depends for the high service standards that have been the hallmark of America's commercial aviation industry.

As indicated in editor Jean McKelvey's preface, this was a void that the June 1987 Air Transport Labor Relations Conference was de-

---

1. Testimony before the House Budget Committee Task Force on Tax Expenditures, Government Organization, and Regulation (July 14, 1977).

2. Statement to Congress dated April 18, 1977, by the Airline Labor Coordinating Committee of the AFL-CIO, composed of the Air Line Pilots Association (ALPA), Brotherhood of Railway and Airline Clerks (BRAC), Flight Engineers International Association (FEIA), International Association of Machinists (IAM), and Transport Workers Union (TWU), quoted in M.L. Kahn, *Airlines*, in COLLECTIVE BARGAINING: CONTEMPORARY AMERICAN EXPERIENCE 339 (G.G. Somers, ed., Industrial Relations Research Association, 1980).

signed to fill, and all of the papers in this volume were initially prepared for that conference.

Airline deregulation prompted a surge of nonunion "upstart" carriers. Of 128 that entered the field, only 37 have survived,[3] but their inroads have encouraged a variety of anti-competitive responses by the major airlines, including a wave of mergers; bilateral code-sharing arrangements between major carriers and regional and commuter lines, where small carriers are listed and operate under a large carrier's name; use of computer reservations systems for marketing advantages;[4] hub-and-spoke route structures, with major-carrier domination of hub airports; restriction of access to terminal gates, especially at hubs, by major carriers;[5] and "frequent-flyer" programs that encourage fidelity to major carriers.

Meanwhile, during the nine years since deregulation, external economic and political events have exerted substantial influence on developments in the airline industry. Notable among these events were a threefold increase in fuel prices and substantial inflation (1978–80) followed by a deep recession (1980–83) during which employment in the industry fell from 361,000 to 329,000. Many of the low-cost upstart airlines were born during this recession, aided by the availability of laid-off airline employees and surplus aircraft. It was also during this recession that the federal government effectively broke the August 1981 strike called by the Professional Air Traffic Controllers Association (PATCO) and discharged the strikers. And it was near the end of the recession, on September 24, 1983, that Continental Airlines declared bankruptcy under Chapter 11, abrogated its collective bargaining agreements, cut its pay scales in half, and resumed business on a nonunion basis. Braniff also

---

3. See Sapulkas, *Young Airlines Stagger*, N.Y. Times, Nov. 23, 1987, at 24, 30.

4. United's Apollo CRS and American's Sabre CRS handle 70 percent of all passenger bookings by U.S. travel agents. The other major CRSs are Systemone (Texas Air Corp.), DATAS II (Delta), and PARS (TWA/Northwest).

5. According to Walter Adams and James W. Brock, "The airline oligopoly blocks potential competitors by tying up gates through exclusive long-term leases and by obstructing expansion plans by local airport authorities. In some cases gates go unused because established carriers either refuse to lease them or demand astronomical rents." *Why Flying Is Unpleasant*, N.Y. Times, Aug. 6, 1987, at 23.

declared bankruptcy and persuaded its unions to accept wage rates comparable to those at Continental.

The creation of holding companies facilitated expansion and diversification. Texas Airlines' holding company, Texas Air Corporation, created New York Air in 1980 as a distinct, nonunion, low-cost carrier and accomplished a hostile takeover of Continental in 1981. The unions' inability to upset Texas Air's "double-breasting" tactic through either the courts or the National Mediation Board became a significant inhibition on union bargaining power and a basis for demanding stringent "scope" clauses in current agreements.

At the collective bargaining table, carriers that found themselves in economic difficulty pressed hard for and secured concessions through pay freezes and cuts and through changes in work rules that reduced labor costs. The unions, in return, demanded a quid pro quo through stock ownership programs, profit-sharing schemes, and similar arrangements. Financially healthy major carriers, with prederegulation pay scales and benefits, pushed for a lower pay level for all new hires at so-called "market rates," that is, at or close to those of the nonunion upstarts. On this basis, they argued, expansion on a competitive basis would become feasible. In sharp contrast with the broadly comparable national patterns and levels of compensation established prior to deregulation, as discussed by Jalmer Johnson in this volume, negotiations became heavily enterprise-oriented and employee compensation became increasingly disparate among carriers.

The national economy, and with it the airline industry, began its recovery in 1984. Airline employment rose from 329,000 in 1983 to more than 400,000 in 1986. A pilot surplus became a severe shortage as new hires jumped from one thousand per year in 1980–82 to seven thousand per year during 1985–87.[6] A wave of mergers swept the industry in 1985 and 1986, leaving many carriers unwilling or unable to rely on earlier hopes for internal expansion.

Mergers and acquisitions during 1985 included Southwest-Muse, Carl Icahn–TWA, People Express–Frontier, and United–Pan Am Pacific. In 1986, the list included Piedmont-Empire, Northwest-Republic, Texas Air–Eastern, TWA-Ozark, People Express–Britt and PBA, Delta-Western, Alaska–Jet America, Texas Air–People

---

6. See Cook, *Wanted: A Lot of Good Pilots*, U.S. News & World Report, Nov. 9, 1987, at 83–84.

Revenue Passenger Miles of Top Nine Airlines

1979		1987	
Carrier	% of RPMs	Carrier	% of RPMs
United	19.4	Texas Air Co.	20.7
American	13.9	United	17.7
Delta	12.0	American	15.1
Eastern	11.4	Delta	12.6
TWA	10.2	Northwest	8.3
Western	4.7	TWA	6.7
Braniff	4.6	USAir	5.2
Continental	4.4	Piedmont	3.1
Northwest	4.1	Southwest	2.5
TOTAL	84.7	TOTAL	91.9

Express, American–Air California, Alaska-Horizon, and USAir-PSA. Three of these mergers were approved by the Department of Transportation over objections by the Department of Justice.[7] The percentage of the airline industry's domestic revenue passenger miles flown by the nine largest carriers, which had fallen from 84.6 in 1979 to 74.3 in 1985, rose to 91.9 percent by May 31, 1987.

As shown in the table, the top nine airlines, based on shares of domestic scheduled revenue passenger miles (RPMs), changed quite dramatically from 1979 to 1987.[8] Seth Rosen of the Air Line Pilots Association observes in the first chapter of this volume:

> [T]he rules governing mergers ... have become increasingly unclear, resulting in more tumultuous mergers. First, no longer has there been a CAB [Civil Aeronautics Board] to impose labor protective provisions to ensure an orderly process for the establishment of seniority. ... Second, the courts rejected enforcement of contractual provisions that would have ensured the survival of the working agreements when representation issues were deemed to exist and be subject to the jurisdiction of the National Mediation Board.

---

7. United–Pan Am Pacific, Northwest-Republic, and TWA-Ozark. Former CAB Chairman Alfred Kahn and others have been critical of the U.S. government for its failure to use the antitrust laws to bar some of these mergers. See Adams and Brock, supra note 5.

8. Data from Department of Transportation for the twelve-month period ending September 30, 1979, and the twelve-month period ending May 31, 1987.

Rosen also notes that carriers in holding companies could elect to operate acquired airlines as separate subsidiaries and "pit one group [of employees] against the other."

In spite of these traumatic changes in industry structure, airline unions have been regaining some of the leverage lost during the 1980–83 recession years. Tighter labor markets, especially for pilots, have contributed to the negotiation of higher pay scales for new hires than were originally conceded and to reductions in the number of years before pay scales merge. The unions have also learned how to intervene in airline merger activities, using concession offers as major bait. They prevented a Texas Air takeover of TWA by facilitating Carl Icahn's acquisition. United's pilots, unhappy with the policies of holding company Allegis Corporation, offered to purchase United for $4.5 billion and were instrumental in effecting a change in corporate management. A Pan American union coalition, seeking a change in top management, has offered significant cost concessions in return.

Union-management relations will continue to be a vital process in the airlines. All of the major carriers remain substantially organized except for Continental (within which Eastern remains a well-unionized unit) and Delta (a high-standard employer where only the pilots and dispatchers are unionized). Deregulation spawned an era of much bitterness and hostility in airline labor relations, as well as a host of inventive responses to unprecedented challenges. There are many indications that as oligopoly, although now unregulated, restrains and moderates price competition, and in the presence of healthy consumer demand and tighter labor markets, unions will remain a strong force in the airline industry and will recoup some of the bargaining power that was dissipated by deregulation.

Parts 1 and 2 provide a wealth of insight from varied perspectives on postderegulation collective bargaining and on the labor market context in which the process has operated. Part 3 explores significant and complex issues relating to union representation in airline mergers, an area in which the National Mediation Board devised new procedures that were announced on July 31, 1987. In part 4, job and seniority rights in the post-CAB era, as well as the role of successorship clauses, are subjected to analysis and debate.

Under deregulation, airlines have made vigorous efforts to provide service during strikes, not only by urging striking employees to cross picket lines but also by hiring strike replacements. Part 5 examines the practice and effectiveness of mediation as a means of avoiding or shortening strikes, as well as the critical legal issues pertaining to the strike behavior of airlines, unions, and airline employees.

Part 6 examines grievance arbitration in the airlines by tripartite system boards of adjustment, including efforts to expedite the process. Readers will not be surprised that the emergence of hostility and confrontation between a carrier and a union can impair the effectiveness of system boards.

Part 7 is an intensive consideration of substance abuse in the airline industry. Because the problem pervades our society, the airline experience can provide important insight to all employers and unions. As the three chapters in this part indicate, the courts are involved in issues relating to whether public policy considerations (i.e., air safety) can provide a valid basis for exceptions to the principle of deferral to arbitration awards.

Part 8 completes the volume with a look at the present and future of airline labor relations. Three presidents of airline unions (the machinists', flight attendants', and pilots'), the CEO of a healthy mega-carrier (American), and the vice president of personnel of a sturdy survivor (Midway) present their differing but hopeful perspectives. The appetizer preceding this main course is an up-to-date look at airline deregulation by its principal "architect," economist Alfred Kahn.

Some observers believe that the shakeout in air transportation will soon lead to a large dose of reregulation. This volume should help ensure that whatever public policies are in store, labor relations considerations will not be neglected again.

Part 1
Collective Bargaining

A Union Perspective

Seth D. Rosen

On October 24, 1978, Congress enacted the Airline Deregulation Act (ADA),[1] thus ending approximately forty years of economic regulation in the airline industry. Deregulation eliminated the regulatory scheme that controlled airline start-ups, entries and exits out of markets, rates, and mergers. As stated in the preamble, the ADA was enacted to "encourage, develop and attain an air transportation system which relies on competitive market forces to determine the quality, variety, and price of air services."

Congress was aware that deregulation could have negative effects on airline employees who "entered the industry and shaped their careers in reliance on a regulatory system which gave them a measure of job security as well as existing careers."[2] Congress believed, however, that eventually deregulation would increase the total number of jobs by creating a more competitive environment. Congress envisioned a ten-year phase-in period in which the competitive capabilities of the carriers and their ability to adjust to the new environment would be tested.[3]

Regulatory changes were intended to promote more competitive pricing activity, establish greater flexibility to respond to changing

---

Significant contributions to this chapter were made by Jane Schraft, Bruce York, Ana McAhron-Schultz, and Eileen Betit.

1. Airline Deregulation Act of 1978, 49 U.S.C. §1301, et. seq.
2. S. Rep. No. 631, 95th Cong., 2d Sess. 113 (1978).
3. *Id.* at 116.

market demands, and increase management incentive to improve overall efficiency. As with other cost increases, wage increases could no longer be automatically passed on to consumers through increased ticket prices. As the established carriers adjusted to deregulation, they became better able to fend off challenges to their markets. Alfred Kahn, the former chairman of the Civil Aeronautics Board (CAB) and the "architect" of airline deregulation, now acknowledges that airline deregulation has not worked out as planned. Rather than fostering greater competition, deregulation has produced a group of mega-carriers with feeder networks offering potentially far less competition than had been intended.[4]

The issues and demands raised in collective bargaining since deregulation have not been unique. There had been similar requests for concessions, hard bargaining, and confrontations in the years before deregulation. Never before, however, had so many unions been faced with confrontational negotiations and requests for concessions at the same time. And not since the early days of unionization in the airline industry had groups faced a management so willing to engage in self-help to achieve its "bottom-line" objectives. Frank Borman, former head of Eastern Airlines, summarized the situation best: "In the final analysis, the Deregulation Act, if it was nothing else, was the greatest anti-labor act ever passed by an American Congress."[5]

Deregulation did not turn the airline industry upside down overnight. Many of the free-market provisions in the act contained delayed implementation dates. For example, not all of the entry and pricing barriers were eliminated until 1983, and the CAB was not eliminated until December 1984.

This chapter examines how collective bargaining in the airline industry has changed over the past nine years under deregulation. It is useful in examining this period to divide it into three phases.

Phase I (1978–81): The New Environment

INDUSTRY CONDITIONS

During the first phase of deregulation, the incumbent carriers were faced with new operating rules. Management had no choice but to

---

4. *Competition Thins Out at 30,000 Feet*, N.Y. Times, June 29, 1986.

5. Presentation by Frank Borman at Lehman Brothers Kuhn Loeb Airline Industry Seminar, New York (Feb. 11–13, 1982).

develop and implement new strategic plans to function in an open-market environment. The established carriers needed to make fundamental decisions about their future structure, including whether to expand or realign their route structures, maintain or expand their market shares, expand through internal or external growth, or restructure themselves into holding companies.

No single path was followed by the carriers; a decision that succeeded for one carrier could be the demise of another. Braniff, the early "darling of deregulation," responded by expanding rapidly. It was the first to use the liberalized rules governing market entry. Other carriers also adopted the philosophy that expansion and "critical mass" were essential to long-term viability and attempted to achieve growth through mergers and acquisitions. These carriers included Texas International, Continental, Pan American, North Central, and Flying Tiger. Others, such as Pacific Southwest, Piedmont, and USAir, expanded more gradually. New carriers also entered the marketplace, including Midway (1979), Muse (Transtar) (1980), People Express (1980), and New York Air (1980). Other carriers adopted a wait-and-see approach to expansion.

The creation of People Express, Muse, Midway, New York Air, and other expansionist airlines created fierce competition in the marketplace and ultimately at the bargaining table. These new competitors entered the market with used aircraft acquired at bargain prices; minimal overhead because they contracted for maintenance and other services from the established carriers; a surplus of airline employees, especially pilots; and low labor costs because they hired new employees at entry-level pay rates. Deregulation enabled the new entrants to compete directly with the established carriers in major markets. The influence of new airlines, coupled with increased competition from established carriers for a share of the market, resulted in fare cuts of as much as 75 percent on previously lucrative routes. Hardest hit were the financially weakened established carriers that had to compete directly with the new airlines and that had little choice but to match the new low fares, and even operate at a loss, to preserve their market shares.

In general, management responded slowly to the increased competition and erosion of profitability. After recognizing the importance of route configuration, some carriers began to realign their route structures into "hub-and-spoke" systems rather than the linear route structures prevalent before deregulation. Hub-and-spoke systems permitted carriers to better control the flow of passenger traffic, limit the diversion of traffic to other carriers, and improve internal operational efficiency.

Some airlines developed new marketing strategies to attract and maintain customer loyalty, especially among the business travelers who normally flew at higher fares. In 1981, American Airlines introduced the first frequent-flyer program, known as the American Advantage plan. Other carriers soon followed with frequent-flyer programs of their own. The success of these early programs eventually led to complementary arrangements with other carriers, hotels, car-rental firms, and cruise lines.

In addition, the use of computer reservations systems (CRSs) as another marketing tool emerged during phase I. Carriers began to recognize the importance of the ownership and use of CRSs. Today, the ownership of a CRS is considered one of the essential requirements to an airline's long-term survivability. Although such systems existed before deregulation, their use has expanded dramatically since 1978. By 1984, approximately 90 percent of travel agents used computer reservations systems to book airline travel.[6]

In addition to the changes in marketing strategies, another development was to have long-term consequences for airline labor relations and collective bargaining: corporate restructuring, which began to occur throughout the industry. Conglomerates, parent companies, subsidiaries, and vertical and horizontal corporations were not new to American industry. What was new, however, was the airline industry's application of these structures in the unregulated environment. Some of the uniqueness and mystique of airline industry was being stripped away.

Even before deregulation, many airlines had begun to develop and implement business strategies based on vertical and horizontal expansion. Flying Tiger acquired the North American Car Corporation in 1971; TWA acquired Hilton International in 1967, Canteen Corporation in 1973, Dunhill Personnel Systems in 1977, and the Milnot Company in 1978; and UAL, United Airlines' holding company, acquired Western International Hotels (Westin) in 1970 and GAB Business Services in 1975.

The use of a holding company as a means of diversifying or expanding became more prevalent during phase I.[7] Not only was this

---

6. M.A. Brenner, Airline Deregulation 65 (Eno Foundation for Transportation, 1985).

7. The following airline holding companies have been formed since

strategy used by airline management as a tool to increase flexibility and profitability, but, as will be discussed later, it was also used as a tool against labor to avoid contractual obligations or threaten implementation of other alternatives. Management now emphasized the holding company's profitability and survival, not the individual airline's. In many instances, the assets of the original airline began to be diverted and its revenues and profits depleted. The formation of holding companies and the pursuit of expansionary objectives became a major threat to airline unions, in that this structure encouraged the establishment of non-union alter ego carriers.

THE PATCO STRIKE

The air traffic controllers' strike of 1981 was unquestionably the most cataclysmic event during phase I and the least expected. It will long be remembered as a watershed in American labor relations history. No doubt the government's reaction to the PATCO strike set the tone for the labor relations climate that followed. As transportation specialists Frank A. Spencer and Frank H. Cassell said, "The firing of 11,000 air traffic controllers established clearly in the minds of businessmen and union leaders a pro-management stance by the government."[8]

The scheduling restrictions first imposed by the Federal Aviation Administration (FAA) that summer continue today in some form. The establishment of regulations on airport use, slot and gate allocations, and traffic flow resulted in lessening the overall impact of the new entrants. The restrictive regulations also placed expanding carriers in a difficult predicament because there was no economically practical way to retreat from expansion. The PATCO strike further exacerbated the decline in the industry's revenue and the downward trend in its collective bargaining settlements.

---

deregulation: phase I, Trans World Corporation (1979), Texas Air Corporation (1980); phase II, AMR Corporation (1982), Frontier Holdings (1982), Dalfort (Braniff) (1983), USAir Group (1983), Air Wisconsin Services (1983), Capitol Holding Corporation (1983), Aloha, Inc. (1984), Ozark Holdings (1984), NWA, Inc. (1984), Pan Am Corporation (1984), Mid Pacific Air Corporation (1984), HAL, Inc. (1985), Alaska Air Group (1985).

8. F.A. SPENCER & F.H. CASSELL, AIRLINE LABOR RELATIONS UNDER DEREGULATION: FROM OLIGOPOLY TO COMPETITION AND RETURN? 5 (Northwestern University, Transportation Center, 1986).

During this first phase, the incumbent airlines were adversely affected by the changes in the operating environment created by deregulation, a weakening economy, and ultimately the PATCO strike. These changes increased competition for market shares and caused a significant erosion in profitability. In the three years immediately following deregulation, the established major and national carriers suffered operating losses of more than $400 million.[9] Between 1978 and 1981, operating expenses for the majors and nationals increased by 66.4 percent, fuel prices by 154.4 percent, and interest expenses by 109.2 percent.[10] Consequently, by the end of 1981, activity at the bargaining table had changed largely to dealing with many carriers, in *extremis.*

COLLECTIVE BARGAINING

The hostile environment for unions representing employees in the airline industry reached new heights after deregulation and created new challenges for union leaders. In particular, the structure and state of the airline industry no longer permitted airline unions to maintain as strong a position in collective bargaining. Strategies that had proven effective in a regulated environment were no longer effective. Unlike unions in the railroad and trucking industries, airline unions had never adopted industrywide bargaining as the accepted form for collective bargaining. The absence of centralized bargaining was felt by the unions for the first time. Decentralized negotiations with substantial local autonomy exposed the unions to reverse whipsawing at the bargaining table. Other conditions also contributed to labor's difficulties in responding initially to deregulation. High unemployment and escalating inflation, for example, shifted the focus of collective bargaining toward job security.

These conditions notwithstanding, little noticeable change occurred in collective bargaining during the first two years of deregulation. Wages, which had generally increased before deregulation, continued to move upward between 1978 and early 1981. For example, between 1975 and 1978 the average hourly wage for a captain of a B–727, B–737, or DC–9 aircraft increased by 32.4 percent, from $52.74 an hour to $89.83 an hour. Between 1979 and 1981, the same average hourly wages increased by 23.5 percent, from $76.56 to

---

9. I.P. Sharp, Department of Transportation Form 41 data.

10. It is important to note that average annual compensation in the airline industry, adjusted for inflation, actually declined during this period.

$94.53 respectively. Even the demise of the Mutual Aid Pact[11] did not result in any immediate change in the use of self-help. Strikes continued to occur at a number of carriers, including Northwest, United, Continental, and Pacific Southwest. Unions remained ready to exhaust the procedures of the Railway Labor Act and were prepared to engage in self-help. No union was prepared to work under imposed terms and conditions of employment. In retrospect, it seems clear that neither side had yet fully appreciated the potential impact deregulation would have on airline operations and collective bargaining.

Mergers consummated during this period continued to be handled through traditional means, that is, through methodical collective bargaining over a "fence agreement"[12] and contract amalgamation.[13] The existence of the CAB allowed for the traditional conduct of bargaining. The statutory requirement for CAB approval, which involved extensive review by the CAB, provided added time for employee groups and companies to resolve problems at a more deliberate pace. More important, as acknowledged by the courts, the CAB recognized the potential for severe disruption and routinely provided a "floor" of employee protection in the form of labor protective provisions (LPPs).[14]

Even during this period of relative calm there were signs that the climate for resolving merger-related problems would be much less temperate in the future. In the Pan Am–National merger, the CAB announced its intention not to impose LPPs in the future, stating that deregulation, by permitting free entry into markets, would prevent serious disruption to systemwide air transportation during strikes.[15]

---

11. The Mutual Aid Pact, formed in 1958, created a system whereby airlines subsidized other airlines undergoing a strike. The pact was eliminated by the ADA in 1978.

12. Fence agreements generally provide for the interim allocation of flying routes and schedules for the merging carriers, different sets of work rules, continued recognition of collective bargaining representatives, and often a process for the orderly integration of seniority.

13. Mergers are potentially destabilizing events affecting all aspects of the workplace, including the status of the employee collective bargaining representative, if any; employee seniority; survival of working agreements and the terms thereof; furloughs; and so on.

14. International Bhd. of Teamsters (IBT) v. Texas Int'l Airlines, 717 F.2d 157, 163–64 (5th Cir. 1983).

15. Texas International–National Acquisition, *appeal docketed*, CAB No. 33112; Pan American Acquisition of Control and Merger with National, *appeal docketed*, CAB No. 33283 (1978).

Not only did the CAB put the parties on notice, but the courts also indicated that they would take a passive role in disputes between a carrier and its employees during a merger when such disputes, even arguably, involved representation or contract questions.[16] At the same time, the National Mediation Board (NMB) decision in *Republic Airlines*[17] was interpreted by management as allowing it to choose between different unions that represented the same craft or class of employees at the premerger carriers. Although it still seemed to be "business as usual" for collective bargaining and labor relations in mergers, significant changes loomed on the horizon.

Phase II (1982–85): The Shake-Out

INDUSTRY CONDITIONS

The industry was still reeling from the continued decline in the economy in 1982. Rising fuel prices and interest rates, fare wars, and increased competition for market shares contributed to the decline. The responses by management during the first phase of deregulation had not restored the carriers to a profitable state.

Nothing underscored the risks and potential for disaster in the marketplace more than Braniff's filing for Chapter 11 in bankruptcy court in May 1982. Braniff had financed its rapid expansion primarily through increased debt and was now left with few reserves to shelter it from high fuel costs, rising interest rates, and low-cost competition. The partial liquidation and sale of its South American operations, coupled with half-price tickets and massive wage conces-

---

16. International Ass'n of Machinists v. Northeast Airlines, 536 F.2d 975, 977 (1st Cir. 1976), *cert. denied*, 429 U.S. 961 (1976); Air Line Pilots Ass'n v. Texas Int'l Airlines, 656 F.2d 16 (5th Cir. 1981).

17. Republic Airlines, 7 NMB at 21 (1979); 8 NMB at 49 (1980). In the view of the Air Line Pilots Association (ALPA), not only was this decision contrary to established NMB and judicial precedent, but it has been used by carriers and courts as an argument to extinguish collective bargaining agreements unilaterally, regardless of their successorship or duration provisions. *See* NMB File No. M/A 11860, Letter of Position filed by ALPA, Mar. 16, 1987.

sions, were not enough to stop the financial hemorrhaging. Its sudden shutdown and instant disappearance from the marketplace was a sign to all that this could happen at other airlines too.

Emergency plans, especially measures to improve cash flow, were hastily drawn at other endangered airlines. All those involved in the collective bargaining process understood that the "have-not" carriers were consumed with the struggle for immediate survival and had little opportunity to develop long-range strategies.

Indeed, the full pitch of this cry was still to be heard. In September 1983, Continental filed for protection under Chapter 11 of the Bankruptcy Code, unilaterally abrogated all of its labor contracts, and imposed the now-infamous emergency work rules, slashing wages and eliminating almost all the previously established work rules. Although all unions struck, Continental became the first major carrier to operate successfully in Chapter 11 by resuming partial operations as a low-fare full-service carrier with labor costs at a level less than 50 percent of the other major carriers. Along with low-cost new entrant People Express, Continental continued to expand in 1983 and 1984. The impact of the two airlines on fare levels, profitability, and negotiations in the industry was enormous.

Meanwhile, the financially strong carriers were developing their strategies for the future. Airlines such as American, Delta, Northwest, and United established a primary goal of expansion through internal growth. To help achieve this corporate objective, innovative and beneficial arrangements were negotiated to finance the acquisition of new equipment.[18]

Yield-management programs were instituted to better track the use and availability of the ever-growing array of discount fares. Marketing techniques, such as fares directed to the discretionary traveler and frequent-flyer programs aimed at the business traveler, became more prevalent during this period. In addition, the major carriers placed greater emphasis than in the past on controlling passenger traffic and market shares.[19] These actions resulted in higher profits

---

18. As a result, five hundred new aircraft were delivered to carriers between 1985 and 1986.

19. Rather than compete on a low-fare basis, other airlines turned to service competition to find a profitable niche in the marketplace. New York Air and Midway shifted their low-fare marketing emphasis to an upgraded service approach. Air Atlanta and Air One entered the market offering

for the industry. In 1984 and again in 1985, the industry's net profits exceeded $850 million.[20]

In addition, management continued to redesign its route structures. Major carriers made efforts to add international routes to their systems and to extend their hub-and-spoke operations. As part of this restructuring, larger airlines realized that it would be advantageous to develop arrangements with regional carriers to ensure traffic feed to the larger carrier's hub, where the major carrier would transport the passengers to their final destinations.

Ultimately, the regional feeder strategy swept the industry. It led to marketing agreements between various carriers and, in some cases, ownership interest in the regional carrier. These arrangements became widely known as code-sharing alliances and enabled the carriers to control passenger flow from a passenger's first flight segment.[21]

The prevalence of the airline parent or holding company became even more noticeable during the second phase of deregulation. One after another, airline companies formed parent corporations to provide greater flexibility and control over corporate assets and, in some instances, to avoid or bypass contractual obligations to unions. Airline conglomerates were now transferring various assets from the operating airline and forming new subsidiaries and potential profit centers for training, aircraft leasing, data processing, reservations, travel packages, frequent-flyer programs, maintenance, and other services.

The tidal wave of deregulation broke over the airline industry during phase II. No period tested corporate and union ingenuity more. Deregulation also took a significant toll on key management personnel. Of the thirteen major carriers in 1978, eleven changed chief executive officers by 1985. Corporations went through major personnel changes, especially in the labor relations area, as they

---

upgraded service, and the "new" Braniff also reentered offering upgraded service rather than low fares.

20. I.P. Sharp, Department of Transportation Form 41 data.

21. This arrangement was not a new concept. In 1967, Allegheny (now USAir) withdrew service from some smaller airports and franchised these routes to commuter or regional airlines. These regionals had smaller, less sophisticated aircraft and could earn money by flying into small airports and by providing flights to Allegheny's hub airports.

enlisted new managers, with fresh perspectives, from other industries.

COLLECTIVE BARGAINING

From a labor relations standpoint, the years from 1982 to 1985 were the worst of times for unions. In the aftermath of the PATCO strike and recession, unions had no public support and were beset by internal dissension as well as disunity. That fact coupled with the availability of ample replacements for strikers doomed the chances of waging a successful strike. The realization that a strike was no longer an effective bargaining tool profoundly altered the balance of power in the collective bargaining process.

Before deregulation, the airline unions, in round after round of negotiations, approached the table with the attitude, "How much are we going to get in this round of negotiations?" Typically, their negotiating goals were higher wages, improvements in pensions, insurance, and other fringe benefits, better working conditions, and job security provisions.[22] Conversely, management approached negotiations with the objective of containing the increase in the cost of the new contract and delaying that increase for as long as possible. Unions traditionally beseeched the NMB to process the negotiations quickly through mediation and to release the parties to engage in self-help. Management would often slow the process down, finding ways to keep negotiations from reaching an impasse.

Those roles certainly were not reversed following deregulation. Unions were in no hurry to see the end of the status quo period and become subject to the imposition of a last offer or use of self-help. Companies were examining strategies and carrying out plans that would have been unacceptable before deregulation.

After Braniff filed for bankruptcy, the threat of bankruptcy and/ or partial liquidation often began to be mentioned as the only option if unions could not agree to concessions. It did not matter whether negotiations were conducted under section 6 of the Railway Labor Act or not. The demands were not tied to such legal niceties.

Several major collective bargaining events occurred in 1983: Braniff employees agreed to substantial concessions as part of a potential

---

22. There are times when certain financially weak companies needed relief, and concessions tailored to their specific needs were negotiated.

reorganization, the American Airlines agreements established non-merging B-scales (two-tier wage structure), and Continental filed for bankruptcy and imposed emergency work rules. All these events reflected the shift in collective bargaining and established new parameters for labor negotiations in this period.

Although B-scales were not a new concept, their initial format was unique to the airline industry. Under the system established by American, pay rates for new employees would never merge with those of current employees. American's employees agreed to this two-tier pay structure because they believed that furloughs were the only other alternative. In return, American's management offered them what was termed "blueprints of the future." These "blueprints" consisted of a variety of management promises, including job security, higher wages and benefits, and job-creating expansion. By the end of 1983, the unions representing American's pilots and flight attendants, as well as its mechanics, dispatchers, and other ground personnel, had agreed to new contracts in which compensation for new employees was permanently lowered to levels significantly below previous levels. Newly hired pilots, for example, were to be compensated at a rate of 50 percent lower than incumbents for the duration of their careers.

At financially healthy carriers such as United, Delta, USAir, and others, American became the model for establishing two-tier provisions. In 1983, eight two-tier wage contracts in the airline industry were concluded; in 1984, the number grew to thirty-five, and by 1985, the number doubled to sixty-two.

Against the backdrop of the Braniff reorganization, the American settlement in August 1983, and the imposition of emergency work rules at Continental in September 1983, management now approached the bargaining table with enormous strength and an agenda to match. In most instances, the issue was no longer how much management would give but how much it would get back. Management's principal bargaining goals were more flexibility through cross-utilization and the use of part-timers, increased productivity, reductions in fringe benefits, and an overall reduction in compensation.

The bargaining objectives of financially sound carriers included pay freezes or small percentage increases, lump-sum payments in lieu of pay increases, and the establishment of a two-tier pay system.[23]

---

23. The use of the lump-sum payment to reduce the consequences of an

All these methods limited the roll-up cost of fringe benefits. Financially troubled carriers sought a decrease in A-scale rates and related fringe benefits, the establishment of B-scales for future use, and the establishment of variable compensation schemes, including profit-sharing and stock plans. Temporary concessions that snapped back at a future date to previously higher levels were no longer acceptable. Management wanted long-term permanent concessions so as to establish a lower fixed-cost base for developing their long-range planning.

Management used whipsaw bargaining techniques to achieve concessions. Each time a carrier received concessions, employees at other carriers knew that similar or deeper cuts would be demanded. Midterm negotiations became commonplace. Threats of shutdowns, partial liquidations, lockouts, or massive furloughs were heard everywhere. Attempts to engage in Boulwarism through manipulative direct negotiations with employees, as well as corporate restructuring, were additional tactics used to undermine the resolve of unions and employees. With little risk of confrontation, management increasingly adopted a "take it or leave it" attitude at the bargaining table.

Heightening the tensions in negotiations at Pan Am, Eastern, and Aloha were threatened terminations of retirement plans as well as refusals to honor snapback agreements, which would have reinstated previous compensation levels and work rules on a specific date. The refusal to uphold snapback agreements clearly signaled that short-term concessions had not cured the carriers' financial problems, and the resulting litigation over this issue only served to put unions further on the defensive.[24]

---

across-the-board increase became so prevalent during this period that by 1987 the Department of Labor created a new index that measured compensation keyed to the lump-sum factor.

24. Aloha, for example, claimed it was legally prohibited from abiding by the snapback provision because the snapback date fell within the status quo period under section 6 of the Railway Labor Act. The U.S. District Court refused ALPA's request for an injunction and, as a result, the snapback language negotiated between the parties was rendered temporarily meaningless. The district court did ultimately uphold ALPA's position with provision for damages but not until years after the request for the injunction was denied. ALPA v. Aloha Airlines, No. 82–0788 (D. Haw. Mar. 17, 1987). *See also* ALPA v. Pan American World Airways, 765 F.2d 377 (2nd Cir. 1985).

Increasingly, management used its leverage to gain concessions from its unions and to undermine the employees' faith in labor's strength. Although labor gave significant relief to many carriers during this period, much of it was used by management to subsidize the ongoing fare wars and to continue the corporations' diversification strategies rather than to improve airline operations.

Labor's goals shifted dramatically as well. Unions and employees began to question management's actions and to resist further concessions in wages and working conditions. Labor argued that concessions without concrete changes in operating procedures, and in some instances in management, would not restore a carrier to profitability. As such, employees began to demand a return for their concessions. The "return" took the form of profit-sharing plans, employee stock ownership plans (ESOPs), employee and management coalitions, representation on company boards of directors, job security provisions, and, in some instances, replacement of top management.

An ESOP was one method management agreed to to give labor a return for its concessions. ESOPs take two forms, unleveraged and leveraged.[25] Unleveraged plans were introduced during this phase of deregulation at Eastern, Western, Republic, and Pacific Southwest airlines. Attempts at leveraged ESOPs were introduced during this period at Frontier, Trans World, and Transamerica.

One successful unleveraged ESOP was that of Republic. In 1983, four of the airline's five unions formed the Coalition of Unions of Republic Employees (CURE). The unions realized that further concessions were necessary to ensure the airline's survival and prevent filing for bankruptcy, but they wanted something in return. After months of negotiations, an ESOP was agreed to in which the employees would receive $93 million in stock in exchange for $300 million in concessions over a three-year period. Employees received a substantial return when Republic rallied and became an attractive acquisition for Northwest.[26]

---

25. Under an unleveraged ESOP, the company contributes stock to the employees in the form of stock bonus plans or profit-sharing plans. Under a leveraged ESOP, money is borrowed from financial institutions to buy the company's stock. The company agrees to contribute regularly to the plan, and funds from the ESOP eventually pay off the loan. As this occurs, the stock is moved to the participating employees' accounts, and the employees become total owners of the company's stock.

26. Republic's pilots got an average return on their ESOP of $5,000 per

This period was also marked by greater attempts by labor to work with management. The Eastern Air Lines employee agreements of 1983 provided a positive model for other airlines. Under this experiment in codetermination and cooperation, members of the Air Line Pilots Association (ALPA), the International Association of Machinists and Aerospace Workers (IAM), and the Transport Workers Union (TWU) joined together to determine the level of concessions required to keep the airline financially viable and the measures of protection that should be given in exchange. Management and labor selected outside consultants to conduct the review of Eastern's financial position and make recommendations. The result was that the pilots agreed to significant wage and work rule concessions in exchange for representation on the company's board of directors and an equity stake in the company, along with other quid pro quos.

Unfortunately, by 1984, inroads made by ALPA and other unions and management to cooperate in finding workable solutions to financial difficulties were for the most part destroyed. The unions' inability to overturn Continental's anti-labor actions through either a strike or legal action further weakened the strength of the airline unions. Even Eastern's management, which had achieved significant relief from its pilots in June 1983, was now—only one year later—demanding further concessions and threatening bankruptcy as an alternative.

The industry began to rebound, however, at the end of 1984. Expansion resumed with full vigor. The demand for pilots grew tremendously. In 1984, 5,465 pilots were hired by commercial carriers, and the number increased 43 percent, to 7,872, in 1985. Consequently, with the new demand for pilots, management was forced to review its position on entry-level pay rates and even its willingness to undertake a strike.

During this time, labor unions also were successful in obtaining legislative reform of the Bankruptcy Code.[27] The new amendments prevented a company like Continental from unilaterally imposing

---

pilot—for two thousand pilots—for a total of $10 million. Republic's stock rose from $9 a share when the ESOP was established to $16 a share two years later when the ESOP was liquidated.

27. Bankruptcy Amendments and Federal Judgeship Act of 1984, Pub. L. No. 98–353.

terms and conditions of employment, the emergency work rules, on employees without review and approval.[28]

Added to the code was a new provision, section 1113, that required a company operating under Chapter 11 to have court approval before it could reject or make interim changes in its collective bargaining agreement. The language of the amendment and subsequent cases made clear that the debtor had to fulfill several requirements before a contract could be rejected.[29] The amendments to the Bankruptcy Code clearly affected labor relations and collective bargaining.

Also on the positive side from the union's perspective, management's confrontational actions had ultimately resulted in increased unity among labor groups. The clearest example of this new unity was the United pilots' strike in 1985. Management's demand for a nonmerging two-tier pay scale for new employees and the pilots' refusal to agree to such a system resulted in a strike that lasted for twenty-nine days. Despite costly efforts by the company to break the strike, United was unable to persuade sufficient qualified personnel to cross the picket line to maintain the airline's operations.[30]

Having learned from the Continental strike, ALPA undertook sophisticated means to support the striking United pilots, such as family-awareness programs, video presentations, national teleconferences, and a toll-free hotline to keep members and their families informed before and during the strike. In addition, programs were

---

28. The Supreme Court approved the company's action in National Labor Relations Bd. v. Bildisco, 104 U.S. 118 (1984).

29. These included (1) making a proposal to the union; (2) including in the proposal *only* those modifications "necessary" to permit reorganization of the debtor; (3) treating all parties fairly and equitably; (4) providing the union with relevant information; and (5) meeting with the union at reasonable times in good faith to reach an agreement. Further, the court could authorize rejection only if the union had refused to accept the debtor's proposal without good cause and the balance of the equities clearly favored rejection of such agreement. Wheeling-Pittsburgh Steel v. United Steelworkers, 791 F.2d 1074 (3rd Cir. 1986). The debtor is permitted to obtain interim relief from the court if "essential to the continuation of the debtor's business, or in order to avoid damage to the estate." *See also* In re Wright Airlines, 144 Bankr. 744 (Bankr., N.D. Ohio 1984); In re Salt Creek Freightways, 46 Bankr. 347 (Bankr., Wyo. 1985).

30. Not only did United suffer enormous losses over the next year rebuilding its operation, but the strike also enabled many weak carriers to improve their financial position significantly.

established to help alleviate the financial and emotional problems of the strikers.

A Union's Response

The benchmark effort at United was not an isolated response. Aided by a return to profitability at many companies, the depleted job pool, and a healthy expanding industry, unions reexamined their structures and policies and developed new strategies and techniques for future collective bargaining. Like the management at many airlines, the unions had reacted slowly to deregulation at first but were now rebounding.

In 1980, ALPA's first response to deregulation was to set a priority on organizing all non-ALPA carriers and to form the National Collective Bargaining Committee to study deregulation. Clearly this was not enough to ride out the wave of deregulation. By the second phase of deregulation, ALPA had been restructured internally to provide for more centralized and coordinated collective bargaining and for membership ratification.[31] Among other changes in 1984, the collective bargaining committee developed a detailed bargaining policy for concessionary negotiations. Highlights included snapback clauses to return the benefit to its preconcession level; job security (furlough protection); scope, successor, and labor protective provisions clauses; pension plan protection, including establishment of a retirement board to oversee administration, the funding of waiver protection, the selection of trustee and investment managers, and plan termination and disposition of any excess assets; a payback provision for wage deferrals or cuts such as security, cash, stock, bonds, or ESOPs; increased input by ALPA in management decision making; and profit sharing.

In addition, the final and binding authority of the president of ALPA over collective bargaining agreements was reaffirmed. This change reinforced centralized control of negotiations and stopped any further trend toward decentralized collective bargaining. Quarterly negotiation conferences were started to increase the level of communication and information exchanged between pilots' representatives. At these conferences, members of negotiating committees

---

31. ALPA negotiates separate agreements for each of the forty-three carriers it represents. Approximately twelve section 6 negotiations are under way at all times.

from different airlines met to discuss management's approaches and tactics at the bargaining table, and suggestions and recommendations for negotiations were developed. These conferences continue to be held today.

An example of the effect of this increased coordination can be measured by reviewing ALPA's handling of the B-scale issue after the American settlement in 1983. Although ALPA was unable to prevent two-tier pay systems for other pilots, by acting in concert it restricted their parameters. Under all the two-tier systems negotiated by ALPA, pilot B-scale compensation merged at some point, usually after five years, with the A-scale.

In response to the United strike and the potential for others to follow the same confrontational course of action, a special meeting of the ALPA Board of Directors was convened in June 1985 to establish and maintain a major contingency fund of $100 million. This fund was established to ensure the financial ability of the union to combat major threats to pilots in the future.

Although the Continental bankruptcy and strike were the low points in this period from a union perspective, the strike by United's pilots and the TWA-Icahn agreements were the most positive events and slowed down the negative slide in collective bargaining for airline unions.[32] Both events reflected the renewed ability of unions to fashion strategies to cope with difficult and potentially devastating situations. If strikes or negotiations were handled properly, unions could once again engage in self-help and effectively shut down a major carrier. Likewise, unions could enter the financial world and make arrangements that would enable airline employees to determine ownership of their companies.

Unusual measures were required to meet the challenges of deregulation and the current operating environment. No one foresaw that unions would become experts in corporate takeovers, leveraged buyouts, and ESOPs. The activities at Trans World, Frontier, Transamerica, Texas Air, United, Republic, Eastern, and other airlines, however, demonstrated the need to develop such strategies and to apply them to the collective bargaining process. Nor had anyone foreseen before deregulation that airline unions would engage in massive communications programs involving coalitions of employ-

---

32. Coupled with these events was the conclusion of the Continental pilots' strike at the end of 1985.

ees, corporate campaigns, family-awareness programs, and satellite teleconferencing to deal with management actions.

Phase III (1986–present): The Consolidation

INDUSTRY CONDITIONS

The airline industry entered phase III ready to continue its expansion and growth strategies. Between 1985 and 1986, available seat miles increased by 6.7 percent for the majors and by 9.9 percent for the nationals. Hiring in 1986 totaled 6,341 pilots and is expected to continue at a rapid pace through the end of the 1980s.

Airline analysts agree that to guarantee profitability and survival in phase III, an airline needs access to three vital components. First, it needs a strong balance sheet. This includes not only a strong cash position but also a strong debt-to-equity ratio. Second, an airline must have a route structure that includes dominant hubs, a feeder system, and international routes. Maintaining dominance at these hubs has proven to be a strong protection against new airlines and against competition from existing carriers. Third, an airline needs at least an ownership interest in a computer reservations system.

Few airlines entered 1986 with all three components essential to future viability. In fact, only three airlines—American, United, and Delta—had strong balance sheets, hub dominance, and ownership in computer reservations systems. Those airlines lacking in these elements realized that the best way to obtain them was by merging with an airline that had them. Even the three airlines mentioned above believed they needed to strengthen certain aspects of their structure and acted accordingly.

During the third phase of deregulation, management has tailored its strategies to achieve these three vital objectives. Airlines have increasingly used commuter and regional carriers for traffic feed. Meanwhile, regional carriers have sought out larger airlines with which to form an alliance. In many cases, larger carriers have obtained outright or substantial ownership of the regional carrier to ensure continuation of the code-sharing arrangement. These alliances have become an integral part of the airline industry. By 1986,

80 percent of the regional airlines had alliances with a major or national carrier.

The major strategy management employed, however, was expansion through external growth. By far the most significant change taking place within the airline industry in this third phase of deregulation has been the consolidation of airlines. In 1986 alone, more mergers took place within the industry than in any other year in its history. A total of twenty-five airlines were involved in fifteen mergers. This resulted in the market share of the five largest airlines dramatically increasing from 54.3 percent in January 1986 to 72.5 percent in January 1987 (assuming all pending mergers are approved). Today, the top eight airline companies control 93.7 percent of market share.

Many events and conditions led to these mergers. No doubt the attitude toward antitrust law and favorable tax treatment influenced the decision to merge and consolidate operations. The pool of potential employees had been substantially depleted as employment increased in the expanding industry and management was forced to abandon its internal growth plans in favor of instant expansion and costly integration.

Mergers and acquisitions notwithstanding, little has changed since the 1970s. Although deregulation encouraged competition by allowing new airlines into the marketplace, it did so for only a short time. Not only are the major airlines that survived the same ones that were the industry leaders in 1978, but they have even greater dominance in the marketplace and are fully equipped to fend off any new competition.

The final major change to take place in this phase of deregulation is related to the increased development of holding companies, discussed below.

Many questions remain unanswered about the final shape of the industry. Analysts vary in their predictions, but most agree that five or six mega-carriers will emerge with more concentrated strength than ever before. One thing seems certain. All the remaining major carriers will possess similar basic characteristics, and all will be part of a holding company.

COLLECTIVE BARGAINING

The bargaining trends of the preceding years continued in phase III. Management still approached negotiations from a position of strength, seeking overall cost reductions to remain competitive with new airlines and such low-cost carriers as Continental. Management's key objectives were pay freezes or small percentage increases, lump-sum payments, containment of fringe benefits, B-scales, increased productivity, and relief from scope clauses restricting the development and ownership of regional carrier networks. Long-term settlements were sought to establish a base for expansion and consolidation.

In the case of financially unhealthy carriers, demands were made or imposed for substantial permanent concessions. At Eastern and Trans World, permanent cost reductions of 20 percent or more with additional productivity gains, fringe benefit reductions, and "deep" merging B-scales were agreed on after bitter negotiations during which unions were threatened with bankruptcy, liquidation, or sale of substantial assets. At TWA the pilots gained an equity interest in the company and job security provisions, including protection of the pilots in future mergers or sales and restriction on the sale of an airline's assets in partial exchange for permanent concessions.

Even Delta requested mediation for the first time in its history in 1986 and had difficult negotiations with its pilots before reaching settlement. Included in Delta's settlement were productivity increases, a modest, merging B-scale,[33] a pay freeze for one year followed by modest pay increases, and fringe benefit containment. In exchange, the pilots obtained improved job security provisions and a commitment to a business plan predicated on substantial growth. Significantly, the parties agreed on new provisions to accommodate the carrier's desire to build a regional feeder network and to cover future mergers.

The general trend set by the pilots at Delta in 1986 was followed at other strong carriers such as American and Piedmont in 1987. American's pilots' agreement is especially noteworthy for two reasons. American initially triggered the B-scale phenomenon. Driven by the dwindling pool of available pilots and much less restrictive B-scales at other healthy carriers, American agreed to pilots' demands to modify its B-scale; the A-scale was merged with the B-scale, and substantial increases were provided in B-scale rates.[34] Man-

---

33. Delta's B-scale provided for new-employee pay rates that were an average of 36 percent above the industry's previous benchmarks, American and United.

34. Pilots on the B-scale received increases ranging from 11 to 28.5 per-

agement's need for relief from its pilots' scope clause was addressed as well, providing American with the ability (subject to significant restrictions) to develop fully and own its regional carrier group.

As it turned out, two interrelated strategies—holding companies and mergers—had the most bearing on collective bargaining during this period. The continued development and refinement of holding companies to achieve long-term stability and increased profitability led to the immediate strategic decision to expand externally to achieve the critical mass necessary to meet those goals. United's acquisition of Pan American's Pacific operation in the spring of 1985 kicked off the consolidation of the industry.

Unlike the mergers that took place immediately following deregulation, the rules governing the mergers occurring during this latest phase have become increasingly unclear, resulting in more tumultuous mergers. First, no longer has there been a CAB to impose labor protective provisions to ensure an orderly process for the establishment of seniority.[35] The few pilot groups that have been able to negotiate LPPs in their contracts since 1978 have thus been well served.[36] Second, the courts rejected enforcement of contractual provisions that would have ensured the survival of the working agreements when representation issues were deemed to exist and be subject to the jurisdiction of the National Mediation Board.[37]

More than ever, carriers were able to act at will in mergers. Fence agreements between the unions of carriers that were being merged and the surviving company became increasingly difficult to negotiate. Carriers with holding company structures were not in a position to operate separate subsidiaries for an indefinite period of time and carefully evaluated when to merge their operations. Of course, the management at some airlines used this new-found flexibility to pit one group against the other to gain leverage in negotiations over

---

cent. A-scale pilots received a 6 percent increase over three years, and the A- and B-scales were to merge at the end of the ninth year.

35. *See also* Independent Union of Flight Attendants v. Department of Transportation (DOT) and Pan Am, 803 F.2d 1029 (9th Cir. 1986); ALPA v. DOT, 791 F.2d 172 (D.C. Cir. 1986).

36. Some of these included Republic, Western, Flying Tiger, and TWA.

37. IBT v. Texas Int'l, *supra* note 14; Republic Airlines, 798 F.2d 967 (7th Cir. 1986); Air Transport Employees v. Western Airlines, 55 U.S.L.W. 3675, 124 L.R.R.M.(BNA) 3192 (1987).

the integration of work forces and the amalgamation of their respective agreements.

Many of these mergers are in progress today. In May 1987, the NMB recognized the instability of the present situation and interceded to develop appropriate procedures to provide, at least in part, an orderly process for the resolution of disputes associated with mergers.[38] The NMB now requires carriers to invoke the Board's services to determine whether a labor organization's status as collective bargaining representative can be terminated. The Board undertook investigations pursuant to this procedure in the cases of *Delta v. Western* and *American v. Air Cal* and issued new rules governing mergers and acquisitions in July 1987.

Obviously, the further development of the holding company structure and mega-carrier has increased the need for unions to negotiate parent, alter ego, and scope protection. The unions now must counter the move toward ownership and control of regional feeders by major and national carriers. The primary concern regarding this new relationship between the majors and nationals and their affiliated regionals is the allocation of current and future aircraft among the various airlines. Although 19-seat aircraft cannot be considered a threat to 150-seat jets in major markets, the acquisition by regional airlines of larger aircraft increases the potential for problems, including service substitution and alternatives to growth.

ALPA has responded to these developments in a number of ways, including drafting scope clauses that limit service substitution based on the size of the aircraft operated by regional affiliates or subsidiaries; developing formal lines of communication and coordination between the various airline families; and organizing the affiliated regional airlines. Since 1981, ALPA has organized twenty-three regional airlines; these airlines currently comprise 45 percent of the airlines represented by ALPA.

In another area, airline unions have refined their ability to deal with today's new corporate structures. Labor has increased its use of ESOPs, for example, as a means to deal with management. Participation in earlier ESOPs led in 1986 to the development of a formal ESOP policy by ALPA. Union expertise in this area is now unquestioned, as efforts in 1987 by United's pilots attest.

---

38. R. Watkins, Hearing Officer for the NMB, Opening Remarks, NMB File M/A 11860.

The United pilots' ESOP initiative is an outgrowth of the strained labor-management relations that had existed since the 1985 pilots' strike. Since then, United's pilots and other employees have become increasingly dissatisfied with United's (now Allegis Corporation) diversification policy. The previously mentioned transfer of three of the airline's subsidiaries to the holding company further exacerbated the pilots' discontent with management's strategy, especially since United's management had already announced that they expected further concessions from their unions, particularly the pilots' union, in 1988 negotiations.

In response, the pilots made a $4.5 billion offer to purchase the airline and the computer reservations system via a leveraged ESOP. The pilots have encouraged all the airline's employees to participate and have obtained the backing of two prominent investment banking firms, Lazard Freres and Solomon Brothers, with additional support from a team of other technical experts. The United pilots' ESOP initiative demonstrates the level of sophistication to which labor has advanced in the financial world. It has already precipitated a change in senior management and the sale of nonairline companies.

In this third phase of deregulation, labor has demonstrated that it has learned from past events, and it has now emerged much stronger and better equipped to deal with the new challenges. Strikes have become increasingly risky for management, which certainly contributes to this renewed strength, as does the shift in recent court decisions.[39] This phase holds promise for future stability in airline labor relations.

One troublesome question, however, remains for the future of collective bargaining in the airline industry: What does the future hold for Eastern, Continental, and Texas Air? If Texas Air succeeds in breaking the unions at Eastern and creating a low-cost, low-fare mega-carrier, it will surely have negative ramifications for collective

---

39. *See* ALPA v. Transamerica Airlines, No. 85–2455 (9th Cir. 1987) (district court has subject matter jurisdiction in a case involving alter ego and bad-faith bargaining claims); Burlington N. R.R. v. Brotherhood of Maintenance of Way Employees, 125 L.R.R.M.(BNA) 2073 (1987) (secondary boycotts found permissible under the RLA); Independent Fed'n of Flight Attendants v. TWA, No. 86–2197 (8th Cir. 1987) (returning striking employees are entitled to displace "crossovers" with lesser seniority); Alaska Airlines v. Brock, 54 U.S.L.W. 3575 (1987) (first right-of-hire provisions in ADA available for employees displaced as a result of deregulation).

bargaining in the airline industry. If the unions are successful in working out agreements with Texas Air compatible with industry standards, no doubt that will have a stabilizing effect on collective bargaining and industry labor relations. Only time will tell.

A Management
Perspective

C. Raymond Grebey, Jr.

Frank Lorenzo, president and chief executive officer of Texas Air and one of the few airline officials who testified against deregulation, characterized it as an anti-labor action—an action he has taken advantage of! Alfred Kahn, who played a central role in bringing about deregulation, offered another, more positive, perspective:

> Deregulation has done most of the things we expected it to do. There has been an enormous increase in the intensity of competition. It has resulted in dramatically reduced fares. It has aligned fares much more closely with costs. It has offered travelers a greater variety of price/quality choices than they had before. It has imposed enormous pressures on companies to increase efficiency, and it has put downward pressure on grossly inflated wages. Small towns have had, on average, an increase in weekly departures.[1]

Let us assume there has been a transfer of wealth, or benefit, to airline passengers. My question, however, is one to which the renowned economist Alfred Kahn does not advert:[2] What has been the impact of deregulation on collective bargaining and on the industry's industrial relations system?

Robert L. Crandall, another keen observer and the very successful chief executive officer of American Airlines, offered this opinion in 1986:

---

1. USA Today, Oct. 10, 1986, at 58B.
2. *See* Kahn, *In Defense of Deregulation, infra* p. 343.

37

While Fred Kahn may be right about the bill being pro-consumer, it is also profoundly anti-labor.

The goal was to achieve greater productivity and lower prices, and that has certainly happened. However, it is important for everyone to recognize that lower ticket prices have occurred primarily because there has been a massive transfer of wealth from airline employees to airline passengers. Whether that is good or bad depends, I suspect, on whether you are Fred Kahn, who looks at things from an economist's point of view, or a consumer, who looks at things from an economist's point of view, or an airline employee, who, I can assure you, looks at things through very different eyes.

The third participant in the creation of this problem—the Government—has essentially walked away from the bargaining table. The Government has created a situation in which every successful carrier must be a low-cost producer, and reality dictates that to be a low-cost producer we must have competitive labor rates. And now, labor and management are left with the very hard task of working out a resolution to that problem.[3]

Although Crandall recognizes the impact of deregulation on the industrial relations system (i.e., "The Government has walked away from the bargaining table...labor and management are left with the task"), his statement is an observation, not a verdict.

As an individual who has spent most of his career working outside a regulated environment, I do not find it unusual that the industrial relations system, that is, labor and management, is "left with the task" of resolving the problems. Who is better suited and equipped to deal with the effects of labor costs on wage and benefit levels, conditions of employment, and the impact of those labor costs on product markets than the principals involved, the spokespeople for labor and management?

Unfortunately, it appears in retrospect that the drafters and implementers of deregulation, for reasons unknown, ignored the desirability of avoiding a precipitous change in the existing airline culture and failed to provide for an orderly and gradual transition from a government-dominated industrial relations system to the more traditional two-party system. Maybe they just took this culture shock for granted, or perhaps their belief in the flexibility of the collective bargaining process led them to conclude that the transition would be trauma-free. Whatever the suppositions, trauma and turmoil have prevailed.

---

3. R. Crandall, The Airline Industry—Still in Transition, paper delivered at Northwestern University (Feb. 27, 1986).

From the perspective of someone who was an outsider in 1978, it is apparent that no one in the industrial relations system prepared for the inevitable consequences of deregulation. No structure for substantive industry-to-union communications was effectively in place. No hierarchy of established dialogue existed between national union and industry leaders. There was no forum for the mutual discussion of broad economic trends and future industry issues.

As a result of deregulation, the industry quickly moved from stable pattern bargaining, in which wages were essentially removed from competition, to an environment in which an individual company's labor relations was a critical component of its business strategy. Each carrier focused on its own resources, with a heavy emphasis on cost effectiveness, including the cost of labor.

This turnabout occurred at a time when the industrial relations systems in the industry were being buffeted by other forces, namely the PATCO strike, foreign competition, and a recession. Obviously, this was not the best of times for unstructured major change in the industry's industrial relations system.[4]

Has collective bargaining worked in this environment of change and culture shock? As a first step in answering this question, certain measurement criteria need to be identified and applied: union-management advocacy, work stoppages, the extent of unionization, employment trends, wage levels, NMB activity, and new innovations. I have drawn some conclusions, generally subjective, about each criterion.

Union-Management Advocacy

The decibel level of union-management advocacy in the airline industry is unequaled in any other industry today. The memories of most observers do not include as many "good guy, bad guy" personalities as have emerged in the news headlines during the past five years. There is no need to detail the events. The mere mention of the names will excite one's recall: Frank Lorenzo of Texas Air, Charles Bryan and Frank Borman of Eastern Airlines, among others.

---

4. F. SPENCER & F. CASSELL, EIGHT YEARS OF U.S. AIRLINE DEREGULATION: MANAGEMENT AND LABOR ADAPTATIONS. RE-EMERGENCE OF OLIGOPOLY 11–12 (Northwestern University, Transportation Center, 1987).

This observation is the basis for the following principle: When collective bargaining becomes the occasion of a titanic personality struggle and when issues of substance become submerged in rhetoric, the process is in jeopardy. Mature and stable relationships in such an atmosphere are a long way off.

Work Stoppages

Airline strikes for the period 1969–78 averaged 3 per year. For the postderegulation period 1979–86 they averaged 2.9 per year.[5] Admittedly, the number of work stoppages in the first year following deregulation, 1979, hit an all-time high for both periods: 9. But the frequency has shown a downward trend, as indicated by the 2.9 average. These data strongly imply that both parties have had compelling incentives to avoid strikes. Even without the help of the old CAB mechanisms, management and labor have used the collective bargaining process to resolve their differences.

Extent of Unionization

There is no doubt that the external forces mentioned earlier initially worked against organized labor. Union status and power were diminished by the PATCO strike, government attitudes toward unions, and the economic recession. This last condition resulted in high unemployment among established carriers, the effects of which were exacerbated by the ability of "instant" airlines with nonunion employees to come into the domestic marketplace at the bottom of the business cycle. Many of these new entrants, such as Southwest, Pacific Southwest, and Air Florida, are gone or have become unionized.

All in all, the level of unionization in the airline industry—nearly 90 percent—far exceeds the extent of unionization in industry in the United States—less than 20 percent. In the main, unions have not been thrown out, but the low-cost nonunion carriers are falling out. A strong reason for this high dropout rate, in tandem with the economic changes and industry reconcentration, is the collective bar-

---

5. Airline Industrial Relations Conference data, April 1987.

gaining process. It is alive, well, and working, as Wallace Hendricks, Peter Feuille, and Carol Szerszen predicted in 1980:

> It may seem paradoxical that at the conclusion of an analysis in which we tentatively demonstrated a positive regulatory impact on union power we reverse direction and predict that deregulation also may provide a favorable environment for the unions. We see nothing inconsistent in our prediction, for it seems to us that the industry and unionization characteristics that developed over forty years of regulation have created a bargaining environment that should not change substantially in the near future. In other words, airline collective bargaining should continue to reflect the continuing impact of the former regulatory environment.[6]

Employment Trends

At the outset of deregulation, there was speculation that there would be a decline in employment levels in the airline industry. This phenomenon would be the result of the clash between the companies' labor relations policies, reflecting their individual business strategies, focused on the restraint of controllable costs, and the inevitability of pattern settlements, with their concomitant pressures on labor costs. Data refute this notion. For example, the average number of employees has increased year by year, from 313,522 in 1978 to 364,080 in the third quarter of 1986.[7]

Even subtracting the number of part-time employees reported for 1984, the last data available, there has been a steady growth in full-time employment. In general, growth has been sufficient to overcome the impact of personnel cuts and the layoffs precipitated by the bankruptcies or failures of thirty-six air carriers since deregulation. Collective bargaining has had a constructive influence on this growth. The bargaining process has resulted in agreements that instituted meaningful job security protection for senior employees, as exemplified by the settlements of the Transport Workers Union at American Airlines and Pan Am.

---

6. Hendricks, Feuille, & Szerszen, *Regulation, Deregulation and Collective Bargaining in Airlines*, 34 INDUS. LABOR REL. REV. 81 (1980).

7. Airline Labor Relations Conference, Labor Cost Index.

Wage Levels

One certain way to start a "no-win" controversy is to take a position on the effect of deregulation on wages in the airline industry. But that is not the question under consideration. My comments on wage levels are not intended as a judgment of deregulation, only of whether the collective bargaining process has worked. According to the Air Transport Association, before deregulation, employees in the airline industry did better than employees in most other industry groups. In 1979, the wages of airline employees were 207.8 percent of their 1970 level, and fringes were 336.6 percent of their 1970 level. In that same year, the United States Bureau of Labor Statistics consumer price index was only 186.9 percent of its 1970 level. It has been suggested that the carriers were able to sustain these wages and benefits because they could pass the costs on to the consumer. Another suggestion is that the public utility style of regulation that controlled the industry created a closed environment set off and free from the market forces that press on other nonregulated consumer service enterprises. Critics say the industry measured itself with a mirror, and the collective bargaining process, functioning within permitted government limits, was a sort of intramural exercise with government administrators as the ultimate referees. Sensitivity to the market was not a real consideration at the bargaining table.

Deregulation turned the mirror into a window. The negotiators on both sides of the table were forced to look outside the industry. Airline wages were, by the stroke of a legislative pen, placed in competition with all wages, not merely those paid to employees of the airline industry.

As noted earlier, the architects of deregulation made no provision for this transition, and most of the participants were ill equipped or unprepared for the task. Frank Spencer and Frank Cassell described the scene:

> Aided by high unemployment, wage and working conditions became unhinged from a 40-year industry pattern. Instead, wages often became idiosyncratic to the individual firm and its philosophy. Wages came to be governed mainly by economic conditions peculiar to the individual carrier and its relationships with its employees. Occupational wage rates for pilots, co-pilots, and attendants diverged increasingly from carrier to carrier. This disparity was reflected in the widening inter- and intra-

occupational divergence of pay as individual carriers introduced and unions reluctantly accepted two-tier pay systems and other schemes to reduce pay or make costs variable through pay reductions in exchange for profit- or stock-sharing or promises of recovery ("snap backs") in better times.[8]

The many consequences that have been written about and debated are two-tier wage scales, wage cuts, wage deferrals, and no-increase contract settlements. The critical point is that they are all the products of a market-sensitive and product-sensitive collective bargaining process as defined by John R. Commons.

Admittedly, the absence of industrywide bargaining and industrywide labor agreements has limited the effectiveness of labor at the bargaining table and, compounded by the initiatives of individual carriers, has produced settlements that are less favorable to labor. In other deregulated markets, such as trucking and railroads, interunion cooperation or the dominance of a single union has acted to perpetuate industrywide contracts and to temper the impact of deregulation.

Even in the traditionally deregulated sectors of the economy, some unions have achieved industrywide influence and impressive bargaining leverage. In the airline industry, however, our bargaining traditions and the inherited system of carrier-by-carrier crafts and classes are formidable, although not insurmountable, obstacles to similar efforts by airline unions. In any event, regulation is not an essential precondition to the removal of wages from competition.

One union that seems to have come to a similar conclusion is the Air Line Pilots Association (ALPA). Although it has given the greatest percentage of concessions in the industry, ALPA appears to have taken internal steps to protect itself from future property-by-property erosion of its bargaining strengths. ALPA appears to have evolved a strategy that integrates a candid recognition of external market forces with an institutional objective of taking wage competition out of the labor market for new employees. ALPA's single-standard approach to B-scales following the United strike (i.e., six-year scales and uniform step rates, industrywide) exemplifies this strategy.

---

8. F. Spencer & F. Cassell, *supra* note 4, at 13.

In summary, it is realistic to expect that wage levels will continue to be affected by developments in the industrial relations patterns of the airline industry and by the dynamics of the collective bargaining process. These influences will interact with the particular economic and business considerations of the individual carriers. Finally, as the economics of the industry change, marginal wage levels will be eliminated by union bargaining.

NMB Activity

The role of the NMB in the administration of the Railway Labor Act is well documented. I am not a lawyer and do not intend to debate the legalities of NMB administrative rulings, procedures, and related court cases.

As an outsider coming into the airline industry, I initially found the NMB to be something of an enigma. Having negotiated under the National Labor Relations Act, I certainly found the differences dramatic and puzzling. The degree of government influence over the collective bargaining process was novel and, frankly, somewhat disconcerting.

Looking at the performance of the NMB as it relates to collective bargaining since deregulation, however, and recognizing and accepting its defined role as set forth in the Railway Labor Act, one can only conclude that the NMB has made sincere, strong, and reasonable efforts to facilitate the process of collective bargaining.

It is no longer unheard of for a union and carrier to reach settlement before the amendable date of the contract or to have a mediator assigned to the negotiations in advance of the amendable date. The NMB has tried to speed up the process and bring the parties to the day of decision more rapidly than during the days of regulation. In some cases, this has meant a proffer and early release. The parties are left with the responsibility of settling their differences without the aid of continuing, mandatory mediation. In making its decision to release the parties, the NMB is faced with the difficult task of resolving a policy dilemma between the parties' interest in an early economic confrontation and the potential injury such a confrontation poses to the general public.

In short, the collective bargaining process under the Railway Labor Act seems to have become more responsive to the preferences of individual carriers and trade unions as affected by product market considerations. At the same time, the NMB's decisions must continue to reflect its overarching statutory responsibility to avoid interruptions to commerce.

Innovations

From my perspective, the most valid measure of success or failure of the collective bargaining process in the years since deregulation is whether the process has resulted in stagnation and repression in the industrial relations system or in creativity and progress. Has the process identified new frontiers for the parties? Even a cursory review of the settlements in the industry, carrier by carrier, union by union, suggests that collective bargaining during the postderegulation period has been the catalyst for such innovations as ESOPs and employee ownership, union representation on boards, regulation of corporate expansion through scope clauses and related provisions, market rates, job security, and seniority integration, in addition to the more traditional wages, hours, and work rule agreements now common across the airline industry.

One example of innovation attributable to postderegulation collective bargaining was the agreement produced by Pan Am in its negotiations with ALPA. On March 17, 1987, Pan Am and ALPA concluded what was announced as a B-rate agreement for first officers of 727–200 aircraft. Similar rates of pay were agreed to with Pan Am's flight engineers' union for all aircraft. The novelty of this agreement was not in the "B" rates that were agreed to; most other carriers had already adopted this approach to market rates for new pilots. The timing of this aspect of the Pan Am agreement was simply a result of the necessity to exhaust its recall lists of laid-off pilots before attempting to establish new-entry market rates. More to the point, this agreement recognized particular product market needs for Pan Am and the changing characteristics of the labor market that provides newly employable pilots to major carriers. At the same time, the agreement acknowledged ALPA's interest in being the union representative for *all* individuals being placed on the Pan Am seniority list.

Both Pan Am and ALPA realized that the labor markets for pilots was changing. It would not continue to provide pilots with multiengine jet experience and commercial or military flying experience. Although many such candidates were available, as evidenced by Pan Am's recent hiring program, the company and the union recognized that the applicant profile was changing and the need to anticipate further changes in the labor market. As a result, Pan Am identified a source of pilots not previously exploited—the commuter or feeder carrier. Accordingly, Pan Am worked out an agreement that provided, through a series of market rates and seniority integration procedures, the movement of new-entry pilots from the open labor market to a subsidiary commuter carrier to Pan Am. This provided Pan Am with an early opportunity to screen, evaluate, and test pilots who would move up through the ranks, from twin-engine propeller planes to first officer or flight engineer positions (after appropriate training and qualification) on 727–200 and airbus jet equipment. This innovative approach provided a new source of pilots, managed the turnover on the commuter carrier, and guaranteed seniority integration from date of hire for individuals who successfully moved up.

Although my measurement criteria are admittedly subjective, in the main they serve to illustrate that (1) the collective bargaining process under deregulation has performed effectively and has not failed to deal with the basic elements of the labor-management relationship, namely seniority, rates of pay, and job security; (2) although the results are diverse across the industry, the process has produced results; the industrial relations system has been strengthened and the initial turmoil is beginning to subside, although it is far from over.

A scorecard on collective bargaining under deregulation should include the following: (1) whether one likes the results or not, collective bargaining has worked; (2) deregulation, in and of itself, is not anti–collective bargaining; (3) labor unions, carriers, and their collective industrial relations systems are free to engage in virtually the same bargaining process as other deregulated industries have successfully followed since the 1930s.

Are there other problems with deregulation? That is not the question I am trying to answer. Can improvements be made in the industrial relations system and the collective bargaining process? Definitely. That is the challenge for the future. Despite the government's failure to provide for an orderly transition from regulation to deregulation, collective bargaining has survived and the industrial relations system is growing stronger. Thus a collective bargaining framework is in place that is conducive to innovation as well as to labor-management participation and cooperation. Within this framework, I am certain collective bargaining can be more effective than it was under regulation.

An Economist's Perspective

Peter Cappelli

Even casual observers of the airline industry have noticed that in the period since deregulation, bargaining power and indeed the initiative in labor relations have shifted from the unions to management, especially compared to the period before deregulation. Less obvious is why this change has occurred and what management will do with its new power.

The deregulation of the airline industry was by any estimation a giant experiment based on academic ideas about how the delivery of air transportation might be improved from the standpoint of the consumer, and, as John Dunlop noted, no one paid any attention to what effects this experiment would have on labor relations.[1] At

I would like to thank the German Marshall Fund for the fellowship I received while this paper was being written.

1. Dunlop, *Trends and Issues in Labor Relations in the Transport Sector,* TRANSP. RES. NEWS, May-June 1985, at 1. The case for deregulation was based almost entirely on empirical findings of inefficient delivery of air transport associated with regulation (*see Insight into CAB Practices and Procedures, Hearings Before the Subcomm. on Administrative Practice and Procedures of the Senate Comm. on the Judiciary,* 94th Cong., 1st Sess. [1975]). The argument for deregulation put forward by the academic community was therefore a counterfactual one: get rid of the regulations, the inefficiencies will disappear as well. The argument for a complete deregulation of the market was furthered a few years later by theoretical arguments, again from the academic community, that suggested that the threat posed by new airline entrants would keep fares down and prevent profiteering even in those

the time, it seemed that deregulation would work to the advantage of the unions. The process of making routes competitive meant that carriers were much more vulnerable to strikes because their markets might be taken away by competitors while the carriers were shut down. As part of the Airline Deregulation Act, the carriers' strike assistance plan (the Mutual Aid Pact) was abolished, and the criteria for any new plan were made so restrictive that they were essentially prohibited. Both actions shifted bargaining power to the unions by making strikes more costly for management.

Explaining Union Losses

In the period immediately following deregulation, from 1978 through early 1981, labor in fact appeared to be doing well in collective bargaining. Management generally gave in under the threat of strikes (or did so shortly after strikes began), and the unions fared well in settlements. The position reversed sharply, however, after the industry recession in 1981 and the subsequent increase in union concessions. A popular explanation for this reversal was that competitive pressures from new, low-cost airlines had forced the trunk carriers to cut costs and, in turn, led to union concessions. This view fit in well with the predictions about how deregulation would work: anyone could start an airline now, and the threat of entry into established markets would bring the costs and fares down in all markets.

Despite the popularity of this view, there is little evidence to support it. Upstart carriers such as People Express had an important influence on fares in many regional markets, but all told they never held more than about 4 percent of the market for passenger traffic. The unions began making concessions not because the carriers were forced to cut costs to compete with low fares but because they needed to cut wages to generate cash flow to help stave off bankruptcy. The main financial pressures on the carriers were the industry recession—the first sustained decline in passenger demand in airline his-

---

markets that were too small to sustain competitive service. *See* Kyle & Phillips, *Airline Deregulation: Did Economists Promise Too Much or Too Little?* 21 Lo-gistics & Transp. Rev. 3 (1985), for an interesting discussion of the role of academic arguments in the deregulation process.

tory—and the bloody fare wars, not with the upstart carriers but with other trunk airlines. Just as the New Deal regulators of the industry had predicted, carriers responded to temporary excess capacity by slashing fares to fill empty seats, thus forcing their competitors to do likewise and eventually driving revenues below any reasonable break-even level.

Given the considerable job investment that airline employees have in their carriers (especially pilots and flight attendants because of their steep seniority pay), it is not surprising that they agreed to wage concessions to help prevent financial bankruptcies and the potential loss of their jobs.[2] A good analogy is the situation of the United Automobile Workers (UAW) during the Chrysler bailout in 1979. The first unions to make wage concessions, in 1981, were those at Braniff, Western, and Pan Am, as each of these carriers rocked close to bankruptcy. Similar financial crises and concessions followed shortly thereafter at Continental, Eastern, and Republic.[3] Some people refer to such a situation as "survival bargaining."

Although it took a year or more, unions at financially solvent carriers made concessions as well, and then continued to make them, indeed made more, even as the financial health of the industry improved; the steepest cuts in wages preceded economic hard times by several years.[4] The important question is, Why did increasing numbers of unions make concessions, and why have they continued to make them?

The pervasiveness of the bankruptcy-related concessions throughout the industry is surprising for several reasons. For one, the airline industry is not like steel where the ever-present threat of low-cost foreign competition continues to exert pressure on unions in the United States. Indeed, even in the auto industry, where the foreign competition is intense, the UAW's concessions at Chrysler did not extend to Ford or General Motors, and the number of unions making concessions did not accelerate over time as it has in the airlines. Nor was there a substantial low-cost nonunion presence in airlines of the

---

2. Indeed, similar developments took place six years earlier at Eastern, when unions responded to a financial crisis by agreeing to wage concessions in the form of the variable earnings plan.

3. Cappelli, *Competitive Pressures and Labor Relations in the Airline Industry*, 24 INDUS. REL. 316 (1985).

4. P. CAPPELLI, *Airlines*, in COLLECTIVE BARGAINING IN AMERICAN INDUSTRY 135 (D.B. Lipsky & C.B. Donn eds. 1987).

type that resulted in the widespread concessions in the meat-packing industry. Indeed, the airline industry had a higher percentage of union members than any other industry in the United States. Further, the financial health of the industry was improving and, if anything, the structural changes associated with deregulation increased the unions' power.

There are two reasons for the prevalence of union concessions. The first concerns the incentives for management to seek concessions and the new tactics and strategies it has used to put pressure on unions. Before deregulation, restrictions on fares and routes prevented labor cost cuts from being used to lower fares and take markets away from competitors. Further, increases in labor costs could be passed on to consumers through fare increases with varying ease depending on the regulations in force at the time. With the end of regulations, management no longer had these protections. It now had much more to gain from concessions and much more to lose if competitors' labor costs fell below its own.[5] After the floundering airlines secured concessions in 1981 to help stave off bankruptcy, the remaining carriers, which were much healthier financially, had a reason to demand equal treatment. The labor cost cuts at the six struggling carriers had given those carriers a competitive advantage that could be translated into lower fares and more business. The stronger carriers secured roughly similar concessions a year or so later on the grounds that the competitive advantage the weaker carriers gained through concessions had to be countered.

The question that remains, however, is, Why did the unions continue to make concessions once the initial concessions had been matched, and even as the overall health of the carriers improved? Certainly part of the problem is that the struggling carriers continued to get concessions. Indeed, Braniff (through negotiations) and Continental (through bankruptcy) took wages and work rules down to market levels, setting an invidious comparison for other carriers. But the main pressure to make additional concessions arose from the new strategies being pursued by management.

---

5. This helps explain why the concessions at Eastern in 1975 did not affect any other carriers: they did not give Eastern a competitive advantage that other carriers needed to counter.

New Management, New Strategies

The increased ability of airline management to put pressure on its unions, even when bankruptcy was not an issue, is the second important reason more and more unions made concessions. This increased ability arose from new strategies for dealing with labor, which in turn stemmed from the new management teams that began to take over the industry after deregulation.

Some observers have suggested that the chief task of management during regulation was to deal with the government regulators, and the expertise this entailed was useless after deregulation. Instead, deregulation demanded entirely new sets of management skills, ones associated with traditional market-driven businesses. Of course, the carriers had ready-made models for this management style in other competitive industries. One of the interesting characteristics of the hierarchical structure in American management is that the strategies and orientation of firms can be changed almost overnight with the introduction of a new top-management team. Most airlines transformed their management in this fashion and did so rather quickly. At Western, for example, less than 20 percent of the top-management team in 1985 had been with the carrier for more than two years. Industrial relations also went through this transformation. The vice presidents for industrial relations at six of the largest twenty-four carriers in the industry were replaced within six months during 1983, the period when the pressure for concessions really took off. Indeed, TWA got rid of its entire industrial relations department. Part of the reason for the speed of the change in industrial relations was that the previous management team was associated with (and took the blame for) the expensive system of labor relations that had developed over the previous forty years, which no longer seemed like a good system to top management. Certainly this pressure on industrial relations management was not unique to airlines, but it did seem particularly abrupt here.[6]

The most immediate consequence associated with these changes in management was a new willingness to maintain operations during

---

6. T.A. Kochan & P. Cappelli, *The Transformation of the Industrial Relations and Personnel Function*, in Internal Labor Markets 133 (P. Osterman ed. 1983).

strikes. As Northrup noted, before deregulation, airline management did not try to operate during strikes and routinely shut down operations when strikes occurred.[7] Ever since the 1979 ALPA strike at Northwest, virtually all carriers have operated during strikes, generally with success. Further, carriers have increasingly threatened to hire permanent replacements for strikers and in several cases have done so (most recently for flight attendants at TWA). These tactics were always open to airline management, but it was not until the introduction of postderegulation management that the change occurred.[8]

Perhaps the most important new tactic used by management has been the reshaping of airlines to influence collective bargaining outcomes. This includes the use of double-breasted operations to avoid union contracts and the use of bankruptcy proceedings to void contracts, both tactics pioneered by Texas Air. Many carriers made decisions about expansions or contractions explicitly contingent on the outcomes of collective bargaining, in the process putting severe pressure on employees eager for security and on the unions to agree to management's terms.[9]

The second major element contributing to the unions' continued willingness to agree to concessions and the shift of power to management had to do with the structure of the unions and of collective bargaining in the industry. The Railway Labor Act helped decentralize bargaining by establishing separate bargaining units for each craft or class of worker. There was little incentive for unions to represent workers across crafts at the same carrier or even to coordinate bargaining across crafts because each craft appeared able to shut the carrier down independently with a strike. The airline unions themselves, especially ALPA and the flight attendants'

---

7. Northrup, *Airline Strike Insurance: Comment*, 30 INDUS. & LAB. REL. REV. 364 (1977).

8. No doubt other considerations were also important, such as the end of the Mutual Aid Pact, which made it more costly to be shut down, as well as the ability of competitors to take a carrier's markets away if operations were shut down.

9. Examples are United's threat to discontinue B–737 service in 1981 unless ALPA agreed to two-person crews and American's threat in 1983 to sell planes and significantly shrink its operations unless unions agreed to work rule concessions and two-tier plans. Management at both carriers offered limited job security if the changes were granted.

unions, have almost from their inception been decentralized as well. Most of the attention of the international unions was directed at government lobbying in Washington, whereas local unions at each carrier were given considerable autonomy in their bargaining decisions.

The result was a decentralized model of collective bargaining paralleled perhaps only in the construction industry. This bargaining structure was not suited to the competitive environment following deregulation because it could not establish and maintain uniform contracts across carriers, which was essential now that product market regulations no longer provided this protection. Further, because the unions at each carrier responded individually to the strategies and pressures generated by their management, the international unions soon found themselves being whipsawed as each concession generated demands for concessions at the other carriers.

As organizations based on democratic processes and elected leadership, unions have considerably more inertia than management and are much slower to react to changes in the environment. For example, it was not until 1985 that ALPA made changes in its structure to give the international union more control over local settlements so as to help prevent concessions from spreading across carriers. Because of this inertia, unions not only in airlines but throughout the United States economy have often found themselves reacting after the fact to management initiatives.

Airline unions, however, have been far more creative than most unions in responding to management initiatives. In general, the responses have been to establish a link between management's business strategies and the outcomes of collective bargaining. In this sense, the unions have been aided by the RLA, which, unlike the Wagner Act, does not draw the distinction between permissive bargaining items (such as the new business strategies) and mandatory items (terms and conditions of employment). The unions generally have responded by negotiating contracts that restrict management strategies unbeneficial to employees. For example, limits on double-breasted operations were secured at four carriers.

The difficulty with these union innovations is that because they are now part of the collective bargaining agreement, enforcement becomes a matter of legal interpretation, and it is impossible to tell what will happen when the courts get involved in interpreting collective bargaining issues. When Delta bought Western, for example, the unions were frustrated in their attempts to enforce contractual restrictions on the merger.

Unions have had surprisingly greater influence outside of collective bargaining, where they have been able to tip the balance of decision making by influencing the financial markets. Unions drove the merger decisions at TWA, sought out the merger partner at Frontier (People Express), effectively drove the merger decision at Eastern, and are at present trying to shape a merger at Pan Am. At Eastern, the unions negotiated directly with the carrier's banks to establish a relationship between contract levels and loans, while at United, ALPA spent 1987 trying to take over the finances of the carrier altogether. The frustrations experienced by unions in their attempts at innovation in collective bargaining, combined with management's increasing use of strategies outside of collective bargaining to influence labor issues, no doubt pushed the unions to seek other forms of influence over employee relations. Together, these developments suggest that the pressures on labor are likely to continue even if the finances of the airline industry stabilize.

Evolution of Airline Union-Management Relations

Examination of the postrecessionary union-management scene across the United States, especially in the manufacturing sector, reveals continued hard bargaining and a fair amount of conflict but also many examples of unions and management working together, at least on some issues, to pursue mutual goals. These efforts include redesigning jobs to reduce costs and increase security, changing basic compensation structures to provide incentives for performance, and, perhaps most important, instituting programs to increase the sense of participation and commitment that unions and individual workers feel toward the firm.[10]

What is striking about union-management relations in air trans-

---

10. *See* Walton, *Work Innovations in the U.S.*, 57 Harv. Bus. Rev., July-Aug. 1979, at 88, for examples of high commitment; and Cappelli & McKersie, *Management Strategy and the Redesign of Work Rules*, 24 J. Mgmt. Stud. 441 (1987), for examples of how jobs have been redesigned.

port is that we see almost none of these industrial relations innovations now in place elsewhere in the economy. Although innovations abound in the form of management strategies for combating unions and union countertactics, there have been relatively few innovations in cooperative and mutually beneficial solutions to the problems faced by unions, workers, and management. Instead, relations have concentrated on confrontational bargaining over traditional issues.

For example, even though the number of strikes has decreased (in part because they are potentially much more costly than before deregulation), most observers suggest that the levels of conflict in union-management relations have reached all-time highs. Certainly it is difficult to imagine levels of trust getting much lower. From the union perspective, no doubt this is because of the steady supply of new management strategies designed to avoid unions (double-breasted and bankruptcy tactics, hiring permanent replacements for strikers, and so on).

Yet several carriers have formalized arrangements for union-management cooperation in recent years: board membership for union representatives at Republic, Pan Am, Eastern, and Western, as well as additional more elaborate union participation at Eastern (the employee-involvement plan) and at Western (the partnership plan). All these programs were introduced in times of crisis, generally as a quid pro quo for union contract concessions. The extent of cooperation typically followed a "yo-yo" pattern: growing stronger when crises occurred, then breaking down when the crises passed.[11] At Eastern, for example, the quality of union-management cooperation seemed to change almost every quarter as the financial fortunes of the carrier changed.

These cooperative arrangements between labor and management did do some good, however. They seemed to contribute to significant improvements in productivity at Eastern, and they were part of the overall program that restored Western from the brink of bankruptcy to profitability.[12] There is also strong evidence that when employees

---

11. Hammer & Stern, *A Yo-Yo Model of Cooperation: Union Participation in Management at the Rath Packing Company*, 39 INDUS. & LAB. REL. REV. 337 (1986).

12. For an account of the Eastern case, *see* LABOR-MANAGEMENT CO-OPERATION AT EASTERN AIRLINES, FINAL REPORT, from the Harvard–

saw union-management cooperative programs and board membership as effective, employees were more committed not only to their
employer but to their union as well. They were also more satisfied
with their work and even with their pay.[13]

In collective bargaining, negotiations since deregulation have remained focused on such zero-sum issues as wage levels and have
continued to be driven by management demands for concessions.
With the exception of some swaps of job security for concessions
(pilots at United in 1979 and more broadly at American in 1983), it
is difficult to think of any examples of mutual gains being achieved
through collective bargaining. Again, with the possible exception of
American, restructuring of union-management relations was not a
major goal.

One of the difficulties with achieving competitiveness by cutting
wages is that it has profoundly adverse effects on employees' attitudes and behavior. Likewise, letting wages decline below levels prevailing in the industry may produce similar effects. Survey data
suggest that the greater the gap between workers' pay and average
wage levels in the industry, the less commitment employees feel
toward the carrier and the less satisfied they are with their work,
their supervision, and, of course, their pay.

The replacement of senior, well-paid workers with new, lower-
paid workers, or indeed starting a new organization to achieve the
same end, may also have considerable costs. Anecdotal information
from manufacturing firms suggests that the skills and firm-specific
expertise held by senior workers can be worth a great deal, especially
when firms need to make rapid changes in products or the delivery
of services. There is also evidence that although workers new to an
organization, or workers in a new organization, may be satisfied with
wages below the industry level, satisfaction declines as their tenure
increases and they become more concerned about their pay relative

---

Brigham Young University study for the U.S. Department of Labor. For
the Western case, *see* K. Wever, Power, Weakness, and Membership Support
in Four U.S. Airline Unions (1986) (unpublished Ph.D. thesis, MIT).

13. The references throughout this section to studies of satisfaction
among airline employees are to the forthcoming article by Cappelli & Sherer,
*Satisfaction, Market Wages, and the Restructuring of Labor Relations: An Airline
Case*, INDUS. REL., and to P. Sherer, M. Morishima, & K. Wever, A Trans-
actional Model of Union and Company Commitment (1987) (unpublished
manuscript).

to the outside market. Some observers point to Pacific Southwest as an example of a new, low-cost organization that eventually grew up and started to look more like its competitors: the young, inexperienced workers who began with salaries well below industry levels eventually unionized and demanded higher wages.

Efforts to increase the productivity of the work force have proceeded along similar zero-sum lines. They have concentrated on securing work rule concessions through collective bargaining, concessions that in many cases look rather like Taylorism—increasing working time and reducing restrictions on schedules, reducing staffing levels, and shifting to cheaper forms of labor such as subcontracting. Again, there is evidence that many of these changes have adverse effects on employees' attitudes. In particular, changes that affect schedules and working time have strong negative effects on the satisfaction of airline employees with all aspects of their jobs. (Surprisingly, however, employees seem to be more satisfied with work rule changes that increase the variety of tasks they perform and the amount of responsibility they have. These changes apparently are not viewed as concessions.)

There have been virtually no efforts in air transport to increase productivity by tapping the hidden potential of airline workers through participative and employee-involvement programs, the current rage in the human resources field. For example, only three carriers claim to have any quality-of-work life programs by which to obtain workers' ideas and involve them in decision making. It is not clear whether any of these programs have in fact amounted to much, but there is strong evidence that workers in the United States want these arrangements[14] and that such arrangements are associated with improvements in work[15] and even in attitudes toward their unions.[16] Our studies suggest that when airline workers feel they have influence over their jobs, they are more satisfied with all aspects of their jobs and are more committed both to their carriers and to their unions.

---

14. T.A. KOCHAN, H.C. KATZ, & N.R. MOWER, WORKER PARTICIPATION AND AMERICAN UNIONS: THREAT OR OPPORTUNITY? (1983).

15. Katz, Kochan, & Gobeille, *Industrial Relations Performance, Economic Performance, and QWL Programs: An Interplant Analysis*, 37 INDUS. & LAB. REL. REV. 3 (1983).

16. Thacker & Fields, *Union Involvement in QWL Efforts: A Longitudinal Investigation*, 40 PERSONNEL PSYCHOLOGY 97 (1987).

Reasons for the Lack of Innovation

There appear to be several reasons why the more constructive innovations in union-management relations have not developed to the same extent in airlines as they have in other industries. First, the general lack of cooperative relations between management and labor seems due largely to a justifiable lack of trust between the parties. On the management side, the new interest at many carriers in getting rid of their unions altogether or at least in destabilizing them obviously makes the unions reluctant to engage in cooperative arrangements. The incredible turnover in the executive ranks since deregulation may have contributed to this lack of trust by making it difficult for the unions to develop any relationship or personal trust with management.[17]

Unions have traditionally been conservative organizations with respect to change, and there has been great inertia in adapting to the many changes in the airline industry and in introducing innovations. Union leaders are vulnerable to the risks associated with cooperative programs and with other labor relations experiments that might appear to be sellouts if they fail; they are elected officials who are routinely tossed out of office if programs do not work. Certainly the competition between unions within many of the crafts also increases the risks of innovation: a serious mistake can lead not only to a change in union leaders but to a change in unions. And the lack of cooperation between unions within the same carrier makes them reluctant to make changes individually for fear of ending up with worse outcomes than other crafts.

Furthermore, compared to their counterparts in the manufacturing industries, neither airline unions nor management have had as much experience in crisis bargaining and in working to save financially plagued operations. Even in periods when industries such as automobile manufacturing were stable and profitable, there were always plants in danger of being closed and labor negotiations designed to save those plants. In contrast, financial crises in air trans-

---

17. That many in the new management teams have come from outside the industry and are at least initially unfamiliar with (and perhaps unsympathetic toward) the idiosyncrasies of long-standing union-management relationships may make them more inclined to break those relationships as well.

port never involved labor negotiations before deregulation because the CAB always arranged mergers almost immediately to bail out the carriers.

Second, the current focus on wage and zero-sum work rule issues as a way to achieve efficiency is at least in part a reaction to the success of airline unions in the decades before deregulation. Union wages were so much higher than those in the outside market, especially for unskilled jobs, and work rules were so restrictive, especially for pilots and other skilled positions, that in management's view there was a great deal of "fat" that could be easily cut. The relative lack of effort to redesign jobs to improve productivity has occurred as a result of several problems. Because most airline jobs are service jobs, it has sometimes been difficult to identify the conditions affecting productivity or even its measures; in many cases, productivity is virtually identical to staffing levels (e.g., the number of pilots or flight attendants). Further, many of the characteristics that define how jobs are performed are set by FAA regulations and cannot be altered. In other words, the airlines may not have as much flexibility as other industries to redesign jobs to increase productivity.

The nature of bargaining also works against many job redesign innovations. Because airline jobs are categorized by craft, it is difficult to introduce work rule changes that expand the scope of jobs and to widen the range of responsibilities without cutting across those craft lines. Dealing with several unions—each of which typically demands treatment equal to or better than that received by the other unions—can make it very difficult for management ever to get agreement on general innovations in labor relations or in contracts. Rarely have all the unions at a carrier reached agreement among themselves about common concessions and other union-management issues.[18]

Third, efforts to develop job involvement and commitment to the organization are hindered by several conditions. Participative arrangements, such as quality-of-work life programs, that increase job involvement are more difficult to operate in air transport not only

---

18. In some cases, such as the adoption of industrywide ESOP plans or changes in some pension arrangements, agreement among all the unions is required by law. In other cases, such as policies to encourage or avoid mergers, agreement is a practical necessity. But such agreement rarely comes, as evidenced by the conflicts among unions at TWA, Eastern, and Pan Am, over attempts to shape merger decisions.

because there may be less inherent discretion in how jobs can be performed but also because the nature of work schedules makes it difficult for employees to get together to participate in decision making. Certainly the craft identification in air transport works against commitment to the carrier; pilots, for example, may see themselves as pilots first and employees of the carrier second. The often turbulent relations between crafts and unions also make it difficult to get employees to identify with the work force and the carrier as a whole. Finally, firms in other industries have the threat of foreign competition as a faceless, common enemy around which both labor and management can rally to improve productivity and gain a competitive advantage. But in air transport, workers know that gains in productivity may increase competition among carriers, which may in turn lead to cost cutting at one's own carrier.

Of course, management also contributes to the failure to introduce productivity-enhancing innovations and encourage job involvement and commitment. One way to assess management's position on these issues is to see how they operate in the absence of unions: how do they treat their nonunion employees? In most other industries, the most innovative employee relations systems are introduced for the nonunion employees, who are generally treated at least as well as the unionized workers. In airlines, the nonunion employee relations system is rarely innovative, and, if anything, these workers appear, on average, to be treated worse than their unionized counterparts.[19] Their pay cuts are often sharper than those of unionized workers,[20] they have little if any say in the changes (concessions) in the terms and conditions of employment, and they have been effectively disenfranchised from important corporate decisions, such as mergers, in which at least unions have given their members some voice.

The 1990s

The dominant influence shaping airline labor relations in the 1990s will be developments in the structure of the industry. The original

---

19. There are obviously exceptions, the most notable being Delta, which has a long history of managing its largely nonunion work force in an exemplary manner.

20. P. CAPPELLI, *supra* note 4.

promise of the deregulators—an airline industry with plenty of new entrants and competition to keep fares down, even in regional markets—clearly seems lost. Virtually all of the new entrants are now out of business, and it is difficult to imagine circumstances in which new carriers could ever be more than bit players. After the long wave of mergers, the market for air transport has become an oligopoly of six major carriers. By itself, that development does not tell us much about the future. Some oligopolies, as in the automobile industry, have been very profitable, while others have experienced continuous price cutting and very low profits, as in meat packing. The key has been whether the competitors have been able to differentiate the market and avoid competing on the basis of price. Since the bloody fare wars during the recession, the airlines appear to have learned to differentiate their markets somewhat by establishing dominant regional markets (developing the feed around hub-and-spoke route systems) and by preventing low-price entry into those markets through the threat of matching fare cuts. As the original regulators of the industry knew, however, battles for market shares in airlines can turn bloody very, very fast. When airlines have excess capacity (as in a recession), there are strong incentives to reduce fares to almost nothing to fill planes. In the process, they take business from competitors, which respond in kind, driving fares and profits through the floor.

How much pressure there will be from the carriers to cut labor costs will depend on how well they can differentiate the product market and avoid fare wars. At the moment, they appear to be doing that very well. The unions, of course, may counter cost-cutting pressures from management with centralized systems of bargaining that take wages out of competition. Even low-profit, cutthroat industries like meat packing had highly paid union workers for that reason. It is especially important now for unions to take wages out of competition because, for the first time, a low-wage, nonunion competitor, Continental Airlines, is creating pressure on other carriers to restrain labor costs.

The industry's move to an oligopoly structure should help the unions toward that goal. First, because the number of carriers is reduced (and, in particular, many of the more financially vulnerable carriers are gone), it is less likely that there will be struggling carriers demanding concessions from their relatively immobile employees. In other words, the weakest links in the industry's chain of labor contracts are gone. Second, the consolidation of carriers also means a consolidation of unions. The larger bargaining units that result are more efficient and thus easier to service and, because the surviving units are more similar, reduce the potential for conflicts in governance. We know from research in other industries, however, that if unions do not centralize bargaining, they may be able to do well in collective bargaining when business is strong but gains will collapse when markets weaken. Each management team seeks an advantage in negotiations that works against labor's goal of establishing uniform labor costs across employers. Attempts to secure such an advantage may soon shift from pressure on wages and zero-sum work rule issues toward innovations that increase productivity by capitalizing on the motivation and commitment of the employees. A shift in this direction would have several advantages for the carriers. First, wage cuts and other concessions can be cut only so far before carriers reach market rates and resistance from workers and their unions becomes too costly (or unions are formed at nonunionized airlines).[21] Second, gains in productivity through innovations in employee relations cannot be easily copied and therefore are likely to provide a more permanent competitive advantage than those gained from union concessions, which have proven to be remarkably ephemeral. The important point about such competition between carriers is that the possibilities for employee gains (through greater satisfaction, improved job security, and so on) suggest that it is not necessarily competition at the expense of the workers. Surely such competition is good for society as well.

---

21. There is evidence that this level has been reached, at least with B-scale rates for pilots; hence recent decisions at American and other carriers to raise the B-scale.

Part 2
Pay and Labor Markets

Trends in Pilots' Pay and Employment Opportunities

Jalmer D. Johnson

Early Years of Deregulation

In 1979, the industry's experience with deregulation involved primarily the amount of freedom that would be allowed in setting fares and establishing routes. Few new airlines entered the market, and thus there was minimal financial pressure on the incumbent airlines. Major and national airlines earned a sizable net profit—$384 million.

Pilots also experienced pay increases in the first few years of deregulation. From 1975 through 1978, salaries of pilots at major airlines increased by 8.6 percent annually, outstripping the average annual inflation rate during this period by 1.3 points.[1] In 1979 and 1980, a period in which nine of these pilot groups signed contracts, pay continued to increase at an annual rate of 8.2 percent, only two-thirds of the rate of inflation for this period.

The relative success that airlines and their pilots experienced in the early years of deregulation was short-lived, however. Beginning in 1980, the industry entered a period in which it was buffeted by (1) higher fuel prices, which escalated from 58 cents per gallon in 1979 to 89 cents per gallon in 1980 and $1.04 per gallon in 1981;[2] (2) the PATCO strike in August 1981, which forced the Federal

---

1. ALPA, Negotiator's Summary of Pilot Agreements (1975–80).

2. Merrill Lynch Capital Markets, Airline Industry Historical Data Book—Annual Operating and Balance Sheet for the Years 1975 through 1984 (1985).

Aviation Administration to institute capacity restrictions at the twenty-two largest airports, initially reducing their air traffic capacity by up to 50 percent; and (3) a nationwide recession. Although these conditions had a definite negative impact on airline profitability, a fourth factor arguably had the greatest impact on the airlines' profitability and therefore on employees' (and specifically pilots') compensation: the entry of low-cost airlines.

New Entrants

Although the first new entrant, Midway Airlines, began service in November 1979, the "new-entrant era" did not begin in a serious way until the start-up of New York Air in December 1980 and People Express in April 1981. The routes served and the services provided differed among new entrants, but they all shared two characteristics: a low overhead and low compensation.

The industry slowdown that began in 1980 created an ideal environment for the new entrants to attract employees. Hiring of pilots at incumbent airlines—which was maintained at a healthy rate of 3,200 pilots per year in 1978 and 1979—slowed to between 800 and 1,000 per year from 1980 through 1982 (fig. 1).[3] Moreover, a decline in traffic growth and an increase in operating losses forced some airlines to reduce capacity and furlough pilots. In 1980, 1,760 ALPA pilots were furloughed, followed by 990 in 1981 and 250 in 1982. Because pilots had limited opportunities at the incumbent airlines, new entrants were able to attract qualified pilots despite the low wages and minimal benefits. In 1981, the average annual salary for a senior captain at both New York Air and People Express was $30,000, and at Midway it was $42,000, compared to the ALPA average of $87,000 for comparable equipment.[4]

The industry's eroding economic condition, combined with the inability of incumbent airlines to compete effectively with the new entrants, reduced net income for major and national airlines from a profit of $32.1 million in 1980 to a net loss of $219.2 million in

3. Future Aviation Professionals of America, FAPA Update and FAPA Job Report (1978–82).

4. Future Aviation Professionals of America, Update 96, Pilot Employment Guide (1981); ALPA, Age/Wage Analysis (1981).

Figure 1. Pilots Hired at Major, National, and Regional Jet
Airlines (1978–86)

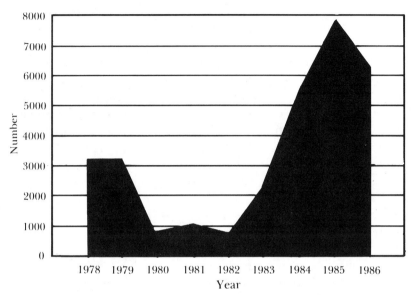

SOURCE: Future Aviation Professionals of America, FAPA Job Report
(1978–86).

1981 and $905.2 million in 1982. These losses forced many airlines
to scramble to find ways to remain financially viable. The conclusion
was that the most direct approach was to reduce employee costs.

Compensation and Financial Viability

At 28 percent of total employee expenses and nearly 10 percent of
total operating expenses in 1981, compensation of pilots was a primary focus of the airlines' cost-reduction efforts. Although reluctant
to give up any of their pay, benefits, or working conditions, pilots
were more willing than other employee groups to provide short-
term relief for their airlines because of their highly structured seniority system, which prevented lateral movement between airlines.
From late 1981 through 1982, thirteen pilot groups represented by
ALPA at major and national airlines agreed to significant pay and
work rule concessions. Of these thirteen groups, ten agreed to tem-

porary across-the-board pay cuts ranging from 6 to 25 percent (table 1).

Before 1982, pilots' wages at major airlines were kept, on average, within 9 to 11 percent of the average industry wage. Beginning in 1982, however, while pilots at struggling airlines saw their wages temporarily reduced, those at profitable airlines continued to experience steady increases (table 2 and fig. 2). This period, therefore, saw the first major split in wages among pilots at major airlines; the disparity in some cases was now more than 50 percent (tables 3 and 4 and fig 3).[5] The disparity increased further in 1983 as Continental filed for Chapter 11 bankruptcy and used its bankruptcy filing to abrogate its labor contracts and implement new wage rates and work rules. Pilots' wages alone were reduced by 46 to 62 percent.

Industry Profits Improve

As the industry continued to recover, incumbent airlines became more effective in competing with their low-cost counterparts through the use of yield-management plans, frequent-flyer programs, and hub-and-spoke route systems. In 1983, the industry cut its net loss from the previous year by more than 80 percent and subsequently posted net profits in excess of $850 million in both 1984 and 1985.

Another competitive strategy adopted by the more profitable airlines was to resume their internal expansion plans, which had been derailed by the industry downturn. To take better advantage of expansion, airlines again concentrated on ways to reduce labor costs. Instead of focusing on pay cuts for existing workers, they demanded reduced pay rates for workers yet to be hired. Enter the B-scale.

B-Scales and Industry Expansion

The benchmark B-scale was adopted at American in November 1983, permanently reducing pay for newly hired pilots by 50 percent.

---

5. Tables 2 and 3 and figures 2 and 3 present wage comparisons, including and excluding Braniff and Continental, to show that although the wage rates established by the airlines that filed for Chapter 11 significantly increased the disparity in industry wages, the disparity in wages increased two to three times even independent of the bankruptcies.

Table 1. Concessions Accepted by ALPA Pilots at Major Airlines (1981–82)

Airline	Date	Summary of Concessions
Aloha	1/81	Pay cap increased from 75 to 80 hours for six months without increase in pay
Air California	6/82	Wages cut by 10% and frozen for one year
Braniff	2/81	Wages cut by 10%
	10/81	10% wage cut extended
	12/81	Pay cap increased from 75 to 85 hours
Continental	10/81	10% wage deferral
	8/82	9.25% pay deferral; pay cap increased from 75 to 78 hours
Eastern	9/81	Pay reduced by 4.5 to 15%
Flying Tiger	5/82	Pay cap increased from 75 to 80 hours
Hawaiian	12/82	Pay reduced by 24 to 47%; pay cap increased from 75 to 85 hours
Pan Am	10/81	Pay reduced by 10% and wages frozen through 12/31/82
Piedmont	12/81	Pay cap increased from 80 to 85 hours
Republic	8/81	Wages reduced by 15% in exchange for company stock
	1/82	Wages reduced by 10% for six months; scheduled raise deferred until 7/1/82
	2/82	Wages reduced by 25% for four months
	10/82	Wages reduced by 10% for two months, plus an additional wage cut of 5% for three months
TWA	4/82	Pay frozen effective 1/82 through 12/82; wages reduced by 20% for 200 least senior pilots
United	8/81	Flat salary; pay cap increased from 77.5 to 81 hours; work rules relaxed
Western	1/82	Pay cut by 10% through 7/31/82
	5/82	Pay cut by 10% through 12/31/82

SOURCE: ALPA.

Following American's lead, other airlines began to demand similar packages. Subsequent B-scales for pilots agreed to in 1984 varied significantly from the American structure. The B-scales ranged from the Pacific Southwest (PSA) agreement, which extended its twelve-

Table 2. Maximum Hourly Pay Rates for Boeing 727 Captains at Profitable versus Unprofitable Incumbent Major Airlines

	*Profitable Incumbent Airlines**	*Unprofitable Incumbent Airlines*	
1986	$133.72	$80.74[†]	$91.04[‡]
1985	130.79	85.08	99.87
1984	125.68	77.84	91.15
1983	120.57	94.51	97.29
1982	111.36	91.90	92.32
1981	99.67	95.30	96.39
1980	89.80	85.99	84.45
1979	79.62	78.12	77.94
1978	73.07	71.35	71.87
1977	67.54	65.73	65.86
1976	61.45	58.04	58.54
1975	56.35	53.88	53.97

SOURCE: ALPA.
*American, Delta, Northwest, Piedmont, United, and USAir.
[†]Braniff, Continental, Eastern, Pan Am, Republic, TWA, and Western.
[‡]Rates for Braniff and Continental were not included in calculating figures in this column.

year pay scale to fifteen years by inserting new pay rates in the second through fourth years (these were an average of 36 percent below previous rates), to the Piedmont agreement, which produced an approximate 30 percent disparity for new pilots and did not provide for parity until pilots were in their third year as captains.

The B-scale that came out of the agreement ending the United pilots' strike in June 1985, which created pay rates for newly hired pilots for their first five years, established a more uniform structure on which subsequent B-scales have been based. Although United's pay rates for pilots in their sixth year and beyond are subject to negotiations, ALPA has been successful since the United agreement in keeping parity for nearly all B-scales to six years or less. This "industry standard" six-year parity was supported by the arbitrated decision reached at Alaska in June 1986.[6]

In large part because of B-scales and lower fuel prices, the industry has steadily increased capacity since 1985. In 1985 and 1986, major

---

6. Alaska Airlines–ALPA 1986 Contract Arbitration (June 11, 1986).

Figure 2. Maximum Pay Rates for Boeing 727 Captains at
Profitable versus Unprofitable Incumbent Major Airlines

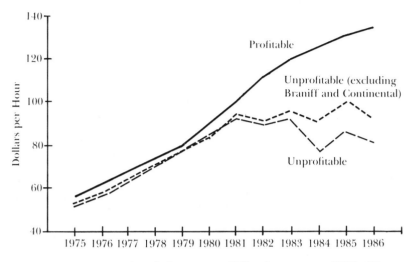

SOURCE: ALPA, Negotiator's Summary of Pilot Agreements (1975–86).

Table 3. Maximum Pay Rates for Boeing 727 Captains at
Incumbent Major Airlines

	Average Hourly Wage	Maximum Hourly Wage	Minimum Hourly Wage	Maximum Percentage above Average	Minimum Percentage below Average
1986	$105.19	$143.33	$47.25	36.26	−55.09
1985	106.18	143.33	44.09	34.99	58.47
1984	99.92	133.35	43.01	33.46	56.95
1983	107.54	127.26	80.63	18.34	25.03
1982	100.88	117.27	85.06	16.24	15.68
1981	97.32	105.62	88.46	8.53	9.11
1980	87.62	97.24	76.93	10.97	12.20
1979	78.76	88.32	73.68	12.13	6.46
1978	72.08	81.06	67.14	12.46	6.86
1977	66.51	73.47	61.48	10.47	7.56
1976	59.50	64.50	52.34	8.41	12.04
1975	54.94	62.57	51.58	13.89	6.11
1975–81	73.82	81.83	67.37	10.85	8.73

SOURCE: ALPA, Negotiator's Summary of Pilot Agreements (1975–86).

Table 4. Maximum Pay Rates for Boeing 727 Captains at
Incumbent Major Airlines (excluding Braniff and Continental)

	Average Hourly Wage	Maximum Hourly Wage	Minimum Hourly Wage	Maximum Percentage above Average	Minimum Percentage below Average
1986	$114.32	$143.33	$76.15	25.38	−33.39
1985	116.74	143.33	76.15	22.78	34.77
1984	109.98	133.35	82.09	21.24	25.36
1983	109.99	127.26	85.06	15.70	22.66
1982	102.70	117.27	85.06	14.18	17.18
1981	98.18	105.62	92.38	7.58	5.91
1980	87.13	97.24	76.93	11.60	11.70
1979	78.78	88.32	73.68	12.10	6.48
1978	72.47	81.06	67.14	11.86	7.35
1977	66.70	73.47	61.48	10.15	7.83
1976	59.99	64.50	52.34	7.52	12.76
1975	55.16	62.57	51.58	13.43	6.49
1975–81	74.06	81.83	67.93	10.49	8.27

SOURCE: ALPA, Negotiator's Summary of Pilot Agreements (1975–86).

and national airlines collectively took delivery of five hundred air-craft. As a result, the demand for pilots, which began to grow in 1983 and 1984 as new entrants continued to expand, increased dramatically. In 1985 alone, 7,840 pilots were hired, an increase of 43 percent over 1984.[7] Hiring continued at a brisk pace in 1986, when 6,341 pilots were hired. Even American hired nearly 2,000 pilots during this two-year period. Many came from regional airlines, contributing to an average annual attrition rate of nearly 40 percent.

The market for pilots since 1985 contrasted sharply with the market that existed during the first few years of deregulation. Given the choice, pilots began more readily to accept employment at incumbent airlines, which offered better pay, benefits, working conditions, and job stability. As a result, to meet their ambitious expansion plans as well as to slow the attrition rate of current pilots, low-paying airlines were forced to increase their compensation to attract new pilots. One example is People Express, which created a seniority-based pay structure and in 1986 increased the pay for senior captain to $68,300 to

7. FUTURE AVIATION PROFESSIONALS OF AMERICA, FAPA JOB REPORT (1983–86).

Trends in Pilots' Pay

Figure 3. Maximum Pay Rates for Boeing 727 Captains:
Percentage Difference from Average for Incumbent
Major Airlines

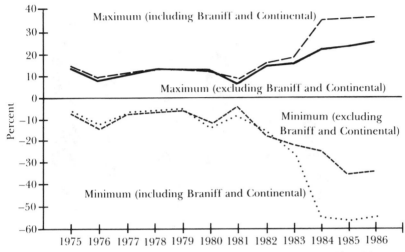

SOURCE: ALPA, Negotiator's Summary of Pilot Agreements (1975–86).

stem an attrition rate that had reached 25 percent the year before.[8]
Another example is Continental, which in 1985 restored its seniority-
based system and raised the pay for a senior captain from $43,000
to $62,500 per year. In June 1987, the rate reached $71,000 and in
June 1988, $74,500. The combination of a more competitive work-
place and more senior pilot groups forced Midway, New York Air,
and People Express to increase their pay for senior captains at an
annual rate of 13.7 percent between 1981 and 1986 (fig. 4).

The growing shortage of pilots also affected the higher-paying incumbents by placing upward pressure on B-scale rates. Following the
benchmark United contract, American was forced to respond. In August 1985, American eliminated its existing scale and replaced it with
new hourly rates for the first four years of service and agreed to negotiate rates for the fifth year and beyond. American increased its hourly
rates by an average of 25.9 percent, setting them at a level that was an
average of 11.2 percent higher than United's B-scale rates (fig. 5). The
rates for subsequent first-time B-scales continued to rise. In August

---

8. *Pilot Pool Is Drying Up*, AIR TRANSPORT WORLD (June 1985).

Figure 4. Average Hourly Wage for Senior Captains at Midway, New York Air, and People Express

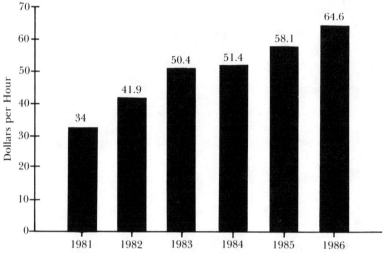

SOURCE: ALPA, Negotiator's Summary of Pilot Agreements (1975–86).

1986, Delta pilots agreed to a B-scale that contained pay rates averaging 36 percent higher than United's rates. In March 1987, American modified its B-scale even further, increasing pay rates by an additional 15 to 29 percent—an average of 32.5 percent above its prevailing rates—and establishing parity at ten years. In addition, Piedmont reduced its parity level to six years.

Unequal Participation in Industry Profitability

Unfortunately, not all airlines benefited from the industry's recovery and growth. Eastern, Pan Am, Republic, and Western, for instance, continued to post significant net losses: in 1983, their combined net loss was $400 million. These losses forced these airlines, which had previously obtained concessions from their employees, to ask for additional concessions. The pilot groups at each airline agreed during 1983 and 1984 to extend or increase previously approved concessions. New pay cuts ranged from 12 percent at Pan Am to 22 percent at Eastern, 23 percent at Republic, and up to 30 percent at Western.

Figure 5. American Airlines B-Scale Hourly Wages for First
Officers on DC-9s

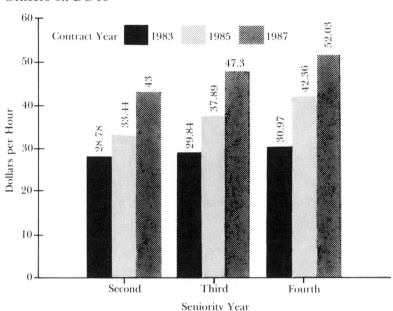

SOURCE: ALPA, Negotiator's Summary of Pilot Agreements.

In exchange for these concessions, employees at Eastern, Republic,
and Western demanded a partial payment in the form of stock and
representation on the airlines' boards of directors (employees at Pan
Am had already received stock as part of their 1981 concessions).
Employee ownership also emerged at PSA in 1984, where employees
agreed to a 15 percent reduction in pay at the national airline. Initial
stock holdings by employees ranged from 12 percent at Pan Am to
32 percent at Western (table 5). In addition to obtaining further
concessions for stock, both Republic and Western changed top management. These changes, combined with a revamping of operations,
enabled both Republic and Western to return to profitability and
subsequently become attractive candidates for mergers. In 1986,
employees at TWA agreed to concessions of up to 22 percent to
attract Carl Icahn to purchase their airline and received 20 percent
of the airline's outstanding stock in return.

Profit-sharing plans were also negotiated by six ALPA airlines
between 1983 and 1985 as an additional way to offset concessions

Table 5. Employee Stock Ownership Plans at Airlines Represented by ALPA

Airline	Year	Employee Stock Holdings*
Eastern	1983	25%
Pan Am	1981	12%
PSA	1984	15%
Republic	1984	15%
TWA	1986	20%
Western	1984	32%

SOURCE: ALPA.
*Initial stock holdings when plan was implemented.

(table 6). Because such plans were adopted by financially unstable airlines, however, few employees actually benefited. In fact, in 1985, only employees at Air California and Western received profits (approximately $900 and $1,000 respectively), and in 1986, only those at Air California did (an average of $400 each).

Current Trends

The compensation system for pilots has undergone drastic changes since deregulation. From bankruptcies to B-scales, there has been continual downward pressure on pilots' wages and benefits. Recent developments, however, suggest that this trend is changing and that salaries are leveling off. This leveling off—which has occurred on both ends of the pay scale—has arisen primarily for four reasons: (1) the increased demand for pilots; (2) the inability of some unprofitable airlines to take advantage of previous concessions; (3) the increase in profitability industrywide; (4) the trend toward consolidation.

DEMAND FOR PILOTS

Pay rates for new pilots increased during the late 1980s largely because of a shortage of pilots. The combined effect of continued industry expansion and an increase in retirements should keep pilots in a seller's market into the 1990s. Major and national airlines had 450 aircraft on order for delivery in 1987 and 1988 and have more than 900 on order or option for delivery in subsequent years. Re-

Table 6. ALPA Profit-Sharing Plans

Airline	Year Adopted	Distribution Base
Western	1983	15% of first $25 million, 20% thereafter, of pretax profits, excluding extraordinary gains or losses; per employee basis.
	1984	15% above the original 20% pretax profits, excluding extraordinary gains or losses exceeding $75 million; proportion based on salary.
TWA	1983	100% of first $10 million, 20% of next $50 million, 25% of next $50 million, and 30% of profits over $110 million, all of pretax profits, excluding extraordinary items and preferred dividends; proportion based on salary.
	1986*	20% of operating income minus interest expense, preferred stock dividends, and income taxes.
PSA	1984	15% of pretax earnings; 50% cash, and 50% stock; proportion based on salary.
Air California	1984	15% of pretax earnings; proportion based on W-2 income.
Braniff	1984	10% of pretax operating profits in excess of $30 million.
Eastern	1985	All net income in excess of $90 million; proportion based on W-2 income; only for calendar year 1985

Source: ALPA.
*Profit sharing went into effect in 1987.

tirements will begin to play a larger role in determining the industry's demand for pilots, since more than 600 pilots are expected to retire each year for the rest of the 1980s. This rate will increase to more than 1,500 each year in the following decade; ALPA estimates that the industry will need to hire between 4,000 and 6,000 pilots each year through the mid-1990s.

Table 7. Profits of Eastern Airlines (1978–86)

	Operating Profit (in millions)	Net Profit (in millions)
1978	$ 96.8	$ 67.3
1979	111.1	57.6
1980	1.9	(17.4)
1981	(50.0)	(65.9)
1982	(18.8)	(74.9)
1983	(100.1)	(183.7)
1984	189.6	(37.9)
1985	221.6	6.3
1986	65.0	(130.8)

Source: DOT Form 41, I.P. Sharp database.

RESISTANCE TO FURTHER CONCESSIONS

Incumbent airlines, which have recorded a steady flow of losses since deregulation, have encountered increasing resistance from their employees to making concessions. The inability of these airlines to capitalize on their employees' earlier concessions to improve finances has raised doubts about the advisability of granting additional concessions.

At Pan Am, employees have been granting major wage, benefit, and work rule concessions since 1981. Pilots, for example, agreed to keep their wages 10 percent or more below their 1981 levels for more than four years. Despite these continued concessions, Pan Am has been losing nearly $1.2 billion since 1981. Concerned about Pan Am's continued demand for concessions, pilots and other employees have begun searching for ways to have greater input into the future direction of their airline.

Employees at Eastern, who have made concessions since the mid-1970s, have had a similar experience. As Eastern's losses began to mount in the 1980s (table 7) employees accepted temporary wage reductions and other concessions. From 1981 to 1984, pilots' wages were reduced by 4 to 22 percent, and in March 1986, the pilots accepted a 22 percent reduction for an additional two years. Pilots' wages in 1987 were thus below their 1981 levels. Although employee concessions have enabled Eastern to post $476 million in operating profits since 1984, the airline continues to record net losses. Pilots have vigorously opposed demands by Eastern's new owner to increase their concessions by an additional 29 percent.

The wisdom of resisting continual requests for concessions has been confirmed by success stories at Republic and Western. In each case, new management and a new operating plan—not just employee concessions—took the airlines from the brink of bankruptcy to profitability. Subsequently, each airline was purchased by profitable, higher-paying airlines.

Pilots throughout the industry have become increasingly resistant to carrying the lion's share of the cost-savings effort. Pilot compensation as a percentage of total employee compensation among major airlines declined steadily, from a peak of 28.1 percent in 1980 to 24.2 percent in 1986. Pilots' share of total compensation, however, declined 13.9 percent during this period. The reallocation of compensation has been even more dramatic at airlines such as Western, TWA, and Continental, where pilots' proportion of total compensation from 1980 to 1986 declined by 20.8 percent, 27.8 percent, and 28.8 percent, respectively.

WAGES AND PROFITABILITY

Industry profitability has also affected the growing leveling off of pilots' wages. Record profits have weakened managements' arguments regarding the need for concessions by pilots and other employees, and airlines have found ways to compete effectively in a lower fare environment even though the low-cost airlines have the larger combined market share. Pilots at profitable airlines, including American, Delta, Piedmont, Southwest, United, and USAir, have continued to negotiate pay increases, although the percentage has decreased (along with the inflation rate) compared to previous periods. Moreover, the success of these airlines suggests that there is not a direct correlation between low wages and profitability. Of the fourteen largest airlines in 1986, four (USAir, American, Delta, and Republic) were ranked among the top six in both net profit margin and average compensation per employee (table 8). The airline with the highest average compensation, Delta—which is predominantly nonunion—produced a healthy 4.3 percent net profit margin. In contrast, Delta's primary competitor, Eastern, experienced a 2.9 percent net loss, even though the salaries of Eastern's employees are an average of $10,000 per year lower.

Table 8. Average Compensation and Net Profit Margins for the
Fourteen Largest Airlines (1986)

	Average Compensation	Net Profit Margin	Rank
Delta*	$50,639	4.31%	5
USAir	46,572	4.99	2
United	45,512	− 1.21	10
American	42,789	4.26	6
Republic[†]	41,981	4.44	3
Northwest	41,684	2.35	7
Eastern	40,642	− 2.89	11
Southwest	39,882	8.01	1
Pan Am	39,092	−17.17	13
Piedmont	35,069	4.37	4
Western	35,014	0.55	9
TWA	34,774	− 3.34	12
People Express[‡]	31,500	−17.98	14
Continental	29,350	0.87	8

SOURCE: DOT Form 41, I.P. Sharp database.
*Listed as they were ranked for compensation.
[†]Compensation figures estimated based on separate operating results through third quarter of 1986.
[‡]Compensation figures are for 1985 because data were incomplete for 1986.

In the 1980s, cash flow has become an even more important measure of corporate viability. As with net profit margin, comparing cash flow as a percentage of revenue with the average salary of each employee shows that there is not a direct correlation between low pay and strong cash flow (table 9). In 1986, the same four airlines were ranked in the top six in both categories.

INDUSTRY CONSOLIDATION

The current trend toward rapid consolidation is clearly reshaping the structure of the industry. Since January 1986, twenty-five airlines have been involved in fifteen mergers. The market share of the five largest airlines jumped from 54.3 percent in January 1986 to 72.5 percent in January 1987.

Industry consolidation is also having an upward influence on pilots' wages. Since January 1986, ten major airlines represented by ALPA, plus American, which is represented by the Allied Pilots Association, have been or are currently involved in eight mergers.

Table 9. Average Compensation and Cash Flow for the Fourteen Largest Airlines (1986)

	Average Compensation	*Cash Flow as a Percentage of Total Operating Revenue*	*Rank*
Delta*	$50,639	10.77%	3
USAir	46,572	10.11	5
United	45,512	6.14	8
American	42,789	10.23	4
Republic†	41,981	9.49	6
Northwest	41,684	8.90	7
Eastern	40,642	4.42	11
Southwest	39,882	16.98	1
Pan Am	39,092	−10.57	13
Piedmont	35,069	11.10	2
Western	35,014	5.15	9
TWA	34,774	4.12	12
People Express‡	31,500	−11.59	14
Continental	29,350	4.84	10

SOURCE: DOT Form 41, I.P.Sharp database.
*Listed as they were ranked for compensation.
†Compensation figures estimated based on separate operating results through third quarter of 1986.
‡Compensation figures are for 1985 because data were incomplete for 1986.

Seven of these mergers have resulted, or are expected to result, in the integration of the respective airlines.[9] The wages for pilots at the surviving airline were higher after six of these seven mergers (table 10). In fact, wages were up to 65 percent higher. The net effect of industry consolidation has been a reduction in the wage disparity among pilots at incumbent airlines.

Outlook for the Future

The compensation scale for pilots has come nearly full circle since deregulation. Salaries, which were on a strong upswing at the be-

---

9. The merger agreement between Texas Air and Eastern (amendment to Form S–4, filed with the Securities and Exchange Commission Oct. 2, 1986) states that "for a period of at least two years following the Effective Time, Eastern will retain its independent identity as a separately operating subsidiary of Texas Air."

Table 10. Impact of Mergers on Pilots' Pay Rates (June 1, 1987)

		Maximum Hourly Wages		
Merger	*Representative Aircraft*	*Surviving Airline*	*Merging Airline*	*Percentage Difference*
American–Air California	MD-80/737	$126.62	$ 99.29	+27.5
Delta-Western	B-727	143.33	86.81	+65.1
Northwest-Republic	B-727	139.23	87.26	+59.6
TWA-Ozark	MD-80	92.52	114.41	−19.1
United–Pan Am Pacific	B-747	173.05	146.89	+17.8
USAir-PSA	DC-9	135.14	111.67	+21.0
USAir-Piedmont	B-727	139.36	138.39	+ 0.7

SOURCE: ALPA, Negotiator's Summary of Pilot Agreements (December 1986).

ginning of deregulation, began to vary as the financial fortunes of airlines began to change. Pilots' salaries plummeted to record lows from 1982 to 1984 as the industry faced both sizable low-cost new entrants and reborn incumbents. The downward direction of pilots' wages began leveling off in the mid-1980s, however. An upward pressure on wages for newly hired pilots arose as the industry scrambled to attract pilots to meet its ambitious expansion plans. Low-cost airlines began having to increase wages at a rapid pace not only to compete against higher-paying airlines for applicants but to meet the needs of a more senior group of pilots. Although pilots at some airlines have continued to work under concessionary agreements, the size of this group will diminish as mergers are completed. Those who continue to work at reduced wages are resisting further cuts and instead are placing the responsibility for improving profits on their management.

Pilots at the profitable mega-carriers will likely continue to accrue pay increases, albeit at a lower annual rate than before deregulation. B-scale rates will continue to rise, increasing the probability of the eventual eradication of the lower-tier pay structure.

Pilots will take a cautious approach to alternative compensation, specifically profit sharing. Although the limited sucess of profit sharing in the industry has been a direct result of low profits, pilots in general have looked at claims of financial hardship with skepticism, particularly since some holding companies have spun off profitable operations (i.e., UAL, Inc., spinning off its computer reservations systems, and Texas Air spinning off Eastern's CRS).

To develop a guaranteed pool of qualified pilots, major airlines will look more toward their regional code-sharing partners and will eventually institute a formal procedure of graduating regional pilots to the major airlines. Finally, the consolidation of airlines will improve ALPA's ability to coordinate bargaining strategies among its member pilot groups.

From Jerusalem
to Dallas:
The Impact of
Labor Markets on
Airline Negotiations

Martin C. Seham

The return of competitiveness to the airline industry has revived the law of supply and demand in the industry's labor market. The conditions affecting this market are new for the airlines but standard for what remains of the nonregulated sector of American industry.

During the days of regulation, limited competition, and limited entry, the labor market in the airline industry reflected the commercial stability of the industry itself. Labor supply was only one component of the bargaining process. Foremost among the other components was the capital-intensive nature of the industry. The high cost of capital and the relatively low ratio of labor costs to capital investment encouraged companies to avoid confrontations whenever peace could be bought with a relatively small increase in labor costs.

Of course, another deterrent to confrontation was and continues to be the structure of the Railway Labor Act, which looks to a delay in the parties' use of economic power to give full range to the play of the negotiating process. Nonetheless, before deregulation, management and labor were free to calculate the damage of a confrontation only in terms of the injury *they* might do to each other; to a large extent they were insulated from the danger of injury from other quarters. Regulation gave some guarantees that new entrants would not leap into the vacuum created by a labor-management confrontation and take unlimited financial advantage of a shutdown. Indeed, for a substantial time, under the Mutual Aid Pact a struck carrier was assured of being reallocated a substantial portion of the market share that had been redirected to competitors. For some carriers the net result was higher profits (or at least lower costs) than operating during an off-peak season. It has also been suggested that the Mutual Aid Pact was designed to reduce costs among the carriers involved, at the expense of labor, and that the pact created a disincentive to reach agreements. In short, during regulation neither management nor labor had reason to fear the loss of long-term job security or company viability from industrial confrontations. Instead, such confrontations may even have been a device to adjust industry capacity to market needs.

The American Example

Deregulation and its consequences placed very different stakes on the table and offered the participants new kinds of chips with which to play. As general counsel to the Allied Pilots Association (APA), the independent certified representative of the American Airline pilots, I was close to the negotiations that resulted, in 1983, in one of the earliest realizations of the two-tier system. APA was not faced with an insolvent or failing carrier; it was, however, forced to deal with an economic environment that had changed dramatically because of the effects of deregulation and was, by virtue of its independence, mandated to reach an agreement consistent with the needs and objectives of its constituency.

During the period of negotiations surrounding the new pay system, American conducted a major "education" campaign for the purpose of explaining the economic environment in which it operated and options available to it. This campaign occurred during the term of the labor contracts and thus required the airline to be particularly persuasive in selling its pay proposals to the unions. Because of deregulation, the airline could effectively argue that it was faced with new entrants offering low fares and expanded fares but that were free of the burdens of high labor costs.

American claimed it had capital investment decisions to make and that they had to be predicated on the expectation of a fair rate of financial return. American argued that it could retrench and limit its operation to the most profitable routes or expand by making capital investments in new aircraft and services. The American pilots were told, with a combination of threat and promise, that they in effect had to make a contribution to that capital investment if its fruits were to be realized. The promised advantages to the American pilots were job security (with an explicit promise that pilots currently furloughed would be recalled) and opportunities for promotions, all at the cost of reduced salaries for newly hired pilots. The union was not enthusiastic about creating a two-tier system and was well aware of the institutional and bargaining problems such a system would produce in later years. The union was also convinced, however, of the reality of American's investment discretion and the competitive environment, as well as the availability of thousands of well-qualified, and often desperate, pilots who had been squeezed out of positions with failed carriers such as Braniff or retrenched carriers such as Pan Am. Thus the job market had a direct impact on APA's decision-making process and, without any attempt at quantification, contributed to the agreement that was reached.

Only a few years later, in 1987, American and its pilots again found themselves in negotiations. The agreement under which two tiers had been established had done its service for both parties. American had committed itself to a major investment program, was in the process of creating new hubs and services, had recalled the furloughed pilots, and, in exchange for certain concessions on working conditions, was now prepared to offer lifetime job security for the expanded pilot complement. In the meantime, APA had become sensitized to the problems arising from having a disparity in wages (two tiers) for the performance of identical work in the cockpit. APA's original, reluctantly made concession had served its purpose and needed to be revised to meet current needs. American Airlines was briskly hiring new pilots—even lowering some entry-level requirements to fulfill its hiring goals—and was battling with the union over attempts to penalize new pilots who wanted to leave American after their training period. The same pool of qualified pilots that had threatened APA's earlier negotiations simply did not exist in 1987. At the same time, American had to consider United's unsuccessful attempt to displace its pilot work force. Negotiators for the pilots have stated that another pilot pool existed of regular employees of new entrants who might have been enticed to change jobs in the event of a confrontation at American. The negotiators thus did not believe the general shortage of pilots played a significant part in American's negotiations.

The earlier fears stemming from when the labor market was saturated had obviously dissipated. This was the time to repair the discrepancies in compensation that had arisen from the introduction of two tiers. The result was a negotiated increase for the second-tier group amounting to 32 percent over three years, compared to only 6 percent for the more senior first-tier pilots. The contract also provided for a merger of the two scales at the time of promotion to captain or after ten years of employment. The influence of the labor market on the parties' negotiations was palpable, and American's willingness to respond was a reflection of the entrepreneurial imperative that exists in a deregulated industry.

The El Al Example

The other example I wish to recount is in some literal ways about as far removed from the American Airlines situation as one can imagine, but this disparate example may help in arriving at some common conclusions.

The collective bargaining agreement between El Al Israel Airlines and the International Association of Machinists (IAM) expired on March 15, 1983, and I was retained by the company to serve as its chief negotiator. The condition of the company was financially perilous, and at that time it was already in the hands of a receiver in bankruptcy appointed by the Israeli Court, which had before it a plan of liquidation. There was no question that the airline's finances were severely aggravated and perhaps caused by the "open skies" policy of international deregulation. As the flag carrier of Israel, El Al had basically one destination, and it quite rapidly saw many new carriers actively competing for its routes and the potential of still more competition from other carriers operating in Israel on a marginal profit basis.

The airline appealed to the president of the IAM for special attention to its needs and received a letter from his subordinate some eleven months later referring the matter back to negotiations at the local level. In particular, the airline sought the union's assistance in developing a cost-reduction plan. The airline had already implemented such a plan by agreement with the Israeli union and the unions representing local staff throughout its worldwide system. In short, El Al sought a concessionary agreement from the IAM that would match the concessions it had received elsewhere, as well as support its argument to the bankruptcy court that liquidation was not necessary and continued operation was feasible. The reaction of the local union committee was to serve a conventional list of demands for increases in wages and benefits and to reiterate that the union "would not move back."

In most other industries the conflict would have been immediately apparent and the confrontational impasse would have been swift. The union had at its disposal the procedures of the Railway Labor Act, however, which were designed for the purposes of delaying self-help in order to avoid interruptions in commerce. The net result was that the procedures of the act were not finally exhausted until March 15, 1984, and, to no one's surprise, a strike took place on that date. One of the consequences of the long delay was necessarily to provide an opportunity to the work force for self-education and for opinion molding by the parties themselves.

The employees' reaction to the strike reflected their awareness of the deregulated environment that governed both the airline's fate and their own. Concurrent with the union's strike action, the airline implemented virtually all the proposals on which it had conceded. These included the elimination of certain employee groups who had previously been immune to layoff, the subcontracting of several operations, and the implementation of a wide range of scheduling, premium pay, and work rule changes. The union characterized these changes as creating a "slave labor" environment. The airline made it plain, however, that it intended to continue to operate despite the strike and appealed to its employees to cross the picket line.

The strike was a saga that would take volumes to tell. It lasted twenty-eight months and ended only when the parties agreed to submit their economic differences to an interest arbitration that, at this writing, has still not been concluded. In the interim, employees are working under the conditions established by the airline during the strike.[1]

The airline's operation was not injured or delayed in any measure during the years of confrontation and, indeed, airline officials claim

---

1. Since writing the above, the arbitrator Clair Duff has rendered an award that confirms most of the larger number of changes instituted by the company. Duff was chosen by the parties from lists supplied by the National Mediation Board.

that service improved. Before the strike was over, more than 50 percent of the unionized employees had crossed the picket line and come to work on the airline's terms. During the course of the strike a group of El Al employees formed an independent union, which through a National Mediation Board election ousted the IAM as representative of the office clerical unit. Within the first two weeks of the strike, some 25 percent of the work force had returned to work, and the percentage grew swiftly. Within the first three months of the strike, more than 40 percent of the IAM work force had returned to work, and by the end of the strike, more than 50 percent had returned. After waiting for a couple of weeks to determine the size and impact of the returning work force and the impact of its subcontracting and supervisory employees on the maintenance of the operation, the airline in mid-1984 began to advertise for replacements. The result was a veritable flood of job applicants, many of whom had experience with such carriers as TWA, United, New York Air, People Express, and a range of foreign flag carriers, and some of whom left their jobs to take higher-paying positions at El Al. This response came despite the requirement that prospective employees sign a form acknowledging the possibility that they might be displaced pursuant to a union or company back-to-work agreement.

The implications of this experience are clear. The impact of deregulation had driven the airline to a financial position that had emboldened it, perhaps required it, to take a confrontational position with the union. The weakness of the carrier became its source of strength as it acted from desperation and necessity. The union's thesis throughout the negotiations and strike was that it would not depart from "industry standards" in dealing with El Al. This argument clearly was not persuasive to a large number of El Al unionized employees, who were forced to recognize that although the union principle might be vindicated, their jobs could be sacrificed, at a time when jobs were scarce.

The personnel involved in negotiations at El Al included cargo, reservations, and traffic agents, as well as office clerical workers and a limited number of maintenance employees. Although these employees undoubtedly needed training in the airline's procedures, there were no regulatory hurdles they had to clear, as there would have been for pilots. The work force El Al was using was highly fungible with the rest of the industry and, indeed, with work skills from outside the industry. As in the case of American's pilots, the availability of labor replacements was a decisive consideration in resolving the confrontation at El Al. In the case of the Israeli airline, at no point was the work force insufficient to meet the requirements of the carrier under the terms and conditions the airline offered. Moreover, the hiring requirements were relaxed enough to ensure that positions could be filled quickly.

There are, of course, differences in the nature of the work forces at El Al and American. In both instances, however, deregulation contributed to the availability of the work force, and that availability, in turn, affected the outcome of the economic struggle.

As long as deregulation continues, both unions and management will use an individualized approach to bargaining. This strategy is the product of intercompany competition, which is manifested also as job competition. This individualized approach must, of course, operate within the context of the general labor market. With the continued pressure of competition comes continued restraint in making improvements in wages and benefits. Junior employees will perceive less incentive for personal growth within any particular company—and possibly less value in seniority and job security—and these highly mobile employees will weaken the unions' bargaining positions. In many ways smaller carriers, such as the foreign flags, will have an advantageous bargaining position over the larger carriers because of the relatively few jobs they would have to fill in a strike, the availability of alternative labor options such as subcontracting, and their less demanding hiring requirements. The logistics of training large numbers of employees for positions in cargo, traffic, and reservations also reduce bargaining flexibility for the larger airlines.

The impact of the labor market on cockpit crews may be a different matter. The need for employees with substantial qualifications and skills hampers easy and rapid replacement. Indeed, now that fewer pilots are being processed through the military than in earlier years, the commercial airlines may experience shortages of pilots. Larger carriers can offset this shortage, but only partially, by hiring pilots from smaller carriers who are seeking greater long-term growth. Add to these restraints the greater professional sense of community of interest that exists among cockpit crews and their organizations, which promotes unity of response. Thus at any given moment deregulation imposes severe restraints on the freedom of companies with respect to the hiring of cockpit crews. The rapid expansion of many major carriers during the 1980s imposes a demand for pilots that may be difficult to satisfy. Yet companies must incur risk and invest substantial time in training pilots. Deregulation therefore imposes restraints on both employees and management, possibly leading to settlement instead of confrontation.

Part 3
Union Representation following Mergers and Acquisitions

A Note on the National Mediation Board

At the time the following chapters were prepared (late spring of 1987), the National Mediation Board had already announced (in April 1987) that by August 1, 1987, it would issue new procedures governing union representation questions on merged airlines, following submissions by interested parties. This solicitation followed the Board's *TWA-Ozark* decision in which it stated that "[e]xperience has shown that existing procedures are inadequate to provide for a fair and orderly resolution of representation matters put into flux by a merger."[1] Eleven proposals and eight reply comments were received by the Board. Not surprisingly, a diversity of views was expressed in these submissions. This diversity is mirrored in the chapters that follow. To some degree these chapters read like briefs addressed to the Board, advocating the respective positions of various unions and companies in response to the Board's request for guidance.

Most of the nine unions submitting proposals or comments urged that carriers be required to submit information to the NMB at the time they announce their plans for acquisitions or mergers. Some advocated that an acquiring airline should be required to recognize the unions representing the acquired carrier for a specified period of time or until all representation issues had been disposed of by the Board or until seniority lists had been integrated. Others argued that the Board should defer to past arbitration decisions regarding successor agreements.

The carriers urged that the Board codify its criteria for determining whether a carrier had merged two airlines into a single entity, based on the assumption that unions for the surviving carrier would continue as exclusive representatives of all employees in the merged craft or class, and also that only the surviving carrier have authority to invoke the Board's services in representation disputes. They further advocated that the Board issue orders to show cause why cer-

---

1. 14 NMB at 218 (1987).

tifications of minority unions should not be extinguished. Some of the carriers argued strongly against dual representation of any kind even for a short time, since to permit continued recognition of minority unions would obstruct the operation of a single transportation system, create labor instability, and ignore the fact that mergers are business transactions.

After considering these responses, on July 31, 1987, the NMB issued its new procedures for handling representation issues resulting from mergers, acquisitions, or consolidations in the airline industry, effective the following day.[2] The new procedures governing single-carrier status require the airlines involved to give the NMB immediate notice of plans for mergers or acquisitions at the time they file for Department of Transportation approval. The aim is to avoid the postmerger representation problems that arose from the Board's earlier decisions, discussed in detail in the following chapters. If after investigation, the Board terminates certifications on the acquired carrier, incumbent unions normally will have sixty days from the date of decision to file a representation application demonstrating at least a 35 percent evidence of interest by the combined craft or class. Such evidence may include authorization cards, dues check-off authorizations, or integrated seniority lists with a carrier involved in the merger. The Board promised to give priority to holding representation elections after the requisite showing of interest so as to expedite its final decision on representation rights.

These new procedures have no impact on voluntary recognition agreements or the processing of pending grievances. Disputes over successor agreements are to be referred to the appropriate system adjustment board for resolution through arbitration.

---

2. 14 NMB at 103, File No. C–5956.

Procedures for Determining Representation following Mergers and Acquisitions

John J. Gallagher

The National Mediation Board has exclusive and unreviewable authority to determine whether two entities involved in a corporate acquisition or merger should be considered a single carrier for representation purposes. This authority is part of the NMB's general charge to investigate representation disputes and issue union certification pursuant to section 2, ninth, of the Railway Labor Act.[1] The NMB historically has been unwilling to decide the single-carrier issue in a merger case before issuing regulatory approval of a proposed merger.[2] Following such approval, or following consummation of a merger, the Board has usually entertained a representation dispute and addressed the single-carrier issue at the request of any affected union. By that late date, however, the carriers involved in the merger have generally taken unilateral action to extend voluntary recognition to the union they understand to be the survivor.[3]

The NMB apparently will still decide the single-carrier issue in merger cases but no longer will there be the usual requirement of a certain percentage showing of interest. This issue is one of many that is currently under consideration by the Board.[4]

---

1. Switchmen's Union v. NMB, 320 U.S. 297 (1943).

2. Republic–Hughes Air West, 7 NMB at 432 (1980).

3. *See, e.g.,* Republic Airlines, 8 NMB at 49 (1980); Northwest Airlines, 13 NMB at 399 (1986).

4. *See, e.g.,* TWA–Ozark Airlines, 14 NMB No. 24 (1987).

Standards for Deciding
Single-Carrier Status

The starting point for determination of the single-carrier issue under section 2, ninth, is the statement contained in the NMB's *First Annual Report* and cited in many later cases:

> Although the term "carrier" is clearly defined in the Act, questions have arisen in connection with representation disputes which made it necessary for the board to interpret its meaning. Where a railroad system is composed of a number of subsidiary corporations, employees have been in dispute as to whether one vote should be taken of a craft or the whole system or whether the subsidiary corporations are carriers within the meaning of the Act whose employees are entitled to separate representation. The board has ruled generally that where a subsidiary corporation reports separately to the Interstate Commerce Commission, and keeps its own pay roll and seniority rosters, it is a carrier as defined in the Act, and its employees are entitled to representation separate from other carriers who may be connected with the same railroad system. If the operations of a subsidiary are jointly managed with operations of other carriers and the employees have also been merged and are subject to the direction of a single management, then the larger unit of management is taken to be the carrier rather than the individual subsidiary companies.[5]

Because the purpose of section 2, ninth, is to determine the appropriate unit for representation, it makes sense that past representation patterns would be relevant. In some cases, the patterns of labor-management relations have been the NMB's central focus in determining whether a single carrier or multiple carriers are involved.

For instance, in *Airlift International, Inc.*, one airline acquired the assets of another.[6] As part of the acquisition agreement, the CAB required the purchaser to hire the acquired airline's employees and assume their labor contract. The Board decided that a union election should be held for the combined operation, paying particular attention to the fact that labor relations policies were being administered by the same individuals:

> In resolving the issue of the carrier's status ... the Board must of necessity take into consideration ... whether or not the employees of the

---

5. NMB, First Annual Report 22 (1935).
6. 4 NMB at 142 (1967).

carrier or carriers have, in fact, been merged and are subject to the direction of a single management having the sole authority to supervise and direct the manner of rendition of the services to those employees.[7]

The unification of labor policy outweighed the fact that the employees of the two consolidated companies had separate collective bargaining agreements.

In *Ross Aviation, Inc.*,[8] the Board found that one air company was so closely controlled by an airline that it was a "carrier" for jurisdictional purposes under section 1, first, of the RLA. The NMB found, however, that the two related companies were not a single carrier for representation purposes. The Board found that the two companies were not similar in their labor aspects because there was no community of interest among the respective pilots, who operated different aircraft, were on separate seniority lists, had to meet different qualifications, were not exchanged between the companies, and were served by different personnel offices and policies. The NMB therefore ruled that the two companies were separate carriers for purposes of section 2, ninth.

In *Air Florida, Inc.*, the NMB outlined the criteria it would consider in making a determination of single-carrier status.[9] In a representation petition involving Air Florida, the issue arose whether Air Sunshine, a wholly owned subsidiary of Air Florida, was in reality a part of Air Florida and could therefore have its employees grouped with those of Air Florida for representation purposes. In a preliminary ruling on the proper scope of the investigation, the Board stated: "Subsidiary corporations will be deemed to be part of the parent carrier where the management and operation of the subsidiary are closely aligned with or controlled by the parent." The matter subsequently became moot when Air Sunshine merged with Air Florida before the NMB had decided on the representation dispute.

The NMB's decision in *Republic Airlines, Inc.*,[10] was significant because it announced the Board's policy not to foster multiple bargaining units in the deregulated airline industry if separate bargaining units would detract from rational labor-management relations. Republic acquired Hughes Air West (renamed Republic

---

7. *Id*. at 145.
8. 5 NMB at 145 (1972).
9. 7 NMB at 34 (1979).
10. 8 NMB No. 15 (1980).

West), but the two airlines retained their separate corporate identities and finances because of tax considerations. Republic announced its intention to present itself to the public as a single carrier, with a common schedule, integrated routes, and identical planes, uniforms, and insignia. Although there were two separate payrolls for accounting purposes, there were to be functional integration, common ownership, and common directors and management, including a common labor relations staff under the direction of Republic's vice president for industrial relations. Maintenance would be performed by Republic. The Board concluded:

> The CAB may approve of a two corporation set-up for purposes of economic regulation, however, this board may pierce the corporate veil for purposes of rational labor-management relations. A finding that Republic West is a separate carrier would exalt form over substance.

In *Northwest Airlines, Inc.*,[11] the Board affirmed that Republic and Northwest had become a single carrier, or "single transportation system":

> There will be a common management, common labor relations and personnel functions and a combined workforce. All ground and air service will eventually be integrated and conducted under the name Northwest Airlines. Additionally, on August 12, 1986, Northwest filed a single integrated flight schedule which will be effective October 1, 1986.

In *TWA–Ozark Airlines*,[12] the NMB found that TWA and Ozark had become a single carrier on October 11, 1986, based upon unification of management, consolidation of reservations systems, a combined flight schedule, and efforts to remove publicly visible Ozark insignia and uniforms or aircraft livery. The NMB especially emphasized that the two previously separate carriers were being held out to the public as a single system:

> We recognize that there may be differences between two carriers' intent to hold themselves out to the public as a single carrier and the public's perception of whether there is a single system. That is why the Board looks into such practical considerations as whether a combined schedule

---

11. 13 NMB at 399 (1986).
12. 14 NMB at 28 (1987).

is published; how the carrier advertises its services; whether reservation systems are combined; whether tickets are issued on one carrier's stock; if signs, logos and other publicly visible indicia have been changed to indicate only one carrier's existence; whether personnel with public contact were held out as employees of one carrier; and whether the process of repainting planes and other equipment, to eliminate indications of separate existence, has been progressed.

Although the Board found TWA and Ozark to be a single carrier, for the first time it indicated, as discussed below, that various crafts or classes could be considered separate for representation purposes.

Clearly, under the RLA, single-carrier status for representation purposes is not automatic for two related corporations. The NMB appears to recognize the legitimate business reasons for structuring a corporate family with more than one legal component. It has relied on a number of objective criteria in determining whether two or more commonly owned corporations should be regarded as a single carrier. These criteria have evolved over the years to include assessment of the level of integration of operations, the "holding out" to the public of a single entity, and common management, especially centralized control of labor relations. These criteria are similar to those applied under the National Labor Relations Act (NLRA) in determining single-employer ("double-breasted") status.

NMB's Representation Procedures

Before the *TWA-Ozark* decision, the NMB had found in a series of mergers that when a formal corporate merger or an operational merger created a single system for representation purposes, there was only one collective bargaining representative in each of the merged crafts or classes. This conclusion was based on the Board's long-standing doctrine that representation under the RLA is "system-wide."[13] It is also based on the proposition that a carrier may negotiate with the majority representative and "no other."[14] Moreover, the NMB consistently has taken a position against fragmenting

---

13. *See* Switchmen's Union v. NMB, 135 F.2d 785 (D.C. Cir. 1943), *rev'd on other grounds*, 320 U.S. 297 (1943); Seaboard Coast Line R.R., 6 NMB at 63 (1976).

14. Virginian Ry. v. System Bd. No. 40, 300 U.S. 515 (1937).

bargaining units,[15] recognizing that multistate labor-management relations require one representative in each postmerger craft or class:

> To [operate a single transportation system] it needs to be able to integrate its work force. The current agreement restrictions which apply to mechanics and jurisdictional restraints on work or aircraft demonstrate the inherent inefficiency in a two-carrier system for representative purposes.[16]

Because there can be only one majority representative, the NMB held in *Republic* that the certifications of unions on the carrier disappearing in the merger were "extinguished by operation of law." Accordingly, the carrier was free to withdraw recognition from the disappearing union.

The NMB's approval of Republic's actions clearly indicated that a carrier could withdraw recognition from one union after a merger. In past mergers, the NMB had consistently refused to issue status quo orders to prevent such a result. When Southern was merged into North Central to create Republic, the carrier withdrew recognition from the Aircraft Mechanics Fraternal Association (AMFA), which had represented mechanics at Southern. Republic recognized the IAM, the representative of the North Central mechanics, as representative of the combined craft. When AMFA petitioned the Board to clarify its representative status, the NMB held:

> [T]he Civil Aeronautics Board . . . has allowed the merger of Southern Airways, Inc. into North Central Airways, Inc. . . . . That combination will occur on July 1, 1979, at which time Southern Airways, Inc. will cease to exist as well as all certifications by the National Mediation Board of collective bargaining representatives for crafts or classes of employees of Southern Airways, Inc. It has been a longstanding policy of the NMB that it will not inject itself into questions of voluntary recognition by a carrier of a labor organization except where such recognition would be in derogation of our existing Board certifications. However, as noted, all certifications issued by the NMB to Southern Airways, Inc. will cease to exist on [date of the merger].[17]

---

15. *See* American Airlines, 3 NMB at 49, 50 (1959); Northwest Airlines, 6 NMB at 105, 107 (1977).

16. Republic Airlines, 8 NMB at 49, 55 (1980).

17. Republic Airlines, 6 NMB at 817 (1979).

Thus the NMB emphasized that one corporation ceased to exist after a merger. Further, the representative status of the unions at the surviving carrier continued, whereas the NMB certifications issued to the unions at the carrier that did not survive were "extinguished." On April 10, 1987, the NMB issued a decision in the *TWA-Ozark* merger case that represented a marked departure from previous Board policy on mergers.[18] In *TWA-Ozark*, the Board retreated from the proposition accepted in *Republic* and *Northwest* that in a merger union certifications on the nonsurviving carrier are "extinguished by operation of law," holding instead that Board action was required to extinguish a certification. The Board proceeded, however, to make its conventional factual analysis of whether a single carrier had been created by the merger. The Board announced in the decision that it would soon initiate procedures to review and redefine Board policy in representation disputes arising from airline mergers. The Board issued its new representation rules on August 1, 1987.

---

18. 14 NMB at 218 (1987).

An Employer's Perspective on Representation Rights

Terry M. Erskine

An understanding of the status and significance of union representation rights in airline mergers lies in the answers to at least four entwined questions, three of which will be discussed in this chapter. First, to what extent do the collective bargaining contracts of an acquired air carrier survive a merger? This fascinating but complex issue will not be discussed here. Second, which (if any) NMB representation certifications of labor organizations on either carrier should survive a merger? Third, in the event there are conflicting premerger class or craft patterns in the two airlines involved, what patterns are appropriate in the merged carrier? And fourth, can or should a class or craft in a merged carrier be fragmented for representation purposes until a postmerger representation election has been completed?

Can a Class or Craft Be Fragmented?

With respect to the last question, it is fair to say that policy put forth in the Railway Labor Act and NMB precedent is clear and to change it would be inviting the destabilization of labor relations in merged carriers. Two well-settled principles of the NMB's administration of the RLA are (1) there can be only one certificated labor organization for each systemwide class or craft of employees at an airline; and

(2) the NMB will certify a labor organization as a representative only if a majority of the employees of the class or craft has indicated that it wants to be organized, by participating in a representation election, and that the organization has been chosen by majority vote. In no recent NMB airline merger case, except the *TWA-Ozark* decision in 1987, has the NMB permitted two different representation certifications to remain in effect for the same class or craft after an operational merger. And in that case, it did so only for the postmerger period in which TWA voluntarily continued to negotiate with the minority union. In its 1987 proceeding in the Delta-Western merger, for example, the NMB was asked by the minority unions to reverse the hallmark RLA principle of majority rule by systemwide class or craft. The NMB was requested to order nonunion Delta to recognize the minority unions of Western after the date of the carriers' operational merger. Consider the irony that, had such an order been issued, to dislodge the minority Western unions under NMB rules, the majority nonunion employees of Delta somehow would have had to become organized enough to be able to invoke the NMB's services to conduct a representation election in which they would have had no intention of voting. (Staying true to the RLA principle of majority rule, the NMB rejected the union's request.)

What Is the Appropriate Structure?

On the issue of what the appropriate class or craft structure for a merged carrier should be, the NMB has consistently permitted the surviving carrier to maintain its class or craft structure unless that structure is challenged and changed in a later representation election. Once it has been asked to consider the appropriateness of a postmerger class or craft structure, the NMB adjudicates on a case-by-case basis. In the event there are conflicting community-of-interest patterns in the premerger carriers, the class or craft structure of the surviving carrier may or may not remain intact. In its decision involving the Northwest-Republic merger,[1] for example, the Board brushed aside a community-of-interest pattern that had existed for forty years at Northwest and, over the objection of the surviving carrier and its unions, found that the appropriate class or craft

---

1. 13 NMB No. 22 (1986).

structure for ground service, passenger service, and clerical employees was not that which had historically existed in the surviving carrier (Northwest) but rather that which had existed in the acquired carrier (Republic). The facts of this case were unique, however, and it is not likely that it will set any useful precedent for future mergers except perhaps those involving Northwest.

Which Representation Certifications Should Survive?

The courts have consistently held that under the RLA resolution of representation disputes involving airline employees is the exclusive jurisdiction of the NMB. In carrying out that responsibility in mergers, the Board has issued a series of decisions setting forth the policies and procedures that are to govern the rights and obligations of the parties.

In a leading case involving the merger of Republic and Hughes Air West,[2] the Board announced that once the integration of two carriers had progressed to the point that they had eliminated or were committed to eliminating their separate existences, the carriers would be a single transportation system for RLA purposes. The Board affirmed that the precise date of the merger would be determined by the carriers. A union challenging the carrier's position would be permitted to invoke the Board's services and obtain an after-the-fact review of whether the carriers had, as of their announced date of merger, taken sufficient steps toward integrating their systems to meet the Board's test for single-carrier status. In its *Republic* decision, the NMB sent a clear signal to the airline industry that carriers could plan future mergers with confidence that the representation certifications of the minority labor organizations at the nonsurviving carrier would automatically be extinguished once single-carrier status was achieved.[3]

The Board reinforced its *Republic* decision six years later in a

---

2. 8 NMB at 49 (1980).

3. *See* Gallagher, *Representation Procedures in Mergers, supra* p. 99, for a discussion of the criteria the Board uses in determining single-carrier status.

decision involving the merger of Northwest and Republic.[4] In this case, the Board confirmed that complete integration of the two airline systems was not required for there to be a finding of single-carrier status. In both the *Republic* and *Northwest* cases, the Board found that the carriers had passed the test of single-carrier status by showing they were committed to eliminating their separate existences as soon as practical and had taken significant steps along that path. In the case of the Northwest-Republic merger, the Board confirmed that single-carrier status had occurred on the day funds were transferred, consummating the formal acquisition of Republic by Northwest.

In 1987, the Board applied the same criteria to the determination of single-carrier status in the TWA-Ozark merger.[5] The Board announced a twist, however: the achievement of single-carrier status would not extinguish the representation certification of the minority union as long as the surviving carrier continued to negotiate with that union for collective bargaining and contract administration purposes. Although this temporary estoppel principle would appear to be at odds with the rationale of prior Board decisions, it could be viewed as the paddle the Board used to spank TWA for not voluntarily recognizing its majority incumbent union, the Independent Federation of Flight Attendants (IFFA), as the representative of all flight attendants on the merged airline.

The historic NMB practices for extinguishing representation certifications have arguably functioned in many past mergers, including Delta-Northeast, Pan Am–National, Republic–Hughes Airwest, Continental–Texas International, Flying Tiger–Seabord, and Northwest–Republic, to fulfill the basic RLA principle of majority rule in an orderly manner. In April 1987, however, the Board announced that with respect to more recent mergers (presumably referring to TWA-Ozark, American–Air California, USAir-PSA-Piedmont, Delta-Western), there was such "confusion and inequity" in the application of Board principles that new procedures governing representation issues in mergers and acquisitions had to be issued.

Not to be overlooked is that airline mergers are business transactions with implications for union representation, not the reverse. Mergers touch the lives of thousands of employees and involve the

---

4. 13 NMB at 399 (1986).
5. 14 NMB No. 63 (1987).

expenditures of millions of dollars. They often involve at least one failing carrier and take place in an environment of cutthroat competition. Throwing up unnecessary barriers to the integration of work forces and the operations of the new airline while it is at its most vulnerable stage is contrary to the purposes of the RLA and to the long-term interests of the employees, shareholders, and public. For example, a rule freezing the premerger "status quo" until new union representation elections have been completed would cause irreparable harm to the enterprise by effectively preventing *any* integration of work forces. The same would be true of a rule that permitted minority unions to bootstrap themselves, via premerger contract successor clauses, into representing employees in the merged carrier without first going through the rigors of a representation election. It would not further the interests of the public, shareholders, or employees to encumber a merged carrier with minority union albatrosses.

The industry's position before the NMB's promulgation of its new rules governing union representation issues in mergers and acquisitions was based on the following specific suggestions:

1. The Board should codify and publish a checklist of criteria for determining when a single transportation system is created by the corporate merger of two or more airlines. The criteria should be in conformance with those announced in the Board's *Republic* and *Northwest* decisions. In applying those criteria, the Board should continue to find that a single transportation system exists even when a complete integration of operations is still being phased in. Delaying the extinguishment of representation certifications of minority unions until many months after a merger, which would occur if this principle were not applied, would thereby retard the consolidation of operations and the integration of work forces and internal systems, as well as deny carriers, their employees, and most of all their owners the full economic benefits the merger was designed to achieve.

2. The Board should continue to follow the doctrine that certifications of minority unions are extinguished automatically as of the date the Board determines that single-carrier status was achieved. The Board should not adopt any rule that would fragment a class or craft by keeping in effect the representation certifications of minority unions until related representation elections are complete. Any rule that permitted certifications of minority unions of an ac-

quired carrier to survive for even one moment after single-carrier status had been achieved would undermine the "majority rule" principle of the RLA and threaten the viability of the enterprise. A single carrier simply cannot function with a major and minor union hydra that is incapable of speaking with one voice for a single systemwide class or craft of employees.

3. Once a carrier has provided sufficient information to the Board, including a specific date of merger, the carrier should be permitted to proceed with certainty that the representation certifications of the minority unions of the acquired carrier will be extinguished unless the Board issues a contrary determination. If a carrier has no such assurance, it will remain in limbo until the Board has issued a formal determination.

4. The Board should continue on the presumption that the class or craft structures of the surviving carrier will remain in place after the merger, pending the disposition of any applications seeking to change such structures.

5. The Board should permit only carriers to initiate proceedings before the Board for the purpose of disclosing their detailed merger plans. The date on which to invoke the Board's services should be decided by the carriers and should not be tied to the date of filing with the Department of Transportation. It is unrealistic to expect the carriers to have detailed plans for operational merger until well after they have filed with the Department of Transportation. To permit the unions to invoke the Board's services would result in premature proceedings involving unfinalized plans.

6. After reaching a finding based on the carrier's written submission that a credible prima facie showing has been made, the Board should issue an order showing why the representation certifications of the minority unions for each appropriate class or craft should not be terminated on the planned date of the merger. Inquiries should be limited to whether the Board's criteria for single-carrier status have been sufficiently satisfied. The inquiry should not be reduced to an attempt to obtain premature commitments from carriers on such subjects as labor protective provisions or contract survival.

7. The Board's procedures should provide for expeditious action so that a final determination on extinguishment of representation certifications can be issued well in advance of the planned date of the merger.

8. The only remedy the Board should provide to a minority union seeking to be a certified representative for the merged carrier is an expedited representation election upon a sufficient showing of employee interest.

The history of airline mergers has demonstrated that they have strengthened the industry for employees, shareholders, and the traveling public. In a deregulated environment, a newly merged carrier is especially vulnerable to competitive market forces and must be able to implement its plans for operational and work force integration rapidly. It must have the certainty of knowing from the start with which single union, if any, it is obligated to negotiate for each of its classes and crafts of employees. It is hoped that the NMB will promulgate rules governing union representation in airline mergers that will facilitate the business purposes of future airline mergers and be faithful to the "majority rule" principle of the RLA.

Protecting Employees' Rights following Mergers and Acquisitions

Asher W. Schwartz

The Railway Labor Act guarantees employees of any carrier the right to select representatives of their own choosing and imposes on the carrier an obligation to negotiate exclusively with those representatives on matters of pay, work rules, and working conditions.[1] Employees in the airline industry have exercised this right almost universally. Following an acquisition or merger, however, the collective bargaining agreements of the acquired carrier are voided. An acquisition or merger therefore has serious implications vis à vis the pay, rules, and working conditions, especially seniority rights, of employees.

What recourse do or should such employees have under the RLA to protect their interests? Whether the employees of the acquired carrier are represented by the same or a different organization, or by no organization, the transition not only engenders conflicts with their new employer but, in the area of seniority, creates competitiveness among employees in the same craft or class. Labor protective provisions could go a long way toward mediating these conflicts.

Scope of Labor Protective Provisions (LPPs)

Until the Pan Am–National merger in 1981, the Civil Aeronautics Board imposed LPPs as a condition for its approval of a merger or

---

1. Virginian Ry. v. System Bd. No. 40, 300 U.S. 515 (1937).

acquisition.[2] LPPs, which were modeled on the Washington Job Agreement that governed railroad mergers, granted displacement and dismissal allowances for employees. Even more important, LPPs provided a mechanism whereby employees were entitled to negotiate with the acquiring carrier and the organization representing the class or craft on that carrier to adjust their seniority status and other conditions and had recourse to arbitration if no satisfactory resolution could be reached.[3] Even if employees moved from a carrier with a craft or class representative to one without, or vice versa, the employees were entitled by the LPPs to bargaining and arbitration to adjust seniority rights fairly and equitably.[4]

Since 1981, however, employees have been denied independent representation following an acquisition or merger. Without such recourse, employees are subject to unilateral and possibly unfair decisions by the acquiring carrier or to agreements reached between the carrier and a representative they did not choose. Further, such representatives tend to act on behalf of the craft or class within which the incumbent members have a predominating role.

In the Delta-Northeast merger,[5] in 1972, for example, the Northeast flight attendants were represented by the Transport Workers Union and the Delta flight attendants were unrepresented. The TWU proposed to continue representing the former Northeast flight attendants and, if necessary, to arbitrate a fair seniority arrangement for the Delta flight attendants. Delta refused to recognize the TWU as the representative of the former Northeast flight attendants, and the CAB, to whom the TWU appealed, refused to direct Delta either to recognize the TWU or to arbitrate, sections 3 and 13 of the LPPs notwithstanding.[6]

The CAB dismissed the TWU's petition on two grounds: (1) the TWU did not demonstrate a basis for CAB intervention; and (2) the TWU was not a "representative" of the former Northeast employees merely because it had represented them before the merger. The CAB stated, "No such agreement [between Delta and TWU] was in fact reached, and it does not appear that TWU's status as collective

---

2. Pan Am–National Merger, Order 79–12–163/164/165.
3. Allegheny-Mohawk Merger, Order 72–431,32, §§ 3 & 13(a).
4. Delta-Northeast Merger, Order 76–9–129.
5. Order 72–5–73/74.
6. Order 73–9–42.

bargaining representative of Northeast employees for Railway Labor Act purposes survived the merger."[7]

The Northeast flight attendants retained independent counsel, who appealed to the circuit court of appeals in the District of Columbia. On May 27, 1975, the court directed the CAB to consider the merits of the Northeast flight attendants' claim, which it did, and on September 23, 1976, the CAB directed Delta to participate in the selection of an arbitrator for an arbitration to be conducted in conformance with section 13(a) of the LPPs. The CAB did not, however, modify its decision that Delta did not have to recognize the TWU as a party to the arbitration proceeding and so ruled.[8] A committee of Northeast flight attendants then proceeded to arbitration by an attorney.

Without LPPs, What Happens Next?

Deregulation and a virtual abandonment of LPPs by the Interstate Commerce Commission (ICC) and the Department of Transportation have made labor issues more acute than they were in earlier years.[9] The new, intensely competitive environment, characterized by takeovers in which there is no concern for the rights of employees or shareholders, necessitates a remedy under the auspices of the NMB. The NMB has determined that in a nonacquisition or nonmerger situation, a collectively bargained agreement continues to apply to employees in a craft

---

7. *See* Air Line Employees Association [ALEA] v. CAB, Order 73–9–42, at 5. ALEA attempted to require the acquiring airline to be bound by the agreement negotiated by ALEA on behalf of employees at the acquired carrier. The CAB refused to sustain ALEA's claim, a decision upheld by the court of appeals for the District of Columbia. "Insofar as any dispute existed over the representational rights of ALEA with respect to some or all of the passenger service employees in the merged unit, such a dispute was within the exclusive jurisdiction of the National Mediation Board under Section 2, Ninth, of the Railway Labor Act." ALEA v. CAB, 413 F.2d 1094 (D.C. Cir. 1969).

8. Order 76–9–129.

9. *See* Flight Attendants v. DOT, 803 F.2d 1029 (9th Cir. 1986) (denying petition to review DOT decision not to impose LPPs on Pan Am's sale of its Pacific routes to United).

or class even when there has been a change of representatives.[10] It would seem more appropriate for the NMB to rule that when a carrier is acquired the representative status of the unions at each carrier not be disturbed until the employer has had a reasonable chance to make adjustments in seniority, either by agreement or arbitration. Once those adjustments were made, the employees' representative would under present rules represent the craft or class at the acquiring carrier until a decision upon an application to the NMB for a representation decision was reached. There have been a large number of cases in which the handling of disputes in this transition period has been critical not only for the employees but for the stability of the collective bargaining process.

When Pan Am acquired National in 1981, LPPs were still applied, and the pilots and flight engineers at each airline had separate unions—and conflicting claims, including bid rights (flight and equipment selection). Bid rights in the cockpit mean money. In the absence of an agreement between the representatives and Pan Am on seniority rights, the integration of the two airlines was virtually impossible without job action or litigation. The four union representatives agreed to submit their contentions to an arbitrator without the participation of Pan Am. Integration of the airlines' routes and equipment came to a halt pending the arbitrator's decision. Had there been no binding determination of their contentions on seniority, the chaos created by the conflicting claims would have threatened Pan Am's ability to merge its operations with those of National.

There have been, and will continue to be, numerous acquisitions by carriers. Unless the NMB devises some method to compel carriers and labor organizations to recognize the representation rights of employees during a transition period, the purposes of the RLA in this context will not be fulfilled. It is easy enough to assume either that employees will not protest or that agreements will be reached voluntarily, but that is not likely to happen. To prevent resolutions from being forced onto employees without the assistance of representatives of their own

---

10. ADMINISTRATION OF THE RAILWAY LABOR ACT BY THE NMB (1934–1970) 78 (1970).

choosing, the NMB should adopt rules covering representation for an interim period following a merger.

Republic Revisited

In 1987, the NMB announced that it wished to establish procedures for handling representation matters resulting from airline mergers. It observed that "[e]xperience has shown that existing procedures are inadequate to provide for a fair and orderly resolution of representation matters put into flux by a merger."[11] A case in point is TWA's takeover of Ozark.

The Department of Transportation approved TWA's acquisition of Ozark on September 12, 1986. On November 10, 1986, the Association of Flight Attendants, which represented Ozark's flight attendants, filed an application alleging a representation dispute among flight attendants. The Aircraft Mechanics Fraternal Association (AMFA), which represented Ozark's maintenance personnel, filed an application to represent mechanics, fleet service helpers (cleaners), and fuelers. Later in November, the Independent Federation of Flight Attendants (IFFA), which represented TWA's flight attendants, filed its application. Six days of hearings were held.

The NMB acknowledged that its decision in *Republic*[12] was the leading case but ruled that certain language in that case—"all certifications on Airwest were extinguished by operation of law upon Airwest's acquisition by Republic"—had been misinterpreted by carriers. The NMB held that "[a]bsent Board approval, neither the present certifications at Ozark nor any other certification may terminate by action of a carrier."[13] Thus the Board disapproved TWA's applications unilaterally, informing the prior Ozark representatives (AFA and AMFA) that their certifications were defunct.

The Board identified the issues before it as follows:

---

11. TWA-Ozark Merger, 14 NMB at 218 (1987).
12. 8 NMB at 49 (1980).
13. 14 NMB at 235. The NMB noted that "in analyzing the present case the Board will use the legal standards set forth in the *Republic* and *Northwest* decisions because they were controlling at the time the events underlying this action transpired" (14 NMB at 236).

(1) Whether TWA and Ozark combined to form a single transportation system, for purposes of the Railway [Labor] Act, on October 26, 1986; (2) If a single transportation system was created, what effect if any does this have on the representation certifications of the Organizations at Ozark and when did the effect occur?
(3) Whether representation elections are warranted for the crafts or classes of Flight Attendants and Mechanics and Related Employees.[14]

In making its "single transportation system" determination, the Board looked to criteria previously identified in *Republic* and reaffirmed in *Northwest*: (1) Are the two systems held out to the public as a single carrier (published schedules, advertisements, reservation systems, tickets, signs, logos, uniforms, painting of planes and other equipment)? (2) Have the carriers combined their operations in terms of management and labor relations (integration of the labor relations and personnel function, common management, corporate officers, interlocking boards of directors, combined work force)?[15]

Applying these criteria, the Board ruled that TWA annexed Ozark and a single transportation system came into being on October 26, 1986. It went on to rule that AMFA's certification to represent Ozark's mechanics and related employees ceased to exist on that date, observing that (1) on October 26, TWA held itself out to the public as a single carrier and had common management and labor relations; (2) the mechanics had a combined work force at that time; (3) TWA and the IAM had negotiated a transition agreement effective October 26 providing for representation by the IAM; (4) TWA had informed AMFA on October 14 that it would not recognize AMFA as representative as of October 26; and (5) AMFA had transferred pending grievances to the IAM on October 24.

The Board found that the flight attendants' situation was far more muddled. Not until December 24, 1986, did TWA inform AFA that its certification had been extinguished as of October 26. On the contrary, TWA negotiated with AFA about wages and working conditions after October 26, did not enter into a transition pact, and did not negotiate with IFFA about the merger.[16] The Board issued an Order to Show Cause why AFA's certification should not terminate as of December 24, 1986.

---

14. 14 NMB at 220 (1987).

15. 13 NMB at 399 (1986).

16. As the carrier pointed out, "[T]here was an ongoing labor dispute between TWA and IFFA which had made negotiations difficult" (14 NMB at 239).

In announcing its intent to revise its merger proceedings, the Board pledged to promulgate a notice soliciting comments from air carriers and unions. The notice, issued April 23, 1987, invited carriers, unions, and other interested parties to provide written proposals for new NMB merger procedures. The Board issued the new procedures on August 1, 1987.[17]

An Alternative, but Not an Answer

The AFL-CIO Internal Disputes Plan (article XX of the AFL-CIO Constitution) may also have an impact on representation rights during and after a merger. Article XX requires each affiliate of the AFL-CIO to respect the established bargaining relationship of every other affiliate. Thus, when the employees in a craft or class are transferred to another carrier on which the craft or class is represented by a different affiliate, an article XX complaint is in the making.

The NMB is not governed by any decision of the AFL-CIO. The Board will, however, postpone a decision for up to thirty days if it is notified that a claim under article XX is pending. In some cases the representation conflict is resolved without an NMB determination because it so clearly comes under article XX. An affiliate that is found to be in violation of article XX is subject to sanctions within the AFL-CIO but is not subject to court action. A union may, however, withdraw its claim to representation to avoid sanctions if it is determined to be in violation of article XX. Such determinations are made through arbitration before an impartial umpire.

In 1969, umpire David Cole explained:

> The Internal Disputes Plan has been applied to numerous disputes arising out of acquisitions, mergers or consolidation of enterprises. The essence of our rulings has been that if the established collective bargaining relationships can be preserved and protected, they should be. Whether they can be is determined by the form and manner of operations after the transaction is completed. The form of acquisition or merger in terms of corporate structure has been treated as of secondary importance. It is the nature of the employer-employee relationship with which we are concerned.[18]

In *Penn Central*, Penn Central acquired the New Haven Railroad. The carmen employed by the New Haven were represented by the

---

17. *See A Note on the National Mediation Board, supra* p. 97.
18. TWU & BRC (Penn Central), No. 69–27, at 228 (June 3, 1969).

Brotherhood of Railway Carmen (BRC), AFL-CIO. Those employed by Penn Central were represented by the Transport Workers Union (TWU), AFL-CIO, which respected the BRC's established bargaining relationship with the New Haven. But the BRC insisted that the acquisition resulted in a new bargaining unit under the Railway Labor Act and it applied to the NMB for certification as the representative of all the carmen on the Penn Central system.

The impartial umpire reviewed the facts of the employer-employee relationship:

> The New Haven BRC labor agreement has remained in force. The employees continue to work under its terms, represented by the BRC, the union of their choice. They are working at their accustomed locations, under the same supervisors, doing work indistinguishable from that which they were doing before this acquisition. They have not been told that because their smaller operation has been acquired by the vastly larger Penn Central system they have been absorbed into the Penn Central unit and are now represented by some other labor organization.
>
> When the Pennsylvania and New York Central were merged the parties recognized this as a genuine consolidation and conducted an election to select the bargaining representative of the carmen. Now, a few months later, on the occasion of the acquisition of the relatively small New Haven (675 employees as compared with almost 9000), the representative of the small group insists there should be another election involving all 9600 of these employees. Usually in such circumstances the representative of the smaller groups seeks to protect itself against absorption. Here we have the reverse. The large surviving group urges that its established collective bargaining relationship should be recognized and respected by the smaller group; that it realizes that it in turn is required by Article XX to respect the established collective bargaining relationship in effect in the smaller unit.
>
> Considering the facts and circumstances, the finding is that we have two separate and identifiable bargaining relationships that have continued as such despite the acquisition of the properties of the New Haven by the Penn Central.[19]

The NMB ruled otherwise, having determined that there was one craft or class on the extended Penn Central system as contended by the BRC and, over the TWU's objection, conducted an election encompassing the entire system.[20] The TWU won the election and

---

19. *Id.* at 229.

20. In re Representation of Employees of Penn Central, No. R–4084 (Dec. 5, 1969).

thereafter represented all the carmen employed by Penn Central, including those employed in the New Haven division.

The BRC was determined by the AFL-CIO umpire to have violated article XX when it applied to the NMB for certification as representative of the Penn Central system and was placed under sanctions by the Executive Board of the AFL-CIO. The sanctions were later lifted by mutual agreement.

The AFL-CIO procedure, which has served its constituents well over the years, is equally applicable to such disputes in the airlines.[21] Because it does not bind the NMB and does not entail participation by the carrier or employers, it can be a workable solution to merger representation problems, but only in a minority of cases.

---

21. Flight Eng'rs Int'l Ass'n & ALPA, Nos. 65 & 89 (Dec. 5, 1966).

Ensuring Union Protection following Mergers and Acquisitions

Marvin L. Griswold

In the eight years preceding passage of the Airline Deregulation Act, eight mergers and acquisitions involving air carriers occurred. In the eight years following deregulation, fifty-two air carriers were involved in thirty-nine mergers or acquisitions. Of those fifty-two transactions, more than two-thirds occurred between late 1985 and early 1987.

This major restructuring and transformation of the airline industry has occurred at a tremendous cost to airline employees. Dismissals, furloughs, and the uprooting of families are commonplace following a merger and often occur without regard to seniority. Moreover, the resolution of contract survivalship and union representation issues following a merger—when employees most need such protection—currently rests in an interstitial area. This situation is the result of a transfer of jurisdiction from the now-defunct Civil Aeronautics Board to the Department of Transportation, the courts, and the National Mediation Board.

Labor Protective Provisions and the DOT

Before enactment of the ADA, the CAB generally imposed employee labor protective provisions as a condition of its approval of an acquisition or merger. In a 1950 decision involving United-Western's acquisition of Air Carrier Property, the CAB enunciated its rationale

125

for embracing employee LPPs under the public interest requirements of the Federal Aviation Act:

> A route transfer or a merger or a similar transaction presumably in-
> volves benefits to the stockholders of the company who are parties to
> it. On balance, it must also benefit the public as a whole, otherwise, we
> would disapprove it. Very often, these benefits to the stockholders and
> to the public will be at the expense of some of the employees of the
> companies involved. We think it only equitable that in such circum-
> stances the hardships borne by adversely affected employees should be
> mitigated by provisions for their benefit.[1]

In 1961, the CAB extensively reviewed its policy of imposing conditions to minimize the adverse impact on airline employees of mergers, consolidations, and route transfers and standardized the
conditions it would require for the protection of employees (*United-
Capital* LPPs).[2] In 1972, the CAB again reviewed the standardized
LPPs and adopted clarifications that resulted in the *Allegheny-Mohawk*
LPPs.[3] The *Allegheny-Mohawk* LPPs provided for the fair and equitable integration of seniority; protection against reduction in compensation; a dismissal allowance for employees deprived of
employment as a result of the merger; the continuation of benefits
such as medical coverage; an option to resign and collect a lump-
sum separation allowance under certain conditions; reimbursement
for traveling and moving expenses if relocation was required; compensatory protection against losses attributable to the sale of a home
for less than its fair value or cancellation of an unexpired lease;
prohibition against a carrier rearranging or adjusting its work force
to deprive employees of LPP coverage; and final and binding arbitration of disputes arising under the LPPs, including disputes over
the fair and equitable integration of seniority lists.

Although neither the ADA nor its legislative history contains any
directive that the CAB should no longer impose LPPs as a condition
for approval of airline mergers, in 1979, in the Texas International–

---

1. United-Western Acquisition of Air Carrier Property, 11 CAB 701,
708 (1950), *aff'd sub nom.* Western Airlines v. CAB, 194 F.2d 211, 213–15
(9th Cir. 1952).
2. United-Capital Merger, 33 CAB 307, 342–47 (1961).
3. Allegheny-Mohawk Merger, Order 72–431, 32.

Pan Am–National acquisition,[4] the CAB "put all labor parties on notice that the labor protection in the future will be provided only if and when the Board determines that it is required by special circumstances. LPPs will no longer be imposed as a matter of course, or because tradition dictates their use. We therefore advise labor to negotiate its own merger protections through the collective bargaining process at the first opportunity." The CAB continued, however, to impose LPPs in subsequent merger cases.

Lending support to the conclusion that Congress did not intend the CAB or the DOT to deviate from the established policy of imposing LPPs in airline merger cases, Congress enacted legislation in 1982 to maintain the CAB's section 408 jurisdiction until sunset. Senator Nancy Kassenbaum (R-Kansas) stated, "We request that the CAB continue to impose these standard labor protective provisions in a manner consistent with its handling of Section 408 transactions prior to the enactment of the Airline Deregulation Act of 1978."[5]

Despite congressional intent, and despite section 408 of the Federal Aviation Act, the DOT has held that the justification for imposing LPPs was to preserve the stability of the air transportation system, not to improve the general welfare of airline employees. Moreover, since January 1, 1985, when the CAB's authority over airline mergers was transferred to the DOT, the department's policy has been to refrain from imposing LPPs unless they are necessary to prevent labor strife that could disrupt the national transportation system or are warranted because of special circumstances. The DOT's philosophy is that collective bargaining is the proper method of ensuring protection for workers.

Irrationality pervades the new DOT standard, in that it is based on false premises both factually and legally. The obvious question is, How can unrepresented workers without a collective bargaining representative obtain LPPs through the collective bargaining process pursuant to section 6 of the RLA? Moreover, LPPs obtained for represented workers through the collective bargaining process could be worthless if the collective bargaining agreements did not survive the acquisition or merger, as a result of the NMB's lack of assertiveness and/or the rulings of Reagan-appointed federal judges.

---

4. Order 80–7–20 (1980).
5. 128 CONG. REC. H57236 (daily ed. June 21, 1982).

Contract Survivalship and the Courts

In response to the wave of acquisitions and mergers affecting air carriers and the DOT's departure from established CAB policy on LPPs, the Teamsters Airline Division began introducing proposals relating to LPPs into its section 6 notices. In contract negotiations with two carriers, Western and PSA, the Teamsters Airline Division negotiated LPPs and postmerger employee protections as the quid pro quo for carrier need concessions.

WESTERN AIRLINES

Western and the Teamsters Airline Division, representing three crafts or classes of employees (mechanics and related employees, stock clerks, and flight instructors), negotiated a letter of agreement in October 1983 as a result of Western's critical financial situation. After much bargaining, Western demanded and received from its employees a 10 percent wage reduction, a freeze on the quarterly unlimited cost-of-living adjustments, and substantial work rule concessions. The union was justifiably concerned about granting concessions without guarantees of job security. Western agreed that the quid pro quo for the wage and work rule concessions would be the protection of employees against the adverse consequences of mergers and acquisitions.

Merger protections were agreed to by and between Western and the Teamsters Airline Division as follows:

7.A. In the event of a merger, consolidation, or acquisition of Western Airlines with another airline or entity, the facilities of Western Airlines as they existed prior to the merger, consolidation, or acquisition shall not be integrated with the facilities of the other airline or entity involved in the merger, consolidation, or acquisition without agreement of the Teamsters Airline Division or until such time as the seniority lists for the crafts or classes inclusive of such employees are integrated. In the event of a merger, acquisition, or consolidation of Western Airlines with another airline or entity the Mechanic and Related, Stock Clerk, and Flight Instructor employees of Western Airlines as represented by the Teamsters Airline Division prior to the merger, acquisition, or consolidation shall not be integrated with the employees of the other airline or entity involved in the merger, acquisition, or consolidation without agreement of the Teamsters Airline Division or until such time as the seniority lists for the crafts or classes inclusive of such employees are integrated.

B. In the event of a merger, consolidation, or acquisition of Western Airlines with another airline or entity, the merger, consolidation, or acquisition agreement will be conditioned upon the acceptance of Labor Protective Provisions no less favorable than the Labor Protective Provisions specified by the CAB in the Allegheny-Mohawk merger by Western Airlines and their merging, consolidation or acquiring airline or entity and covering the Mechanic and Related, Stock Clerk or Flight Instructor employees of Western Airlines as now represented by the Teamsters Airline Division.

C. Western Airlines agrees that it will not enter into any merger, consolidation, or acquisition without the language contained in Paragraph 7 of this Agreement between Western Airlines and the Teamsters Airline Division being incorporated into and made a part of such merger, consolidation or acquisition agreement.

D. Western Airlines shall require the mergering, consolidating, or acquiring carrier or other entity to assume the obligations of the IBT [International Brotherhood of Teamsters] collective bargaining agreements. Notice of the existence of this Agreement shall be given to any airline or other entity involved in a merger, consolidation, or acquisition with or of Western Airlines. Such notice shall be in writing with a copy to the Teamsters Airline Division. Western Airlines shall be liable to the Teamsters Airline Division and to the covered employees for all damages sustained as a result of such failure to require assumption of the terms of this Agreement, and the IBT collective bargaining agreements.

12.A. Western Airlines, Inc., agrees that it will not create or be a part of a New York Air type operation engaged in FAR [Federal Air Regulations] Part 121 operations unless the work performed by this craft or class, or any portion thereof, is assigned to employees within the scope and operation and in accordance with the terms and conditions of the agreement between Western Airlines and the Teamsters Airline Division respecting this class and craft.

B. Further, it is understood that the company may not divert or transfer any of its aircraft or assets to a new or existing Part 121 operation substantially owned or controlled by Western Airlines, Inc., unless the work performed by this craft or class, or any portion thereof, is assigned to the employees within the scope and operation and in accordance with the terms and conditions of the agreement between Western Airlines, Inc., and the Teamsters Airline Division.

C. Moreover, all work recognized as work coming within this class or craft and covered by the collective bargaining agreement between Western Airlines and the International Brotherhood of Teamsters shall continue to be assigned to and performed by employees covered by said collective bargaining agreement whether such work is performed by the company, or any subsidiary, division, or parent, or successor of the company, or subsidiary of such parent, or successor and shall be recognized as work coming within the jurisdiction of the union and covered by the collective bargaining agreement between Western Airlines and the International Brotherhood of Teamsters for this craft or class.[6]

In 1984, Western and the union concluded new collective bargaining agreements for each of the three crafts or classes of employees, effective from September 1, 1984, to January 1, 1987. The new agreements incorporated the previously agreed-to merger protections, with the exception of 7D, which was replaced with the following language contained in a September 1, 1984, letter of agreement:

> It is mutually agreed and understood between Western Airlines, Inc. and the International Brotherhood of Teamsters as follows:
> In the event of an unfriendly takeover effort, as determined by the International Brotherhood of Teamsters, Western Airlines shall require the merging, consolidating, or acquiring carrier or other entity to assume the obligations of the IBT collective bargaining agreements. Notice of the existence of this Agreement shall be given any airline or other entity involved in a merger, consolidation, or acquisition with or of Western Airlines. Such notice shall be in writing with a copy to the Teamsters Airline Division. Western Airlines shall be liable to the Teamsters Airline Division and to the covered employees for all damages sustained as a result of such failure to require assumption of the terms of this Agreement, and the IBT collective bargaining agreements.[7]

On September 9, 1986, Delta, DL Acquisition Corporation (a subsidiary of Delta), and Western entered into an agreement and plan of merger. Under the merger agreement, DL Acquisition would be merged into Western, and postmerger Western would become a wholly owned subsidiary of Delta. On September 18, 1986, Delta and Western filed a joint application for an exemption for approval of acquisition of control with the DOT.

---

6. Letter of Agreement between Western Airlines and the Teamsters Airline Division, Oct. 1983.

7. Letter of Agreement between Western Airlines and the Teamsters Airline Division, Sept. 1984.

On or about October 15, 1986, the union met with the chairman of Western, who was advised that the union had determined that the terms of the September 1, 1984, merger letter of agreement were applicable to the acquisition of Western by Delta. The union was advised that Western did not know what position Delta intended to take with respect to continuation of the basic agreements. Western was subsequently advised that unless the union was informed by October 31, 1986, of Western's intent to comply with the obligations contained in the September 1, 1984, merger letter of agreement, the union would assume that Western did not intend to comply and therefore would pursue all available legal and contractual remedies. On or about October 30, 1986, the president of Western responded by asserting that Western did not believe the September 1, 1984, merger letter of agreement was applicable to the merger agreement.

The union filed separate class-action grievances on behalf of mechanics and related employees and flight instructors and stock clerk employees, respectively, asserting that Western had violated the September 1, 1984, letter of agreement and the basic agreements by refusing to compel Delta to assume the Teamsters Airline Division collective bargaining agreements with Western. The union requested that Western not finalize its merger with Delta until it complied with the terms of the collective bargaining agreements and the September 1, 1984, letter of agreement. It also requested that the grievances be referred directly to the arbitration board. Western asserted that it did not believe the matter set forth in the grievances was covered by the collective bargaining agreements between Western and the union and subsequently notified the union that it would refuse to arbitrate this matter.

On December 5, 1986, the union filed a complaint[8] in the United States District Court for the Central District of California against Western and Delta. It sought to compel arbitration of its grievance concerning Western's failure to require Delta to assume the collective bargaining agreements between Western and the union and to enjoin the sale of Western to Delta pending the resolution of the union's grievance through binding arbitration. On December 5, 1986, the union moved for a temporary restraining order to enjoin the approval of the merger agreement by Western's shareholders. On De-

---

8. No. CV 86–7921 JMI (PX).

cember 10, 1986, the district court denied the motion for a temporary restraining order.

The DOT approved the merger agreement on December 11, 1986. On December 16, 1986, the shareholders ratified the merger agreement, and on the following day, Delta terminated all members of Western's board of directors and replaced them with directors Delta had selected. Under the merger plan, Western would continue its operations and retain its corporate identity until April 1, 1987. As such, it was subject to its collective bargaining agreements with the union and to the jurisdiction of the system board of adjustment.

On December 29, 1986, the union moved for partial summary judgment on count 1 of the complaint. In so doing, the union sought an order compelling expedited arbitration of its grievance that Western had breached the successorship provisions of the collective bargaining agreements and its memorandum of understanding, to which it was signatory with the union. On the same day, Western and Delta filed a motion to dismiss the complaint or, in the alternative, for summary judgment. The union filed its response to Western's and Delta's motion on January 20, 1987. Western and Delta responded to the union's motion for partial summary judgment on January 18, 1987.

On February 13, 1987, the district court issued a final order and memorandum opinion granting Western's and Delta's motion to dismiss. The court concluded that "the union's action for an injunction and arbitration of a grievance in a merger raises a representation issue." The complaint was dismissed on the basis that representation disputes are within the exclusive jurisdiction of the NMB.[9]

An appeal was presented to the Ninth Circuit Court of Appeals asserting that the decision of the district court should be reversed and remanded with instructions to compel Western expeditiously to arbitrate the union's grievance. The district court's failure to compel Western to arbitrate was a reversible error because the successorship provisions on which the union based its grievance did not obligate

---

9. The district court did not state the basis for its conclusion that a representation dispute existed. Apparently no weight was given to the parties' dispute over the meaning and application of the contractual successorship provisions agreed to by Western. That dispute is by statute within the exclusive jurisdiction of the system board of arbitration and not the NMB.

Western to engage in any unlawful action or violate any federal policy. An arbitrator could have awarded the union only monetary relief or directed Western not to merge with Delta until Western was able to secure Delta's assumption of the bargained agreements with the union. Neither remedy would have violated the law. Nor would either have infringed on the jurisdiction of the NMB because no representation dispute among Delta's employees was involved. The union did not seek any relief against Delta. No relief awardable by the district court or the system board of arbitration against Western would have resulted in the representation of current Delta employees by the union. No precedent established that representation disputes arise from the operation of successorship clauses. Cases held only that representation disputes could not be settled by the courts. There was no authority for the proposition that to compel arbitration under an existing agreement when no representation dispute exists was nonjusticiable because it involved successorship provisions or that successorship provisions were voidable at the whim of the carrier. This case concerned Western's contractual premerger obligations to its employees, no more and no less.

The court was advised on March 2, 1987, that without an expedited hearing and determination of the appeal before April 1, 1987, the operational merger of Delta and Western would be finalized, employees would be forced to relocate or lose their jobs, the subject matter of the dispute would be destroyed, and the Board of Arbitration would lose its power to remedy the union's grievances.

On March 17, 1987, the court of appeals entered an injunction pending appeal that directed the parties to arbitrate expeditiously the question whether Western, as a condition for merging with Delta, was obliged to require Delta to assume Western's collective bargaining agreements and otherwise comply with contractual merger protections.[10] The parties selected arbitrator Robert O. Harris to hear and decide their contract dispute. The arbitration hearing commenced on March 30, 1987, the same day the court of appeals heard oral argument, and the evidentiary record was closed on March 31, 1987. Summation, to be presided over by Harris, was scheduled for April 1, 1987. On March 31, 1987, the court of appeals entered a comprehensive final order reversing the district court's judgment[11]

---

10. Order 87–5657 (9th Cir. 1987).
11. No. CV 86–7921.

and remanding the case "with instructions to enter order compelling arbitration"; denying Western's motion for reconsideration of its March 17 order directing arbitration pending appeal; and enjoining the contemplated merger of Delta and Western pending arbitration or the carrier's stipulation that the result of arbitration would be binding on the successor corporation. Delta and Western sought an ex parte stay from Justice Sandra Day O'Connor, circuit justice for the Ninth Circuit, shortly before midnight on March 31. Two and one-half hours later, the court of appeals' injunction against the merger was stayed "pending the timely filing and disposition of a petition for a writ of certiorari." The union was not served with the carrier's application for stay until approximately five minutes before the stay was issued. The Ninth Circuit Court of Appeals issued its opinion later, on April 1. Thus Justice O'Connor had the benefit of neither opposing arguments nor the court of appeals' opinion when she acted in the early morning hours of April 1. Under the cloak of the stay, Western was merged into Delta at approximately 8:30 A.M. EST, on April 1, 1987. Later that day, when the arbitration proceeding reconvened in Los Angeles, Western declined to proceed on the ground that the adjustment board had lost jurisdiction. On April 2, 1987, Justice O'Connor amended her order, stating that the order by the court of appeals that had compelled arbitration was also stayed. The union's motion to vacate the stay was denied by the United States Supreme Court on April 6, 1987.

PSA

PSA and the Teamsters Airline Division negotiated four collective bargaining agreements covering mechanics and related employees, station agents, flight attendants, and reservation agents in January 1984. In these negotiations, PSA sought and obtained wage concessions from the union under the threat that the holding company (PSA, Inc.) would liquidate the airline absent the concessions. Employees represented by the union agreed to concessions representing approximately a 15 percent cutback in wages inclusive of substantial changes in work rules and conditions. In exchange for these concessions, the union obtained comprehensive successorship language providing protection for the PSA employees in the event of a merger, consolidation, or acquisition. In view of the then-emerging trend toward consolidation in the airline industry, the union would not agree to concessions without strong language protecting its members in the event of a merger, takeover, or other form of buyout. The protective provisions of all four agreements are substantially identical and state in part:

Section 1. Single Carrier and Separate Airline Operations
A. In the event of a merger, consolidation or acquisition of or by PSA with another carrier engaged in interstate, intrastate or foreign air transportation under circumstances where the operations of the two carrriers are to be integrated so as to create a single carrier within the meaning of the Railway Labor Act:
2. Where the majority of employees in the . . . class or craft of the post-merger carrier were employees of a carrier other than PSA immediately prior to the merger, the following shall apply:
a. The consolidated, post-merger carrier shall assume the obligations of the IBT Collective Bargaining Agreement, and shall maintain that agreement as to PSA employees represented by the Teamsters Airline Division prior to the merger until it is changed in accordance with Sections 2, 5, and 6 of the Railway Labor Act. The provisions of this Section shall not apply to the employees in the . . . class or craft of the post-merger carrier who are represented by an individual or labor organization other than the Teamsters Airline Division or to employees who are unrepresented unless the requirements of subsection (c) are satisfied.
b. The consolidated, post-merger carrier shall recognize the Teamsters Airline Division as the representative of the employees in the post-merger . . . class or craft who were previously represented by the Teamsters Airline Division at PSA. If a question of representation is raised and placed before the [National Mediation] Board, recognition of the Teamsters Airline Division will be continued during the pendency of the representation matter for such employees.
c. If the employees of the other carrier within the . . . class or craft are unrepresented, the post-merger carrier shall recognize the Teamsters Airline Division as the representative of all employees in the . . . class or craft if within twelve (12) months of the merger the union is able to present evidence of a majority showing among all the employees of the class or craft. A majority showing shall consist of written and dated authorizations demonstrating that a majority of employees in the . . . class or craft of the post-merger carrier desire representation by the union for the purpose of collective bargaining. Where the union makes the required showing of majority interest, representatives of the post-merger carrier and the union will meet to negotiate pay and working conditions to be applicable to the employees of the . . . class or craft.
3. The consolidated, post-merger carrier shall extend to PSA employees in the . . . class or craft, who were represented by the Teamsters Airline Division prior to the merger, labor protective provisions no less favor-

able than the Labor Protective Provisions specified by the Civil Aeronautics Board in the Allegheny-Mohawk Merger Case at Sections 3, 4, 5, 6, 7, 8, 9, 10, 11, 12 and 13. To the extent that the existing provisions in the collective bargaining agreements covering said affected employees provide, in whole or in part, protections or benefits equivalent to the Allegheny-Mohawk LPPs, such pre-existing protections or benefits shall be considered as satisfying or contributing to the obligations prescribed by this paragraph.

4. The facilities of PSA as they existed prior to the merger, consolidation or acquisition shall not be integrated with the facilities of the other airline or entity involved in the merger, consolidation or acquisition without agreement of the Teamsters Airline Division or until such time as the seniority lists for the post-merger . . . class or craft are integrated pursuant to the arbitration procedures outlined below. The employees of PSA, as represented by the Teamsters Airline Division prior to the merger, acquisition or consolidation, shall not be integrated with employees of the other carrier involved in the merger, acquisition or consolidation without agreement of the Teamsters Airline Division or until such time as the seniority lists for the post-merger . . . class or craft are integrated pursuant to the arbitration procedures outlined below. In the event the integration of seniority lists has not been completed sixty (60) days from commencement of negotiations concerning such integration, then that issue (seniority integration only) shall be submitted to final and binding arbitration before an arbitrator pursuant to the provisions of Section 13 of the LPPs. All seniority integration disputes shall be submitted to a single arbitrator.

C. PSA and/or PSA, Inc. agree that they will not enter into or execute any agreement of merger, acquisition or consolidation of corporate entities without the language contained in this Section being incorporated into and made part of such merger, acquisition or consolidation agreement, so that the requirements of this Section will be binding on the post-merger, acquired, acquiring or consolidated carrier in accordance with their terms. Notice of the existence of this Agreement shall be given to any airline or other entity involved in such a merger, acquisition, or consolidation. Such notice shall be in writing with a copy to the Teamsters Airline Division. PSA and PSA, Inc. shall be liable to the Teamsters Airline Division and to the covered employees for all damages sustained as a result of any violation of the provisions of this paragraph.[12]

PSA agreed with the language in the merger protective provisions and understood its effect. PSA responded that it needed the conces-

---

12. Mergers, consolidations, and acquisitions provisions contained in each of the 1984 through 1987 collective bargaining agreements between PSA and the Teamsters Airline Division.

sions and that these merger protections constituted an acceptable quid pro quo. In an address to PSA employees, the chairman of the airline stated that the company needed the concessions to remain competitive and that, in recognition of the employees' willingness to sacrifice, the company had agreed to provide PSA employees with the greatest merger protections in the industry.

On or about December 8, 1986, PSA and its parent corporation, PS Group, Inc., entered into an agreement and plan of merger with USAir Group, Inc., a holding company of which USAir is a wholly owned subsidiary. Under the merger agreement, AL Acquisition, a newly created wholly owned subsidiary of USAir Group, would merge with and into PSA and thereby become a wholly owned subsidiary of USAir Group. Despite the chairman's representation to the employees of PSA, the merger agreement failed to incorporate the language contained in the merger protection clauses or to require USAir to assume the obligations of the collective bargaining agreements of the Teamsters with PSA. In fact, section 7.3(g) of the agreement and plan of merger provided that, as a condition to approval of the merger, PSA would negotiate and execute agreements with its employees' union representatives "which modify and render inapplicable to the Merger" between PSA and USAir "any provision of any collective bargaining agreement to which [PSA] is a party which by its terms applies to mergers, consolidations, acquisitions, coordinations or other corporate or operational transactions."[13]

On December 12, 1986, USAir Group, Inc., PS Group, Inc., and PSA filed with the DOT a joint application for an exemption to permit USAir to acquire PSA. On December 15, 1986, the union filed group grievances covering the four crafts or classes, protesting PSA's failure to abide by the merger clauses of the agreements. Specifically, the grievances protested that the merger agreement did not include or incorporate the language contained in the merger protection clauses and that neither PSA nor PSA Group would ensure that the requirements of the merger clauses would be binding on USAir Group and its subsidiaries. The union requested that the grievances be referred directly to final and binding arbitration. On December 19, 1986, PSA responded to the grievances by stating that

---

13. Agreement and Plan of Merger among USAir Group, Inc., AL Acquisition Corp., PS Group, Inc., and Pacific Southwest Airlines, Dec. 8, 1986, at 35, § 7.3(g).

"the dispute which the union seeks to have arbitrated, through its 'group grievances' is, in reality, a representational dispute within the exclusive jurisdiction of the National Mediation Board. Such a dispute is not arbitrable under these or any other collective bargaining agreements governed by the Railway Labor Act."[14] PSA again declined to arbitrate the dispute on December 31, 1986, in response to the union's appeal of the grievances to arbitration.

On January 28, 1987, the DOT tentatively approved the proposed merger between PSA and USAir. In its January 28, 1987, order to show cause why tentative approval of the acquisition should not become final, the DOT declined to impose LPPs as a condition of the acquisition, stating that labor-management relations in the airline industry "are determined not by government regulations, but by private sector decisionmaking—*in this case through collective bargaining.*"[15] The union filed action in the United States District Court for the Northern District of California on February 2, 1987, requesting an order compelling PSA expeditiously to arbitrate the dispute with the union on the issue of interpretation or application of the four collective bargaining agreements. The essence of the case was PSA's attempt to evade the obligations of freely negotiated successorship provisions that had since become inconvenient for the company. After a hearing on March 10, 1987, the district court on March 20 issued an order dismissing the union's complaint "since this complaint raises representational issues over which the court has no jurisdiction."[16]

As union counsel advised the Ninth Circuit, "With deference, we must insist that the district court misunderstood the successorship provision at issue, uncritically read plainly distinguishable authorities, ignored this Court's decision in *Western Pacific,*[17] and erroneously viewed its function as searching for 'representational issues disguised as arbitrable contract disputes.'" This all-encompassing decision, if upheld, means that employees cannot protect themselves against an unprecedented, impermissible intrusion into private collective bargaining.[18]

---

14. Letter from Paul George, Vice President, Employee Relations, PSA, to Marvin Griswold, Teamsters Airline Division (Dec. 19, 1986).

15. Order 87–1–53 (emphasis added).

16. Order CV–87–0402 MHP No. CA.D.C. (SFO).

17. 809 F.2d 607.

18. No. 87–1846 (1987).

The NMB and Union Representation Following a Merger

The Board has used the *Republic* merger doctrine since 1980 to determine whether air carriers have combined their operations to form a single transportation system for purposes of the RLA. In *TWA-Ozark*, the Board pointed out that "when the Board found in *Republic* that Republic and Republic West will operate as a single carrier for purposes of the Railway Labor Act" and as a result "all certifications on Airwest were extinguished by operation of law upon Airwest's acquisition by Republic," the understanding was that Republic would voluntarily recognize the organizations on its property as the representatives for each craft or class on the acquired carrier, enhancing the goal of stable labor relations by providing one representative for each craft or class. The Board further pointed out that stability was enhanced on Republic because there was continuity in collective bargaining representation for all employees, particularly those on the acquired carrier, who, as a result of the merger, were likely to experience the most turmoil.[19]

Recently, however, the Board's *Republic* merger doctrine has been misperceived and misapplied by merging carriers.

Without question, the recent wave of mergers has had an unsettling effect on the continuity of collective bargaining and employee representation in the airline industry. The Board has given recognition to this fact by its recent decision in *TWA-Ozark* and in the Notice of the Development of New Procedures for Handling Representation Issues Resulting from Mergers, Acquisitions, or Consolidations in the Airline Industry.

It has been the policy of the Department of Transportation to refrain from imposing LPPs in merger cases, on the ground that such matters should be left to the parties to resolve through collective bargaining. Several court decisions have held that collectively bargained merger protections cannot be enforced either by the courts or adjustment boards because mergers of air carriers invariably involve representation issues over which the NMB has exclusive jurisdiction. Without question, the ball is in the NMB's court. The NMB should clearly and forcefully affirm that certifications are not extinguished in contractual successorship disputes arising as a result of an acquisition or merger until the adjustment board issues a final and binding award. This action would serve to unravel the gordian knot created by the DOT, the courts, and the carriers.

---

19. 14 NMB at 234 (1987).

Part 4
Seniority and Job
Rights Issues in
Mergers and Acquisitions

Seniority Integration in the Absence of Mandatory Labor Protective Provisions

Robert H. Nichols

Wesley Kennedy

Few people would argue that stable, amicable labor relations are in the public interest and that labor disputes have adverse consequences for employees, employers, and the public. This goal clearly underlies federal labor policy in the airline industry.[1] Stable labor relations are in the interest of employees, who wish to pursue livelihoods without the hardship of disputes with their employers; employers, who wish to sell their services without the uncertainty and costs of disputes with their employees; and airline passengers, who wish to travel without the delays and disruptions that can be caused by labor disputes.

The issue of seniority is particularly important to the achievement of these public policies in the airline industry, for no employment issue is dearer to airline employees. Seniority has even more significance to airline employees than to employees in other industries in which seniority is measured predominantly by an employee's tenure in one location. In the airline industry, seniority is predominantly

---

1. Among the declared purposes of the RLA are "[t]o avoid any interruption to commerce or to the operation of any carrier engaged therein"; "to provide for the prompt and orderly settlement of all disputes concerning rates of pay, rules or working conditions"; and "to provide for the prompt and orderly settlement of all disputes growing out of grievances or out of the interpretation or application of agreements covering rates of pay, rules, or working conditions." RLA § 2, 45 U.S.C. § 152 (1926). *See* NLRA § 1, 29 U.S.C. § 151 (1935).

"system seniority," measured across the carrier's entire system. Seniority dictates not only individuals' wages and compensatory benefits, but also their jobs, residences, shifts, hours, and virtually every other important aspect of their employment. This is particularly true of in-flight employees—pilots and flight attendants—who work in multimillion dollar "plants" traveling thousands of miles each day. Accordingly, disputes concerning seniority endanger stable labor relations.

No situation creates a greater risk of acrimonious seniority disputes than does the merger of two carriers. The harsh consequences that can befall employees as a result of the integration of two seniority lists are readily apparent: integration creates direct clashes between separate groups of employees who must frequently work side by side. Although such conflicts can be particularly acrimonious when the premerger groups were represented by separate bargaining representatives and seniority issues become entangled with representational issues,[2] passions can run high and disputes can become intense even when the employee groups share the same union.[3] These conflicts can provoke direct employee actions against travelers[4] and, in extreme cases, make air travel dangerous.[5]

Given the highly charged nature of this issue, disputes should not be resolved by sheer political or economic power at the expense of the legitimate seniority expectations of the employee groups at the merging airlines. For many years before deregulation, a fair process, culminating in arbitration, was provided by sections 3 and 13 of the standard labor protective provisions routinely imposed by the Civil Aeronautics Board as a condition of its approval of mergers, ac-

---

2. Such representational questions are beyond the scope of this chapter. These issues do, however, have a good deal of currency. *See* Western Airlines v. IBT, 107 S. Ct. 1515 (1987) (O'Connor, Circuit Justice); TWA-Ozark Airlines, 14 NMB at 218 (1987).

3. These representational questions are discussed in Wilder and Lurye, *Successorship Clauses: A Union Perspective, infra* p. 169.

4. *See, e.g., Sabotage at Northwest Air*, CRAIN'S DETROIT BUS., Feb. 2, 1987.

5. Thus, for example, there have been reports in the news media, in connection with the Northwest-Republic merger, of isolated instances of aircraft sabotage. Given the level of employee hostility generated in such situations as the Texas Air–Eastern merger (*see, e.g.,* Wall St. J., Jan. 22, 1987, at 6), one can reasonably anticipate that such occurrences may continue.

quisitions, and similar transactions. Section 3 of the standard LPPs provides for the "fair and equitable" integration of seniority lists in each craft or class of employees when a merger affects seniority interests and for the resolution of those issues through arbitration under section 13 of the LPPs if the issues cannot be resolved through collective bargaining or an alternative procedure. Some airline unions have also developed their own internal policies to augment the provisions of sections 3 and 13.[6] Following deregulation, however, the Department of Transportation has effectively taken the position that LPPs will *never* be imposed as a condition of its approval of mergers or similar transactions and that carriers and their employees are left to their own devices to resolve seniority issues arising in mergers.[7]

The laissez-faire posture adopted by the DOT, under which the process of collective bargaining has been depended on for the solution to all merger-related labor issues, has significantly altered the environment in which seniority integration disputes are resolved. In fact, this approach has proven wholly inadequate for resolving the conflicts that arise in the integration of seniority lists. Instead, the process that now prevails in the industry and that has replaced the orderly procedures of sections 3 and 13 is the "law of the jungle," under which the stronger premerger employee group—particularly when it is supported by management at the merged carrier—is able to impose its will on the smaller premerger group.

To redress this imbalance of power, some process, such as sections 3 and 13 of the standard LPPs, should be imposed by statute for the resolution of seniority issues arising out of airline mergers and acquisitions.

Development of CAB and DOT Rules Regarding LPPs

THE IMPOSITION OF LPPS BEFORE DEREGULATION

The standards governing the imposition of LPPs as a condition of regulatory approval of airline mergers or similar transactions have

---

6. *See infra* pp. 146–48.
7. *See infra* pp. 148–51.

their roots in the treatment of similar issues in the railroad industry. Since 1950 the CAB has routinely imposed LPPs as a condition for the approval of airline transactions adversely affecting employees,[8] and the validity of this policy has consistently been upheld by the courts.[9] The CAB standardized its LPPs in 1961 in the *United-Capital Merger* case[10] and thereafter imposed those LPPs in numerous cases. In 1972, in the *Allegheny-Mohawk Merger* case,[11] the CAB reviewed its policy and, with minor modifications, reaffirmed its commitment to the formula adopted in *United-Capital*. The standard LPPs have since been known colloquially as "*Allegheny-Mohawk* LPPs."

Beginning no later than *United-Capital*, the standard LPPs expressly covered seniority issues. Section 3 of the *United-Capital* LPPs, which remained unchanged after *Allegheny-Mohawk*, provided that

> [i]nsofar as the acquisition or merger affects the seniority rights of the carriers' employees, provisions shall be made for the integration of seniority lists in a fair and equitable manner, including, where applicable, agreement through collective bargaining between the carriers and the representatives of the employees affected. In the event of failure to agree, the dispute may be submitted by either party for adjustment in accordance with Section 13.[12]

Section 13 of the standard LPPs, both under *United-Capital* and *Allegheny-Mohawk*, established a procedure for the resolution of disputes, culminating in final and binding arbitration.

The CAB made no determination in section 3 of *how* seniority lists were to be integrated, beyond the general standard that the integration be "fair and equitable." Instead, the Board left this decision to the parties in each case. Over time, internal union procedures—supported by the obligation to arbitrate under section 13 of the

---

8. United-Western Acquisition of Air Carrier Property, 11 CAB 701, 708 (1950), *aff'd sub nom.* Western Airlines v. CAB, 194 F.2d 211 (9th Cir. 1952).

9. *See, e.g.,* ALPA v. CAB, 4775 F.2d 900 (D.C. Cir. 1973); American Airlines v. CAB, 445 F.2d 891 (2d Cir. 1971); Oling v. ALPA, 346 F.2d 270 (7th Cir. 1965); Kent v. CAB, 204 F.2d 263 (2d Cir. 1953), *cert. denied,* 346 U.S. 826; Hyland v. United Air Lines, 254 F. Supp. 367 (N.D. Ill. 1966).

10. 33 CAB 307, 342–47 (1961), *aff'd sub nom.* Northwest Airlines v. CAB, 303 F.2d 395 (D.C. Cir. 1962).

11. 59 CAB 22 (1972).

12. United-Capital Merger, 33 CAB 307 (1961) (App. A).

LPPs—were developed for those cases in which both premerger employee groups in a particular craft or class were represented by the same labor organization. The most prominent of these internal union procedures has been, of course, the ALPA Merger Policy, which was developed beginning in the late 1940s. That policy, which has since been amended on numerous occasions and is a continual source of debate within ALPA,[13] provides for a three-stage process for integrating seniority lists, with each stage to be completed within a specified time period: (1) data collection and verification; (2) negotiation and, if necessary, mediation; and (3) in the event no resolution has been achieved through negotiation or mediation, arbitration before a board of ALPA members, chaired by a neutral person from outside the association.[14] The outcome of this process is binding upon ALPA[15] and becomes the position of the association in negotiations and, if necessary, in arbitration with the merged carrier under sections 3 and 13. ALPA Merger Policy has governed the integration of pilot seniority lists in virtually every airline merger since the early 1960s in which both premerger pilot groups were represented by ALPA.

The process established under sections 3 and 13 has served the interests of all concerned. It guarantees that an impartial resolution will be achieved, through arbitration if necessary, and thus protects the interests of all airline employees in resolving seniority integration conflicts. Moreover, from the perspective of the affected carriers, seniority integration under sections 3 and 13 has been essentially a "no-cost" item. Aside from marginal cost increases, such as potentially increased training costs,[16] protection of seniority rights between

---

13. *See, e.g.,* REPORT OF THE MERGER POLICY STUDY COMMITTEE TO THE ALPA BOARD OF DIRECTORS (Nov. 1986) (available from authors).

14. ALPA MERGER POLICY BOOKLET 3–8 (Dec. 1, 1986) (available from authors).

15. *Id.* at 8.

16. The legitimate interest of a merging carrier to minimize transition costs, such as training, resulting from seniority integration actually *coincides* with the interest of employees in preserving their jurisdiction over their premerger work. To the extent that the carrier's interests are not sufficiently protected through internal union procedures or other processes adopted by the affected employees, those interests are protected by the merged carrier's right to participate in bargaining and arbitration under sections 3 and 13.

two premerger employee groups through this process is on the whole greatly beneficial to the carriers because an impartial process tends to minimize the inevitable antagonisms that arise from the clash of conflicting seniority interests.

Deregulation and the Emergence of Current LPP Doctrine

Congress turned the airline industry upside down when it enacted the Airline Deregulation Act in 1978.[17] Events since then have demonstrated that airline employees have been profoundly affected by the statute. Although the "Employee Protection Program" (EPP) included in section 43 of the Act[18] demonstrated a recognition by Congress that deregulation could have an undue impact on employees, it seems reasonably clear that Congress gave no substantive consideration to whether the CAB should continue to impose standard LPPs, particularly those in sections 3 and 13, as a condition for approval of airline transactions.[19] The driving force behind dereg-

------

17. Pub. L. No. 95–504, 92 Stat. 1705 (1978).

18. 92 Stat. 1752, 49 U.S.C. § 1552. The EPP has been upheld by the Supreme Court. Alaska Airlines v. Brock, 107 S. Ct. 1476 (1987).

19. Indeed, there are indications that Congress assumed, in enacting the ADA, that preexisting CAB doctrine on the subject would continue unchanged. Thus, although Congress liberalized the CAB's authority to approve airline mergers, the statutory provision empowering the Board to condition approval "upon such terms and conditions as it shall find to be just and reasonable" under the public interest was left unchanged. Federal Aviation Act, § 408(b), 49 U.S.C. § 1308(b). Moreover, Congress added to the definition of the "public interest" under the FAA a provision that the Board "shall consider . . . as being in the public interest, and in accordance with the public convenience and necessity . . . the need to encourage fair wages and equitable working conditions for air carriers." Federal Aviation Act, § 102(a)(3), 49 U.S.C. § 1302(a)(3). This is precisely the language the Supreme Court found in 1939 to authorize the ICC to impose LPPs in the railroad industry. United States v. Lowden, 308 U.S. 225 (1939). S. Rep. No. 631, 95th Cong., 2d Sess., issued in 1978, noted with approval that airline employees had relied on the CAB's LPP doctrine and that deregulation would likely make such protections even more necessary to those employees. Subsequent statements by members of Congress have indicated that Congress assumed that LPPs would be imposed under the same standards following deregulation as had been applied previously. See, e.g., H.R.

ulation was not labor protection but, rather, a desire by Congress that the CAB's treatment of airline transactions be governed more closely by traditional antitrust law.[20]

In 1979, the CAB, while acknowledging in *Texas International–Pan Am–National Acquisition*[21] that the "public interest" standard remained unchanged by the deregulation act,[22] determined that the act required a reevaluation of its previous LPP doctrine. The Board

> put all labor parties on notice that labor protection in the future will be provided only if and when the Board determines that it is required by special circumstances. LPP's will no longer be imposed as a matter of course, or because tradition dictates their use. We therefore advise labor to negotiate its own merger protections through the collective bargaining process at the first opportunity.[23]

Nevertheless, the Board continued to make standard LPPs a condition for approval of airline transactions and indeed has not denied such employee protections in any two-carrier transaction since deregulation.

Following the "sunset" of the CAB's authority,[24] the DOT at the first opportunity made clear—in cases such as the *Midway–Air Florida Acquisition*,[25] *Southwest-Muse Acquisition*,[26] *Pacific Division Transfer*,[27] and *Piedmont-Empire Acquisition*[28]—that it would carry to its logical extreme the CAB's admonition in *Texas International–Pan Am–National* that employees should rely on collective bargaining for protection from the adverse consequences of mergers. The DOT adopted a standard under which LPPs would not be imposed unless necessary to prevent disruption of the air transportation system as

---

REP. No. 882, 99th Cong., 2d Sess. 3 (1986); 128 CONG. REC. 57,236 (daily ed. June 21, 1982); H.R. REP. No. 793, 98th Cong., 2d Sess. 11 (1984).

20. *See, e.g.*, S. REP. No. 631, 95th Cong., 2d Sess. 78–79 (1978); H.R. REP. No. 1211, 95th Cong., 2d Sess. 5–17 (1978); 134 CONG. REC. H13,446–47, S18,796–800 (daily ed. Oct. 14, 1978).

21. CAB Orders 79–12–163/164/165.

22. *Id.* at 59–60.

23. *Id.* at 67.

24. CAB Sunset Act of 1984, § 3, Pub. L. 98–443, 98 Stat. 1703; ADA, § 40(a), Pub. L. 95–540, 92 Stat. 1744; 49 U.S.C. § 1551.

25. Order 85–6–33.

26. Order 85–6–79.

27. Order 85–11–67.

28. Order 86–1–45.

a whole or under "special circumstances" to ensure fair wages and equitable working conditions. In so doing, the department made clear that in its view the impact of airline mergers on employees was entirely a matter for collective bargaining, not regulatory action: "[C]arriers and unions should decide through private negotiations what benefits should be paid airline employees in the event of a merger or acquisition."[29] The DOT consistently reaffirmed this "laissez-faire" policy during a spate of airline merger proceedings during 1986 and 1987.[30] Its refusal to impose LPPs as a condition of approval essentially left carriers and their employees on their own in resolving employee issues in mergers. The DOT also rejected alternative requests by labor parties to impose only sections 3 and 13.[31]

The DOT's standard has been upheld by two courts of appeal, one in a case containing virtually no record of the impact of a transaction on employees,[32] and the other in a case in which the terms of the carriers' transaction took account of the impact on employees.[33] In a recent decision, however, arising from the Northwest-Republic, TWA-Ozark, and Texas Air–Eastern acquisitions, the District of Columbia Circuit overturned the department's application of its LPP standard in the *Texas Air–Eastern* case and remanded the proceeding to the DOT for consideration of the impact of the acquisition on employees. The court indicated that, if collective bargaining proves to be inadequate in a particular case for the protection of employees' interests, LPPs should be imposed.[34] Moreover, as discussed below, events in these cases and others in recent years have

---

29. Midway–Air Florida Acquisition Show Cause Proceeding, Order 85–6–33, at 5.

30. Joint Application of USAir Group, Inc., PS Group, Inc., & Pacific Southwest Airlines, Order 87–3–11; American–Air Cal Show-Cause Proceeding, Order 87–2–33; Delta-Western Acquisition Case, Order 86–12–30; Texas Air–Eastern Acquisition Case, Order 86–10–2; TWA-Ozark Acquisition Case, Order 86–9–29; Texas Air–Eastern Acquisition Case, Order 86–8–77; Northwest-Republic Acquisition Case, Order 86–7–81.

31. *See, e.g.*, TWA-Ozark Acquisition, Order 86–9–29; Northwest-Republic Acquisition, Order 86–7–81; Pacific Division Transfer, Order 85–11–67.

32. ALPA v. DOT, 791 F.2d 172 (D.C. Cir. 1986).

33. Independent Union of Flight Attendants [IUFA] v. DOT, 803 F.2d 1029 (9th Cir. 1986).

34. ALPA v. DOT, 838 F.2d 563 (D.C. Circ. 1988).

underscored the costs to all concerned of not having an orderly mechanism for accomplishing seniority integration. Finally, there are continuing efforts in Congress to compel the DOT to alter its LPP standard.[35] It therefore remains possible that in the future the DOT may be forced to look more favorably on requests to impose LPPs.

INADEQUACY OF THE PRESENT APPROACH

It is the DOT's philosophy that employment issues, including seniority integration, arising from airline mergers or acquisitions should be subject to the same "market" forces that govern entry into the airline market. The absence of a mandatory process for seniority integration puts a premium on economic and political power, both in relations between the merged carrier and its employees and in relations between respective premerger employee groups. Some merged carriers have shown favoritism to one premerger employee group and have pitted employee groups against one another. Similarly, a politically stronger premerger employee group may be given an incentive to impose its will on its weaker counterpart. Under deregulation, the traditional bilateral process of collective bargaining, on which the DOT relies to resolve all merger-related employee issues, is wholly inadequate in preventing such outcomes. Indeed, even when the parties have recognized that establishing an orderly integration process is in their mutual interest, formulating such a process has frequently proved both costly and difficult.

DOT's Laissez-Faire Approach

RECENT HISTORY

Since 1984, when the DOT was first called upon to approve the merits of such transactions, approximately twenty airline mergers and acquisitions have been approved. A partial list of the mergers with significant labor relations implications would include the following: Southwest–Muse (1985), Midway–Air Florida (1985), United–Pan Am (Pacific Division) (1985), Northwest–Republic

---

35. *E.g.*, Aviation Daily, May 14, 1987, at 241–42.

(1986), Texas Air–Eastern (1986), TWA–Ozark (1986), Delta–Western (1986), Alaska–Jet America (1986), Texas Air–People/Frontier (1986), American–Air California (1986), USAir–PSA (1986), and USAir–Piedmont (1987). Rumors suggesting future mergers sweep the industry almost daily. A brief review of how seniority integration was or is being accomplished in each of these cases may be helpful in appreciating some emerging issues confronting the parties in such cases.[36]

In several of these cases, and particularly when by reason of earlier concessionary agreements labor had achieved significant ownership interests and board representation, the acquiring carrier has agreed to accept LPPs "as a matter of contract." What this phrase means in a practical sense is far from clear. Such agreements were reached in *Delta-Western* and *USAir-PSA*.

In *Delta-Western*, Delta stated to the DOT that it would offer provisions no less favorable than the traditional *Allegheny-Mohawk* LPPs to its employees as a matter of contract.[37] This commitment was exacted by Western in the discussions leading up to the agreement between the carriers and reflected the degree to which labor concerns were matters of agenda at that carrier, on whose board of directors labor was represented. Following the merger, this promise was translated into a letter sent by Delta to all its employees, both Western and premerger Delta, purporting to afford to each employee a series of provisions essentially identical to *Allegheny-Mohawk* LPPs, includ-

---

36. In both *Southwest-Muse* and *Alaska–Jet America*, the merged carrier has opted to keep the operations separate and distinct. At Muse, which operated under the Transtar name before its recent cessation of operations, the pilots designated ALPA as their representative. Aviation Daily, May 26, 1987, at 306. The Southwest pilots have their own union, and it reportedly was instrumental in Southwest's determination to keep the two operations separate. Alaska openly announced at the time of the acquisition of Jet America, which it proposed to operate as a nonunion subsidiary, that the deal was undertaken to "keep pressure on the unions [at Alaska] for further cost containment." Aviation Daily, Oct. 31, 1986, at 170. By the latter part of 1987, the carrier reversed course and determined to combine the operations. In negotiations with ALPA, the parties reached an agreement in October 1987 by which the Jet America pilots, without their participation, were placed on the ALPA list. That agreement has been challenged by a group of former Jet America pilots in ongoing litigation. Bernard v. Alpa, No. C87-5400 CAL (N.D. Cal.).

37. Agreement & Plan of Merger among Delta Airlines, Inc., DL Acquisition Corp., & Western Airlines, Inc. § 5.11 (available from authors).

ing sections 3 and 13. Delta was unwilling to make such provisions a matter of contract with AFA, however, which represented Western's flight attendants. Delta's reluctance was not altogether illogical, since the airline's flight attendants were unrepresented. Delta also declined, however, to enter into such an agreement with ALPA, which represented the pilots of both carriers. Discussions between the pilots about seniority integration commenced under the auspices of ALPA, and Delta initially refrained from active participation in the process. As time wore on, however, Delta became impatient and sought to impose deadlines on the groups; it also indicated that it would be unwilling to wait for the full procedure provided by ALPA Merger Policy. Finally, Delta intruded itself more directly into the process and in effect acted to "mediate" the seniority dispute between the pilot groups. For all practical purposes, ALPA was not a player in the resolution of the dispute.[38] The integrated pilot seniority list that resulted from this process is now the subject of litigation.[39]

Delta has systematically refused to deal with AFA on any seniority issues and has even rejected those merger representatives designated by AFA as the appropriate representatives of the former Western flight attendants.[40] Thereafter, no agreed solution having been achieved, Delta imposed what it deemed to be a "fair and equitable" solution. That list was unacceptable to the Western flight attendants, and arbitration under the contractual LPPs is ongoing.

Northwest-Republic represents a slight variant on this theme. Republic's unions had negotiated an obligation from Republic to obtain a commitment from an acquiring carrier that it would agree to contractual LPPs no less favorable than *Allegheny-Mohawk*. At the commencement of the Northwest-Republic DOT proceeding, Northwest claimed to the administrative law judge that it would honor Republic's commitment only "until the procedures for resolving major disputes have been exhausted."[41] For reasons made abundantly clear in the chapter in this volume by Roland P. Wilder, Jr., and William

---

38. As made clear below, TWA—which steadfastly opposed LPPs in any form—had taken an even stronger approach in the earlier TWA-Ozark merger.

39. Herring v. Delta Air Lines, No. 87–5725-RJK (C.D. Cal.).

40. A subsequent ballot conducted by the carrier confirmed these individuals as the desired spokespersons for the Western group.

41. Joint Applicants' Answers to Labor Parties' Information Requests, Mar. 17, 1986, at 4–5 (available from authors).

Lurye, this formulation was unacceptable to the union parties. Finally, Northwest, after considerable prodding by the administrative law judge, agreed to honor Republic's commitment to its employees.[42] Thereafter, recognizing the impossibility of offering sections 3 and 13 only to Republic employees, the carrier made those two provisions available to Northwest's pilots and flight attendants as well.[43]

As far as the pilots are concerned, Northwest has continued to operate the airlines as separate entities and has maintained separate ALPA contracts with each pilot group. Northwest has been content to let the ALPA process run its course, reserving the right to reject the result and trigger its own "section 13" arbitration if it finds the outcome unpalatable. The situation for flight attendants has been confused by the representational issues presented by the contest between the Teamsters and AFA. There too the carrier appears content to let the victorious union, the Teamsters, resolve the dispute without management input. Thus, in many ways, Northwest's response to these issues has been the most traditional.[44]

---

42. Stipulation Regarding Labor Protective Provisions, May 1, 1986 (available from authors).

43. The logic of this arrangement escaped the Republic pilots, who subsequently filed a suit against Northwest in an attempt to arbitrate the integration of the list with Northwest alone (under § 13) without the participation of the Northwest pilots. Northwest resisted this proposition, as did ALPA, which intervened in the case. The Republic pilots ultimately abandoned the litigation. Lawlus v. Northwest Airlines, No. 86–1032-A (E.D. Va.).

44. To complete the picture, however, it is worth noting that this approach extended only to the in-flight employees. When faced with a representational dispute among the office, clerical, passenger, and fleet service employees in 1986, Northwest negotiated an agreement establishing the seniority for portions of this group of employees with the Brotherhood of Railway and Airline Clerks (BRAC), which represented some of these employees. This was accomplished without participation by the ALEA-represented Republic employees, save for a committee of BRAC-selected employees. The result survived court challenge. ALEA v. Republic Airlines, 798 F.2d 967 (7th Cir.), *cert. denied,* 107 S. Ct. 458 (1986). Thereafter, the NMB determined that the appropriate unit was inconsistent with that reflected in these agreements and directed an election. BRAC now has lost the right to represent these employees. What the IAM, the successful union in the NMB election, will ultimately do with this resolution remains to be seen.

United's acquisition of Pan Am's Pacific operations, which included some 430 pilots and 1,200 flight attendants, illustrates yet another approach. At the DOT hearing, United fought vigorously against imposition of any LPPs and prevailed.[45] United then turned in good faith to its own unions to address the issues presented by the transaction, one of which was, of course, seniority.[46] The flight deck crews (United's pilots and Pan Am's pilots and flight engineers), through very sophisticated representatives, quickly established a procedural agreement among themselves and the carrier. The agreement was patterned after the ALPA Merger Policy, although ALPA procedure was not applicable because of the presence of Pan Am flight engineers represented by the Flight Engineers International Association (FEIA). The agreement provided for arbitration among the employee groups if agreement could not be reached in negotiations. United agreed either to accept the result or to arbitrate. The position of the pilot groups, however, was to be established in the initial proceeding. In fact, the issues between the pilot groups were resolved in direct negotiations and accepted by United within a very short time.

The flight attendants presented quite another story. United spent months in negotiations with the union that represented its flight attendants, AFA, in an effort to reach substantive agreement on the integration of seniority lists. When that attempt collapsed, considerable effort was expended in designing an elaborate procedural agreement to resolve the dispute. This was accomplished in direct negotiations, which also dealt with the wages, hours, and working conditions that would be part of the new long-haul routes being acquired by United. The ultimate agreement, which required membership ratification, provided for two-step arbitration between the flight attendant groups, wholly funded by United (including the cost of counsel for the employee groups), and committed United absolutely to accepting the result. The matter was arbitrated under a standard which the neutral found indistinguishable from the LPP standard. In September 1987, approximately a year and a half after

---

45. Pacific Division Transfer, Order 85–11–67 (1985).

46. United declined to involve the Pan Am unions in this process, prompting a challenge to the DOT's determination not to impose LPPs by the independent Pan Am flight attendants' union. The Ninth Circuit rejected this appeal. IUFA v. DOT, *supra*.

the effective date of the transaction, an award was issued by which the flight attendants' lists were integrated.

Midway's acquisition in bankruptcy proceedings of many of the assets of Air Florida presented different problems. In that situation, Midway determined, shortly after reactivating some of Air Florida's operations, that it wanted its pilot groups to be integrated. The groups were represented by different unions, however: by an independent union at Air Florida and by ALPA (which had just been certified) at Midway. The carrier's desires were made clear to both pilot groups through a carefully orchestrated series of actions designed to keep each group uncertain about the carrier's intent in the event they did not reach the desired result. Nevertheless, the pilots were able through intensive direct negotiations, the costs of which were borne by the carrier, to integrate their lists and to designate ALPA as the representative of the combined group.[47]

Texas Air, of course, was unencumbered by significant union constraints. It therefore determined upon its acquisition of Eastern that its New York Air employee groups would be folded into its Continental structure.[48] An arbitral process was imposed by the carrier, which entailed truncated proceedings between the employee groups, including legal counsel for each group paid by the carrier. Many Continental pilots objected strongly to the result. In response, when Texas Air later folded the People Express pilot group into the Continental group, the carrier declined to afford the People Express pilots a comparable arbitration procedure, but instead simply as-

---

47. For whatever reason, to date Midway has not seen any reason to do the same with its flight attendants' units, which remained separate until very recently. The Miami-based former Air Florida group was represented by AFA, which displaced an independent union in 1987. Before the election at Air Florida, AFA had narrowly lost an election among the separate unit of the Chicago-based Midway flight attendants. In June 1987, AFA sought a second election and ultimately was certified in November 1987. Before that certification, however, on September 1, 1987, AFA lost its representational rights in the Southern operation, because as of that date the two operations were formally combined. During the period when no group was represented, the carrier unilaterally combined the groups' seniority lists, based upon length of service with Midway or its affiliated operations.

48. The irony is obvious to anyone who participated in the battles waged over New York Air's separate nonunion status. *See* ALPA v. Texas Int'l Airlines, 656 F.2d 16 (2d Cir. 1981); ALPA v. Texas Int'l Airlines, 567 F. Supp. 66 (S.D. Tex. 1983).

signed positions to the People Express pilots by status. Senior status was assigned to the Continental and New York Air pilots, People Express captains were placed at the bottom of the captain ranks, and so on.

When Continental acquired the assets of Frontier Airlines, the Frontier employees had slightly more leverage by reason of their substantial bankruptcy claims. In exchange for the waiver of these claims, the Frontier employee groups were able to negotiate with Continental a relatively neutral seniority integration process, again at the expense of the carrier, between themselves and their counterparts at Continental. In the case of the pilots, the arbitration award that emerged from this process gave rise to considerable dissatisfaction among the former Frontier pilots. This outcome resulted, at least in part, from restrictions on the arbitrator by the agreement authorizing the arbitration; those restrictions had been insisted on by Continental in order to protect pilots who had flown during the Continental pilot strike, which had commenced in September 1983. The integrations affecting the former Frontier flight attendants and ground employees were conducted under less restrictive provisions; each of those groups was, accordingly, able to reach a settlement more favorable than the arbitration award issued in the pilots' case. Meanwhile, at least pending the outcome of "single-carrier" issues before the NMB, or the imposition of LPPs by the DOT on remand from the court of appeals, the Eastern pilots remain on the outside and have no available mechanism to compel an integration with the Continental pilots.

A final approach is best exemplified by the TWA-Ozark merger. In that case, as will be discussed in considerably more detail below, the carrier openly favored its own pilots. After a series of unprecedented actions, including the assignment of all of Ozark's MD–80s (its premium aircraft) to TWA crews, the furlough of approximately eighty Ozark pilots, and threats of more dire actions to come, a solution was "negotiated" between the two pilot groups.[49] ALPA,

---

49. The issues for flight attendants at TWA are enormously complicated by the unsuccessful strike by the TWA flight attendants' union in 1987 and the aftermath of litigation. Suffice it to say, there is ample evidence that the seniority issues between the Ozark flight attendants, formerly represented by AFA, and the various TWA flight attendants' groups are being used effectively by the carrier for its own purposes.

faced with an explicit threat by the TWA pilots that they would leave ALPA if efforts were made to enforce the arbitration provisions of ALPA Merger Policy, found itself unable to do more than exercise moral suasion on the TWA group to act responsibly, to little or no avail. Needless to say, litigation commenced.[50]

INCENTIVES FOR CARRIERS

As noted above, seniority integration is an issue on which the merged carrier should have little or no legitimate interest beyond questions of training costs and the like. Accordingly, if the carrier is bound to a mandatory process for seniority integration, its involvement in the process is likely to be minimal. If the merged carrier is free not to agree to a process for seniority integration, however, the carrier is able to side with one or the other premerger employee groups by granting or withholding its consent to a particular process or outcome and to play employee groups against one another in order to secure economic or other concessions from the unfavored employees. The incentives to engage in such conduct are particularly strong in the present intense competitive atmosphere in the industry.[51]

INCENTIVES FOR EMPLOYEE GROUPS

Criticism of the current approach to seniority integration cannot be confined only to the conduct of employers. Internal union policies such as ALPA Merger Policy theoretically remain binding on employee groups regardless of the presence or absence of sections 3 and 13. In the absence of an ultimately enforceable process, however, politically powerful employee groups are presented with an opportunity to work their will on weaker groups in the seniority integration process. Even when the two groups share the same collective bargaining representative, the political pressures on the representative are such that it may have little choice but to accede to the wishes of the stronger group.[52]

---

50. Hammond v. ALPA, No. 87–2792 (N.D. Ill.).

51. *See Winners in the Air Wars*, FORTUNE, May 11, 1987, at 68–79; P. Cappelli, *Competitive Pressures and Labor Relations in the Airline Industry*, 24 INDUS. REL. 316 (1985).

52. In theory, the duty of fair representation bars a union from discrim-

Again, the TWA-Ozark merger may be seen as the paradigmatic case. When TWA was acquired by Carl Icahn in early 1987, the TWA pilots obtained an agreement with the company[53] that provided, among other things, that in the event of a subsequent merger the pilot seniority lists of TWA and the acquired carrier could be integrated only with the consent of "ALPA."[54] The TWA pilots' master executive council (MEC) interpreted that agreement as giving it veto power over any seniority integration in the TWA-Ozark merger and made clear that it would consent to such an integration only if the terms were substantially favorable to the TWA pilots and detrimental to the Ozark pilots. The MEC indicated its intention, in the event its demands were not met, to withdraw the TWA pilots from membership in ALPA.[55] ALPA, despite its ultimate agreement with the Ozark pilots that ALPA Merger Policy was binding in the TWA-Ozark merger[56]—an agreement extracted months after the integration process should have begun and with intense political infighting—had little political alternative but to accommodate the demands of the TWA pilots. The outcome was an "agreement" between the two pilot groups, in reality reached outside the confines of ALPA Merger Policy, substantially favorable to the TWA pilots and adverse to the Ozark pilots, entered into by the Ozark pilots under substantial political and economic pressure.[57]

---

inating between employee groups on the basis of political power. *See, e.g.,* Branch 6000, Nat'l Ass'n of Letter Carriers v. NLRB, 595 F.2d 808, 812, & n.15 (D.C. Cir. 1979); Barton Brands v. NLRB, 529 F.2d 793, 798–99 (7th Cir. 1976); Truck Drivers & Helpers Local Union 568 v. NLRB, 379 F.2d 137, 142–43 (D.C. Cir. 1967); Ferro v. Railway Express Agency, 296 F.2d 847, 851 (2d Cir. 1961). It is plain, however, that in the real world, political pressures regarding an issue as central as airline seniority integration might overwhelm the will of a union to adhere to its policies.

53. The "wraparound agreement" is discussed in greater detail below, in connection with the inadequacy of collective bargaining.

54. Letter of Understanding among ALPA, TWA, and Carl Icahn, Jan. 3, 1986 (cited herein as the "wraparound agreement"), § 10 (available from the authors).

55. *See, e.g.,* St. Louis Post-Dispatch, Dec. 5, 1986.

56. Resolution of the ALPA Executive Committee, Nov. 19, 1986 (available from the authors); Letter from Henry A. Duffy, President of ALPA, to Captain M.G. Burkhart, Oct. 14, 1986 (available from the authors).

57. Letter of Agreement between TWA and the Air Line Pilots in the

The Inadequacy of Collective Bargaining

In the view of the DOT, these seniority integration problems can be resolved adequately through the traditional processes of collective bargaining. Traditional collective bargaining is a bilateral process, in which a single employer and a single collective bargaining representative negotiate agreements. By contrast, seniority integration in any craft or class, even in the paradigmatic two-carrier merger, involves as many as four parties—the two employee groups and the two carriers. Moreover, these parties cannot even be identified before the merger, when merger protections and seniority integration procedures are ideally negotiated.[58] Merger protections and LPPs negotiated before a merger by the separate employee groups may thus result in different levels of contractual protection for the two groups[59] and may prove difficult to enforce against a merged carrier, which is necessarily bound by the contracts of its premerger corporations.

The extreme case, once again, is TWA-Ozark. The wraparound agreement was not a collective bargaining agreement; on the contrary, it was negotiated with a third party—Carl Icahn—who was seeking to acquire control of the carrier during the takeover battle with Texas Air. Unfortunately for the Ozark pilots, who at the time of the acquisition were seeking to negotiate LPPs, the TWA-Ozark merger agreement prohibited Ozark from modifying its position in

---

Service of Trans World Airlines, Inc., as Represented by ALPA, Feb. 20, 1987 (available from the authors).

58. Negotiating such protections and procedures after a merger has occurred or been announced is obviously inadequate. At that juncture, the merged carrier has little immediate incentive to negotiate a fair and equitable seniority integration, in that, as discussed above, it then has an incentive to side with one or the other employee group and to play the two groups against each other.

59. To say that the respective groups simply have to live with the consequences of the agreements they chose to negotiate does not take into account that, at the time each group negotiated its protection, it had no way of predicting the merger partner its employer would select. At any rate, such a cliché will hardly prevent resentment on the part of the adversely affected group, which must work closely with other employees who have superior terms and conditions of employment.

any subsequent collective bargaining negotiations.[60] In short, following the merger, the TWA and Ozark pilots were subject to radically different degrees of merger protection solely because the Ozark pilots did not have the good fortune to find themselves in the midst of a corporate raid and had the bad fortune not to have secured contractual LPPs before the merger. Thus the fortuities of timing play a critical role in employees' abilities to negotiate fair and equitable procedures for seniority integration.

Even when employee groups have successfully negotiated full *Allegheny-Mohawk* LPPs with their employers, however, as Wilder and Lurye discuss fully in the next chapter, prevailing labor law successorship doctrine makes their enforcement problematical.

Need for a Mandatory Process

The public interest is ill served by the existing DOT doctrine, which leaves the affected parties to resolve for themselves the nettlesome seniority integration issues that arise in all airline mergers. The passions engendered by these issues, the incentives the current doctrine gives parties to take unfair advantage of their political and economic leverage, and the inadequacy of the system of collective bargaining for resolving these issues all support the conclusion that sections 3 and 13 of the standard LPPs should be made statutory in every merger or similar transaction. Sections 3 and 13 serve legitimate ends: the need for an orderly, expeditious, and impartial system to protect the seniority rights of employees and the legitimate desire of a merged carrier to avoid unnecessary training or other costs resulting from the integration of the premerger work forces. Sections 3 and 13 provide these protections at surprisingly little cost to employees or carriers. These time-honored procedures, which served the industry well for nearly four decades, are perhaps the only available mechanisms by which to carry out the indisputable, basic public policies supporting fair wages, equitable working conditions, and stable labor relations.

---

60. TWA-Ozark Agreement and Plan of Merger, at 20 (available from the authors).

Seniority Integration: A Management Perspective

John B. Adams

The period from 1985 to 1987 saw a major restructuring in the airline industry, primarily through the consolidation of carriers. Some of these consolidations have been the result of marketing considerations that the managements of the carriers deemed necessary to achieve economies of scale. Other combinations have occurred because a partner was in actual or perceived dire economic straits. Although further consolidation is probable among small carriers, or as smaller carriers are absorbed by larger ones, we are unlikely to see mergers of many of the current mega-carriers in the future.

Methods of Seniority Integration

The treatment of employees affected by such transactions has differed not only between the merging carriers but also among different employee groups within the carriers. Despite these variations in treatment, however, the airline industry has not suffered major disruptions. Significantly, these consolidations were successfully achieved, and the seniority and jobs rights issues of affected employees were resolved without government intervention. The parties to these mergers and acquisitions, as well as the employee representatives involved, have demonstrated that they are fully capable of developing solutions to seniority and job rights issues tailored to the circumstances of each individual transaction. Accordingly, there is

163

simply no justification for the government to impose uniform rules and procedures.

One of the first acquisitions after deregulation was Eastern's purchase of the Braniff Latin American route authority. Given the open skies nature of domestic routes, the sale of Braniff's international route authority was the only transaction that required formal approval by the various regulatory agencies involved. Braniff's bankruptcy precipitated the transfer of the routes to Eastern, but no employees from Braniff moved into Eastern as part of the deal. Even though the pilots and maintenance and related employees were represented by the same unions at the two carriers, the unions did not insist that the work forces be combined. Ironically, Braniff had tried to sell its international route authority to Eastern earlier but had been blocked in the courts by the unions; being blocked was the "straw that broke the camel's back" in Braniff's attempt to remain an operating entity. The unions' "success" in blocking the sale ended any prospects of sufficient cash coming into the company to keep it operating.

In other combinations, such as the merger of Southern–North Central–Air West in 1980, which eventually became Republic, there was a very "traditional" full blending of the work forces. Such was also the case with Continental–Texas International in 1982, in which there were the usual integration arguments.

The sale of Pan Am's Pacific Division to United in 1985 was a transaction similar to that of Eastern and Braniff except that the Pacific Division was operating even though Pan Am's financial difficulties were reportedly very acute. Had the transaction not taken place, a scenario identical to that of Braniff and Eastern may have been replayed. In the Pan Am–United transaction, the integration of pilot seniority lists resulted from an arbitration in 1986, and the pilots moved from or remained at Pan Am according to a specified merger process. The flight attendants at United, represented by AFA, insisted that the flight attendants from Pan Am be put at the bottom of United's international seniority list, and no integration was proposed.[1]

Interestingly, the ground personnel of Pan Am were not offered any positions at United. Ironically, they fixed the aircraft being left

---

1. Subsequently, the issue of integrating seniority lists was referred to arbitration by a system board of adjustment—Ed.

behind at Pan Am while the crews who flew the aircraft were absorbed into United.

The Piedmont acquisition of Empire in 1985 is yet another variation. Here the ALPA-Piedmont agreement placed all Empire pilots at the bottom of the Piedmont seniority list, thus not truly integrating them or giving them credit for their length of time with Empire. The various ground staffs were integrated into Piedmont but were given different treatment for pay and seniority to bid on aircraft.

The acquisition of Ozark by TWA resulted in similarly disparate seniority integration procedures when the seniority lists for the pilots were combined in 1986. As part of the integration agreement, Ozark's pilots were precluded for nearly a decade from exercising their seniority to bid on some wide-body aircraft at TWA. Combined with contractual changes in scheduling procedures at TWA, the procedures for integrating the seniority lists resulted in the furlough of eighty-six Ozark pilots.

These examples are not meant to be an all-inclusive treatment of seniority integration since deregulation but are designed to show that a wide variety of methods have been used to integrate seniority lists, whether by agreement, arbitration, default, or design. What the use of these various methods demonstrates is that mergers since deregulation have been substantially different from the traditional airline mergers, such as United-Capital, that occurred in the past. Increasingly, airline employees are covered by seniority and job rights provisions similar to those that are applied to the millions of workers in unregulated industries in the United States that are covered by the Taft-Hartley Act. Under this law, when businesses are combined or closed, employees do not necessarily become a part of the new firm, and, if they do, they are not subject to the same terms as employees in a regulated industry.

It is fair to assume that the airline industry as a whole will continue to expand, although expansion of an individual carrier may mean contraction for others. Thus the airline industry may very well parallel other industries in which a product line can be sold to another corporation with an entirely new work force. In the airline industry this would mean that the transfer of international routes (such as Pan Am–United or Eastern-Braniff), or hubs or facilities at different locations, would be treated no differently than the closure of an automobile assembly plant in one city and the opening of a new one in another.

The sale of planes, gates, and route authorities is a fairly simple transaction but has a far from simple effect on the people involved. Methods of seniority integration and job rights are obviously evolving, with mixed results. When Congress enacted the Airline Deregulation Act, it mandated provisions granting certain employees the ability to remain in the industry, albeit at the disadvantage of starting anew (minus seniority) at a different employer. Although the law called for those affected to be given economic subsidies, Congress never deemed it appropriate to honor those commitments, given the pressures to fund other more basic social programs.

Congress never entertained mandating seniority adjustment procedures for individuals who lost their jobs at one carrier and assumed new ones at another, but it would be interesting to assess the impact on seniority and the perceptions of job rights at carriers such as Piedmont, which hired a substantial number of senior Braniff captains and placed them at the bottom of Piedmont's seniority list. If seniority adjustment procedures had been in effect, the result would probably have been very different, especially given what Piedmont did with Empire's pilots, who were placed at the bottom of the seniority list even though they came from an operating company.

LEGISLATIVE EFFORTS

Further legislative efforts can be expected to shift the burden of economic protection onto the acquiring carrier. Ironically, this will probably decrease the job prospects for employees of failing companies, whose opportunities for employment will be in the hands of bidders at the auction block. The acquiring carrier would receive the assets of the failing company but would not hire its employees except at the bottom of a seniority list.

Legislative job protection provisions will probably result in more Braniff-type transactions than in the absorption of failing companies into operating ones. Just as the end of the Mutual Aid Pact did not mean an end to strikes but to the hiring of permanent replacements, legislatively imposed job protection provisions will probably mean a net loss of jobs that otherwise might have been saved.

The CAB rather quickly phased out mandatory seniority integration procedures and economic transition provisions, deferring such arrangements to private agreement between the affected parties.

That philosophy did not change with the transfer of those responsibilities to the DOT. The DOT's actions are quite in line with the approach of the Interstate Commerce Commission and the deregulation of the trucking industry, which had sixteen thousand pre-deregulation companies and employed far more workers than the airlines and railroads.

COLLECTIVE BARGAINING

The remaining method of addressing seniority and job rights issues has been through unilaterally issued corporate policies or collective bargaining procedures. Again, the results have been mixed; collective bargaining during the TWA-Ozark merger resulted in the furlough of Ozark pilots only, even though the pilots at both companies were represented by ALPA. Attempts to deal with this topic in other than a transaction-specific situation, such as the proposed merger of two carriers, have also had mixed results. The language negotiated between PSA and the Teamsters is probably the best example of serious attention being placed for the first time on seniority and job rights in the collective bargaining context. In this case, the parties agreed that for the acquisition of PSA by USAir to occur, the management of USAir would have to change its job protection provisions. As a result, changes were made that both sides found acceptable, and the acquisition of PSA went forward.

Corporate philosophy has played a major role in how the casualties of deregulation are handled. In the Braniff collapse, the major beneficiaries of the demise of that carrier—American (through the elimination of a major competitor) and Eastern (in the acquisition of Braniff's routes)—made no major effort to employ Braniff's people.

Continental, however, contrary to the self-serving rhetoric of union leaders and opportunistic executives at other carriers, made a concerted effort in its acquisition of a failing People Express and the defunct Frontier to provide jobs to thousands of former employees of those carriers. Texas Air, the parent company of Continental and Eastern, was the only airline or airline holding company willing to intervene in Eastern's near brush with bankruptcy or shutdown in 1986 by purchasing the company. Its intervention saved forty thousand jobs while other airlines watched like vultures on the fence waiting to pick up the pieces. Texas Air can thus take full credit for saving more jobs in the industry than all other carriers or holding companies combined, yet it had no legislative or administrative mandate to do so.

Although job rights issues in mergers and acquisitions have hardly been solved, the airline industry experienced a massive number of consolidations from 1985 to 1987—the largest in its history—yet had little disruption. The common thread throughout this period, if there is one, is that Congress in giving approval to strong pro-competitive policies in the airline industry, as it did in trucking and telecommunications, left it up to the parties involved to achieve the objectives of their respective constituencies. The airline industry did not collapse despite the lack of government interference in several of the major transactions. Perhaps the lesson is that having accomplished so much during this most trying of times, the airline industry might best be left alone and the approach of nonintervention continued.

Successorship Clauses: A Union Perspective

Roland P. Wilder, Jr.

William Lurye

Before the enactment of the Airline Deregulation Act, there was little, if any, need for successorship clauses in the airline industry. Few mergers occurred, and those that did were mostly between carriers that were both unionized. Either through recognition agreements or otherwise, employees continued to be represented after the merger.[1] To ensure labor stability during the merger, the acquiring carrier was required by the Civil Aeronautics Board to provide employees with certain labor protective provisions.[2]

Since deregulation, however, mergers and acquisitions have occurred at a seemingly exponential rate.[3] As one commentator noted, the result of this "merger-mania era" has been that "workers are usually the victims, not the beneficiaries, of corporate guerilla warfare."[4] The Department of Transportation, which assumed the responsibilities of the CAB on January 1, 1985, has not continued the CAB's practice of imposing LPPs on acquiring carriers. The DOT has instead held that LPPs will be imposed only when necessary to prevent labor strife that would disrupt the nation's air transportation system. The burden has thus been shifted to employees and their

---

1. *See* TWA-Ozark, 14 NMB at 218, 234 (1987).
2. *See* Allegheny-Mohawk Merger, 59 CAB 22 (1972).
3. *See* TWA-Ozark, 14 NMB at 234 n.2, in which the NMB lists some of the numerous mergers that occurred during the late 1980s.
4. Bernstein, *Airlines Devise a New Way to Bust Unions*, LA Times, May 20, 1987.

chosen representatives to show that such strife would occur.[5] According to the DOT, LPPs are a matter for "free collective bargaining, even though it can lead to strikes and other forms of labor strife" between the carrier and its unions.[6]

---

5. *See* Midway–Air Florida Acquisition, Order 85–6–33. According to the DOT, "With deregulation, other carriers can move quickly to fill gaps in service, so a strike will not disrupt the transportation system." Thus, even in the event of a strike, the DOT does not consider the imposition of LPPs appropriate. In the Northwest-Republic Acquisition, Order 86–7–81, the secretary of transportation rejected an administrative law judge's (ALJ) recommendation that LPPs be imposed. The judge had concluded that there was "the possibility of significant labor unrest, tension and strife and consequent disruption of service." Northwest refused to provide the judge or its own union with any information concerning the integration of the carriers' operations, including the impact of the merger on employees. Northwest would not disclose its plans for employee wage levels, furloughs, layoffs and transfers, consolidation of reservation offices and functions, or its projected staffing level. Northwest-Republic Acquisition, No. 43754 ALJD, slip op. at 79–84 (June 27, 1986), *rev. denied sub. nom.* IAM v. DOT (Northwest Airlines, Inc.), 127 L.R.R.M. (BNA) 2597 (D.C. Cir. 1988).

Until recently, *see infra* note 6, the DOT's standard had withstood judicial attack, with one court of appeals finding that it is "well within the broad zone of discretion delegated it by the [Deregulation] Act." ALPA v. DOT, 791 F.2d 172, 176 (D.C. Cir. 1986). *Accord* Independent Union of Flight Attendants v. DOT, 803 F.2d 1029 (9th Cir. 1986). As expressed to the courts, the DOT's view is that the ADA "directed it 'to promote entry by lower cost, more efficient carriers, which may spur the incumbents to operate more efficiently,' " (ALPA, 791 F.2d at 175, *quoted in* CAB Order 84–7–60 at 13) and that LPPS, because they raise the cost of such transactions, have no place in the deregulated industry (791 F.2d at 175).

6. Northwest-Republic Acquisition, Order 86–7–81, slip op. at 28. *But see* ALPA v. DOT (Texas Air Corp.), 127 L.R.R.M. (BNA) 2597 (D.C. Cir. 1988), in which the court of appeals reversed and remanded the DOT's order approving Eastern's acquisition by Texas Air to the extent it declined to impose LPPs, stating:

> We conclude that, because DOT relies so heavily on the unions' ability to negotiate for pre-acquisition protections through collective bargaining, it acted in an arbitrary and capricious manner in failing to consider the possibility that these bargained-for protections might be lost after the acquisitions were approved. This issue must be addressed by DOT....

Id. at 2599 (footnote omitted).

Further destabilizing the rapidly deteriorating situation was the decision by the Fifth Circuit Court of Appeals in *International Brotherhood of Teamsters v. Texas International Airlines.*[7] In this case, the employees on the larger carrier, Continental, were unrepresented, whereas the employees on the acquiring carrier, Texas International, were represented in part by the Teamsters. Texas International declared that the Teamsters' certification was terminated "by operation of law" when the merger took place, a position upheld by the court of appeals.[8] The appellate court also rejected the Teamsters' contention that the collective bargaining agreement survived the merger even in the absence of a certified employee representative. Their argument relied on the established Railway Labor Act doctrine that a collective bargaining agreement is the *employees'* agreement, not just the labor organization's, and that the agreement survives even when there is a change of bargaining representatives.[9] Application of this principle seemingly mandated preservation of the status quo postmerger.

The court of appeals instead concluded that enforcement of the contract "inescapably entailed the continuance of the Union's role as employee representative for the minority group," which in its view "unavoidably constitute[d] a determination of employee representation." Believing that LPPs imposed by the CAB "assure[d] at least an interim solution" of the "many problems" created by mergers, the court reasoned that "union representation could only fill in the narrow space between the floor provided by the labor protective provisions and the ceiling set by the agreement." The judiciary, in its view, should not enter into that "interstitial area."[10] Thus the court held that the Teamsters' claim raised a representation dispute

---

7. 717 F.2d 157 (5th Cir. 1983).

8. In so declaring, the carrier was relying on the NMB's decision in *Republic Airlines*, 8 NMB No. 49 (1980), which has since become known as the "*Republic* merger doctrine." In *Republic*, the NMB held that in mergers between two organized carriers, the premerger representative of the larger class or craft becomes the representative of the larger craft or class. The NMB, accordingly, revoked the smaller organization's certification. This principle was reaffirmed and clarified by the NMB in TWA-Ozark, 14 NMB at 233. *See also* Delta-Western, 14 NMB at 291 (1987); American–Air California, 14 NMB at 379 (1987); Midway Airlines, 14 NMB at 447 (1987); Airline Industry Merger Guidelines, 14 NMB at 388 (1987).

9. *See* Air Transport Employees v. Western Airlines, 105 L.R.R.M. (BNA) 3004 (C.D. Cal. 1980).

10. 717 F.2d at 161–64.

resolvable only by the NMB. Consequently, employment issues for craft or class employees became subject to the carrier's whims.

Advent of Successorship Clauses

Taking their cue from the DOT, and against the backdrop of the *Texas International* case, unions drew from the experiences under the NLRA as amended[11] and negotiated successorship clauses into their agreements.[12] Successorship obligations are designed to ensure that after an acquisition employees, at a minimum, continue to be represented by the organization they selected rather than by a new union or, in the worst case, become unrepresented altogether. Optimally, the clause obligates the selling carrier to require the purchasing carrier to assume the collective bargaining agreement as a condition of acquisition. If the prospective acquiring carrier thereafter wishes to complete the acquisition and assume the agreements, the result is a voluntary recognition of the union by the acquired carrier. The scope of recognition is limited, however, to only those employees whom the union represented before the merger.[13]

---

11. 29 U.S.C. § 151, *et seq.*

12. Under the NLRA, in lieu of successorship clauses and affirmative acts by an employer to bind its successor to the collective bargaining agreement, the agreement is extinguished upon the sale of the employing entity. Howard Johnson v. Detroit Local Joint Exec. Bd., 417 U.S. 249, 258 n.2 (1974); NLRB v. Burns Int'l Security Services, 404 U.S. 822 (1972). Successorship clauses have received the tacit approval of the U.S. Supreme Court. Howard Johnson, 417 U.S. at 258 n.2 (appropriate to enjoin a sale if the sale would breach a successorship clause). The clauses have also withstood all attacks on their lawfulness and have been held to be a mandatory subject of bargaining. *See* Local Jt. Exec. Bd. v. Royal Center, 796 F.2d 1159 (9th Cir. 1986), *cert. denied*, 55 U.S.L.W. 3468 (Jan. 13, 1987). IAM Local 1226 v. Panoramic Corp., 668 F.2d 276 (7th Cir. 1981); Amax Coal Co. v. NLRB, 614 F.2d 872 (3d Cir. 1980), *rev'd in part on other grounds*, 453 U.S. 322 (1981). Arbitration of breaches of such clauses is common. *See, e.g.,* Martin Podany Associates, 80 Lab. Arb. (BNA) 658 (1983) (Gallagher, Arb.); Sexton's Steakhouse, 76 Lab. Arb. (BNA) 577 (1981) (Ross, Arb.); Hosanna Trading Co., 74 Lab. Arb. (BNA) 128 (1980) (Simons, Arb.).

13. *See* Amax Coal, 614 F.2d at 886–87; United Mine Workers v. Eastover Mining Co., 603 F. Supp. 1038 (W.D. Va. 1985). In *Amax Coal,* the court found a successorship clause lawful because it affected only the terms and conditions of employment of Amax's employees and not the terms and

Further, by keeping the entire collective bargaining agreement in effect after the acquisition and merger, successorship clauses not only fill the representational "interstitial area" created by mergers but also guarantee the retention of all employee protections and benefits achieved during the years of collective bargaining. Successorship clauses also ensure employees that they will have meaningful redress through the continued existence of the system board of adjustment for problems arising during the process of the merger and beyond.

The prospect that voluntary recognition of a union by an acquiring carrier might result in employees in a craft or class being represented by a different labor organization following the merger does not render a successorship clause nugatory. Voluntary recognition is favored and given full effect under the RLA.[14] Indeed, the NMB's policy is one of "noninterference in voluntary recognition matters, 'except where such recognition would be in derogation of an existing Board certification.' "[15] Voluntarily extending recognition to an organization through a successorship clause does not derogate an existing certification on the acquiring carrier because the scope of the recognition is limited to only those employees whom the organization represented on the acquired carrier. The postmerger carrier is obligated to bargain with both organizations and to maintain both organizations' agreements. Further, if employees of an acquiring carrier are not represented by any union, there is no certification to be derogated.

Nor is the NMB's *Republic* merger doctrine (see *supra* note 8) undermined by the operation of successorship clauses. The doctrine was established when "it was the prevailing practice for the acquiring carrier to voluntarily recognize the organizations on its property as representatives of the employees on the acquired carrier."[16] Thus the NMB's focus was on employees' desire to continue to be represented. The successorship clause takes the *Republic* merger doc-

---

conditions of employment of employees who were strangers to the bargaining relationship.

14. Virginian Ry. v. System Board No. 40, 300 U.S. 515, 548 n.6 (1936); Southwest Airlines, 8 NMB at 684 (1981); Galveston Wharves, 4 NMB at 200 (1962).

15. TWA-Ozark, 14 NMB at 234, *quoting* Republic Airlines, 6 NMB at 817 (1979).

16. TWA-Ozark, 14 NMB at 235.

trine one step further. It allows the employees to continue to be represented by the organization duly selected and authorized by them. Because successorship clauses do not impinge on any other organization's certification, and the result is voluntary recognition, they are completely compatible with the *Republic* merger doctrine. They are also in accord with the underlying design of the RLA: to permit employees to choose their own unions.[17]

Beyond Continuing Representation

Successorship clauses are not limited to honoring collective bargaining agreements or employees' choice of unions following mergers and acquisitions. They may also include, for example, the right to negotiate seniority integration provisions before a merger or the integration of the carriers' operations or of a particular craft or class. In the 1984 IBT-Western agreement, for example, the carrier agreed that its facilities and employees would not be integrated with those of the acquiring carrier until seniority lists had been integrated.[18] These provisions on seniority integration before a merger

---

17. *See* Texas & New Orleans R.R. v. Brotherhood of R.R. & Steamship Clerks, 281 U.S. 548 (1930); Aircraft Mechanics Fraternal Ass'n v. United Airlines, 406 F. Supp. 492, 497 (N.D. Cal. 1976).

18. This language read in part:

> In the event of a merger, consolidation, or acquisition of Western Airlines with another airline or entity, the Mechanic and Related facilities of Western Airlines as they existed prior to the merger, consolidation, or acquisition shall not be integrated with the facilities of the other airline or entity involved in the merger, consolidation, or acquisition without agreement of the Teamsters Airline Division or until such time as the seniority lists for the crafts or classes inclusive of such employees are integrated. In the event of a merger, acquisition, or consolidation of Western Airlines with another airline or entity the Mechanic and Related employees of Western Airlines, as represented by the Teamsters Airline Division prior to the merger, acquisition, or consolidation shall not be integrated with the employees of the other airline or entity involved in the merger, acquisition, or consolidation without agreement of the Teamsters Airlines Divi-

are no more restrictive than the more common successorship clause, which conditions acquisition on assumption of bargaining agreements. Integration of seniority lists has been described by one impartial observer as an "inflammatory issue"[19] because it can determine at which location or on which routes an employee may work, and even whether the employee will be actively employed. Resolving seniority integration issues in connection with a merger can therefore only promote labor stability.

In the recent PSA-USAir acquisition, the PSA-Teamsters agreement contained successorship provisions that included honoring collective bargaining agreements, recognizing the Teamsters as the representative of the former PSA employees postmerger, and integrating seniority lists before the merger, or, if after the merger, at least before a particular craft or class was integrated.

In 1984, the Teamster-represented crafts and classes at PSA, totaling about 3,800 employees, made wage and work rule concessions that resulted in labor savings of 30 percent. In return, PSA agreed to a comprehensive merger and acquisition clause that encompassed five pages of the collective bargaining agreement. The clause addressed virtually every type of acquisition or merger to which PSA might be a party.[20] Regarding the acquisition of PSA, the agreement provided that as a condition of any merger or acquisition, the acquiring carrier would recognize the Teamsters as the continuing representative of the former PSA employees.[21] It also mandated that LPPs "no less favorable" than those specified by the CAB in the Allegheny-Mohawk merger would be extended to the Teamster-represented craft or class and that neither the facilities nor the employees of PSA would be integrated with the facilities or employees of the acquiring carrier until the seniority lists for the postmerger craft or class had been integrated. PSA thus agreed not to merge

---

sion or until such time as the seniority lists for the crafts or classes inclusive of such employees are integrated.

Letter of Agreement, Sept. 14, 1984, between Western and the Teamsters Airline Division.

19. Northwest-Republic Acquisition, No. 43754 ALJD, slip op. at 80.

20. The language of this clause is set forth in Griswold, *Ensuring Union Protection following Mergers and Acquisitions, supra* p. 125. —Ed.

21. This obligation took into account the possibility that the NMB might certify another representative for the consolidated postmerger craft or class.

with another carrier unless its employees received substantial protection, including the right to continued representation.

On December 8, 1986, PSA accepted USAir's purchase offer. Although USAir at first indicated its willingness to provide PSA employees with *Allegheny-Mohawk* LPPs, USAir conditioned the purchase of PSA on the waiver of the merger and acquisition clauses by the Teamsters. Initially, the Teamsters refused to waive these provisions and instead filed a grievance over PSA's failure to make assumption of the collective bargaining agreement, as well as the other terms described above, a condition of its acquisition. PSA refused to arbitrate the grievances, contending that they raised representation issues that only the NMB could resolve.

The union brought legal action to compel PSA to arbitrate. The district court, however, concluded that the successorship provisions raised postmerger representational issues over which only the NMB had jurisdiction.[22] The union noted its appeal to the Ninth Circuit Court of Appeals.

Almost immediately, on March 31, 1987, the Ninth Circuit Court of Appeals held that the successorship provisions entered into by the Teamsters and Western, which were very similar to those in question at PSA, generated arbitrable minor disputes, rather than representation disputes.[23] But a few hours later Justice Sandra Day O'Connor, as circuit justice, stayed the mandate of the court of appeals pending application for certiorari and its disposition. In the circuit justice's opinion, the provisions raised representation disputes.[24] One of the cases she cited as precedent was *Pacific Southwest.*[25]

Meanwhile, USAir had issued an ultimatum: either these issues would be resolved quickly or it would back out of the deal. Under these circumstances, the Teamsters and PSA negotiated letters of agreement whereby the Teamsters waived the successorship provisions in return for various employee protections and benefits. The protections included the right to convert to cash all PSA stock held in the employee stock ownership plan, established in 1984 as part

---

22. IBT, Airline Div. v. Pacific Southwest Airlines, No. C–87–0402 MHP (N.D. Cal. Mar. 20, 1987).

23. IBT, Airline Div. v. Western Airlines, 813 F.2d 1359 (9th Cir. 1987).

24. Western Airlines v. IBT, 107 S. Ct. 1515 (O'Connor, Circuit Justice 1987). The Court declined to vacate the stay. 107 S. Ct. at 1621 (1987).

25. *See supra* note 22.

of the quid pro quo for employee concessions, which yielded between $12,000 and $15,000 per employee; the extension of *Allegheny-Mohawk* LPPs to the Teamster-represented employees; the creation of a $3.2 million severance pay fund to provide supplemental severance pay and job-placement services for Teamster-represented PSA employees who would lose their jobs as a result of the merger, allowing, *inter alia,* twelve months' severance pay for employees with five or more years of service; and loss-of-pay protection for employees engaged in negotiating or administering seniority integration agreements. The letters of agreement were ratified by all affected Teamster-represented classes or crafts, although by a margin of only eleven votes in the mechanics and related craft or class. Although employees did not receive all the benefits of the original 1984 bargain—in particular, continued union representation and job security rights—they did receive more generous LPPs than were enjoyed by most other employees involved in mergers.

Need for Continuing Representation

The need for comprehensive successorship clauses giving strongest protection to employee groups is demonstrated by an examination of the merger between TWA and Ozark in 1986. The carrier's abusive tactics reflect the perils employees face in mergers.

On September 12, 1986, the DOT approved the acquisition of Ozark by TWA. By January 1987, virtually all of TWA's and Ozark's operations had been integrated, with the notable exception of the flight attendants. Before the merger, TWA's flight attendants were represented by IFFA, and Ozark's flight attendants were represented by AFA. IFFA represented more than 90 percent of the postmerger class or craft, but TWA continued to recognize and negotiate with the representatives of AFA until late December 1986. Even after TWA took the position that AFA's certification had expired "by operation of law," it refused to acknowledge that IFFA was the representative of the postmerger class or craft. Consequently, a transition agreement could not be negotiated, employee grievances could not be processed, and seniority integration could not be achieved.[26]

---

26. TWA-Ozark Merger, 14 NMB at 229–31.

Rather than permit representatives of the TWA and Ozark flight attendant groups to negotiate an integrated seniority list, or, failing agreement, to arbitrate the formation of the list as called for by the TWA-IFFA agreement, TWA unilaterally imposed an integrated seniority list on active flight attendants. IFFA challenged TWA's stated intention to promulgate a merged seniority list. The district court, however, declined to enjoin TWA's unilateral action on the ground that the dispute was "minor" not "major" and had to be submitted to arbitration for final resolution.[27] On April 6, TWA implemented its unilaterally established seniority list and distributed bid packages, consisting of flights to be flown in May 1987, for selection by attendants on the basis of seniority. They were awarded based on the seniority preferences established by the TWA list. On April 7, IFFA filed a grievance challenging TWA's action. TWA declined to submit the seniority dispute to arbitration, preferring to litigate its arbitrability in court.

Even after TWA and Ozark merger representatives developed an integrated seniority list, TWA declined to accept the list on which the employee representatives agreed. Another grievance was filed; again, TWA declined to arbitrate. Because of these tactics, resolution of the seniority integration dispute was long delayed. At this writing, a final decision still has not been rendered.

TWA's disregard for negotiated employee protection underscores the need for continuing representation of employees in mergers. Without representation, TWA would have gone unchecked, as could a nonunionized carrier in administering voluntarily assumed LPPs and promulgating integrated seniority lists.

Another illustration of the need for continued representation is Delta's action in integrating the craft or class of former Western mechanics and related employees with Delta's comparable employee groups. As noted earlier (see *supra* note 18), the Teamsters-Western agreement called for seniority integration before the merger of the mechanics and related employees craft or class. Instead, Delta unilaterally determined where Western employees would work (e.g., Los Angeles, Atlanta, or Salt Lake City) and then told them to report to their assigned locations; thousands of families were uprooted as a result. By memorandum dated April 30, 1987, about thirty days after Western's operations were integrated into Delta's, Delta un-

---

27. IFFA v. TWA, No. 87–6014-CV-SJ–6 (W.D. Mo. Apr. 3, 1987).

veiled its plan for the "integration of the seniority/service lists of former Western personnel and of Delta Maintenance/Quality Control personnel."[28] After employee representatives of former Western employees and Delta employees were elected and had agreed on a "procedure" for merging seniority, the "procedure" had to be approved by Delta management. Not until June 25, 1987, nearly three months after the operational merger, was this approval forthcoming.[29]

Delta's delay in effecting seniority integration adversely affected former Western employees. Because the Western work force was rearranged before seniority integration, Western employees could not use their seniority to remain in Los Angeles in preference to junior Delta employees. Moreover, under Delta's internal personnel procedures, seniority has limited uses. The seniority list is to be used "only . . . for Line Maintenance station bidding [and not for hanger or shop maintenance positions], for leveling, and in the unlikely event of a furlough of Maintenance Department personnel."[30] The seniority integration agreement finally approved by Delta's management totally failed to protect former Western mechanics and related employees from Delta's unilateral actions upon consummation of the merger. Many of the Western employees who were dislocated had greater seniority than the Delta employees who remained in Los Angeles.

Finally, the Western employees had no recourse if Delta's management did not approve the seniority list agreed on by the former Western and Delta employee representatives. Although Delta asserted before various tribunals that it had voluntarily assumed *Allegheny-Mohawk* LPPs, its demand for the right to disapprove the seniority list was contrary to *Allegheny-Mohawk*, which allowed for binding arbitration over seniority integration disputes. Without the presence of the union, Delta's promise of fair and equitable seniority integration was practically unenforceable. The alternative to reaching an agreement acceptable to Delta, as the employee merger rep-

---

28. Delta Memorandum, Apr. 30, 1987.

29. Delta Maintenance and Quality Control Seniority List Agreement of June 17, 1987, later approved by Delta on June 25, 1987. Although the term "procedure" is vague, it refers to an integrated seniority list developed by employee representatives.

30. *Id.*

resentatives well understood, was a unilaterally imposed seniority integration.

Are Successorship Clauses Enforceable?

Whether a collectively bargained successorship clause is enforceable before a system board of adjustment is a hotly debated question. A grievance over breach of a successorship clause is predicated on an express term of an agreement, and past cases seemingly mandate that it be arbitrated like any other dispute over the application or interpretation of a contract provision.[31] Yet, carriers have routinely refused to arbitrate successorship grievances, contending that such clauses raise representation disputes over which only the NMB has jurisdiction. Three courts, including the only appellate court to hear this specific issue, have rejected the carriers' position and compelled them to arbitrate alleged breaches of successorship clauses.[32] Other district courts, however, have agreed with the carriers' position, as has Justice O'Connor in her capacity as circuit justice.[33]

In *Western Airlines*, the union brought suit to compel arbitration over successorship provisions and to enjoin the merger of Western into Delta pending an arbitral award.[34] The district court summarily dismissed the complaint, finding that "the union's action for an injunction and arbitration of a grievance in a merger, raises a representation issue . . . within the exclusive jurisdiction of the NMB and

---

31. *See* 45 U.S.C. § 184; IAM v. Central Airlines, 372 U.S. 682, 687–89 (1963).

32. *See* IBT v. Western Airlines, 813 F.2d 1359, *vacated & remanded*, 108 S. Ct. 53 (1987); AFA v. Republic Airlines, No. 86 C 3164 (N.D. Ill. June 11, 1986); ALPA v. Texas Int'l Airlines, 567 F. Supp. 66, *motion to stay denied*, 467 F. Supp. 78 (S.D. Tex. 1983).

33. Western Airlines v. IBT, 107 S. Ct. 1515; AFA v. Western Airlines, Civ. No. 87–0040 (D.D.C. Feb. 20, 1987); IBT v. Pacific Southwest Airlines, No. C–87–0402 MHP (N.D. Cal. Mar. 20, 1987).

34. The IBT Airline Division and the Air Transport Employees (ATE) brought separate actions for injunctive relief and orders compelling arbitration. The ATE's action was also dismissed by the district court. ATE v. Western Airlines, No. CV–86–8032-JIM (Bx) (C.D. Cal. Feb. 13, 1987). The appeals by the Teamsters and the ATE were consolidated by the court of appeals. The discussion above concerning the Western-Delta merger focuses on the claims asserted by the Teamsters.

[is] not subject to judicial review."[35] The court of appeals, however, reversed the district court and enjoined the merger "pending completion of arbitration proceedings or until Western and Delta file with the clerk of [the] court a stipulation that the result of the arbitration, subject to appropriate judicial review and all valid defenses, will bind the successor corporation."[36] The court of appeals stated:

> The unions are not seeking either by this action or by arbitration to obtain recognition by Western of their status as the collective bargaining representatives of Western's employees; the unions already have such recognition. Similarly, the unions are not seeking a determination that they are the collective bargaining representative of Delta employees. This action seeks arbitration with Western, not Delta. The arbitration is not likely to make a determination that any union or unions will become the representative of Delta employees, given the scope of jurisdiction of the Systems Adjustment Board. *See* 45 U.S.C. Sec. 184. Instead, the unions seek a determination that Western breached its agreement by agreeing to a merger with an airline that did not agree to voluntarily recognize the unions. Thus, strictly speaking, the actions by these unions are not for resolution of "representation" disputes, but are merely claims that Western has breached its contract.[37]

Underlying the court of appeals decision was the long-standing axiom that "[i]t is the function of the arbitrator, not the courts, to decide the meaning of the contract and to consider appropriate remedies in the first instance."[38]

Western Airlines was the first successorship case under the Railway Labor Act to reach the United States Supreme Court. Unions and carriers alike eagerly anticipated the outcome. Unfortunately, however, the Court did not decide the merits of the dispute. It granted

---

35. IBT v. Western Airlines, No. CV–86–7921-JMI (Px) (C.D. Cal. Feb. 13, 1987).

36. 813 F.2d at 1364. Pursuant to an interim order issued by the court, arbitration commenced before the Western-Teamsters System Board on March 30, and, except for closing arguments, was concluded on March 31, 1987. The Western-ATE System Board was scheduled to convene on April 6, 1987.

37. *Id.* at 1362.

38. *Id.* at 1363. Justice O'Connor's stay order, discussed above, extended to the ongoing arbitration between Western and the Teamsters, which was adjourned, and to the scheduled arbitration between Western and the ATE.

certiorari to the Ninth Circuit Court of Appeals, vacated its judgment, and remanded the case to the appellate court for consideration of mootness.[39] On remand, the court of appeals is considering whether consummation of the Delta-Western merger and termination of the union's certifications by the NMB[40] ended the controversy between the parties by disabling the court from awarding any effective relief to the union. If the case is moot, it will be dismissed; if not, the court of appeals will enter a new judgment appropriate to the changed circumstances.

Conclusion

The effectiveness of successorship clauses in the industries subject to the RLA remains unsettled. But assuming that the successorship concept survives this test, it provides an effective means for protecting employees most affected by a merger—those on the acquired carrier—by assuring continuation of the employees' postmerger seniority rights and other terms and conditions of employment. From the labor perspective, the clauses make mergers a relatively victimless war.

---

39. 108 S. Ct. 53 (1987).

40. Delta-Western, 14 NMB at 291 (1987). The Board's Airline Industry Merger Guidelines, 14 NMB at 388 (1987), however, indicate that certification termination procedures have no impact on voluntary recognition agreements and do "not act to inhibit the processing of pending grievances otherwise permissible under the Act." *Id.* at 394. *See also* Carey v. Westinghouse Electric Corp., 375 U.S. 261 (1964); United Auto Workers v. Telex Computer Products, 816 F.2d 519, 525 (10th Cir. 1987) ("If an agreement allows arbitration of contractual disputes that may affect representational issues, the concurrent jurisdiction of the NLRB will not deprive the parties of their bargain").

Part 5
Handling of Major Disputes

Labor Mediation:
A Management View

William J. Curtin

In the last ten to fifteen years, there has been a broad but largely unexamined disengagement by government from labor relations in the airline industry. This disengagement (or "deregulation") is independent of the market deregulation arising from the Airline Deregulation Act,[1] although the two forms of deregulation have occurred almost concurrently and have the same philosophical roots. The dual deregulation of airline markets and of labor relations has placed unprecedented pressures on the collective bargaining process and mediation. With increasing frequency, deregulated carriers view the outcome of collective bargaining and mediation as bearing on the ultimate question of corporate survival.

Some observers and members of the airline industry have questioned the effectiveness and relevance of the Railway Labor Act, including its mediation procedures, in the postderegulation economic environment. There have been calls for further "privatization" of collective bargaining in the industry through either the repeal or radical modification of the RLA.[2]

---

1. Airline Deregulation Act, Pub. L. No. 90–504, 92 Stat. 1705 (1978) (codified in various sections of 45 U.S.C.).

2. *See, e.g.*, Arouca & Perritt, *Transportation Labor Law and Policy for a Deregulated Industry*, 1 LAB. LAW. 617 (1985). One recent call for the RLA's repeal neglected even to note that the airline industry is covered by the RLA. *See* the editorial *The Railroads' Baggage*, Wall St. J., May 14, 1987. For an analysis of bringing the airline industry under the NLRA, *see* W.J. Curtin

At the same time, the RLA, and especially its mediation procedure, continues to be an effective means for monitoring the collective bargaining process in the airline industry. Mediation is a limited form of government intervention that does not dictate the substantive outcome of collective bargaining. Given that the deregulation of labor relations in the airline industry has removed both substantive and procedural constraints on collective bargaining, mediation is the only remaining viable form of government intervention.

Although market and labor deregulation have placed new pressures on the mediation process, mediation under the RLA is not in conflict with market deregulation of the airline industry. Mediated collective bargaining comports with the private economic decision making that characterizes market deregulation. More pragmatically, mediation postderegulation has assisted many carriers and unions in reaching agreements on complex and confrontational collective bargaining issues.

Deregulation of Airline Industry Labor Relations

As the term is used in the airline industry, "deregulation" generally refers to market deregulation and the substantial economic reconfiguration of the industry as a result of the ADA. Much has been written concerning how this new competition among the airlines, and the resulting entry of low-cost and nonunion carriers, has affected labor relations in the industry.[3] Some analysts conclude that such market deregulation has had an unintended adverse impact on labor relations in deregulated industries.[4]

& H.A. Rissetto, The Railway Labor Act and the National Labor Relations Act: A Comparative Appraisal for the Airline Industry. A Report to the Air Transport Association of America (Mar. 1983) (unpublished manuscript).

3. *See* Cappelli, *Competitive Pressures and Labor Relations in the Airline Industry*, 40 INDUS. REL. 316 (1985); Comment, *Deregulation of the Airline Industry: Toward a New Judicial Interpretation of the Railway Labor Act*, 80 Nw. U.L. REV. 1003 (1986); P. CAPPELLI, AIRLINE INDUSTRIAL RELATIONS AFTER DEREGULATION (Wharton School Working Paper No. 615, 1986).

4. J. DUNLOP, *Deregulation and Industrial Relations*, in TRANSPORTATION LABOR ISSUES FOR THE 1980's 1 (1982); Dunlop, *Trends and Issues in Labor Relations in the Transport Sector*, TRANSPORT RES. NEWS, May-June 1985, at 1.

There has been a broader and less closely examined process of labor deregulation in the airline industry that has also substantially affected collective bargaining. This labor deregulation preceded the Airline Deregulation Act by several years but has continued concurrently with market deregulation. Labor deregulation is characterized by the same laissez-faire economic approach as market deregulation and has been adopted by the executive, legislative, and judicial branches of the government.

EMERGENCY BOARDS AND CONGRESSIONAL ACTION

The most important deregulation of the collective bargaining process in the airline industry has been the discontinuance of the availability of the RLA's emergency board procedure. During the Nixon administration, Secretary of Labor George Shultz informally promulgated a policy whereby such procedures would no longer be used in the industry.[5] Subsequent administrations have continued that policy, with only one congressionally imposed exception.[6] Although historically the emergency board procedure under the RLA has been less frequently used in the airline industry than in the railroad industry,[7] airline emergency boards have occasionally had important impact.[8]

Emergency board procedures under the RLA and special congressional legislation now remain only theoretical possibilities in the air-

---

5. C. REHMUS, THE NATIONAL MEDIATION BOARD AT FIFTY 41 (1984).

6. Emergency Board No. 95–504 (Nov. 2, 1978) (Wien Air Alaska and ALPA). The appointment of that emergency board was part of a political compromise that led to the enactment of the ADA. *See* REHMUS, *supra* note 5, at 41.

7. *See* D. CULLEN, *Emergency Boards under the Railway Labor Act*, in THE RAILWAY LABOR ACT AT FIFTY 154–56 (1976). One airline emergency board has been established since 1976 (in 1978), bringing the total to 34. By contrast, there were 165 emergency boards for rail disputes between 1926 and 1975 and 47 since 1975. This difference is attributable in part to the absence of airline industry national bargaining and the lack of any analogy to those local commuter disputes that have precipitated emergency board appointments in the railroad industry. *See* REHMUS, *supra* note 5, at 48–53.

8. In 1966 the IAM bargained collectively with a group of five major air carriers; this led to the appointment of Emergency Board No. 166, to a forty-three-day nationwide strike, and eventually to congressional action. Curtin, *National Emergency Disputes Legislation: Its Need and Its Prospects in the Transportation Industries*, 55 GEO. L.J. 786 (1967).

line industry. The absence of special presidential intervention through the emergency board procedure or congressional intervention through special legislation means that the only mechanisms for resolving collective bargaining disputes in the airline industry will be agreement and self-help.

LABOR PROTECTIVE PROVISIONS

A more recent and significant deregulation of airline labor relations, which has both substantive and procedural aspects, is the Department of Transportation's refusal to impose labor protective provisions as a condition for approval of mergers and acquisitions among carriers. Since the sunset of the CAB and the transfer of functions to the Department of Transportation, the department has consistently taken the position that it will no longer impose standard *Allegheny-Mohawk* LPPs unless there is a threat of industrywide disruption of transportation.[9] Despite a wave of mergers and acquisitions in the mid–1980s that resulted in the largest consolidation in the history of the airline industry, the DOT has remained firm in its position that LPPs are a subject for collective bargaining, not government imposition.[10] This development has been substantive in that the economic provisions of the LPPs are no longer automatically applicable in airline transactions. The impact of this change on the bargaining process is evident in the lifting of mandatory seniority integration, which, in effect, imposed a bargaining obligation on a surviving carrier and the unions involved in a merger or acquisition.

This form of deregulation, however, may be short-lived. In 1986 and 1987, some carriers adopted the *Allegheny-Mohawk* LPPs voluntarily or through collective bargaining,[11] and there are legislative proposals pending to reinstitute LPPs.[12] Further, the NMB may fill

---

9. *See* Independent Union of Flight Attendants v. DOT, 803 F.2d 1029 (9th Cir. 1986) (approving standard for imposition of LPPs) and People Express–Frontier Acquisition, Order 85–11–58, at 7. *See also* Texas Air–Eastern Acquisition, Order 86–4–24, at 13–15, and Texas Air–Eastern Acquisition, Order 86–7–21, at 28–31.

10. *Id.*

11. Delta-Western Acquisition, Order 86–12–30. USAir-PSA Acquisition, Order 87–3–11.

12. Pending bills H.R. 3051 and S. 1485 would require LPPs in all mergers and related transactions. The House passed H.R. 3051 on October 5, 1987. The Senate passed H.R. 3051 on October 30, 1987, but amended the bill to contain the text of S. 1485. The bills are currently in committee.

this regulatory vacuum with the *TWA-Ozark* representational procedures.[13] Nonetheless, the largest consolidations in the industry's history have occurred without the constraints of LPPs.[14]

JUDICIAL ABSTENTION

The forgoing examples involve "deregulation" of airline labor relations as a result of executive or congressional action. There also has been a judicial tendency to abstain from involvement in Railway Labor Act collective bargaining disputes, which can be described as a form of "deregulation." Thus, in contractual disputes concerning mergers or acquisitions, the federal courts have exercised restraint under the RLA by declining to become involved, deeming such controversies as representational disputes within the exclusive jurisdiction of the NMB.[15] In applying the organizational rights provisions of section 2, third and fourth, the courts have rejected analogies to the NLRA and have interpreted the RLA's limitations narrowly.[16] Furthermore, the courts have often characterized substantial labor controversies as "minor disputes" and have referred them to adjustment boards, thereby avoiding substantive involvement in airline labor disputes.[17]

In many of these decisions the courts correctly interpreted the RLA and properly referred disputes to the adjustment boards or the NMB. The federal courts should not, after all, be in the business of determining the substantive outcome of airline collective bargaining disputes. These decisions, which appear to be based on a

---

13. TWA-Ozark Airlines, 14 NMB No. 63 (1987).

14. Pacific Division Transfer, Order 85–11–67; Piedmont-Empire Acquisition, Order 86–1–45; Texas Air–Eastern Acquisition, Order 86–7–21; Northwest-Republic Acquisition, Order 86–7–81; TWA-Ozark Acquisition, Order 86–9–19. Since writing the above, the D.C. Circuit has remanded the *Texas Air Merger* case for reconsideration of the decision not to impose LPPs. *See* ALPA v. DOT, 838 F.2d 563 (D.C. Cir. 1988).

15. *See* Western Airlines v. IBT, 107 S. Ct. 1515 (1987) (O'Connor, Circuit J.); Air Line Employees Ass'n v. Republic Airlines, 798 F.2d 967 (7th Cir. 1986), *cert. denied*, 105 S. Ct. 458 (1986).

16. *See, e.g.,* Independent Union of Flight Attendants v. Pan American World Airways, 789 F.2d 139 (2d Cir. 1986); IAM v. Northwest Airlines, 673 F.2d 700 (3d Cir. 1982).

17. *See, e.g.,* ALPA v. Pan American World Airways, 599 F. Supp. 108 (E.D. N.Y. 1984), *aff'd*, 767 F.2d 908 (2d Cir. 1985) (freeze of pension accruals).

laissez-faire approach to labor relations, can be taken too far, however. Federal courts do have a role in policing the collective bargaining process under the RLA.

The major exceptions to this trend of judicial abstention are cases growing out of the 1987 United-ALPA and TWA-IFFA strikes, which addressed issues pertaining to replacement workers.[18] Although the specific holdings of those cases may not be correct, it is clear that the courts felt they were intervening only to police the collective bargaining process and to preserve bargaining relationships.

Summary

The result of this trend toward government disengagement from airline industry labor disputes has been the removal of many traditional substantive and procedural constraints on collective bargaining. Previously, carriers and unions could anticipate executive or judicial policing of the collective bargaining process or intervention to prevent labor disputes. Moreover, government (wage guidelines) or labor protective provisions often determined the outcome of substantive collective bargaining issues. Airline labor relations now operate in an environment free of such regulation.

Postderegulation Mediation

Deregulation of airline markets and labor relations has greatly increased the number, complexity, and difficulty of the issues to be addressed in collective bargaining and mediation. Further, this more complex bargaining and mediation must occur in the postderegulation environment without many of the traditional benchmarks that have served to guide the collective bargaining process.

The Deregulated Bargaining Environment

Market deregulation, the resulting increased competition among carriers, and the entry of low-cost and nonunion carriers clearly have

---

18. IFFA v. TWA, 819 F.2d 839 (8th Cir. 1987); ALPA v. United Air Lines, 614 F. Supp. 1020 (N.D. Ill. 1985), *aff'd in part & rev'd in part*, 802 F.2d 886 (7th Cir. 1986), *cert. denied*, 107 S. Ct. 1605 (1987).

made airline labor relations more confrontational. Carriers have been under extreme economic pressure to control labor costs to compete. As the NMB commented several years ago, "The overriding goal of the carriers in bargaining has been to put costs on a comparable basis with those of the post-deregulation carriers and reorganized established carriers such as Continental and Braniff."[19]

The airlines under deregulation have viewed their ability to reduce labor costs as crucial to survival. The unions, in contrast, have viewed deregulation as unfairly eroding airline employees' economic positions and requiring unrealistic cost comparisons between unionized and nonunionized carriers.

In addition to this change in bargaining climate, deregulation has affected the type of proposals the parties have presented in collective bargaining and the persistence with which they have pursued those bargaining goals in mediation. Economic competition and the need to control labor costs have led carriers to be more innovative in collective bargaining proposals. Among the issues seriously pursued by the airlines are the institution of two-tier wage scales, subcontracting, the use of part-time employees, and various methods of increasing productivity, such as cross-utilization.[20]

The unions, in contrast, have been in the more defensive bargaining posture of attempting to preserve the historically attractive wages and working conditions of the airline industry. Many unions, however, have attempted to respond to the concessionary pressures from the carriers by developing their own innovative bargaining agendas. Among the obvious examples have been the negotiation of contractual labor protective provisions and other job security proposals,[21] as well as the establishment of various stock proposals and other forms of employee ownership and union participation on boards of directors.[22]

---

19. *Two-Tier Wage Structures: The Airline Experience*, 49 NMB ANNUAL REP. 55 (1983).

20. *Id.*

21. The high water mark of contractual labor protective provisions were the provisions of the PSA-IBT agreements negotiated concurrently with economic concessions in 1981. Daily Lab. Rep. (BNA), No. 73, at A-7 (Apr. 20, 1987).

22. *See* Daily Lab. Rep. (BNA), No. 40, at A-1 (Mar. 3, 1987) (summarizing TRADING STOCK FOR WAGES: EMPLOYEE OWNERSHIP IN THE AIRLINE INDUSTRY [National Center for Employee Ownership 1987]).

The deregulation of airline markets and labor relations has forced labor and management to address difficult issues in an environment of great uncertainty. Traditional industry wage and work rule patterns have diminished in importance because new, and often nonunion, competitors have operated at low labor costs. Comparisons to traditional competitors are no longer helpful: the innovative approaches developed by their competitors, or the managerial concessions demanded by the unions, do not necessarily translate to other airlines. Further, the forms of labor deregulation discussed earlier have left the parties without the various substantive and procedural benchmarks of government regulation in collective bargaining and mediation.

A good example of this uncertainty involves the negotiation of LPPs. During the era of government-imposed LPPs in mergers and acquisitions, the issue of labor protection was removed from collective bargaining and mediation.[23] Carriers and unions that have negotiated LPPs since deregulation have done so without a clear understanding of the enforceability of such provisions.[24] Further, the parties have had to assess the likelihood of new legislation[25] and the evolving role of the NMB.[26]

In short, since deregulation, labor and management have entered mediation with more proposals, novel positions, and anxiety about an uncertain economic and regulatory environment. Airline deregulation obviously has not made the mediator's task any easier.

THE POSTDEREGULATION MEDIATION RECORD

The NMB has continued to mediate airline industry disputes in a postderegulation environment by applying traditional mediation skills to new collective bargaining problems.[27] Sometimes mediation has succeeded; sometimes it has not.

The NMB has historically had a 97 percent success rate in me-

---

23. IAM v. Northeast Airlines, 536 F.2d 975 (1976).
24. *See supra* note 21 and Western Airlines v. Teamsters, 107 S. Ct. 1515 (1987).
25. *See supra* note 12.
26. TWA-Ozark Airlines, 14 NMB No. 63 (1987).
27. *See* W. WALLACE, *Mediation and the Airline Industry*, in LABOR RELATIONS YEARBOOK—1984, at 186–87 (1985).

diating airline and railroad collective bargaining disputes.[28] This rate has been sustained under deregulation. From 1982 to 1984, the strike rate was the lowest in the history of the airline industry in the United States.[29] Since 1984, there have been several highly publicized and important work stoppages: Pan Am–TWU, United-ALPA, and TWA-IFFA. Self-help may have been inevitable in those cases, given the polarized positions of the parties, but mediation may have assisted in narrowing the issues in dispute.

Although they do not make the headlines, many airline collective bargaining disputes have been resolved in mediation during deregulation. One example is the American-APA negotiations, which were resolved by agreement in 1986. In no sense does the record of airline mediation since deregulation indicate that the mediation process has failed and that radical change in the RLA is warranted.

A CONTINUING ROLE FOR MEDIATION

The deregulation of the airline industry does not justify any further "privatization" of the collective bargaining process. As a theoretical matter, there is nothing inconsistent in continuing the role of mediation in the airline industry while market deregulation continues. Deregulation is designed to eliminate the government imposition of economic constraints on the airline industry and to allow the free forces of competition to determine results. Collective bargaining is a private process between parties, and mediation is only a limited form of government intervention to facilitate the private resolution of labor disputes. Mediation does not result in the government imposition of substantive terms on the parties involved; rather, it assists the parties in reaching agreements.

Concern about disruption of air transportation services, which underlies the RLA, remains in a deregulated environment. Although many airline unions have been hesitant to strike lest employees be replaced, airline work stoppages still have a substantial impact on the nation's commerce. Indeed, in the wake of the Supreme Court decision in *Burlington Northern* there is a substantially increased risk of the proliferation of work stoppages.[30] If mediation is successful

---

28. 50 NMB ANNUAL REP. 46 (1984).
29. *Id.* at 4, 37.
30. In the *Burlington Northern* decision, the Supreme Court concluded that the RLA does not prohibit secondary boycotts in lawful work stoppages

in preventing even a limited number of strikes, then the RLA mediation procedure will have fulfilled an important public purpose.

Suggestions have been made for radical alterations in the mediation procedure of the RLA. Such changes, however, would leave the parties without an important stabilizing asset: the ability of mediators and the NMB to assist in resolving disputes.

Given the deregulation of labor relations in the airline industry, mediation is currently the only real form of government intervention in the collective bargaining process in the industry. Mediation thus continues to ensure that the parties have exerted every reasonable effort to make agreements consistent with the mandate of the RLA.[31] Considering the judicial disengagement from RLA enforcement in the mid–1980s, mediation may be the only effective mechanism for ensuring that the RLA and collective bargaining in the airline industry work.

Critics of RLA mediation should ask themselves: What alternative form of government intervention would arise if mediation were no longer available? A hint may exist in two 1986 labor disputes. The TWA-IFFA strike, which was ineffective, precipitated extensive litigation. In the 1987 American Airlines–Association of Professional Flight Attendants (APFA) dispute, the union decided not to strike but filed numerous lawsuits challenging the actions of the carrier, including its implementation of bargaining proposals. Carriers can successfully defend against meritless litigation. Litigation is not a productive alternative to mediation, however, in the resolution of airline labor disputes. In the absence of mediation, airline unions will increasingly attempt to enmesh the federal courts in the resolution of labor disputes, and there will always be a risk that some federal district court judge will resist the trend toward judicial abstention and not only police the collective bargaining process but effectively impose a resolution on the parties.

Finally, mediation can have a stabilizing effect on labor costs, a goal consistent with deregulation. With the disappearance or con-

---

after exhaustion of the RLA's procedures. The Court's decision followed extensive litigation arising from a labor dispute between the Maine Central Railroad and the Brotherhood of Maintenance of Way Employees (BMWE) which affected rail carriers throughout the country. 107 S. Ct. 1851. Burlington N. Ry. Co. v. BMWE, 793 F.2d 795, 802–3 (7th Cir. 1986); Central Vermont Ry. v. BMWE, 793 F.2d 1298, 1303 (D.C. Cir. 1986).

31. § 2, First, 45 U.S.C. § 152, First.

solidation of low-cost carriers in the industry, the airlines may be entering a period of stable labor costs. Mediation could be a vehicle by which industrywide patterns for such costs could be reestablished through collective bargaining. This would ultimately enable carriers to compete on the basis of service and not on the ability to reduce labor costs.

The mandate of the RLA—that the NMB is to "use its best efforts by mediation, to bring [the parties] to agreement"—remains good law and good policy. There should be no "sunset" of the NMB, as some critics have advocated. Indeed, given the additional pressures that deregulation has placed on the collective bargaining and mediation processes, the increased importance of the NMB's mediatory role should be acknowledged and supported with both resources and staff.

Conclusion

Mediation has played an increasingly important role in the post-deregulation airline industry. Although mediation has become more difficult because of the complexity and uncertainty in collective bargaining in the airline industry, it has aided many parties in reaching settlements and avoiding work stoppages. The policy considerations that led Congress to view mediation as a desirable vehicle for resolving transportation industry labor disputes, some hundred years ago when it enacted the first railroad labor legislation, remain applicable today. A decade of deregulation in the transportation industry does not, and should not, negate one hundred years of successful experience with labor mediation.

Labor Mediation: A Union View

William L. Scheri

Since its creation, the National Mediation Board has successfully settled thousands of disputes and has helped avert many strikes. Thus the stated goal of the Railway Labor Act—to "properly put itself in communication with the parties to a controversy and [to] use its best efforts, by mediation, to bring them to agreement"—for the most part has been achieved. Despite its successes, however, the NMB suffers from weaknesses in its mediation process that increasingly are compromising its effectiveness. This chapter identifies several of these problems and proposes some solutions in hopes of improving the Board's mediation function.

When followed through to the end, the collective bargaining process under the RLA works as follows: a notice under section 6 of the statute must be served when a party seeks a change in the collective bargaining agreement affecting rates of pay, work rules, or working conditions. The parties then must meet and bargain concerning the proposed changes. Although the parties are required to meet and bargain, either party may declare that bargaining has become unsuccessful and an impasse has been reached. At that time or within ten days of the impasse, either party may request mediation by the NMB. Alternatively, the NMB may on its own proffer its services. Once the case is docketed by the Board, a staff mediator is assigned and mediation commences. The status quo must be maintained during the mediation process. If mediation is invoked and initiated by the NMB, the bargaining process must continue until the parties are released from mediation by the Board. Rates of pay, rules, or working conditions cannot be altered until then.

Weaknesses in the Mediation Process

MEDIATORS' LACK OF EXPERIENCE

The first problem that diminishes the ability of the Board to accomplish its goal of bringing the parties to an agreement is the lack of negotiating experience of several of the staff mediators. Even though most staff mediators have experience in the railway or airline industry, many do not have mediation experience. The skills required of a mediator are highly specific. The step from advocate, the background of many of the mediators, to conciliator is often a long one. To acquire the minimum skills necessary to make them effective mediators, staff mediators need to perform the job for at least a year.

To alleviate this problem, the Board should reinstitute its program whereby new mediators served an apprenticeship before being assigned sole responsibility for mediating a dispute. The extent of supervision and training would, of course, vary with the experience of the individual mediator. Although such a system would initially require extra work for the senior mediators, time would be saved in the long run because effectiveness would be increased.

REASSIGNMENT DURING NEGOTIATING

The second problem in NMB negotiation is the increasing tendency to change mediators during the negotiating process. During the El Al negotiations, for example, no less than five mediators were assigned to the case over the course of negotiations. Bringing each mediator up to speed caused delays and disruption in the negotiations, significantly extending the negotiating period (March 1984 to July 1986). Superficially, it is appealing to reassign a mediator when negotiations are in recess rather than have the mediator unoccupied during this period. Assigning a new mediator after the recess poses significant problems, however, because continuity is lost and the progress of the negotiations invariably is slowed.

In my experience, negotiations in which two or more staff mediators have been involved have resulted in protracted negotiations:

the parties maintained the position they held before the recess while the new mediator became familiar with the facts of the case. This process ultimately reduced the prospects for negotiating an agreement. Negotiations may of course last for years. Nevertheless, the Board should make every effort to ensure that one mediator sees each negotiation through to its conclusion.

PREMATURE INVOLVEMENT BY BOARD MEMBERS

The third problem that works against the Board's goal of bringing the parties to a negotiated agreement is the increasing tendency of Board members to become involved in negotiations prematurely. The effectiveness of the staff mediator is reduced when the parties know that a Board member will be called in at an early stage in the negotiations if they hold firm to their respective positions rather than engage in meaningful give-and-take bargaining with the staff mediator. Board members often become involved in disputes before the negotiations under the mediator actually have reached a standstill, further reducing effectiveness. In past years, Board members stayed out of negotiations until only a short time before the parties were released. Consequently, the appearance of a Board member carried more clout than it does today. Board members should restrict their involvement in negotiations until just before the date on which the Board projects it will release the parties from the mediation obligation.

An additional change that would enhance the mediation process is to relax the increasingly formalized communication system among the parties and the Board. The NMB mediation process does not presume that a mediator will assume a judiciallike role in which it is improper to have off-the-record communications with the parties. On the contrary, the system functions best when contacts between the mediator or the Board and individual parties are frequent and open. My experience strongly suggests that the most effective mediators are those who welcome, even solicit, contacts from the parties.

PRO-CARRIER TILT

The final, and perhaps most serious, problem is the pro-carrier tilt of the current Board. Because the three members of the Board are appointed by the president of the United States, individuals tend to be selected on the basis of their pro-management or pro-labor positions, depending on the party in power. The current Board has tended to favor management to such an extent that the carriers hold far more sway with the Board than was the case during past administrations. The carriers' positions on issues in negotiations, the timing of Board members' involvement in the negotiations, and the timing of the release of the parties seem to be more favorably considered by the Board than are the positions of labor. This view is shared by many, if not all, airline labor organizations.

Despite its shortcomings, the NMB has helped avoid many long and destructive economic battles. As the airline industry passes through this era of "merger mania," however, it is critical that the Board act in an evenhanded and effective way to ensure industrial peace.

Standards Governing Permissible Self-Help

James E. Conway

The deregulation of the airline industry changed the economic ground rules on which both carriers and unions had traditionally relied in formulating collective bargaining strategy. With the price of a ticket now a significant instrument of competition, carriers were pressured not just to contain costs but to reduce them to survive. Wages and work rules—which unlike other costs such as fuel were at least somewhat within the carriers' control—quickly became the focus of efforts to cut costs. Proposals by carriers for wage concessions, B-scale wages for new hires, and increased productivity became the norm. The stakes were high, and the years immediately following deregulation were years of confrontation and tough choices, prompting both the carriers and the unions to prepare for, and in several instances to accept, a strike as the only means of determining where the economic balance would be cast. There have been twenty-three strikes in the airline industry since 1979, and in each case wage concessions or increases in productivity in one form or another were key issues.

For the first time this decade, and after a steady six-year decline, strikes in the United States are on the increase in industry at large. Labor analysts theorize that the unions feel they have come to the

I would like to thank my colleague Charles L. Warren for his valuable contributions to this chapter.

end of the line on givebacks, while economic conditions, particularly in manufacturing, are still working against them. The number of major strikes, the number of strikers, and the number of lost workdays increased significantly in 1986 over 1985—lost workdays, for example, increased by 68 percent. Similarly, labor's pursuit of increasingly more limited resources in the airline industry continues to collide with the carriers' objective of cost cutting and augurs for more labor unrest in the future, not less. Although lawful airline strike activity has remained relatively level—carriers averaged 3 strikes annually from 1969 through 1978 and 2.9 from 1979 to 1987—the average strike since deregulation has lasted twice as long, 115 days, as opposed to 71.[1]

One consequence of this steady level of strike activity has been the development of a modest but still far from settled body of law dealing with the economic weapons available to the parties in a strike. In particular, several decisions have dealt with the right of carriers to replace striking employees and the right of employees to honor picket lines and to engage in sympathy strikes. Additionally, economic conditions causing labor stress have, over the last several years, often coincided with employees' reluctance to take the risks associated with a work stoppage and a greater resolve on the part of management to do whatever is necessary to prevail if struck. As a result, the increasingly frequent use by unions of alternative, less risky means of bringing economic pressure to bear on a carrier may ultimately be of even greater interest than the strikes themselves. "Corporate campaigns," extensive use of media and communications technology to gain public support and maintain membership solidarity, and new alliances with Wall Street investors are becoming almost standard union tactics. Occasionally adjunct to, but more often in lieu of, a work stoppage, such activity is designed to keep the membership shoulder to shoulder—and on the payroll—while the union seeks to attain its ends without sacrificing jobs or job security. Although the effectiveness of these techniques is far from

---

1. With only fifty or so strikes involved, the "sample space" for these data may be too small and the "standard deviation" too high to produce a meaningful average. Nevertheless, in the airline labor relations business, we have all—unions and carriers—learned to be comfortable with small spaces and all manner of deviants.

proven, the increasing use and sophistication of such tactics suggests that they are rapidly becoming standard weapons in the unions' arsenal.

Carriers' Rights to Engage in Self-Help during a Strike

USE OF STRIKE REPLACEMENTS

The right of an employer to hire permanent replacements for strikers is well established in labor law.[2] Under the RLA, this right is further bolstered by the carriers' statutory *duty* to provide service.[3] Some courts have suggested that the right to hire permanent replacements under the RLA is limited by the duty to make only those changes in the status quo that are reasonably necessary to keep operating during a strike.[4]

These principles are illustrated by the decision of the United States Court of Appeals for the Eleventh Circuit in *Empresa Ecuatoriana de Aviacion v. District Lodge No. 100*.[5] The carrier in that case replaced certain striking employees during an unlawful IAM strike over a minor dispute, without first seeking an injunction against the strike. The carrier then obtained an injunction ending the strike but did not reinstate those strikers who had been replaced. The district court found that four strikers had been replaced unnecessarily and ordered them reinstated but held that the remaining strikers had been validly replaced because the carrier needed to continue operations.

Cautioning that it was not establishing a per se rule that a carrier may replace strikers before seeking injunctive relief any time a union engages in an illegal strike during a minor dispute, the Eleventh

---

2. *See* NLRB v. Mackay Radio & Tel. Co., 304 U.S. 333 (1938) (NLRA employer has right to hire permanent replacements for strikers because of its right to continue to operate business).

3. *See* BRAC v. Florida E. Coast Ry., 384 U.S. 238 (1966).

4. *See* ALPA v. United Air Lines, 802 F.2d 886, 909 (7th Cir. 1986), *cert. denied*, 107 S. Ct. 1605 (1987); National Airlines v. IAM, 416 F.2d 998, 1006 (5th Cir. 1969).

5. 690 F.2d 838 (11th Cir. 1982), *cert. dismissed*, 463 U.S. 1250 (1983).

Circuit nevertheless upheld the district court's decision as a proper exercise of its equitable discretion.

> The court carefully considered and balanced the competing interests. It held that the carrier was justified in replacing employees as needed in order to continue to meet its cargo and passenger flight schedules, perform its necessary internal business functions, and avoid losing customers and revenue to competitors. It found that the carrier struck a proper balance between its twin obligations to serve the public and to attempt reasonably to maintain the employer-employee relationship.[6]

The appellate court listed several reasons for supporting the lower court's decision.

> The airline did not carry out a mass, punitive discharge the moment the strike began. It sought to operate with supervisory employees and their friends, who worked long hours. It hired replacements as and when needed for the tasks at hand. It attempted to persuade some strikers to report to work. Also the carrier acted with reasonable dispatch in seeking injunctive relief; there is no basis for any inference that it delayed going to court in order to get rid of strikers. When the strike was ended by the TRO, strikers who had not been replaced were reinstated, no one was denied reinstatement because of misconduct, strikers replaced were told that if their replacements left or other positions opened up they would be recalled, and pursuant to this promise several strikers were reinstated.[7]

The court noted that the rationale for upholding the carrier's right to replace strikers in this case differed from that in *National Airlines,* in which the strikers had not been replaced until *after* an injunction had been obtained and the strikers had refused to return to work; and from *Florida East Coast,* in which the cooling-off period had expired so that the union was free to strike and injunctive relief was therefore unavailable. The court found that neither case supported the union's argument that the carrier could not replace strikers until injunctive efforts had been exhausted.[8]

In *International Brotherhood of Teamsters v. World Airways,*[9] a district court denied a union's motion for a preliminary injunction that

---

6. *Id.* at 844–45.

7. *Id.* at 845 (footnote omitted).

8. *Id.* at 845–46.

9. 111 L.R.R.M. (BNA) 2170 (N.D. Cal. 1982).

would have prevented the carrier from conducting a training program to prepare substitute crews to be available in the event of a work stoppage. The carrier initiated the training program before the amendable date of the agreements at issue and before the NMB released the parties to engage in self-help. The court held that the training program did not constitute a status quo violation "so long as it is separated from the continuing operations of the Company."[10] The court also rejected the union's contention that initiation of the training program violated the carrier's duty to bargain in good faith. "Considering the Company's precarious financial condition, the conduct of a replacement training program cannot be considered an act of bad faith bargaining. ... The training program is an alternative in the event of a work stoppage, not a device to circumvent the requirements of the Act."[11]

The status of individuals hired as *temporary* replacements in the event of a strike that never occurred was the subject of an arbitration proceeding in December 1986 involving Pan Am and the Independent Union of Flight Attendants. Responding to a IUFA sympathy strike that began in February 1985 and anticipating that IUFA would call its own strike after April 1, 1985, the release date set by the NMB, in mid-March 1985 Pan Am sought temporary flight attendants from among 1,300 flight attendant trainees. Although the temporary flight attendants were paid at the same rate as regular flight attendants, some of their benefits exceeded those of regular flight attendants, they were not placed on the seniority list, few actually performed the duties of flight attendants, and all were terminated in May 1985 when it became apparent that a strike would not occur. After several hundred of the temporary flight attendants were hired as permanent flight attendants in August 1985, the union filed a grievance contending that Pan Am's creation of a new "temporary" flight attendant category had been improper, that the "temporary" flight attendants had been furloughed when they were released in May, and that when they were reemployed in August they should have been paid at the A-scale rates rather than the lower B-scale rates used for new hires. The arbitrator, Mark L. Kahn, found, however, that the actual use the carrier made of the temporary flight attendants differed significantly from its use of regular

10. *Id.* at 2172.
11. *Id.* at 2173.

flight attendants, noting that they were "obviously not hired as permanent replacements for strikers, nor were they misled into believing that they had been placed on a permanent footing." The arbitrator concluded that the temporary flight attendants did not belong to the IUFA bargaining unit, were not entitled to union representation, and did not acquire any rights under the IUFA contract.

The status of strike replacements who never performed any work was also the subject of the Seventh Circuit's decision in *ALPA v. United Air Lines*.[12] In late 1984, in anticipation of a need for additional pilots, United began selecting and training five hundred candidates for pilot positions. Contrary to its prior policy of treating pilot candidates as employees from the first day of training, however, United told these trainees that they would not be offered employment until the company had reached a new collective bargaining agreement with ALPA. As negotiations with the union proved unsuccessful and the end of the cooling-off period neared, United offered jobs to the five hundred pilots effective May 17, 1985, the date the NMB had set to release the parties to self-help. United did not, however, make the offers of employment contingent on an ALPA strike. On May 17, ALPA did call a strike, but only a few of the five hundred pilots crossed the picket lines to work. After the conclusion of the strike, United took the position that it would not hire any of the five hundred pilots who had failed to report to work, except for cases of extreme hardship or extenuating circumstances.

ALPA filed a lawsuit challenging United's failure to offer post-strike employment to the five hundred pilots, arguing that they had become employees on May 17 even though they refused to cross the picket line and hence were entitled to reinstatement as returning strikers. The district court first ruled that the five hundred pilots should be restored to employee status and assigned immediately to line positions but later amended its order to provide that as striking employees who had been permanently replaced during the strike, the five hundred were entitled only to recall as vacancies occurred.[13]

The Seventh Circuit reversed this portion of the district court's ruling. The court found that because the five hundred pilots had "never performed any work for United nor did they ever submit to

---

12. 802 F.2d 886 (7th Cir. 1986), *cert. denied*, 107 S. Ct. 1605 (1987).
13. 614 F. Supp. 1020 (N.D. Ill. 1985).

United's supervision of them in their work," they did not satisfy the definition of an "employee" entitled to the protection of section 2, fourth, of the RLA.[14] Section 2, fourth, prohibits a carrier from interfering with the right of its *employees* to join or remain members of a union.[15] Although the court acknowledged that the result might be different for an employer subject to the NLRA,[16] it concluded that the RLA's clear definition of *employee* required a different result.

The Seventh Circuit also overruled the district court's holding that by requiring the trainees to cross the ALPA picket line to gain employment, United had violated section 2, fifth, of the act,[17] which prohibits a carrier from requiring any person seeking employment to sign a contract or agreement promising to join or not join a labor organization. Agreeing that section 2, fifth, extended protection to applicants for employment, the court nevertheless concluded that, unlike section 8(a)(3) of the NLRA,[18] which broadly proscribes discrimination against union labor in hiring practices, section 2, fifth, was very specific in its restrictions and United had not run afoul of its provisions.[19]

Finally, the appellate court rejected the argument that United had violated the status quo provisions of the RLA by unilaterally changing its procedures determining the point in training when trainees achieved employee status. Noting that the changes in United's training program could potentially violate section 6 of the act[20] if they affected the rates of pay, rules, or working conditions of pilots already employed by United, the court nevertheless found that ALPA had failed to show that the change in training practices had any effect at all on working United pilots.[21]

The most recent court decision dealing with the replacement of striking employees is the Eighth Circuit's decision in *Independent Federation of Flight Attendants v. TWA*.[22] Following a strike by its flight

---

14. 45 U.S.C. § 152, Fourth.
15. 802 F.2d at 911.
16. *See* NLRB v. New England Tank Industries, 302 F.2d 273 (1st Cir. 1962), *cert. denied*, 371 U.S. 875 (1962).
17. 45 U.S.C. § 152, Fifth.
18. 29 U.S.C. § 158(a)(3).
19. 802 F.2d at 914.
20. 45 U.S.C. § 156.
21. 802 F.2d at 916–17.
22. Daily Lab. Rep. (BNA), No. 101, at D–1 (May 27, 1987).

attendants after the NMB's release date, TWA promptly hired 1,220 new flight attendants as permanent replacements. Another 1,280 striking flight attendants crossed the picket lines and returned to work for TWA. Other new flight attendants were hired as trainees during the strike, of whom 463 had not completed training on the date the strike ended. After the strike was over, TWA retained its new hires and cross-overs and recalled formerly striking flight attendants as vacancies came available. The trainees, whom TWA considered to be permanent employees from the date they entered training, were placed in permanent positions as they completed their training.

The IFFA brought suit claiming that TWA had unlawfully denied reinstatement to the more than two thousand striking flight attendants who had been replaced during the strike. The district court held that the new hires and the cross-overs were employed as permanent replacements and were not subject to displacement by the returning strikers. The court held, however, that the trainees had not taken their jobs within a reasonable time after the conclusion of the strike and thus had not acquired permanent replacement status before the strikers perfected their right to return to their jobs.[23]

The Eighth Circuit upheld the lower court's ruling on the new hires, noting that TWA had clearly and unambiguously manifested its intention to hire the new flight attendants as permanent replacements for strikers and not as additions to the work force. The Eighth Circuit went on, however, to reverse the district court's ruling on cross-overs. Explaining that the union security clause of the IFFA agreement had not been the subject of bargaining and thus had remained in effect after impasse had been reached, the court reasoned that the cross-overs had to retain their union membership: "Accordingly, TWA may not accord cross-overs permanent replacement status and prevent full term strikers from displacing cross-overs with less seniority because such action impermissibly discriminates among union members based on the degree of their union activity."[24] The court found that treating cross-overs as permanent replacements gave rise to several of the concerns that the Supreme

---

23. 643 F. Supp. 470 (W.D. Mo. 1986).
24. IFFA v. TWA, 819 F.2d 839 (8th Cir. 1987).

Court in *NLRB v. Erie Resistor Corp.*[25] had found persuasive in disapproving awards of super-seniority to employees who worked through a strike.

> The Court disapproved of super-seniority because the award operated to the detriment of strikers as compared to nonstrikers; it in effect offered an inducement to abandon the strike; and it created a longterm division among the workforce. Although an award of superseniority brings these concerns into a sharper focus than does the conferring of permanent replacement status to cross-overs, these concerns are nonetheless present. Awarding the cross-overs permanent replacement status differentiates employees on the basis of their union activity, induces employees to abandon the strike and is likely to create longterm conflict and division within the workforce of those working together under the union security clause.[26]

The Eighth Circuit therefore concluded that unreinstated strikers were entitled to displace cross-over employees with less seniority.

Finally, the appellate court upheld the lower court's ruling on trainees, but on different grounds than those relied on by the district court. Citing the Seventh Circuit's decision in *ALPA v. United Air Lines*, the court found that the trainees had never become employees within the meaning of the RLA. Acknowledging that, unlike United, TWA had told the trainees that they were employees and paid them a salary during training, the court nevertheless ruled that the RLA's applicability is determined by the work the person performs rather than the label the employer puts on his or her status and that the trainees were not performing any work of the carrier "by any stretch of the imagination." The court found that TWA's historical practice of treating trainees as nonemployees, as well as the "general rule" under the NLRA protecting employees from discharge while on strike, further supported its ruling. The court thus concluded that any trainee who had not yet performed services for TWA by the end of the strike could not be considered a permanent replacement.

OTHER METHODS OF SELF-HELP
AVAILABLE TO CARRIERS

The Seventh Circuit's decision in *ALPA v. United Air Lines* also treated two other aspects of a carrier's right to engage in self-help during

---

25. 373 U.S. 221 (1963).
26. Daily Lab. Rep. (BNA), No. 101, at D–3.

a strike. To induce nonemployee pilots already qualified as captains or first officers to come to work for the company in the event of a strike, United offered to pay them salaries that exceeded what they could otherwise expect to receive as new hires and to guarantee those salary levels even if these new pilots were reassigned to positions as second officers once the strike ended. The replacement pilots were in fact demoted following the settlement of the strike. ALPA claimed that United had unlawfully failed to negotiate with ALPA over the salaries to be paid to the replacement pilots and had violated its duty to bargain in good faith and discriminated against the striking pilots by offering salaries that exceeded those paid to union members in second officer positions. The court quickly rejected the first argument, holding that the duty to bargain does not extend to the terms and conditions of employment for replacements of striking employees.[27] The claim of bad-faith bargaining was based on ALPA's contention that United had offered the replacements more money than was paid to incumbent second officers before the strike and that the replacements' salaries were higher than the B-scale salaries proposed by United for new hires. The court found, however, that the proper salary comparison was between the replacements and the incumbent captains and first officers, whom they had originally been hired to replace. The record showed that the salaries paid to the replacements were lower than those paid to incumbents in those positions. The court found no basis whatsoever for ALPA's claim that an employer violated its duty to bargain by offering replacements salaries that exceeded those it would offer new hires in the future.

The court also rejected ALPA's claim of discrimination and its argument that the only lawful inducement United could offer replacements was the prospect of permanent employment. The district court had expressly found that the guaranteed salaries "were necessary to keep United running." The court further refused to hold that the salary guarantees could remain in effect only during the strike, after which they should be superseded by the new collective bargaining agreement. Citing *Belknap v. Hale*,[28] the Seventh Circuit

---

27. 802 F.2d at 908.
28. 463 U.S. 491 (1983).

noted that permanent replacements could sue their employer to enforce promises made to induce employment.[29]

The court found that one other method of self-help embraced by United failed to pass muster. As part of its prestrike preparations, United had planned to rebid the entire airline to fill vacancies created by the strike. The court found that had it been implemented, this procedure would have allowed junior cross-overs and replacements to impede the future advancement of more senior strikers. Applying *BRAC v. Florida East Coast Railway*, the court held that the rebid could be upheld only if United could show that it was needed for the company to continue operating during the strike.[30] The court concluded, however, that United had made no such showing. United contended that "by rebidding the airline early in the strike it was in a better position to determine its future need so that pilots could be trained for vacant positions in the event the strike were to continue for a long time," and the court agreed that "[i]f this were all that the record revealed, we would be inclined to agree with United that its rebid was necessary to keep the airline flying."[31] The court found, however, that the record showed the rebid to be "an attempt by United either to destroy the union or at the very least discourage union membership."[32]

> The existence of anti-union motivation, by itself, provides a sufficient basis upon which to uphold the district court's decision with respect to the rebid procedure. An employer is not free under the RLA, in the guise of self-help, to act "to influence or coerce employees in any effort to induce them...not to join or remain members of any labor organization." 45 U.S.C. § 152, Fourth...Under the circumstances presented here, we can only conclude that, in the balance between United's right to self-help and its duty to respect ALPA's right to exist and function, the district court did not err in finding that United's actions regarding the rebid violated the RLA.[33]

According to the court, the finding of anti-union motivation made it unnecessary for it to consider several arguments proffered by United to support the lawfulness of the rebid.

---

29. 802 F.2d at 909–10.
30. *Id.* at 898.
31. *Id.* at 899.
32. *Id.* at 900.
33. *Id.* at 900 (footnote omitted).

Unions' Rights to Engage in Self-Help

SYMPATHY STRIKES

The right of employees to engage in a sympathy strike depends on whether or not the employees are contractually bound not to strike. In the absence of an agreement not to engage in sympathy strikes, employees generally have the right to do so. If the applicable collective bargaining agreement contains no-strike language that may or may not apply to sympathy strikes, the determination of the scope of that language may present a minor dispute and the sympathy strike may be enjoinable pending arbitration of that dispute.[34]

The presence of no-strike clauses in collective bargaining agreements thus is crucial to any determination of the employees' right to engage in a sympathy strike. In a 1984 arbitration case, for example, Alaska Airlines sought to have the scope clause of its contract with ALPA construed to prohibit its pilots from refusing to fly the Alaska portion of an interchange flight with Continental. The Alaska pilots had refused to fly the Continental aircraft on Alaska routes in response to a request by striking Continental pilots to support their efforts against Continental. Conceding that its collective bargaining agreement with ALPA did not contain express no-strike language, Alaska nevertheless argued that none was necessary in that the pilots had violated the contract's scope clause in refusing to fly the Alaska route. That clause provided that "[a]ll flying . . . now or hereafter conducted by . . . the Company (including utilization of aircraft under the operational control of the Company) shall, if flown by the Company, continue to be performed by pilots on the Alaska Airlines' Pilots' System Seniority List." The system board ruled that the scope clause did not address concerted action such as a sympathy strike and that the course of dealings between ALPA and Alaska confirmed that interpretation.

In *International Association of Machinists v. Alaska Airlines,*[35] the court found that a contract clause providing that "[t]he union will not cause or permit its members to cause, nor will any member take part

---

34. *See* Trans International Airlines v. IBT, 650 F.2d 949 (9th Cir. 1980), *cert. denied,* 449 U.S. 1110 (1981).

35. 639 F. Supp. 100 (W.D. Wash. 1986), *aff'd,* 813 F.2d 1038 (9th Cir. 1987).

in, any strike or stoppage of any of the Company's operations" constituted a no-strike clause broad enough to prohibit sympathy strikes. The court held that the unqualified reference to *any* strike refuted the IAM's contention that the provision was intended to apply only to primary disputes.

The right of *nonunion* employees to engage in a sympathy strike was upheld in *Arthur v. United Air Lines*.[36] United had terminated five nonunion flight operations training instructors for their failure to cross the ALPA picket line and report to work during ALPA's 1985 strike against United. The five brought suit against United claiming that their termination violated their right to engage in peaceful strike activity under the RLA. The court held that "terminating non-union employees who fail to report to work because they refuse to cross picket lines during a primary strike of their employer is unlawful under RLA absent evidence that such terminations were necessary to prevent disruption of vital transportation services." The court found that the rights of sympathy strikers derive from the right to strike and to picket recognized in *Brotherhood of Railway Trainmen v. Jacksonville Terminal Co.*:[37] "When a union's appeal to non-union employees for support is conditioned by the threat of employer retaliation, the right to strike is significantly impinged." United made no claim that either termination or even replacement of the five training instructors was necessary for it to continue its operations during the strike.

Whether RLA unions have the right to engage in secondary strikes and picketing is a question most attorneys for airlines probably did not worry much about until recently. In light of the Supreme Court's ruling in *Burlington Northern Railroad Co. v. Brotherhood of Maintenance of Way Employees*,[38] holding that the RLA does not proscribe secondary strikes and picketing, those worry-free days are over. Whether the availability of secondary activity encourages or discourages the settling of major disputes is open to argument. What is beyond argument is that if airline unions ever develop sufficiently cooperative relationships among themselves, the house of labor will have at its disposal an awesome new weapon during the period of self-help.

---

36. 655 F. Supp. 363 (D. Colo. 1987).
37. 394 U.S. 369 (1945).
38. 55 U.S.L.W. 4576 (Apr. 28, 1987).

"POLITICAL STRIKES"

One final strike-related incident since deregulation deserves brief comment. For the second time within ten years, ALPA threatened a nationwide work stoppage effective March 1, 1981, over issues principally related to the certification of new aircraft capable of being flown by two rather than three pilots. The shutdown was averted by political compromise, but the novel legal issues were not resolved. Earlier, in 1972, ALPA had announced a twenty-four-hour strike in protest of the alleged ineffectiveness of government efforts to control hijackings. The District Court for the District of Columbia denied the industry's application for a temporary restraining order on the grounds that the issue presented no cognizable labor dispute under the RLA and, in addition, implicated protected First Amendment rights. Although a temporary injunction was issued against the strike by a two-to-one vote of a three-judge court of appeals panel and the action was subsequently withdrawn without a decision on the merits, many carriers were justifiably concerned about the quality of the RLA analysis by the courts and the industry's ability to enjoin a stoppage ostensibly aimed at nonbargainable issues. While it is a truism to recall that the heart of the RLA is the duty to avoid any interruption to the operations of a carrier, that duty is directed to disputes between carriers and employees. The so-called "price of peanut butter" dispute involves some disconcerting case authority. The absence of any clear legal precedent supporting injunction of such actions in the decade since deregulation means carriers will continue to live with this troublesome anomaly.

OTHER METHODS OF SELF-HELP AVAILABLE TO UNIONS

As airline management has become more adept at dealing with strikes through the use of time-honored NLRA tactics such as strike replacements, airline unions have responded by dredging up some old-style alternatives of their own. Eastern pilots picket airports wearing surgical masks; Northwest baggage handlers misroute bags; American flight attendants carry one tray at a time and report safety violations to the FAA. Bollixing the operation from within—the primal form of systematic pressure—is the trend. The AFL-CIO's industrial union department has published a manual designed to teach employees how to do battle while in full-pay status. "The Inside

Game: Winning with Workplace Strategies" acknowledges that strikes can, in the current economy, be beaten back.

The search for effective substitutes for strikes goes beyond conventional—if frequently unlawful—guerrilla warfare. It has, in some cases, entailed a patently unacceptable misapplication of resources. The *United* decision illustrated some of the methods ALPA used to increase its economic clout before, during, and in lieu of a strike. Before the United strike, ALPA mounted a campaign to inform travel agents throughout the country of the impending strike and engaged in informational picketing at airports across the country. The Seventh Circuit stated that although it did not condone ALPA's attempts "to undermine public confidence in United's ability to continue to provide service,"[39] it nevertheless did not find that ALPA's actions had the "consequences of a strike" and thus were not in violation of ALPA's status quo obligations during the cooling-off period. Although not at issue in the *United* litigation, that strike also saw the development by ALPA of a massive "hi-tech" public relations effort designed to maintain the morale of the striking pilots and their families and to enlist public support for the strike.

High-tech communications, teleconferences, family awareness groups, computer networking, Hollywood stars, celebrity lawyers, and Washington lobbyists may all represent innovative forms of permissible collective action. But if the sponsoring union commits its resources to those efforts, has a strike nonetheless, and raises its dues by 37 percent, is it unfair to inquire whether the organization might not have served its members better by putting its emphasis on effective collective bargaining?

One other form of self-help, which until now has been confined to the merger and acquisition context, could as well be employed in a work stoppage, and even more dramatically coincides with an unwillingness to engage in effective collective bargaining. Both Frontier Airlines and TWA became enfeebled because they could not effectively compete.[40] That inability, in turn, stemmed from, among other causes, excessive labor costs, which the carrier and unions were un-

---

39. 802 F.2d at 906–7.

40. Variations were seen at Eastern and, most recently, at United, where ALPA's apparent success in using its bargaining leverage to oust Richard Ferris was surely as attributable to lingering strike-related problems as to dissatisfaction with corporate strategy.

able to repair. Although unwilling to grant the concessions sought by incumbent management, labor became actively involved in the negotiations leading to the selection of the successful bidder and granted significant concessions in each case to such third parties. One management RLA practitioner has applauded these events as "creative problem solving." In fact, the unions' role in these transactions was an abdication of the statutorily prescribed processes. The unions owed a duty under the act to bargain with the carriers. That duty was exclusive. Bargaining with "white knights" and investment bankers was the antithesis of responsible union action, not laudable creativity.

Implications and Trends

The North Carolina commissioner of agriculture once said that traditional southern ideas were slowly dying, "like a frog in warm water." He explained: "You throw a frog in hot water, and he'll jump out of there. But you put him in warm water, and soften him up a little bit and he'll just sit there while you slowly cook him."

The body of strike-related case law developed under the RLA since deregulation is not unmanageably large. Taken one by one, cases seem to establish few remarkable principles and generally speak at length about the need to consider and balance carefully all competing interests. When the cases are examined closely, however, it appears that the courts have accepted some bad arguments. They have unnecessarily qualified the parties' rights even when reaching sound conclusions. Important issues remain unsettled. The balance struck by the courts, when the cases are considered collectively, seems oddly out of sync with the statutory purpose. From this perspective, it is not unreasonable for carriers to think about the commissioner's frog.

Consider strike replacements. *Empresa* affirmed the carrier's right to replace wildcat strikers without first seeking to enjoin the strike. But the case also suggests a willingness on the part of the federal court to require the carrier to establish that an employee is necessary for the operation of the airline before replacements will be sanctioned. The inherent complexity and subjectivity of many such judgments, particularly when considered in relation to the operations of a major carrier, may leave the practitioner agog.

Similarly, in *IBT v. World Airways* the carrier's prestrike replacement training program was upheld and the Teamsters' charges of status quo violations dismissed. But consider the rationale. The program was permissible as long as it was "separated from the continuing operations of the Company" and was not an act of bad faith "considering the Company's precarious financial condition." What are we to conclude from the district court's analysis—that if any airline were to train in its normal facility, without a cloak of poverty to shield it, the result might differ? If so, why?

Independent Federation of Flight Attendants seems equally puzzling in its handling of the cross-over issue. If cross-overs cannot be assured of having their jobs after a strike is over, who will cross? And if opening on and bargaining over eliminating union security is required to terminate those provisions at impasse, impasse is virtually assured, since the unions not only cannot agree to such demands but may well be forced to charge the proposing carrier with bad-faith bargaining for so proposing.

The sympathy strike issue is one that leaves carriers with a taste difficult to describe. Considered in conjunction with the state of the law on secondary activity and political strikes, the rights of carriers may be briefly formulated as follows: Carriers buy and pay for labor peace of some certain duration in collective bargaining agreements with their unions. That peace is not guaranteed. Unions have a right to engage in sympathy strikes. Unorganized employees have, at least in the view of the *Arthur v. United* court, similar rights that are perceived as "derivative." Both the union and nonunion employees have rights to damages against the carrier for termination in breach of those rights. Carriers have no clearly established reciprocal rights against unions. Unions on strike against one carrier may picket other carriers without limitation and without regard to "ally" considerations. It is possible that unions may strike at any time over issues not susceptible to resolution with the carriers (e.g., inadequate improvements in air traffic control).

The basic picture is not encouraging. It might be only a question of time after any significant level of sympathy strike, secondary strike, or political strike activity before Congress would move to effect changes. As someone once said, there are disadvantages to wearing hats with rabbits in them, even for a short time. At the same time, one is prompted to ask whether at this stage such reform might not be just so much more paint on a very old dame. I have, for the first time in twenty years, begun to think that the RLA may have outlived its usefulness.

Grand old notions concerning the "prompt and orderly settlement of all disputes" have been growing dim. The parties too often seem to think of litigation as the problem-solving mechanism of choice, and the courts have not adequately served the parties with clear, crisp, and practical exposition. The NMB can be sharply criticized for its torpor in letting cases such as *Lan Chile* and *Transamerica* languish literally for years without allowing conflict to run its course.[41] Meanwhile, the parties litigate, liquidate, hire Ed Asner, rehearse for the *60 Minutes* show, and bargain with Lazard Freres.

Strikes are not the mark of manhood. They represent failure of imagination. But worse events can befall an enterprise. We can see some examples now. Although strikes are painful, I had, until recently, always thought that the collective action of the strike was vital to the process—that ideally effective bargaining should take place while every effort is made to seek out suitable substitutes. But clearly, not every substitute is suitable. Death by strangulation while the interminable processes of the act run their course is not suitable. If the parties cannot compose their differences in a reasonably short time, they should be free to engage in self-help. Abandonment of bargaining with the appropriate management incumbents in favor of dealing out concessions to takeover artists is wrong—but if acceptable, then abandonment by both parties should be acceptable. Solving all significant problems by litigation is not suitable.

More than ever, a certain sense of blurring is evident in the manner in which the parties operate, and the NMB administers, the RLA. Coalition bargaining itself, with its potential for clouding peoples' statutory rights and obligations, is widely practiced. Coalition bargaining is acceptable when perceived by the unions as effective in containing concessions, but strict statutory craft or class demarcations and union autonomy are emphasized when any carriers seek to deal with all employees as a group. Bright-line distinctions in the major and minor dispute area grow dim. A Boston court enjoins an IAM layoff because it sees irreparable harm; an Alaska court enjoins a suspension of service; a Chicago court orders arbitration of a rep-

---

41. *See* Lan Chile Airlines v. NMB, 115 L.R.R.M. (BNA) 3655 (S.D. Fla.), *appeal dismissed*, 749 F.2d 731 (11th Cir. 1984), and ALPA v. Transamerica Airlines, No. 85–2455 (9th Cir. May 14, 1987).

resentation dispute based on pleadings, calling it a minor dispute. The growing trend toward "status quo" injunctions has left a once relatively settled area in a state as mysterious as Hindu scripture. No aspect of the RLA seems immune from this spreading sense of surprise. The NMB, after initially recognizing the old "1706" configuration as the appropriate grouping for ground service personnel, expressly rejects such craft or class arrangements as no longer valid for a mature industry in every case it considers for roughly a decade. Then, in 1986, it holds just such an arrangement must prevail on the newly merged Northwest-Republic operation. There are other problems. It is now apparently acceptable for someone to step directly from a role as a partisan advocate to membership on the National Mediation Board. Charles L. Woods did exactly that when he left his job as a Teamster organizer to become a member of the NMB in 1985.

For many years, the Railway Labor Act seemed to be a law perfectly attuned to the needs of the parties. It seemed to safeguard adequately the frequently competing rights of air and rail carriers, their employees, labor unions, and the public. Recent experience under the act, some directly strike-related and some destined to enlarge the potential for future unrest, have caused me to question that conviction. Perhaps this sixty-year-old rail-oriented statute, never an ideal fit for the airlines, is simply just one more dinosaur, one more vestige of a regulated era that should be scrapped. Clearly, more certainty, less unpredictability, and quicker turnaround and response times are notions better suited to the competitive, deregulated environment in which we now live. The time for careful reexamination is at hand.

Carriers' Rights to Self-Help during Strikes

Michael H. Campbell
William N. Hiers, Jr.

Carriers' rights to self-help in response to strikes need to be identified with far more certainty and predictability. Unfortunately, it is not much of an exaggeration to say that carriers (and unions, for that matter) tend to find out the law by what happens to them in litigation—during a strike or afterward. Considering the size of carriers and the large number of employees involved, strike-related litigation easily can involve millions of dollars and thousands of jobs.

The Railway Labor Act was conceived as mediatory legislation.[1] It is ill equipped to referee disputes that, despite complete compliance with the rules, lead to open confrontation and self-help. Deregulation of the airline industry has made this failure more acute.[2] As the Eighth Circuit Court of Appeals noted: "[W]e take judicial notice that labor relations in the airline industry have entered a different era, one of strife and turmoil resulting from deregulation and takeovers by 'corporate raiders'...."[3] In this new era, carriers have an

---

1. 45 U.S.C. §§ 151–88. Congress made the RLA applicable to the airline industry in 1936 by passing Title II of the RLA, 49 Stat. 1189–91, 45 U.S.C. §§ 181–88. With certain exceptions, all provisions of the RLA were thereby extended to common carriers by air. 45 U.S.C. § 181, Railway Labor Act, § 201. *See* IAM v. Central Airlines, 372 U.S. 682, 685–89 (1963).

2. The airline industry was "deregulated" pursuant to the Airline Deregulation Act, Pub. L. No. 95-504, 92 Stat. 1705 (1978) (amending the Federal Aviation Act of 1958, 49 U.S.C. §§ 1301–1542).

3. TWA v. IFFA, 809 F.2d 483, 491 (8th Cir. 1987).

increased need for guidance when labor disputes threaten to result in work stoppages.

The Supreme Court has stated: "The major purpose of Congress in passing the Railway Labor Act was to provide the machinery to prevent strikes."[4] Nonetheless, the RLA offers no guidance to carriers regarding the scope of permissible self-help.[5] Thus, by default, the federal courts have become the arbiters of allowable self-help activity. Because strikes in the air (and rail) industries are relatively rare, however—owing to their enormous magnitude and potentially catastrophic financial consequences—the common law in this area has been painfully slow to develop. Moreover, because the initial forum for these disputes is in the federal district courts, which have no specialized expertise in this area, and which in turn are bound, by the doctrine of *stare decisis*, to follow the few relevant appellate court decisions, little consistent legal precedent has developed. The need for consistency is particularly compelling in the case of airline strikes because airlines typically operate in all twelve federal judicial circuits. The situation is compounded by the RLA requirement that bargaining units be systemwide (i.e., nationwide). Thus inconsistent—or nonexistent—precedents in various circuits can lead to conflicting results in the same strike. The need for guidance cannot be understated.[6]

---

4. Detroit & Toledo Shore Line R.R. Co. v. United Transportation Union, 396 U.S. 142, 148 n.13 (1969), *quoting* Texas & New Orlean R.R. Co. v. Brotherhood of Ry. & Steamship Clerks, 281 U.S. 548, 565 (1930).

5. *See* Brotherhood of Ry. Trainmen v. Jacksonville Terminal Co., 394 U.S. 369, 378 (1969) ("Nowhere does the text of the Railway Labor Act specify what is to take place once these procedures have been exhausted without yielding resolution of the dispute. Implicit in the statutory scheme, however, is the ultimate right of the disputants to resort to self help..."). During congressional debate on the RLA, proposals for mandatory binding arbitration and anti-strike provisions were considered and rejected. *See* 67 Cong. Rec. 4508, 4512–13, 4517–18, 4648, 4702, 8814, 9205–6 (1926).

6. Not surprisingly, when faced with strikes governed by the RLA, courts have frequently recognized the inadequacy of legal precedent. Thus, particularly in light of their own inexperience with the RLA, courts have taken refuge in the relatively extensive development of case law under the NLRA. Despite thinly veiled disclaimers that there are fundamental differences between the NLRA and the RLA, courts have attempted to adapt the more familiar concepts of the former to resolve problems that arise under the latter. These attempts have generated confusion regarding when NLRA case law will be grafted onto the RLA. *See, e.g.,* ALPA v. United Air Lines,

Right of Carriers to Engage in Self-Help

Under section 2, seventh,[7] a carrier may not unilaterally establish or change rates of pay, rules, or working conditions affecting represented employees until the collective bargaining and mediation procedures set forth in the RLA have been exhausted. The obligation to maintain the status quo during a major dispute applies not only to contractual conditions but to working conditions established by past practice.[8] Likewise, the union may not exert economic pressure to establish or change rates of pay, rules, or working conditions until these procedures have been exhausted.[9]

If all the channels of mediation have failed, however, the parties are then free to engage in self-help.[10] This right is implicit in the

---

614 F. Supp. 1020, 1041 (N.D. Ill. 1985) ("In considering the general boundaries of permissible self help under the RLA, the court may resort to the National Labor Relations Act . . . for assistance. . . . To the extent, however, that the policies of the RLA and NLRA differ, the Court may not incorporate into the RLA the 'panoply of detailed law developed by the National Labor Relations Board and courts under [the NLRA]' "). *Compare* IFFA v. TWA, 819 F.2d 839 (8th Cir. 1987) (holding that issues of whether trainees are employees cannot be determined by resort to NLRA case law) *with* ALPA v. United Air Lines, 614 F. Supp. 1020, 1041–44 (N.D. Ill. 1985) (concluding, at least partly on the basis of NLRA cases, that trainees become employees under certain conditions) *and* IFFA v. TWA, 643 F. Supp. 470, 477–79 (W.D. Mo. 1986) (same conclusion).

7. Railway Labor Act, § 2, Seventh, provides: "No carrier, its officers, or agents shall change the rates of pay, rules, or working conditions of its employees, as a class, as embodied in agreements except in the manner prescribed in such agreements or in Section 156 of this title." 45 U.S.C. § 152, Seventh.

8. *See, e.g.*, Detroit & Toledo Shore Line R.R., 396 U.S. 142 (1969) (status quo extends to all actual, objective working conditions out of which the dispute arose, which includes past practices not covered expressly in the agreement).

9. *See, e.g.*, Chicago & North Western Ry. Co. v. United Transp. Union, 402 U.S. 570 (1971).

10. Brotherhood of Ry. & S.S. Clerks v. Florida E. Coast Ry. Co., 384 U.S. 238, 244 (1966); Brotherhood of Locomotive Eng'rs v. Baltimore & Ohio R.R. Co., 372 U.S. 284, 291 (1963) ("Both parties, having exhausted all of the statutory procedures, are relegated to self-help in adjusting this dispute. . . ."); Pan American World Airways, v. Flight Eng'rs' Int'l Ass'n, 306 F.2d 840, 846 (2d Cir. 1962) ("When the cooling-off procedures of the Act . . . are exhausted . . . it is quite clear that the Act contemplates that fur-

RLA,[11] which grants employees subject to the act the right to strike if they have exhausted statutory procedures.[12]

Likewise, once the status quo period expires, the carrier is free to engage in such self-help measures as implementing the changes it was still proposing to make at the conclusion of bargaining.[13] Much controversy has centered, however, on the extent to which, and under what conditions, the carrier is free to implement other changes not covered by a section 6 notice.

The carrier's self-help rights include hiring permanent replacements for striking employees[14]; however, striking employees who have been permanently replaced are not entitled to reinstatement until vacancies arise.[15] This right has led to numerous disputes regarding returning strikers, whether a carrier may rebid job positions or offer other economic inducements to permanent replacements and crossovers, and whether a carrier may train permanent replacements during the status quo period. Finally, during many strikes, employees who are not on strike refuse to cross the strikers' picket lines. There are many unanswered questions regarding the carrier's right to respond to these sympathy strikes.

---

ther progress toward the determination of the controversy will be left entirely to the interplay of economic forces without further governmental intervention. The parties are then free from all compulsion under the Act and may resort to 'self help' ").

11. Brotherhood of Ry. Trainmen v. Jacksonville Terminal Co., 394 U.S. 369, 378 (1969).

12. *See* Florida E. Coast, 384 U.S. at 244 ("The unions, having made their demands and having exhausted all the procedures provided by Congress, were therefore warranted in striking. For the strike has been the ultimate sanction of the union, compulsory arbitration not being provided"); Florida E. Coast Ry. Co. v. Brotherhood of R.R. Trainmen, 336 F.2d 172, 181 (5th Cir. 1964) ("when the machinery of industrial peace fails, the policy in all national labor legislation is to let loose the full economic power of each [party]. On the side of labor, it is the cherished right to strike"); Jacksonville Terminal Co., 394 U.S. at 382–85 ("Whether the source of [the right to strike] be found in a particular provision of the Railway Labor Act or in the scheme as a whole, it is integral to the Act") (footnote omitted) and at 390 ("[T]he Railway Labor Act permits [employees] to engage in *some* forms of self-help. . . . [S]uch protected self-help includes peaceful 'primary' strikes . . . ").

13. Florida E. Coast, 384 U.S. at 246–47.

14. IFFA v. TWA, 643 F. Supp. at 473.

15. *Id.* at 475.

Duty to Continue Operations

In assessing the scope of self-help available to carriers, the courts have been mindful of what they perceive as the "first duty" of the carriers—the duty to the public of continued operation.[16] Thus the carrier "owes the public *reasonable efforts* to maintain the public service at all times," even when beset by labor-management controversies.[17] Accordingly, the courts have recognized that, during the self-help period, a carrier must be allowed to deviate from the terms of collective agreements.[18]

Right to Implement New Terms and Conditions

The central question a carrier must address when it anticipates a strike is to what extent it may deviate from the terms of its collective bargaining agreement. Some guidance on this important question can be found in two decisions of the Supreme Court: *Brotherhood of Railway & Steamship Clerks v. Florida East Coast Railway* and *Brotherhood of Railway Trainmen v. Jacksonville Terminal Co.* These decisions, however, are not entirely consistent, and two lines of cases have developed. One line has held that a carrier may implement new terms and conditions after a collective bargaining agreement expires by its own terms at the end of the cooling-off period. The other line of cases holds to a narrower view, that a carrier may implement only those proposals that were subject to a section 6 notice in addition to new terms that are "reasonably necessary" for the carrier to continue operations.

---

16. *See* Florida E. Coast, 384 U.S. at 244–45 ("The carrier's right of self help is underlined by the public service aspects of its business. 'More is involved than the settlement of a private controversy without appreciable consequences to the public.' . . . In our complex society, metropolitan areas in particular might suffer a calamity if [the carrier's] service for freight or for passengers were stopped. . . . [W]hole metropolitan communities might be paralyzed"); Arthur v. United Air Lines, 655 F. Supp. 363, 368 (D. Col. 1987) ("an employer has a duty under the RLA to maintain operations during a strike").

17. Florida E. Coast, 384 U.S. at 245 (emphasis added).

18. *Id.*

The narrower view is found in *Florida East Coast*.[19] In that case, the Supreme Court recognized that carriers must be allowed to depart from their collective bargaining agreements during strikes to fulfill their obligation to serve the public.[20] Responding to the argument that a carrier could make *no* change that was not the subject of a section 6 notice, the Court reasoned:

> [T]he practical effect of that conclusion would be to bring the [carrier's] operations to a grinding halt.... For when a carrier improvises and employs an emergency labor force it may or may not be able to comply with the terms of a collective bargaining agreement, drafted to meet the sophisticated requirements of a trained and professional labor force.... [W]hen a strike occurs, both the carrier's right of self-help and its duty to operate, if reasonably possible, might well be academic if it could not depart from the terms and conditions of the collective bargaining agreement without first following the lengthy course the Act otherwise prescribes.[21]

Thus the Court ruled that an employer was not constrained absolutely to follow the dictates of its collective bargaining agreement during the course of a strike. The Court concluded, however, that only those changes that were "reasonably necessary" to the carrier's continued operation could be made in addition to changes that were the subject of a section 6 notice. The Court stated:

> The carrier must respect the continuing status of the collective agreement and make only such changes as are truly necessary in light of the inexperience and lack of training of the new labor force or the lesser number of employees available for the continued operation.[22]

In *Jacksonville Terminal Co.*,[23] just three years after the *Florida East Coast* decision, the Supreme Court again commented on the appro-

---

19. *Id.* at 238.

20. *Id.* at 245 ("The complication arises because the carrier, having undertaken to keep its vital services going *with a substantially different labor force*, finds it necessary or desirable to make other changes in the collective bargaining agreements") (emphasis in original).

21. *Id.* at 246.

22. *Id.* at 248. Moreover, the Court placed the burden on the carrier to show *any* need for alteration of the collective bargaining terms.

23. Brotherhood of R.R. Trainmen v. Jacksonville Terminal Co., 394 U.S. 369 (1969).

priate scope of self-help available to parties under the RLA. In *Jacksonville Terminal Co.*, however, the Court seemed to retreat from the position it had taken in *Florida East Coast*. Noting that the RLA "is wholly inexplicit as to the scope of allowable self help," the Court concluded that the "least unsatisfactory" solution "is to allow parties who have unsuccessfully exhausted the [Act's] procedures for resolution of a major dispute to employ *the full range of whatever peaceful economic power they can muster*, so long as its use conflicts with no other obligation imposed by federal law."[24]

It is difficult to reconcile the language in these decisions, a problem aggravated by the Court's failure in *Jacksonville Terminal Co.* to acknowledge, much less distinguish, its previous approach in *Florida East Coast*. This apparent inconsistency has created a tension between carriers and unions about the extent to which carriers may implement new terms and conditions during self-help.

Although several subsequent cases have addressed whether a carrier has the right to implement terms during the self-help period that were not the subject of a Section 6 Notice, the case law on this point continues to be unclear. The case of *TWA v. IFFA*[25] illustrates this inconsistency.

In *TWA v. IFFA*, the Eighth Circuit held that a carrier may implement only those provisions of a collective bargaining agreement that were included in a section 6 notice as well as those reasonably necessary to continue operations.[26] After the carrier's flight attendants struck, TWA implemented new working conditions, including abrogation of the union security and dues checkoff provisions of the collective bargaining agreement. Although those provisions had not been included in the section 6 notice, TWA contended that the agreement had expired at the end of the status quo period pursuant to the agreement's duration clause and that it therefore was free to implement new terms regarding union security and dues checkoff.[27]

TWA had relied on the decision of the Ninth Circuit in *IAM v. Reeve Aleutian Airways*[28] and its progeny,[29] arguing that the agree-

---

24. *Id.* at 391–93 (emphasis added).
25. 809 F.2d 483 (8th Cir. 1987).
26. *Id.* at 492.
27. *Id.* at 484.
28. 469 F.2d 990 (9th Cir. 1972), *cert. denied*, 411 U.S. 982 (1973).
29. *See* IAM v. Aloha Airlines, 776 F.2d 812, 816 (9th Cir. 1985) ("[The agreement] expired by [its] own terms on March 1, 1983, because the IAM

ment's duration clause was in effect a termination clause that freed the carrier from all provisions of the agreement after the status quo period. TWA argued that its case was squarely on point with *Reeve* and was distinguishable from *Florida East Coast* because there was no termination clause in the *Florida East Coast* collective bargaining agreement.

In ruling against TWA, the Eighth Circuit rejected the Ninth Circuit's approach in *Reeve* and relied instead on *Florida East Coast*:

> In light of our holding that the agreement at issue has not expired, the Supreme Court's decision in [*Florida East Coast*] is controlling here.... TWA may only make those changes "as are truly necessary in light of the inexperience and lack of training of the new labor force or the lesser number of employees available for the continued operation" of the airline.[30]

The answer to the question "What terms can be implemented?" is that it depends on which federal judicial circuit reviews the carrier's self-help actions. In circuits that follow *Florida East Coast* and *TWA*, the rule is that a carrier can implement only those changes that were proposed and negotiated or are deemed "reasonably necessary" for the carrier to operate during the strike. In circuits that follow *Reeve*, the rule is that if the parties have negotiated a duration clause that resulted in the expiration of the agreement at the end of the status quo period, then the carrier has wide latitude to implement changes in rates of pay, rules, and working conditions.

The better rule is that of *Reeve*. Implicit in *Reeve* is the concept that the parties may bargain in advance over what contractual terms shall apply during the self-help period. For parties to decide that

---

had filed a section 6 notice and was seeking to negotiate new and different terms for a new collective bargaining agreement. As of March 1, 1983, there was simply no existing collective bargaining agreement to interpret"); IAM v. Northeast Airlines, 536 F.2d 975, 978 n.2 (1st Cir. 1976) ("In general, the terms of a Railway Labor Act collective bargaining agreement are not controlling after the collective bargaining agreement and any subsequent status quo period expire"); IAM v. Qantas Airways, 122 L.R.R.M. (BNA) 2263 (N.D. Cal. 1985) ("Following termination of the agreements, and exhaustion of the major dispute procedures of the [RLA]...[the carrier] was not bound to continue in effect any of the conditions previously established by the contracts, including the union security and dues check off provisions....").

30. 809 F.2d at 492.

collective bargaining terms shall have a termination date is not a novel precept under the RLA.[31] Any other rule destabilizes labor relations in the air and rail industries by depriving the parties to such agreements of a means of advance self-adjustment of their disputes. Moreover, to extend the terms of an RLA contract artificially following its expiration burdens the carrier with the need to negotiate a host of issues relating to operations during self-help. This process is fraught with difficulty and interferes with the parties' obligation to "exert every reasonable effort to make and maintain agreements." In effect, two collective bargaining agreements need to be negotiated—one pertaining to normal operations and the other to self-help situations. Otherwise, to avoid the limitations identified in *TWA* on a carrier's right to self-help, a carrier would be forced to serve a section 6 notice proposing changes requiring virtual renegotiation of the contract with respect to the carrier's strike contingency plan. Such an exercise would harm the negotiation process and result in both parties taking inflammatory positions. Congress did not intend that course to be followed when it sought to bring stability to air and rail labor relations through the imposition of protracted—but meaningful—negotiations.

Right to Hire Permanent Replacements for Economic Strikers

In keeping with the first duty of carriers to continue operating during a strike, a carrier's right to hire permanent replacements for striking employees is well established.[32] Once a carrier hires permanent replacements, economic strikers are entitled to reinstatement only as vacancies occur. Further, the carrier is not required to

---

31. *See, e.g.,* ALPA v. Pan American World Airways, 765 F.2d 377 (2d Cir. 1985) (holding that parties to an RLA contract may agree that a term will expire on a certain date).

32. *See, e.g.,* Florida E. Coast, 384 U.S. at 244, 246; IFFA v. TWA, 819 F.2d 839, 842 (8th Cir. 1987); ALPA v. United Air Lines, 802 F.2d 886, 907 (7th Cir. 1986); Empresa Ecuatoriana de Aviacion v. District Lodge No. 100, 690 F.2d 838, 844 (11th Cir. 1982); Flight Eng'rs v. Eastern Air Lines, 208 F. Supp. 182, 194 (S.D. N.Y.), *aff'd,* 307 F.2d 510 (2d Cir. 1962); ALPA v. Southern Airways, 49 L.R.R.M. (BNA) 3145 (M.D. Tenn. 1962).

discharge permanent replacements to rehire economic strikers.[33] Several issues have arisen, however, regarding a carrier's right to replace striking employees permanently and particularly the rights of the replacements. Several cases in the late 1980s, including *IFFA v. TWA*[34] and *ALPA v. United Air Lines*,[35] address these issues.

Right to Grant "Junior Cross-overs" Permanent-Replacement Status

A carrier's most immediate concern during a strike is with staffing whatever operations can be maintained. When strikers abandon their jobs, the carrier typically has four sources of personnel to fill vacant positions: supervisory personnel; employees who did not strike; strike replacements; and employees who, after initially choosing to strike, have elected to cross the picket lines and return to work before the strike ends. In the *TWA* case, the Eighth Circuit significantly undermined carriers' self-help rights by holding that cross-over employees were not entitled to the same protection against displacement by returning strikers that has been extended to newly hired strike replacements.

In *TWA*, the carrier refused to reinstate striking flight attendants to their former positions if those positions had been filled either by newly hired replacements or "junior cross-overs" (employees with lower seniority "who either worked throughout the strike or returned to work as flight attendants prior to [the end of the strike]").[36] Relying on NLRA precedent, the district court adopted the general rule set out in *NLRB v. Erie Resistor Corp.*:[37] "An employer may operate his plant during a strike and at its conclusion need not discharge those who worked during the strike in order to make way

---

33. IFFA v. TWA, 819 F.2d 839, 842 (8th Cir. 1987). The cases in this area uniformly rely on NLRA precedent, particularly NLRB v. Mackay Radio & Tel. Co., 304 U.S. 333 (1938), and its progeny.

34. 643 F. Supp. 470 (W.D. Mo. 1986), *rev'd in part, aff'd in part*, 819 F.2d 839 (8th Cir. 1987).

35. 802 F.2d 886 (7th Cir. 1986).

36. 643 F. Supp. at 471. The district court noted that TWA had made a commitment to the crossovers that they would retain their jobs after the strike. *Id.* at 474 n.2.

37. 373 U.S. 221 (1963).

for returning strikers."[38] The district court determined that this rule would protect cross-overs as well as newly hired replacements.[39] Both parties appealed. The Eighth Circuit affirmed the district court's holding that returning strikers were not entitled to displace newly hired permanent replacements.[40]

With respect to junior cross-overs, however, in an unprecedented holding under the RLA, the Eighth Circuit reversed the district court's ruling that the cross-overs were not subject to displacement by returning strikers with greater seniority:

> TWA may not discriminate among union members based on the degree of their union activity. Accordingly, TWA may not accord cross-overs permanent replacement status and prevent full-term strikers from displacing cross-overs with less seniority because such action impermissibly discriminates among union members based on the degree of their union activity.[41]

The Eighth Circuit's decision severely restricts carriers' self-help rights and contravenes the principles that underlie the use of permanent replacements. The premise of granting permanent status to strike replacements arises from an employer's need to offer strike replacements a reasonable inducement to cross a picket line.[42] It has long been recognized that few strike replacements would cross picket lines if, following the strike, they knew they would be displaced by returning strikers.[43]

The Eighth Circuit's rule that differentiates between the inducement necessary to attract a new hire and that reasonably necessary to induce a current employee to cross a picket line and return to work makes no sense. Indeed, the Eighth Circuit has provided far greater job protection for new employees than for veteran employees who remain on the job without striking or veteran employees who

---

38. 643 F. Supp. at 473, quoting Erie Resistor, 373 U.S. at 232.

39. 643 F. Supp. at 473.

40. 819 F.2d at 842.

41. *Id.* at 843 (footnote omitted).

42. *See* NLRB v. Mackay Radio & Tel. Co., 304 U.S. 333 (1938); IFFA v. TWA, 643 F. Supp. 470, 474 (W.D. Mo. 1986); *rev'd in part, aff'd in part,* 819 F.2d 839 (8th Cir. May 26, 1987).

43. Mackay, 304 U.S. at 345–47; TWA, 643 F. Supp. at 474 ("The inducement of permanent rather than temporary employment is deemed presumptively needed to attract new hires").

cross the picket line and return to work.[44] Moreover, the Eighth Circuit's holding has the potential to prolong strikes, thus further destabilizing labor relations in the airline industry. Under this holding, a carrier will be forced to hire more new employees as permanent replacements because there will be less incentive for veteran employees to abandon a strike and cross a picket line. This rule clearly contravenes the purpose of Congress in enacting the Railway Labor Act: to foster stability in labor relations.

Right to Rebid Positions

In the 1985 strike against United by the carrier's pilots, United was faced with an urgent need to attract as many crossovers and new qualified permanent replacements as possible. In anticipation of the strike, United announced several inducements to obtain the needed pilots. The carrier announced to its current pilots that it would allow all nonstriking pilots to bid on all pilot positions vacated by striking pilots. Thus pilots who agreed to work during the strike could achieve dramatic increases in pay and job opportunities normally reserved for pilots with greater seniority. In addition, United indicated that it would hire permanent replacements for striking pilots and guarantee minimum salaries for the replacements, even if they were later forced to accept lower-paying positions.

On May 17, 1985, ALPA called a strike at United. United canceled all pilot assignments and rebid all pilot positions.[45] United also implemented its guaranteed-salary plan to attract "fleet-qualified" pilots to work as permanent replacements.

In June 1985, the parties reached a back-to-work agreement:

> Under this agreement, the pilots would return to work and assume the same positions they had held prior to the strike. Both United and ALPA agreed not to punish either the striking or nonstriking pilots.... Al-

---

44. *See* IAM v. J.L. Clark Co., 471 F.2d 694, 700 (7th Cir. 1972) (Pell, J., dissenting) (Supreme Court decisions regarding permanent replacement of economic strikers give "no indication that the strikers who returned to work during the strike were any less protected than the new employees").

45. These bids were not actually awarded until June 1, 1985, and no pilot was activated during the strike in any assignment awarded during the rebid. 802 F.2d at 893.

though United agreed to restore all pilots to their pre-strike positions, when new vacancies arose, either due to attrition or expansion, United stated it would award the vacancies, in order of seniority, to nonstriking pilots who had been awarded similar positions during the strike rebid. In other words, nonstrikers were to be given preference over strikers.... Finally, United stated that it planned to continue to pay the guaranteed salaries of the fleet-qualified replacements.[46]

As part of the back-to-work agreement, it was recognized that ALPA would continue to pursue a previously filed lawsuit alleging that United's self-help actions had violated the RLA. The district court ruled in favor of ALPA regarding the rebid issue. The court decided in favor of the carrier, however, with respect to the hiring of and paying guaranteed salaries to "fleet-qualified" permanent replacements.[47]

By rebidding the entire airline, the district court held that United had, in effect, illegally granted superseniority to nonstriking pilots.[48] The court found that the rebid violated the RLA because United "failed to justify the rebid as reasonably necessary for its operations during the strike" and because those actions were motivated by anti-union animus.[49]

The Seventh Circuit agreed with the district court's holding that it was illegal to rebid the pilot positions to allow nonstriking pilots preference over those who had struck. The circuit court specifically noted that "throughout the strike no nonstriker actually filled a vacancy that was awarded during the rebid. Yet, at the same time, the rebid significantly harmed those pilots who refused to cross the picket line."[50] Invoking the reasoning of *Florida East Coast*, that a carrier may implement only those changes in the parties' contractual relationship that are "reasonably necessary to keep the operation of the carrier going," the court determined, as had the district court,

---

46. *Id.* at 894.

47. ALPA v. United Air Lines, 614 F. Supp. 1020 (N.D. Ill. 1985).

48. The Seventh Circuit noted an example of the super-seniority effect that the rebid would have: "Group of 500 members who crossed the picket line were able to gain between 2960 and 5090 places on the seniority list in bidding for DC-10 captain positions. In some cases this represented a jump in seniority of between 19 to 29 years." 802 F.2d at 898.

49. 802 F.2d at 897.

50. *Id.* at 898.

that the rebid was unnecessary and therefore illegal because its only possible effect was an attempt to harm the union.

In affirming the lower court's holding that the rebid was illegal, the Seventh Circuit recognized that it "was an attempt by United either to destroy the union or at the very least discourage union membership."[51] The circuit court went further, however, and stated that "[t]he existence of anti-union motivation, *by itself*, provides a sufficient basis upon which to uphold the district court's decision...."[52] Therefore, under *United*, a self-help measure need be not only "reasonably necessary" to continue the operation of the airline during the strike but free of anti-union animus as well.[53] Thus a carrier cannot discriminate against nonstriking employees by rebidding positions for nonstrikers only, unless such an action is reasonably necessary to enable the carrier to continue operations during a strike. It is ironic that United was found to have violated the RLA in part because it did not *implement* the rebid. If it had, United could have argued that the rebid was necessary to permit operations during the strike.

The court's conclusion is troubling. Inevitably, during a strike, both parties develop some level of animus or hostility. Such is the nature of strikes. The high stakes for carriers in these cases, in lost jobs and back-pay liability, should not be decided on such subjective criteria. The better rule would be to assess objectively whether a particular measure of self-help was reasonably necessary to allow the carrier to continue operations.

Right to Use Economic Inducements to Attract Permanent Replacements

To attract "fleet-qualified" permanent replacements,[54] United offered new captains and first officers $75,000 and $50,000 per year,

---

51. *Id.* at 900.

52. *Id.* (emphasis added).

53. The circuit court expressly left open the question of the legitimacy of a rebid in the absence of anti-union animus. *Id.* at 899 n.9.

54. The court explained this appellation: "The term 'fleet-qualified replacements' refers to pilots who were, in most instances, flying for other airlines when ALPA's strike against United began. The district court found that when hired these pilots were ready to serve as captains or first officers on the type of jets flown by United." *Id.* at 907 n.16.

respectively. Moreover, United promised to guarantee these salaries even if the replacements were subsequently forced to take lower-paying positions.[55] ALPA argued in the district court that this scheme violated the RLA because it resulted in a sanction against striking pilots.[56] The district court, however, held that United had not violated the RLA because (1) the pay scales offered replacement pilots were reasonable considering the pilots' experience and qualifications; (2) United's use of the replacement program was soundly based since the strike made it necessary for United to offer a pay scheme sufficient to attract qualified replacements; and (3) the hiring of replacements at guaranteed salary levels "does not disadvantage striking pilots."[57]

On appeal, ALPA argued that the carrier's unilateral implementation of a guaranteed salary program violated its duty to bargain in good faith and was illegally discriminatory. Responding to the good-faith bargaining argument, the Seventh Circuit stated that "[i]t is settled that this duty [to bargain] does not extend to the terms and conditions of employment for replacements of striking employees."[58] The court's response to ALPA's other arguments made it clear, however, that this holding does not permit a carrier wide latitude in attracting permanent replacements with offers of discriminatorily high salaries.

ALPA also challenged the carrier's determination of the *amount* guaranteed to the replacements. Specifically, ALPA argued that it was illegal to offer replacements more than the carrier would offer pilots to be hired in the future. The Seventh Circuit disagreed, holding that there is no violation of the RLA as long as the amount offered replacements is not higher than the amount contemporaneously offered incumbent employees.[59] Thus United's pay plan for permanent replacements did not violate its duty to bargain in good faith.

ALPA's argument that the guaranteed salaries discriminated against strikers did not fare any better. The court held that this

---

55. Indeed, the replacements were demoted following the strike because the new contract entered into between United and ALPA provided for the return of all striking pilots to their prestrike positions. *Id.* at 907.

56. 614 F. Supp. at 1047.

57. *Id.*

58. 802 F.2d at 908, quoting Capitol-Husting Co. v. NLRB, 671 F.2d 237, 246 (7th Cir. 1982).

59. 802 F.2d at 908–9.

action by United did not disadvantage any striker and that the guaranteed salaries were necessary to keep the carrier in operation.[60]

Finally, ALPA argued that the guaranteed salaries "could only lawfully be in effect during the temporary duration of the strike."[61] Noting that ALPA's argument conflicted with *Belknap v. Hale,*[62] the Seventh Circuit held that United was free to make good on its guarantee to the permanent replacements that the promised salaries would be continued following the strike. Thus a carrier has the right to offer reasonable economic inducements to permanent replacements.

In determining whether the inducements are reasonable, courts consider: (1) the experience and qualifications of the replacements hired; (2) the necessity of hiring "qualified" replacements; and (3) whether the inducements materially disadvantage striking pilots. A carrier also has no obligation to bargain over the terms and conditions of employment for permanent replacements.

In addition to the above considerations, the carrier may offer the replacements as much as it was offering incumbent employees, even if subsequently hired employees are to receive less. This standard is an important consideration in this time of two-tier wage schemes. Furthermore, a carrier may offer reasonable guarantees to replacements that their salaries will not be reduced as part of any back-to-work agreement entered into by the carrier. The carrier then is contractually obligated to keep this and any other promises. Otherwise, the replacements may sue to enforce the agreements.

Right to Train Permanent Replacements

One of the difficult issues facing a carrier when it anticipates a strike is whether it will be able to obtain trained permanent replacements

---

60. *Id.* at 909.

61. *Id.*

62. 463 U.S. 491 (1983). *See also* Bubbel v. Wien Air Alaska, 116 L.R.R.M. (BNA) 2473 (Alaska 1984) (holding that permanent-replacement pilot states a cause of action under breach of contract and estoppel theories in a complaint against the carrier, alleging that he was falsely assured that he would not be displaced by returning strikers).

who can begin work as soon as the strike is called. The expense of such a program and its potentially inflammatory effect during negotiations mandate that the carrier know its legal rights.

Several cases have offered insight into the status of trainees as permanent replacements. First, a carrier has the right to implement a training program for permanent replacements without bargaining with the union.[63] Second, the training program can be implemented during the status quo period in preparation for a potential strike as long as the training program is separate from the regular operations of the company.[64] Third, trainees may not displace striking employees except *during* the strike.[65]

UNITED PILOT STRIKE

The issue of using trainees as permanent replacements was raised in the 1985 *United* case. During negotiations, in preparation for a possible strike, United selected approximately five hundred pilots (the "Group of 500") to enter its training program. These pilots each signed an agreement with United stipulating that they were not United employees and that United was under no obligation to offer them permanent employment at any time. Several weeks before the strike commenced, however, United offered jobs to most of the Group of 500. These job offers were to be effective May 17, 1985—the day the cooling-off period would expire and ALPA would be free to strike.

On May 17, ALPA struck, but only a few of the Group of 500 crossed the picket lines and accepted the jobs that had been offered by the carrier. United stated that it would not hire any of the Group of 500 who had not reported to work as directed on May 17.

---

63. IBT v. World Airways, 111 L.R.R.M. (BNA) 2170 (N.D. Cal. 1982).
64. *Id.* The court distinguished this case from Illinois Central R.R. Co. v. Brotherhood of Locomotive Eng'rs, 422 F.2d 593 (7th Cir. 1970), in which the court held that a training program was illegal because the program interfered with the regular operation of the carrier and deprived regular employees of work. 111 L.R.R.M. (BNA) at 2172. The court also rejected the union's contention that the carrier had violated its duty to bargain in good faith by initiating the replacement training program while negotiations were in progress. *Id.* at 2172–73.
65. *See* IFFA v. TWA, 819 F.2d 839, 846–47 (8th Cir. 1987); ALPA v. United Air Lines, 802 F.2d 886, 911–14 (7th Cir. 1986).

After protracted litigation, the Seventh Circuit held that the statutory definition of "employee" in the RLA[66] precluded a finding that the trainees had attained employee status on May 17.[67]

The court concluded: "[U]nless a person has performed services for the employer under that employer's supervision he is not an employee for purposes of the RLA."[68] Thus, because members of the Group of 500 were not "employees," they had no rights under the RLA and were not entitled to jobs at United.[69]

TWA FLIGHT ATTENDANTS STRIKE

The trainee issue also was raised in the TWA flight attendants strike. In *TWA*, the district court considered the carrier's argument that approximately 450 flight attendant trainees who were still in training when the strike ended should be treated as permanent replacements and given preference over returning strikers. Virtually all the trainees were phased into service, under supervision, from May 20 (three days after the strikers offered to return to work) through June 3.

TWA argued to the district court that the trainees "had been upgraded in company records to flight attendants and were being paid as flight attendants, so they should be deemed to be flight attendants for purposes of displacing strikers, regardless of their total lack of on-the-job experience."[70] Without citing any authority, the court responded that "[o]ne must reject the theory that a mere job title and rate of compensation should be deemed to establish status as a flight attendant, sufficient to withstand the claims of returning strikers."[71] Thus the court concluded that the flight atten-

---

66. Section 1, Fifth, of the RLA provides: "The term 'employee' as used herein includes every person in the service of a carrier (subject to its continuing authority to supervise and direct the manner of rendition of his service) who performs any work defined as that of an employee or subordinate official...." 45 U.S.C. § 151, Fifth. In addition, section 201 of the RLA provides that section 1, fifth, extends to "every air pilot or other person who performs any work as an employee or subordinate official of such carrier or carriers, subject to its or their continuing authority to supervise and direct the manner of rendition of his service." 45 U.S.C. § 181.

67. 802 F.2d at 911.

68. *Id.* at 913 (footnote omitted).

69. Subsequently, on its own initiative, United made offers of jobs to the Group of 500. *See* 288 Aviation Daily, Apr. 8, 1987, at 45.

70. 643 F. Supp. 478.

71. *Id.* at 479.

dant trainees should not have been retained in preference to returning strikers and ordered back pay for all strikers who had been displaced by the trainees.

On appeal, the Eighth Circuit reversed the district court on the trainee issue, holding that the Seventh Circuit's *United* decision "is dispositive of this issue."[72] The court stated: "The trainees in question, although hired by TWA, never performed any services for TWA under its supervision prior to the Union's offer to return to work. Thus, they cannot be considered employees within the meaning of the RLA."[73] The court completely discounted TWA's treatment of the trainees as employees. The court summarized its rationale as follows:

> The RLA does not extend its coverage based upon the employer's labelling of persons as employees or the payment of salary. Rather, RLA coverage is determined by the *work the person performs* under supervision of the employer. This performance factor is determinative in trainee situations because it is the only requirement that the statute explicitly includes. Thus, clear statutory language supports the conclusion that the trainees are not employees protected by the RLA because these trainees were not "performing any work" of the carrier by any stretch of the imagination."[74]

Determinations of whether trainees may be considered permanent replacements, who thus receive the legal rights accorded that status, are important in the airline industry, in which many positions are held by employees with unique skills (e.g., pilots, flight attendants). Such employees cannot be replaced unless the replacements have sufficient training. Minimum levels of training for positions such as pilots and flight attendants are, for obvious reasons, required by law. This situation is very different from that in other industries covered under the NLRA in which employees frequently may be replaced by people with little or no formal training. Moreover, because the RLA mandates systemwide bargaining units of crafts or classes (unlike the NLRA), the sheer numbers of employees to be replaced are typically much larger than under the NLRA, making the task of locating pretrained replacements much more difficult and of operating only with supervisors an impossibility.

---

72. 819 F.2d at 845.
73. *Id.* at 845–46.
74. *Id.* at 846 (emphasis added).

Also, unlike employers subject to the NLRA, carriers are under a duty to attempt to continue operations during a strike. It follows that a carrier must therefore train sufficient personnel to prepare for this possibility. The courts should not unduly circumscribe the ability of carriers to use such trainees or the carrier's commitments to the trainees that jobs will be available. In addition, because a carrier faced with a strike cannot accurately predict how long the strike will last, it is unfair to permit a union to hold the carrier hostage by allowing it to expend time, energy, and money in training personnel only to have the strikers reclaim their jobs just before the training is over. Such an injustice deprives the carrier of the benefit of its investment in the trainees, thereby reducing its incentive to train such personnel, and would deprive the trainees of the jobs they expected. The better rule would be to deem as replacements all persons to whom the carrier has made a commitment by having made them employees.

Right to Respond to Sympathy Strikes

When a union strikes it usually establishes a picket line in an attempt to persuade other employees not to report to work. Employees other than the primary strikers who refuse to cross the picket line are deemed "sympathy" strikers. A carrier attempting to operate during a strike must be prepared to react to these strikers as well as to those with whom it has a primary dispute.

Although the law concerning sympathy strikes is fairly well developed under the NLRA,[75] few cases have been decided on this subject under the RLA. The Supreme Court's decision in *Jacksonville Terminal Co.*, although it clearly recognizes the right of employees to engage in peaceful primary strikes, offers little guidance on the rights of carriers and employees in sympathy strikes. Nor until recently had other courts been more helpful in this area.[76]

---

75. *See* M. Hutcheson, Employer's Guide to Strike Planning and Prevention 176–86 (1985); C. Morris, The Developing Labor Law 1026–33 (2d ed. 1983).

76. *But see* Northwest Airlines v. ALPA, 325 F. Supp. 994, 1003 (D. Minn. 1970) ("the right [to appeal to secondary employees] must obviously carry with it the corresponding right of the non-striking employee to respond"),

In *Arthur* v. *United Air Lines*,[77] a case arising from the 1985 ALPA strike against United, the court was squarely faced with the question of what protections, if any, the RLA extends to nonunion sympathy strikers. The case involved five nonunion United employees who were discharged because they refused to cross ALPA picket lines during that strike.

The district court noted that *Jacksonville Terminal Co.* was not particularly helpful and that "[s]ubsequent opinions of the Supreme Court construing the RLA have not addressed the question of what protections, if any, sympathy strikers have from employer retaliation, nor have any other reported decisions of which this Court is aware."[78] Accordingly, the union argued that the court should look to the NLRA to determine the rights of sympathy strikers under the RLA. The court agreed.[79]

The district court ruled that a carrier may not discharge employees for their sympathetic activities in refusing to cross a picket line and report to work.[80] The court stated that "terminating non-union employees who fail to report to work because they refuse to cross picket lines during a primary strike of their employer is unlawful under the RLA *absent evidence that such terminations were necessary to prevent disruption of vital transportation services.*"[81] The court did not elaborate on its condition related to "vital transportation services," and, although this condition would seem to mean that the right of a nonunion employee to engage in sympathy strike activity is not absolutely protected, only subsequent cases will determine whether that condition is more ephemeral than real.

In its ruling, the court determined that the rights of sympathy strikers derive from the effect that a contrary holding would have on the union's right to strike.[82] The court stated: "[T]he right to

---

rev'd and remanded on other grounds, 442 F.2d 246 (8th Cir. 1970), *cert. denied*, 404 U.S. 871 (1971).

77. 655 F. Supp. 363 (D. Col. 1987).

78. *Id.* at 366.

79. *Id.* at 367 ("Such cases are not binding on this Court, but merely serve as analogies in determining what limitations, if any, the RLA places upon an employer's self-help activity").

80. *Id.*

81. *Id.* (emphasis added).

82. *Id.* at 367–68 ("although United's actions in this case are directed against non-union employees, the ultimate effect upon ALPA is the same,

strike recognized in *Jacksonville Terminal Co.*, as well as the policies behind the RLA, are best served by a rule which protects plaintiffs from retaliation."[83]

Several other cases have considered the rights of *unionized* employees to engage in sympathy strike activity. Typically, these cases involved a primary strike by employees in one craft or class and sympathy strike activity by employees of the same carrier in another craft or class.

IBT v. Pan American World Airways[84] and *IAM v. Alaska Airlines*[85] considered the effect under the RLA of sympathy strikes by unionized employees. In both of those cases the courts held that the question of whether unionized employees may engage in sympathy strikes against their carrier is a minor dispute and must be determined by the appropriate system board of adjustment.

In *IBT v. Pan American World Airways*, Pan Am employees represented by the Teamsters (IBT) refused to cross TWU picket lines. Pan Am immediately informed all IBT employees that because of the strike no work existed and they were furloughed until further notice.[86]

Shortly thereafter, Pan Am began to reestablish its flight service. Accordingly, the carrier notified some IBT members to return to work; most refused, however, and remained on strike. Pan Am then notified other IBT members, whose jobs had *not* been reactivated, that work was available and requested that they express their desire to fill certain open positions for the duration of the strike. About two weeks later, Pan Am and TWU reached a tentative agreement and settled their dispute.[87] Accordingly, the carrier began to return to full service. Because returning to full service would take some time, however, the carrier attempted to reach an agreement with

---

albeit less direct: the effectiveness of ALPA's self help measures is diminished").

83. *Id.* at 368.

84. 607 F. Supp. 609 (E.D. N.Y. 1985).

85. 813 F.2d 1038 (9th Cir. 1987), *aff'g* 639 F. Supp. 100 (W.D. Wash. 1986).

86. Pan Am employees represented by ALPA and the Flight Engineers International Union, whose members initially refused to cross the picket lines, entered into back-to-work agreements. IBT, however, continued to strike. 607 F. Supp. at 610.

87. On March 27, 1985, the TWU employees ratified the new contract.

IBT that would provide for the orderly return of IBT employees as work became available. The striking IBT employees then attempted to return en masse. At that time, Pan Am was operating at only about 50 percent of its capacity; the carrier assigned what work was available and furloughed the remainder of the IBT employees.

IBT then sued Pan Am in federal court to enjoin the carrier to follow the seniority, furlough, and recall procedures in the IBT–Pan Am contract, alleging that Pan Am had failed to follow the bid-and-bump procedure set forth in the agreement. The union contended that the recall of employees as implemented by Pan Am constituted a unilateral change in the agreement and thus was a violation of sections 152, third, 152, fourth, and 156. Thus the union argued that it had alleged that the dispute was "major." Pan Am argued that the contract governed this dispute and it therefore was a "minor" one to be resolved by the system board.

The court held that, because the carrier's interpretation of the contract was "plausible," this case was within the exclusive jurisdiction of the system board.[88] The union argued, however, that "the sheer number of employees affected in this case renders this a 'major' dispute."[89] The court rejected this approach, which, given the number of potential sympathy strikers in most crafts or classes, could have had far-reaching application in many sympathy strikes. The court held that, although relegation of the dispute to the grievance process would be "an arduous and, perhaps, prolonged task," the system board nonetheless was the appropriate forum.[90]

Carriers can sometimes enjoin a sympathy strike. In *TWA v. IBT*,[91] the Ninth Circuit held that a sympathy strike by unionized employees may be enjoined if the issue of whether the sympathy strike is permitted by the contract is a minor dispute.[92] In arriving at this conclusion, the court rejected cases arising under the NLRA that reached a contrary conclusion.[93] The court recognized that "where a minor dispute exists the union must first establish its contractual

---

88. 607 F. Supp. at 613.

89. *Id.*

90. *Id.*

91. 650 F.2d 949 (9th Cir. 1980).

92. *Id.* at 964–66 ("The minor dispute arbitration procedure was designed as a substitute for prearbitration strikes..., and we think this includes sympathy strikes of the character presented in this case").

93. *Id.*

right to engage in a sympathy strike before disrupting a carrier's operation."[94] The court noted that this rule may not apply if a carrier is unable to show the traditional standards governing the granting of preliminary relief.

In another case concerning the injunction rights of carriers in sympathy strikes, *IAM v. Alaska Air Lines*,[95] a Washington district court determined that a broad no-strike clause applied to sympathy strikes under the RLA. The court adopted the reasoning of the NLRB on this point in *Indianapolis Power & Light Co. v. Local 1395, International Brotherhood of Electrical Workers*.[96] Thus carriers can expect that broad language in no-strike clauses, absent facts that would indicate that the union did not intend to waive the right to engage in sympathy strikes, will protect against sympathy strike activity.

Sympathy strike issues must be analyzed differently for unionized and nonunionized employees. Strikes against carriers will frequently result in sympathy strike activity by both groups. On the one hand, nonunionized employees are entitled to the same protection against retaliation, enforceable in federal court, that would be extended to a primary striker: they may not be discharged or disciplined for failure to cross picket lines but may be permanently replaced. On the other hand, issues relating to unionized sympathy strikers will frequently be deemed minor disputes subject to the jurisdiction of the appropriate system board of adjustment. Furthermore, it is important to consider whether unionized employees may be prohibited from engaging in sympathy strikes if their collective bargaining agreement contains a broad no-strike clause. The employer may be entitled to an injunction halting the sympathetic strike, pending a determination by the system board.

Conclusion

Although the RLA contains no express limitations on a carrier's right to engage in self-help during an economic strike, the federal courts are whittling away at those measures carriers have used to fulfill their duty to operate. Moreover, the absence of an adequate body

---

94. *Id.* at 966.
95. 639 F. Supp. 100 (W.D. Wash. 1986).
96. 273 NLRB 1715 (1985).

of law that would enable carriers to clarify their self-help rights is troublesome. The tendency to find out what the law is only after a lawsuit frustrates the carriers' ability to react to strikes and can have severe financial consequences. Some degree of certainty about the law is necessary for a stable airline industry. Thus far, the developing law seems to restrict unduly the right of a carrier to engage in self-help when faced with a union intent on shutting it down.

Airline Strikes and the Law

Joseph Guerrieri, Jr.

Stable labor relations were the hallmark of the airline industry when it had regulated fares and routes and a more or less constant number of carriers.[1] The highly competitive market that resulted from deregulation, however, rapidly destabilized labor-management relations. Indeed, even major carriers have demanded wage and rule concessions, claiming they were needed to compete with low-fare, low-cost carriers of the Texas Air and Continental ilk. If resistance to these concessions continues, increased labor-management strife may well result. Nevertheless, in *TWA v. IFFA*, the United States Court of Appeals observed that although the RLA was passed during a period of stability, the law nevertheless applied with equal force in this time of turmoil brought about by deregulation and corporate takeovers.[2]

Barring an unforeseen change in the airline industry or in legislation, self-help can be expected to increase. If it is true, as some analysts have predicted, that disputes are less likely to be settled through the procedures outlined in the act, it is critical to understand the limitations on management's right to change rules, wages, and working conditions when it is finally permitted to engage in self-help. Unions must also be aware of the self-help activities available

---

1. *See, e.g.*, Arouca & Perritt, *Transportation Labor Law and Policy for a Deregulated Industry*, 1 LAB. LAW. 617 (1985).
2. 809 F.2d 483, 491 (8th Cir. 1987).

to them, including secondary picketing when mediation has failed and the status quo provisions of the RLA have expired.

Constraints on Carriers during Strikes

The constraint the RLA imposes on carriers to change wages, rules, and working conditions during a strike was underscored in the *IFFA* case. TWA argued that the entire contract between it and IFFA became void after the procedures of the RLA were exhausted and the parties were entitled to engage in self-help. The TWA-IFFA contract had the following duration clause:

> Except as otherwise specified in this Agreement, this entire Agreement shall be effective August 1, 1981 [and] shall remain in effect until July 31, 1984 and thereafter shall renew itself without change for yearly periods unless written notice of intended change is served in accordance with Section 6, Title 1 of the Railway Labor Act, as amended, by either party hereto, at least 90 days prior to the renewal date in each year.[3]

Even though TWA neither included discontinuance of the union security and dues check-off provisions of the collective bargaining agreement in its section 6 notice nor bargained regarding the issue, the management of TWA believed it could disavow the union security provisions. TWA relied principally on *IAM v. Reeve Aleutian Airways*,[4] in which the Ninth Circuit had determined that a duration clause similar to that contained in the TWA-IFFA agreement terminated the entire agreement in question. That reliance was misplaced.

Both the district court and the Eighth Circuit rejected TWA's interpretation and the holding of *Reeve*. In *IFFA*, the court held that provisions of an agreement not addressed in section 6 notices remain in effect. The Eighth Circuit affirmed the district court's holding that the duration clause of the contract simply defined the point at which the collective bargaining agreement became amendable and not the point at which the entire contract became terminable.[5] The *IFFA* court held that an employer is free to implement only those

---

3. *Id.* at 484.
4. 469 F.2d 990 (9th Cir. 1972).
5. *See also* EEOC v. United Air Lines, 755 F.2d 94 (7th Cir. 1985).

changes proposed in the section 6 notice but that its freedom to change other wages, rules, and working conditions is limited to "only such changes as are truly necessary in light of the new labor force or the lesser number of employees available for the continued operation."[6] Clearly, the union security and dues check-off provisions were not of that type.

The Eighth Circuit based its holding on the policies of the RLA as explicated by the Supreme Court in *Florida East Coast*. In this case, the Supreme Court held that collective bargaining agreements based on the RLA are the product of years of struggle and negotiation and govern the community of striking employees and the carrier. The Court noted that a strike does not destroy this community but is only an interruption in the continuity of the relationships. The *Florida East Coast* court reasoned that "were a strike to be the occasion for a carrier to tear up and annul . . . the entire collective bargaining agreement, labor-management relations would resort to the jungle."[7] A carrier might use a strike on one issue to make sweeping changes in work rules it could not obtain through the statutorily mandated negotiation and mediation process. Moreover, it "might indeed have a strong reason to prolong the strike and even break the union. The temptation might be strong to precipitate a strike in order to permit the carrier to abrogate the entire collective bargaining agreement on terms most favorable to it."[8]

The *IFFA* decision further isolates the conflicting decision of the Ninth Circuit in *Reeve*. The Ninth Circuit's view in *Reeve* has been strongly criticized by both the Eighth Circuit in the *IFFA* case and by Judge Richard Posner of the Seventh Circuit in *Equal Economic Opportunity Commission v. United Air Lines*. The Ninth Circuit is decidedly out of step not only with the Supreme Court in *Florida East Coast* but with the other circuits that have addressed the issue.

The *IFFA* decision left an important issue unanswered, however, by holding that a contract that explicitly provided for total termination in the event of a labor-management impasse would be unlawful under the RLA. The Eighth Circuit did not reach the same conclusion and held that a carrier's unilateral implementation is

---

6. Brotherhood of Ry. and Steamship Clerks, Freight Handlers, Express and Station Employees v. Florida E. Coast Ry. Co., 384 U.S. 238, 248 (1966).

7. *Id.* at 247.

8. *Id.*

limited by the contents of its section 6 notice. It is doubtful, however, that an employer could lawfully hold out in bargaining for a fully terminable duration clause. Indeed, were it to do so, the RLA's purposely "almost interminable" status quo provisions would be defeated.

Secondary Picketing

The Supreme Court made clear in its *Burlington Northern* decision that the Norris-LaGuardia Act precludes federal courts from assuming jurisdiction to enjoin secondary picketing in railway labor cases.[9] The provisions of the NLRA regarding secondary boycotts are powerful and far-reaching, but on this issue the RLA and the NLRA must be considered two entirely separate and distinct bodies of law.

In *Burlington Northern*, the Supreme Court removed all doubt that anything in the Norris-LaGuardia or Railway Labor acts, taken either separately or together, effects the same ban on secondary picketing as the NLRA's section 8(b) (4) and 10(d).[10] The Court also clarified a number of other issues: (1) that section 13(c) of the Norris-LaGuardia Act[11] continues to require a broad definition of the term "labor disputes" from which section 4 of the act removes federal jurisdiction to issue injunctions;[12] (2) that the RLA's failure to create access to the same kind of administrative expertise as found in the NLRA remains a significant reason to distinguish the two acts and should limit judicial attempts to depart from the plain language of section 13 and presumably other provisions; (3) that the president's power to appoint an emergency board under section 10,[13] thereby imposing at a minimum a sixty-day period during which the disputants must return to and maintain the status quo, and the Congress's power to legislate the recommendations of the Board provide mechanisms for avoiding interruptions to commerce; and (4) that "the availability of such self-help measures as secondary picketing may increase the effectiveness of the RLA in settling major disputes

---

9. Burlington Northern Ry. Co. v. BMWE, 107 S. Ct. 1841 (1987).
10. 29 U.S.C. §§ 158(b) (4), 160(d) (1982).
11. 29 U.S.C. § 113(c) (1982).
12. 29 U.S.C. § 104 (1982).
13. 45 U.S.C. § 160 (1982).

by creating an incentive for the parties to settle prior to exhaustion of the statutory procedures."[14]

The Court specifically rejected the "substantial alignment" test developed in *Ashley, Drew and Northern Railway Co. v. United Transportation Union and Its Affiliated Local 1121*.[15] The *Ashley, Drew* test had required courts to determine whether the secondary employer had a close enough relationship to the primary employer that strike activity directed against the secondary employer would further the union's economic interest. The *Ashley, Drew* decision held that if the union's action was not in the employees' interest, such action could not be considered a "labor dispute" under the Norris-LaGuardia Act and could be enjoined.

The Supreme Court found such judicial second-guessing inappropriate. Few would dispute that unions are in a better position than courts to determine what strike activities are worthwhile and to balance the risks of lost wages or employment against the likelihood of success.

Burlington Northern represents an acknowledgment by the courts that labor-management relations in the railway industry are best approached by recognizing that railway companies are interconnected. Because of this interconnectedness, one can presume that two RLA carriers will become substantially aligned once the unions decide what economic activity is likely to be successful. The union in *Burlington Northern* chose carriers with which its employer "interchanged a significant volume of traffic."[16] The RLA allows this range of strike action because, under the NLRA, two carriers are more likely to be interdependent than any two employers. For this reason, the RLA is truly tailor-made for the transportation industry.

Both *IFFA* and *Burlington Northern* should have the effect of encouraging the prompt resolution of labor-management disputes. The *IFFA* decision reduces a carrier's incentive to hold out and provoke self-help in the hope of terminating its entire contract. Under *Burlington Northern*, the lawful use of secondary pressure will bring about a prompt resolution of industrial disputes, thus avoiding drawn-out and debilitating economic struggles.

---

14. Burlington Northern, 107 S. Ct. at 1854.
15. 625 F.2d 1357 (8th Cir. 1980).
16. 107 S. Ct. at 1844.

Part 6
Handling of
Minor Disputes

System Boards of Adjustment: The State of Expedited Arbitration

Stephen E. Crable

Title II, section 184, of the Railway Labor Act requires each air carrier and its employee representatives to establish a board of adjustment with jurisdiction not to exceed that of railroad system, group, or regional boards of adjustment as provided in title I, section 153. Section 153 applies to rail carriers and sets forth, among other provisions, the jurisdiction, composition, and procedure for establishing what is now the National Railroad Adjustment Board. Although sections 184 and 185 allow for the creation of a national air transport adjustment board, no such board has been created either by the National Mediation Board or by individual carriers. Within the airline industry, carrier-by-carrier or system boards of adjustment have become the norm.

Until recently, airline system boards had been praised for being more efficient and less expensive than the National Railroad Adjustment Board. Increasingly, however, unions are finding that system boards have become too slow and costly and are negotiating swifter arbitration procedures. This trend is evidenced in the labor agreements of flight attendants at fifteen carriers: Alaska, Air California, American, Braniff, Continental (prebankruptcy), Eastern, United, Western, Republic, Northwest, TWA (prestrike), Ozark, Pan Am, Piedmont, and PSA.

Structure of System Boards

With only three exceptions (Braniff, Northwest, and PSA), the agreements referred to above all provide for a dispute resolution process that includes both four-member adjustment boards and five- or three-member adjustment boards. The four-member boards are composed of an equal number of carrier and employee representatives and usually hear cases appealed from the last step of the grievance procedure. The five- or three-member boards consist of an equal number of carrier and employee representatives plus a neutral referee or arbitrator and usually resolve deadlocks of the four-member boards. The following language, which created and designated membership on four-member boards for flight attendants, is almost standard in the industry:

> A. *Establishment of Board.* In compliance with Section 204, Title II of the Railway Labor Act, as amended, there is hereby established a System Board of Adjustment for the purpose of adjusting and deciding disputes or grievances which may arise under the terms of the agreement and any amendments thereto, and which are properly submitted to it after all steps for settling disputes and grievances as set forth in Section 26 have been exhausted.
> B. *Membership.* The System Board of Adjustment shall consist of four (4) members, two (2) selected by the Company and two (2) selected by the Union.[1]

When the four-member board deadlocks and is unable to reach a resolution on a case or the agreement does not require submission of the dispute to the four-member board, all contracts, by one method or another, provide for the appointment of a neutral referee and final binding resolution of the dispute by arbitration before either a five- or three-member board of adjustment.

Expedited Four-Member Boards

Processing a grievance through both the four- and five-member boards can be expensive and time consuming. The time investment is aggravated by the fact that four-member boards usually meet only

---

1. United-AFA Agreement, § 26 (1985–86).

a few times a year. This scheduling situation can add several months of delay from the outset of the arbitration process. In light of these delays, the parties have devised a variety of procedures to expedite decisions. To deal with the problem of scheduling meetings, numerous agreements between carriers and unions, including those of American, USAir, Eastern, Alaska, and Pan Am, provide for an emergency board. The language in section 20(H)1 of the 1987 agreement between USAir and the Association of Flight Attendants is representative:

> Upon receipt of notice of the submission of a dispute, the Chairman shall set a date for the hearing, which shall be at the time of the next regular meeting of the Board, or, if at least two (2) members of the Board consider the matter of sufficient urgency and importance, then at such earlier date and at such place as the Chairman and Vice Chairman shall agree upon, but not more than fifteen (15) days after such request for meeting is made by at least two (2) of said members, and the Chairman shall give the necessary notices in writing of such meeting to the Board members and to the parties to the dispute.

An even prompter method of "expediting" four-member boards is to bypass or eliminate them altogether. The Braniff, Northwest, and PSA agreements reflect the latter approach. In this case, following the final steps in the grievance procedure, the dispute is submitted to a three-member board of adjustment, consisting of a company representative, a union representative, and an agreed-on neutral referee.

The less radical bypass method is usually specific to the grievance involved. Thus some agreements provide for bypassing the four-member boards for discipline and discharge cases, whereas others allow bypass for contract interpretation cases. The Eastern, Republic, TWA, United, and Pan Am agreements fall in the former category and thus allow discipline cases to go directly to arbitration. The TWA, United, Western, Republic, and Pan Am agreements all allow contract disputes to skip the four-member board.

Expedited Arbitration

Once a case reaches the five- or three-member board, the delays faced by unions in the airline industry are similar to those faced by unions everywhere: delays in selecting an arbitrator, scheduling hearing dates and locations, and obtaining a decision. Many approaches have been used to deal with these problems. To facilitate the selection of an arbitrator, the United, American, TWA, Continental, and USAir agreements all provide for permanent panels of neutral referees from which the parties select an arbitrator if no mutual agreement is reached. The use of a permanent panel eliminates research time into an arbitrator's background and delays in obtaining panels from a government agency. The Eastern, Northwest, and Republic agreements provide for the appointment of the arbitrator by a government agency, thus avoiding the delay that occurs when one party will not select an arbitrator from a panel because it has not been able to evaluate the arbitrators or the panel. A third approach is the PSA agreement, which requires that an arbitrator be selected within five days of receipt of the names of the panel of arbitrators from the Federal Mediation and Conciliation Service. Although this approach is superficially appealing, it is not apparent what effective remedy exists if the company refuses to select the arbitrator within five days.

Among the most straightforward methods for expediting the arbitration process is included in TWA's agreement, which provides for the following:

(4) *Selection of Referee*: Within ten (10) working days, after the appeal to the five (5) member board as specified above, the Company and the Union shall select a neutral referee in the manner herein provided, to sit with the Board and settle in dispute.

(5) *Hearing Time Limits*: The neutral referee shall set a date for hearing which will be scheduled no later than twenty (20) work days after his/her appointment.

(6) *Decisions*: a) The five (5) member Board shall consider the dispute pending before it, and a majority vote of the Board shall be final, binding and conclusive upon the Company and the Union and anyone they may represent having an interest in the dispute; b) The decision by the five (5) member Board shall be rendered within twenty (20) work days after the close of the hearing.[2]

Such an agreement reduces a carrier's ability to delay arbitration. It does not, however, necessarily eliminate delay caused by the arbitrator.

---

2. TWA-IFFA Agreement, art. 17(c) (1983).

A second method for ensuring prompt arbitration is the one used at United. This method is not obvious from its agreement, however, which creates a four-member board and an elaborate method for resolving deadlocks. In practice, the four-member board is seldom used and all cases go directly to arbitration before a full five-member board. The board typically meets for one full week each month, every month. During October, it establishes a schedule for the following year, including the assignment of dates to the neutral board members (who are selected from a permanent panel). Grievance cases are then scheduled on a monthly basis with priority given to discharge cases and significant contract disputes. With this system in place, a compelling case can usually be processed through arbitration in less than thirty days from the time the grievance is denied at the last step of the grievance procedure. Although there is no contractual requirement that neutral board members render a decision within a specified period, because the neutrals are permanent members, delays are not a significant problem.

Probably the most ambitious attempt to establish an expedited arbitration process is contained in the Pan Am agreement. The stated purpose of the procedure is "to provide an economical, just, speedy and simplified method of resolving disputes"; the procedure is contained in a side letter that can be canceled by either the company or the union after one year of operation. This "expedited grievance procedure" (EGP) allows the union, at its discretion, to process up to five discipline cases a month and allows contractual disputes to be heard by mutual agreement of the carrier and the union.

Within fifteen days from the time a case is submitted for the EGP, an arbitrator must be selected from a permanent panel of neutral referees. If the neutral referee is not available within the timeline for hearing and deciding the case, another arbitrator is selected. Termination cases must be heard within forty-five days (sixty days for other cases) after the arbitrator is selected unless otherwise agreed. No briefs are written and no transcripts taken. Executive sessions, if necessary, must be held immediately following the hearing. The arbitrator is ordinarily expected to make a bench decision but may request an additional forty-eight hours to reach a decision. None of the decisions is precedent setting or accompanied by a written opinion.[3]

---

3. For a more detailed discussion of the Pan Am experience, see Singer, *Pan Am's Experience with Expedited Arbitration Procedures, infra* p. 261—Ed.

Conclusion

What is the state of flight attendants system boards ten years after deregulation? In some cases, the grievance arbitration process has virtually come to a standstill. Typically, delays occur because one or both carriers refuse to commit adequate resources (money and personnel) to resolving contract disputes, one or both parties erect endless procedural and technical obstacles, or one or both parties insist on forcing even the most trivial disputes to arbitration. In these situations, system boards of adjustment are being overwhelmed by grievances and employees are being deprived of their statutory rights under the RLA. Such instances demand that the system board process be streamlined and made more efficient. Yet in other bargaining relationships, identical system board/arbitration procedures are in place and the procedures are working well. In these cases, dozens of grievances are processed through four-member system boards of adjustment in any given year. The majority of the cases are resolved by the system board, and the remainder are arbitrated promptly. The conclusion is obvious: the most important element of an adequate, well-functioning system board/arbitration procedure is not the contractual language but a healthy bargaining relationship between the employer and the union. Unfortunately, healthy relationships are rare in today's airline industry. As a substitute, both parties need to concentrate on expediting the system board process by taking the cue from innovative strategies already being used. While delay and excessive legalism may be in the short-term interest of one party or the other, the long-term costs to the bargaining relationship and the negative effect on employee morale and passenger service greatly outweigh any short-term advantages.

Pan Am's Experience with Expedited Arbitration Procedures

Bonnie Singer

When Congress deregulated air transportation in 1978, cost reductions became necessary as airlines looked for new and innovative ways of doing business. Management sought concessions from the unions. As the unions lost items at the bargaining table, they sought to regain them through the grievance process. At the same time, management staff was reduced. One obvious solution was to streamline the grievance procedure.

Utilization of a "Direct" Five-Member System Board

The flight attendants group at Pan Am has implemented several changes in grievance resolution in the past decade. In 1977, the group voted in a new union, the Independent Union of Flight Attendants (IUFA). Previously, flight attendants had been represented by the Transport Workers Union, which also represented mechanics and certain other ground workers. The grievance procedure for flight attendants under TWU representation was the same as it was for all other TWU-represented members.

Under IUFA's first agreement, which was effective in 1979, handling of the grievance procedure and board of adjustment was, by and large, the same as it had been under the TWU except that the agreement more clearly distinguished between the system board and the field board. The system board's function was to hear grievances or complaints involving two or more bases or when a question of systemwide ramification was raised. The field board's function was to hear matters of discharge, discipline, and qualification.

The only major change attempted in the agreement was never implemented: the selection of a panel of nine referees to hear and decide cases deadlocked by the four-member system board. The parties spelled out detailed procedures concerning this panel but were never able to agree on who should be members. This may have been because of the mutual distrust and skepticism that existed between IUFA and Pan Am following nearly two years of negotiations.

As time passed and the parties gained experience in dealing with each other, it became obvious that certain issues could not be resolved by a four-member board. These issues were either considered too sensitive by the union membership or too explosive politically by the company or the union or involved genuine areas of dispute between the parties. These were cases only an arbitrator could resolve. It was agreed in 1982 that the union could, at its option, bypass the four-member system board and present up to seven cases each year directly to a five-member system board, which consisted of a referee, two management members, and two union members. The parties could agree to bypass the four-member board in an unlimited number of cases.

The parties used this provision to their mutual advantage and avoided the time and expense of presenting cases in which a deadlock was a foregone conclusion and a four-member board just a formality. Because direct five-member boards were so successful, the parties began mutually to agree to present certain disciplinary matters directly to a five-member field board, even though there was nothing in the agreement to permit the union to do so. Through experience, the parties found that the procedure could be streamlined further.

The 1985 agreement was the most radical diversion from past practice, and, again, both the company and the union have greatly benefited. The first provision allows the president of the union to file a grievance directly with the director of labor relations at Pan Am rather than go to the flight service department and hold a first-step hearing.[1] This procedure is used when the operating depart-

---

1. In 1982, the parties replaced the traditional two-step process by eliminating the hearing before the supervisor who had made the initial decision.

ment has no expertise in the area and the issue would normally be referred back to the labor relations department. Typically, such grievances involve pensions, corporate policy, and the like.

The second innovation is a provision for an expedited grievance procedure. This procedure was set up primarily for discipline and discharge cases in which resolving the individual grievance is more important than the precedential value of the case. The highlights of this procedure are as follows:

the four-member board is bypassed;
an arbitrator is selected from a permanent panel;
specific time limits are set for the hearing;
no briefs are written;
no transcripts are taken;
a bench decision is issued by the arbitrator following executive session (unless extra time is requested, not to exceed forty-eight hours);
the decision is nonprecedential; and
no opinion is written.

If the union so requests, the company must agree to decide five field board cases each month. System board cases may be brought only by mutual agreement between the company and the union.

Panel of Arbitrators

The first challenge faced by the parties was to choose permanent panels of arbitrators. Although the agreement provided for one panel for each of the five flight service bases, the parties agreed to have only three regional panels. This was largely in recognition of the fact that years earlier the parties had been unable to agree on even one panel. Surprisingly, selection of arbitrators was fairly easy, probably because both parties were excited about the new procedure and wanted it to work well. The advantage of permanent panels of arbitrators is that the members are acceptable to both sides and therefore selection of an arbitrator is immediate, whereas under the regular grievance procedure, selection normally takes three to four weeks. The parties are so pleased with members of these panels that they often choose members as arbitrators for "regular" arbitrations. Both advocates and board members enjoy working with arbitrators who are known to them; they know what to expect in the conduct of the hearing and do not have to provide the extensive background often required when an arbitrator is unfamiliar with the contract and practices of the parties.

DATES FOR HEARINGS

Once the parties agreed on panels of arbitrators, the next problem was to establish dates for hearings. In many cases in the past, the deadline for holding a hearing could not be met because the arbitrators were booked far in advance. This problem was resolved by having the parties reserve some hearing dates and assign cases to those dates as they arise. If the parties want a particular arbitrator to hear a case, the parties agree to waive time limits and dates are arranged as much as three months in advance.

EXECUTIVE SESSION

The executive session following the conclusion of the hearing seems to play a larger role in the expedited procedure than in the regular process. Because there are no briefs to consider, persuasive arguments, which would normally be made in addition to those in closing statements, are made to the arbitrator by the company and union members of the board. In one termination case, a board member was able to change the arbitrator's mind by arguing the case from a different perspective than that presented by the company advocate.

At Pan Am, the outcome of a case following the regular arbitration procedure has never been changed as a result of an executive session. This may be because the majority of arbitrators prepared their written decisions before the executive session.[2]

BENCH DECISION

One of the major advantages of the expedited grievance procedure is the speed with which decisions are made. This is especially important in discharge cases. If the grievant is returned to work, the company's economic liability is vastly reduced; if not, the grievant is relieved of the emotional turmoil and economic uncertainties much sooner.

Flight attendants at Pan Am have encountered some shockingly

---

2. For a report on this study, done in 1985 by the National Academy of Arbitrators (NAA), *see* Krislov, *Arbitration 1985: Law and Practice*, NAA PROC. 38, app. B.I (1986).

long delays in receiving decisions made through the regular grievance procedure, although the union contract calls for the arbitrator
to make a decision within sixty days of the conclusion of the hearing
or the receipt of briefs. In one discharge case, despite repeated
urging from both the company and the union board members, a
decision was not issued until more than ten months after briefs were
filed.[3] In that case, the arbitrator returned the grievant to work *with
full back pay.*

Nonprecedential Decision and No Written Opinion

Although the expedited procedure calls for no opinions, in about
half the cases the arbitrator has written an opinion explaining the
reasons for his or her decision. Pan Am has found this very helpful
and instructive for the handling of future cases.

Undoubtedly, it is frustrating for both parties not to be able to
cite decisions and opinions favorable to them, particularly when the
arbitrator's language includes a "quotable quote" that could serve to
resolve future disputes. The parties are not willing to allow precedent
to be set, however, since the chance of error is larger in such decisions
because there are no briefs or transcripts.

Present and Future Assessment

Since the inception of the procedure in 1985, two-thirds of the cases
presented to field boards have been heard in expedited arbitration.
The procedure has worked well for both the union and company,
and expedited arbitration procedures will likely be adopted throughout the airline industry.

In 1983, members of the National Academy of Arbitrators were
requested to respond to a questionnaire prepared by the academy
on expedited arbitration. Of the 206 responses received, 122 of the
arbitrators had some experience with it. Overall, the responses supported the conclusion that expedited arbitration has become a valuable addition to dispute resolution by reducing costs "without a

---

3. Briefs were not filed until approximately four months after the conclusion of the hearing.

similar reduction in the quality of justice dispensed."[4] That has certainly been the experience at Pan Am.

Another way to cut costs would be to reduce the number of board members. Two board members from each side, plus an arbitrator, is ideal. Pan Am normally appoints one person from the operating department and one from labor relations; if one person lacks expertise in a certain area, the other usually has it. Board members serve to educate the arbitrator regarding the practice between the parties and can follow up on points the advocate may have missed. During executive session, they can point out errors of fact that the arbitrator may have made or persuade the arbitrator to modify his or her view of the case. (The advantages of this tripartite arrangement seem clear. Yet in a 1983 survey by the National Academy of Arbitrators of its membership, two-thirds of the respondents thought that tripartite arbitration was not worth the expense and delay it might cause.[5])

A compromise method of reducing costs could be to use three-member boards. If three-member boards were used, each party could utilize a board member who not only was persuasive but also familiar with the operation of the airline. Parties could agree to have three-member boards on an experimental basis, either for a fixed period of time or until either party objected. Complex cases could even have five-member boards at the request of either party. This would make the procedure more efficient without causing detriment to either party. If three-member boards were successful in expedited arbitration, they could be used in the regular grievance process, thus greatly improving the efficiency of grievance procedures throughout the airline industry.

---

4. For a report of the survey, *see* Peck, *Arbitration 1985: Law and Practice*, NAA Proc. 38, app. B.II (1986).

5. Krislov, *supra* note 2.

The Varieties of Airline System Boards: A Neutral's Perspective

Charles M. Rehmus

Although tripartite arbitration boards were used by industries such as local transit well before 1926, the Railway Labor Act was the first legislated system of grievance arbitration that provided for partisan representatives to sit with and guide the neutral referees. In those days it was assumed by railroad advocates that the parties' interests were so vital and the neutrals so inexperienced that partisan board members were essential to guide the referees. Fortunately, the air transport industry and its unions avoided section 205 of the amended RLA and evolved their own procedures for interpretation and enforcement of their systemwide agreements. They did, however, adopt the tripartite system board procedure and, almost without exception, have insisted on using it for almost fifty years.

Interestingly, this is not because, either then or now, the National Mediation Board cared whether the airline industry maintained tripartitism or, like most outside industry, relied on arbitration by a single neutral referee. Rather, the Board's sole interest, as its members have said and demonstrated repeatedly, has been that minor disputes be settled peacefully. As long as harmony prevails, the Board does not insist that the parties select neutrals it nominates and appoints or care if they choose their own. The Board does not care how many people sign the arbitration award as long as it is binding and enforceable. Some arbitrators have characterized airline system boards as simple persistence in a bad habit, but an industry that has coped with the immense changes resulting from deregulation could have changed its structure for handling grievances had it wanted to. I conclude that tripartite system boards of adjustment have been maintained in the air transport industry because the parties prefer them.

Practices and Procedures

The next decade, however, will bring increasing experimentation and divergence from what twenty years ago was an almost uniform use of four- and then five-member boards. There have already been dramatic departures from the use of these boards. Pan Am's relationships with ALPA, FEIA, and the TWU illustrate the classic model for how boards work. At the systemwide level, all grievances are heard initially by the four-member board. The case is reheard by the five-member board only if the four-member board formally deadlocks. At one time United, including both its pilot and flight attendant boards, followed this practice and was often successful in settling at the four-member level. But about fifteen years ago United eliminated four-member hearings and went to initial hearings at the five-member level. Much the same evolution has taken place between American and the Allied Pilots Association, so that all their system board hearings are now being initiated at the five-member level. Northwest still uses five-member boards with ALPA but only three-member boards with the IAM. Republic, however, uses five-member boards with the IAM but only three-member boards with FEIA and ALEA. PSA and the Teamsters have eliminated boards entirely and use a single neutral arbitrator. Moreover, in some relationships, as at Alaska Airlines, the parties use boards in some cases but waive them in others.

Practices among the boards are equally varied. In some situations, as on United's and TWA's pilot boards, the partisan members are usually scrupulous in being no more familiar with the grievance than is the referee and attempt to limit their advance knowledge to the submission. This would appear to be the less common practice, however. Neutrals are recurrently troubled by board members who lead witnesses or, perhaps even more serious, testify regarding controverted, important facts. Such testimony may encourage what most neutrals consider the greatest potential evil of system boards: "clarification" or "supplementation" of the factual record by fellow board members during executive sessions. Fortunately, this is uncommon, but when it occurs the proceeding can take on something of the character of a rigged award, sometimes aiding and at other times hurting the side that interpolated the supposed facts. The integrity of system boards of adjustment, of arbitrators, and of the arbitration process itself is threatened whenever this occurs.

EXECUTIVE SESSIONS

Executive sessions themselves are subject to major variations. In some cases they amount to little more than a perfunctory meeting at the close of the hearing in which the partisans merely ask the referee to send them an opinion and award that for all practical purposes will be final. In these cases, one wonders why the parties wish to incur the additional expense for the time of their appointees.

Other boards insist on having a working executive session after a delay to permit time for study of the transcript, exhibits, and briefs. They want the referee to arrive if not precisely with a vacant mind at least with nothing indelible inscribed on it. This time and expense can be worthwhile if the case is close and difficult but may be wasteful otherwise. Finally, some boards agree to have the neutral arrive at the executive session with a decision already *in petto* or even literally in briefcase. Probably the most sensible practice, one followed by quite a few boards, is to decide how much the partisan board members will participate after they know the importance and complexity of the case and, if the neutral is a stranger, how he or she appears to react to it.

Issues that Need Consideration

There are numerous dangers that must be guarded against in the tripartite system board procedure. In addition to the problems mentioned above, another is that the referee becomes "mesmerized," as arbitrator Sylvester Garrett once characterized it. This occurs when there is a great disparity in experience and articulateness among the partisan representatives. In close cases in which effective opposition is lacking, the persuasive partisans may unfairly swing the balance to their side. Referees must constantly remind themselves that, just as in collective bargaining, the force and enthusiasm with which an advocate or a fellow board member espouses a view or a proposed solution does not necessarily reflect its worthiness.

Overall, neutrals should moderate their criticism of tripartite arbitration panels. Parties who remain committed to them apparently do not totally share our confidence in our own expertise. They are willing to accept the delays and increased costs associated with tripartite boards in return for the greater confidence it gives them in both the process and its outcome.

A possible approach in the future would be to abandon tripartite boards in discipline or discharge cases and use them only for cases involving other issues. Although discipline cases are important to individual grievants, they rarely have any substantial impact on the parties' institutional interests. Equally important, they are common, so the financial savings resulting from arbitration by a single neutral referee would be significant. Finally, in discipline cases board members rarely enhance the neutral's understanding of the background facts or issues involved—except through the unethical communication referred to earlier.

There is another kind of case, usually though not invariably disciplinary in nature, in which airline labor and management should abandon tripartite boards altogether. In these cases, the parties may know or suspect that the union's duty of fair representation is involved. Such cases are potentially difficult and costly enough without worsening the situation because grievants and their attorneys suspect, with or without foundation, that the partisan influence on the referee in executive session may be invidious to their interests. At the very least, in duty of fair representation cases grievants and their attorneys should be consulted and perhaps decide whether they prefer a board or a single neutral arbitrator. The lack of this kind of consideration has been raised so many times in subsequent litigation that the parties should be pessimistic about tripartite solutions to duty of fair representation problems.

In contrast, in cases involving contract interpretation or operating rules, the parties' institutional interests are involved. Board members can be of inestimable value in these cases in assisting the arbitrator's understanding of the underlying shoals and reefs. They sometimes suggest and help create compromise settlements that would at best be dangerous and often beyond the appropriate remedial range of a lone neutral. In such cases, grievance arbitration can become akin to negotiations or interest arbitration in which partisan participation is the sine qua non. Settlements of this kind illustrate the virtues of system boards of adjustment at their best.

Part 7
Alcohol and Drugs in Airline Operations

Rehabilitation and Discipline: An Industry View

Thomas R. Miller
Susan M. Oliver

Alcohol and drug use in American industry is an issue that commands a steady stream of headlines in the press and an ever-increasing number of cases for labor arbitrators and the courts. The statistics are staggering. Federal experts estimate that between 10 and 23 percent of all workers in the United States use function-impairing drugs on the job. The National Institute on Drug Abuse estimates that drug and alcohol abuse on the job costs American industry $100 billion a year in lost productivity through absenteeism, sick leave, accidents, and thefts.[1] Moreover, substance abusers expose employers to additional liabilities.[2]

---

1. NATIONAL INSTITUTE ON DRUG ABUSE, DRUGS IN THE WORKPLACE (1986).

2. *See, e.g.,* Pittard v. Four Seasons Motor Inn, 688 P.2d 333 (N.M. Ct. App. 1984) (employer liable for failure to test and remove identifiable drug abusers from positions when the employees present a potential danger to the public or other workers); G & H Equipment Co. v. Alexander, 533 S.W.2d 872 (Tex. Civ. App. 1976) (employer liable for injuries to third parties as a result of intoxicated employee's auto accident); Colwell v. Oatman, 510 P.2d 464 (Colo. App. 1973) (employer liable for negligent hiring when intoxicated employee could not physically perform the work and injured another employee); Otis Eng'g Corp. v. Clark, 668 S.W.2d 307 (Tex. 1983) (employer liable for negligent supervision when employee who was sent home because he appeared intoxicated killed himself and several others in an auto accident); Brocket v. Kitchen Boyd Motor Co., 264 Cal. App. 2d 69 (1968) (employer liable for negligent supervision); Microwave, Inc. v.

The scope of the problem is aptly described by Peter Bensinger, president of the consulting firm of Bensinger, DuPont and Associates, and former administrator of the United States Drug Enforcement Administration: "With 22 million marijuana users, 8 million current cocaine users, and over 10 million Americans using prescription drugs without an appropriate medical prescription, the workplace is literally riddled with substance abusers, both on and off the job."[3]

Clearly, the transportation industry is not immune to the effects of alcohol and drugs in the workplace. Transportation accidents are one of the most serious manifestations of the alcohol and drug abuse problem in our society, as the following examples illustrate:

■ The National Transportation Safety Board attributes a 1983 accident involving a part 135 air carrier to illegal drug abuse. Two crew members died when a cargo flight crash-landed at Newark Airport. Autopsies showed that the pilot had been smoking marijuana, possibly while flying.[4]

■ In March 1985, an air traffic controller who had been injecting 3 grams of cocaine a day at work put a DC–10 jumbo jet on a collision course with a private plane. Fortunately, the pilots were able to avert disaster. At the last minute, the smaller aircraft made an emergency landing.[5]

Workers Compensation Appeals Bd., 45 Cal. Comp. Cases 125 (1980) (employer liable for permanent, total disability from brain damage caused by alcoholism induced by tension at work).

Three passengers involved in a commuter train collision on December 10, 1986, claimed $5 million in damages against the Southeastern Pennsylvania Transportation Authority and its three operating unions for failing to prevent drug use by the train crew. The engineer of one train and a conductor on the other tested positive for marijuana, and a third conductor tested positive for marijuana. Snitow v. Southeastern Pa. Transp. Auth., C.A. No. 4815 (Phila. Ct. C.P., filed Jan. 30, 1987).

3. BNA, ALCOHOL AND DRUGS IN THE WORKPLACE: COSTS, CONTROLS AND CONTROVERSIES 126 (1986).

4. NATIONAL TRANSPORTATION SAFETY BOARD (NTSB) ACCIDENT REPORT, NTSB AAR 84–11 (Aug. 7, 1984). *See also* Castro, *Battling the Enemy Within*, TIME, Mar. 17, 1986, at 52.

5. *Id.*

■ In a March 1986 safety study by the National Transportation Safety Board, the board's records revealed that during the preceding four-year period alone, the board had investigated eighteen railroad accidents in which alcohol or other drugs were either a contributing factor or a primary cause. The board's records further indicated that approximately 10 percent of all fatal general aviation accidents involve alcohol, as do approximately 7 to 8 percent of all fatal commuter/air taxi crashes.[6]

■ As recently as January 4, 1987, an Amtrak passenger train and three Conrail locomotives collided near Baltimore, resulting in the deaths of 16 passengers and injuries to 170 others. Mandatory drug tests, which are required by the Federal Railroad Administration following a serious train accident, showed that the two Conrail personnel responsible had residues of marijuana in their systems. Although drug use has not been determined to be the cause of the accident, Amtrak officials have put the blame on violation of operating rules by the Conrail crew.[7]

Although no accidents attributable to alcohol or other drugs have involved a commercial air carrier certificated under part 121, the facts suggest that the possibility exists.[8] The findings of a newspaper survey conducted in November 1986 by the *Pittsburgh Press* of seventeen drug treatment clinics across the country revealed that in the

6. NTSB SAFETY STUDY, NTSB/SS–86/01 (Mar. 28, 1986); *see also* NTSB SAFETY STUDY, STATISTICAL REVIEW OF ALCOHOL-INVOLVED AVIATION ACCIDENTS, NTSB/SS–84/03 (Mar. 1, 1984).

7. Daily Lab. Rep. (BNA), No. 14, at A–10 (Jan. 22, 1987). In February 1986, federal regulations applicable to the railroad industry were implemented that mandated, among other things, drug testing of rail crews following a major train accident. 49 C.F.R. pt. 219 & pts. 212, 217, 219, & 225, as amended.

8. Based on NTSB records dating to 1964, there has been no instance in which a fatally injured pilot operating a U.S.-certificated air carrier in scheduled service under 14 C.F.R. 121 has tested positive on a blood alcohol test. In 1977, a Japan Air Lines cargo airplane crashed in Anchorage, Alaska, killing all five crew members. Toxicological tests on the pilot revealed a blood alcohol content of 0.21 percent. Although this accident occurred in the United States, Japan Air is a foreign carrier and is therefore not counted as a "U.S.-certificated" carrier. NTSB SAFETY STUDY, STATISTICAL REVIEW OF ALCOHOL-INVOLVED AVIATION ACCIDENTS, *supra* note 6.

period 1984–86, sixty airline pilots from at least ten different carriers either had received or were receiving treatment for cocaine addiction. The newspaper noted that the total may have been higher because many clinics surveyed refused to disclose publicly the number of pilots they treated or to name the pilots' employers.

An alcohol- or drug-related catastrophe in the commercial airline industry could take a far greater toll than an accident in other forms of transportation. A single domestic air disaster can claim as many as 275 lives and result in immense liabilities for the carriers involved. Settlements in the 1982 Air Florida crash at Washington National Airport averaged more than $800,000 per passenger.[9]

The airline industry recognizes the pervasive threat of alcohol and drug use, as evident from the comments of the Air Transport Association to the FAA on the subject of the FAA's proposed rules for the control of drug and alcohol use for people engaged in commercial and general aviation activities: "We know that in the general population, drug use occurs in approximately 10% of the adult population. There is no reason to believe that airline employees are somehow immunized from this problem."[10] As Elizabeth Dole, Secretary of Transportation in the Reagan administration, made clear in a statement on drug abuse initiatives in transportation issued on January 21, 1987: "When it comes to drug use in transportation, there can be no compromise. Transportation affects tens of millions of Americans every day. Nowhere does the private choice to use drugs have more devastating public consequence than on our nation's roads, rails, water and airways."

Despite the high visibility of the issue of alcohol and drugs in the workplace and a clear recognition among employers in United States industry that decisive action must be taken, employers differ greatly in their proposed solutions. Much of the current debate is focused on what approach should be taken when a substance abuser is identified. Employers must choose between discipline and rehabilitation

---

9. Brief of the Air Transport Association and the Airline Industrial Relations Conference, at 2, as amici curiae supporting certiorari, Northwest Airlines v. ALPA, No. 86–1548, *sub nom.* Northwest v. ALPA, 808 F.2d 76 (D.C. Cir. 1987).

10. Control of Drug and Alcohol Use for Personnel Engaged in Commercial and General Aviation Activities, In re Docket No. 125148, Notice No. 86–20. Comments of ATA before the DOT at 6–7 (Feb. 23, 1987).

or elect a combination of both. Employers must balance their legal obligations to maintain a safe workplace with their desire to help employees receive treatment and return to work.

The question of how to achieve the proper balance between a carrier's obligation to maintain rigorous safety requirements and the laudatory goal of returning rehabilitated employees to their past positions has been the focus of several arbitration and court decisions in recent years. This issue arose in a case involving a first officer who was discharged for co-piloting a Northwest jet while under the influence of alcohol.[11] The pilot's discharge was subsequently challenged in a system board hearing chaired by arbitrator George Nicolau. Nicolau concluded that the offenses committed by the pilot were serious. Nicolau reasoned, however, that the offenses were the "unavoidable consequence of the illness of alcoholism," which had subsequently been shown to be successfully treated. Nicolau ordered the pilot reinstated subject to requalification under the FAA's nonmonitoring procedure, Federal Air Regulation section 67.13 (d)(1)(i)(c). The decision was later appealed by Northwest.

On review by the federal district court, the judge overturned the system board's decision and ruled that Nicolau had exceeded his jurisdictional authority and had issued an award that was contrary to public policy.[12]

On appeal by ALPA to the District of Columbia Circuit Court, the circuit court reversed the lower court decision and upheld Nicolau's reinstatement order.[13] Contrary to the lower court's opinion, the circuit court held that the safety issues presented in the system board hearing were presumptively arbitrable and found no violation of public policy in the arbitrator's decision.

Northwest applied to the United States Supreme Court for a stay of the District of Columbia Circuit Court's decision. On February 20, 1987, the Supreme Court ordered the stay of the decision of the circuit court pending the timely filing and disposition of a petition for a writ of certiorari. A petition was subsequently filed by Northwest on March 26, 1987, and a certiorari conference was held on

---

11. Northwest v. ALPA, Pilot System Board Case No. 405–82 (Oct. 29, 1984).

12. Northwest v. ALPA, 633 F. Supp. 779 (D.D.C. 1985).

13. Northwest v. ALPA, 808 F.2d 76 (D.C. Cir. 1987).

May 14, 1987. To date, no decision has been made by the Court as to whether review will be granted or denied.[14]

Another case involving a Northwest pilot who was discharged for violating the airline's alcohol policies had a different result. It was decided by a system board chaired by arbitrator Thomas F. Carey.[15] Contrary to arbitrator Nicolau's award, Carey upheld the airline's actions and sustained the pilot's discharge. In determining that the company's actions were proper, Carey specifically considered Nicolau's decision but declined to consider Nicolau's award a binding precedent.

Carey concluded that he would be acting beyond his jurisdictional authority to hold the alcoholic pilot to a different standard than his nonalcoholic peers if a proven violation of the twenty-four-hour drinking rule (preventing drinking within twenty-four hours of flight time) was persuasively established in the record. Given such a find-

---

14. Whether or not Northwest's petition for certiorari is granted, the Supreme Court addressed the public policy issue, albeit in a non-RLA context, in Misco, Inc. v. United Paperworkers Int'l Union, 108 S. Ct. 364 (1987). The Supreme Court found that the Fifth Circuit had erred in setting aside an arbitrator's award that had reinstated an individual who had used marijuana in his position as an equipment operator on the ground that the arbitration award was contrary to clear public policy. The Supreme Court held that a court's refusal to enforce an arbitrator's interpretation of a collective bargaining agreement is limited to situations in which the contract as interpreted would violate some explicit public policy that is well defined and dominant and can be determined by deference to laws and legal precedents, not from considerations of supposed public interests. *Cf.* E.I. DuPont de Nemours v. Grasselli, 790 F.2d 611 (7th Cir. 1986), *cert. denied*, 107 S. Ct. 186 (1986) (arbitrator's award that reinstated discharged employee who had experienced mental breakdown that led him to attack his supervisor and an operator, and attempt to do further damage, did not violate public policy of providing safe working environment); United States Postal Serv. v. American Postal Workers Union, 736 F.2d 822 (1st Cir. 1984) (arbitrator's award requiring the postal service to reinstate an employee who had been convicted of embezzling postal funds violated public policy and was unenforceable); S.D. Warren Co. v. United Paper Workers Int'l Union, 815 F.2d 178 (1st Cir. 1987) (arbitrator's award reinstating employees who were fired for selling marijuana to an undercover police officer on company property vacated as violating well-defined public policy against the use of drugs in the workplace).

15. Northwest v. ALPA, Pilot System Board Case No. 955–84 (Mar. 25, 1987).

ing, Carey found neither a basis nor a need to address issues of public policy.

A third case involving a Delta pilot discharged for violating an airline's alcohol policies, including operating an aircraft while under the influence of alcohol, was decided by arbitrator Mark Kahn.[16] Like the aforementioned decision by Nicolau, Kahn ordered the pilot reinstated. In contrast to Nicolau's opinion, however, which found the pilot's offenses the "unavoidable result of the alcoholism," Kahn's decision was predicated on a finding of disparate treatment and a determination that Delta had failed to communicate its alcohol policy effectively to its pilots.

Although the pilot's conduct in operating an aircraft while under the influence of alcohol was found to be "egregious," Kahn recognized the pilot's nineteen-year record of satisfactory service with the company and reinstated him without back pay or other benefits but with all costs of rehabilitation to be borne by the company on the same basis as if the pilot had not been discharged and had accepted the rehabilitation option.

Delta filed suit on February 12, 1987, in an effort to overturn Kahn's award. On review by the federal district court, the judge overturned the system board's decision and ruled that Kahn's award was contrary to public policy.[17] An appeal of this decision has been filed by ALPA and is currently pending before the Fifth Circuit.

The reinstatement of pilots who have flown passenger aircraft while intoxicated undermines carriers' efforts to safeguard the flying public. To permit intoxicated pilots to escape discharge for such egregious conduct renders meaningless the effectiveness of a carrier's disciplinary policies. It also sends a message to all employees that even the most flagrant violations of a carrier's alcohol and drug rules may not result in discharge.

Moreover, such arbitration decisions destroy carriers' legitimate efforts to ensure compliance with their statutory obligations to operate with the "highest standards of safety in the interests of the traveling public" through the establishment of safety rules and standards that are "higher" than the FAA's minimum requirements.

The need to preserve a carrier's independence in complying with federal safety policies was underscored by James Landry, senior vice

---

16. Delta v. ALPA, Pilot System Board Case No. 1–85 (Jan. 31, 1987).
17. Delta v. ALPA, C.A. No. C87–239 (N.D. Ga., Sept. 30, 1987).

president and general counsel for the Air Transport Association, in hearings in 1987 before the House Subcommittee on Government and Transportation and the Senate Committee on Commerce, Science and Transportation. Landry spoke of the danger of considering rehabilitation "carte blanche" for any employee who has violated a company safety rule:

> [A] fundamental conflict can arise between safety and rehabilitation: public policy—as reflected in the statutory requirement that airlines operate with the highest possible degree of safety—would dictate that few rehabilitated employees be entrusted with the lives of the flying public. While the goal of rehabilitation is to return employees to their prior positions as productive members of society, *we believe that when the interests of public safety conflict with the interests of individual employees, public policy absolutely requires that the concern for safety prevail....The promotion of safety requires that carriers have the ability to enforce their rules so that standards remain as high as possible.*[18]

In lieu of legislative action specifically addressing the issue, it is clear that the proper balance to be struck between a carrier's duty to ensure public safety and its desire to protect the interests of employees undergoing rehabilitation must await resolution by the United States Supreme Court.

Management and Labor Initiatives

An extensive array of approaches is available to employers to combat the problems of alcohol and drugs. Rarely is one approach used to the exclusion of others. Approaches include such aggressive efforts as undercover investigations by company security and outside law enforcement personnel, as well as searches of employees' lockers, cars, and the like. General Motors used such techniques in 1986 to arrest two hundred employees at its plants on drug-related charges.

Another approach is alcohol and drug testing. In the 1970s, a new front was opened up in the battle against substance abuse when low-

---

18. *Proposed Amendments to the FAA and Federal Railroad Safety Act Concerning Alcohol and Drugs in the Airline and Railroad Industries: Hearings Before the Subcomm. on Commerce, Science and Transportation,* 100th Cong., 1st Sess. (1987) (testimony of James Landry, Senior Vice President and General Counsel, ATA) (emphasis added).

cost scientific processes that detect drugs by urinalysis were manufactured and marketed. Today, drug tests are being used by thousands of employers in the United States.[19] This approach has, no doubt, received additional impetus as a result of the success of the Department of Defense's testing program to curb drug use by uniformed personnel[20] and the recommendations of the president's Commission on Organized Crime, which in 1986 endorsed drug-testing programs for all employers, including those in the private sector.[21]

Alcohol and drug testing can be companywide or directed at a particular group, and the gamut of testing can include any or all of the following:

preemployment screening;
periodic testing during physical examinations;
testing following accidents or injuries;
testing based on a reasonable suspicion that the employee has used alcohol or drugs in violation of company policy; and
random testing.

Although an employer's use of such tests is controversial, existing data demonstrate that testing programs can dramatically reduce accidents and injuries in the workplace:

■ The Southern Pacific Railroad reported a 70 percent reduction in accidents and injuries attributed to human error after beginning drug and alcohol screening.[22]

---

19. BNA, *supra* note 3, at 27.
20. The testing of uniformed military personnel has shown that increased testing, including at random, is an effective deterrent to substance abuse. A 1985 survey conducted by the Research Triangle Institute of the military's testing program showed very positive results. The survey indicated that in 1985, 6.5 percent of military personnel had used marijuana the previous month as compared to 16 percent in the previous month of 1982. With respect to the use of any drug, including marijuana, during the prior month, the 1985 survey demonstrated a rate of 9 percent among the same group. This figure was significantly lower than in 1982 (19 percent) and in 1980 (27 percent). T.J. DONEGAN & R.T. ANGAROLA, 1 EMPLOYEE TESTING AND THE LAW (1986).
21. PRESIDENT'S COMMISSION ON ORGANIZED CRIME, AMERICA'S HABIT: DRUG ABUSE, DRUG TRAFFICKING AND ORGANIZED CRIME 452 (Mar. 3, 1986).
22. EMPLOYEE REL. UPDATE (Nov. 1986).

■ The Georgia Power Company reported a reduction in the accident rate at its Vogtle nuclear power project from 5.4 per 200,000 labor hours in 1981, the year it began drug screening, to 0.49 in 1985.[23]

■ The Federal Railroad Administration reported that the railroad industry's first year of experience under the mandatory postaccident testing regulation had resulted in a reduction from 16 to 5 percent the number of employees who tested positive for either alcohol or drugs, as compared with the relatively high rate of positive readings in tests and autopsies prior to testing.[24] John Riley, a federal railroad administrator, stated that the results of the railroad industry's first year of experience "show, without question, that the testing program is having a deterrent effect."[25]

An innovative approach to combating alcohol and drug problems is to refer employees to evaluation and treatment under the auspices of an employee assistance program. These programs are in keeping with the predominant belief within United States industry that it is beneficial and cost effective to promote the early referral of employees with alcohol or drug problems into evaluation and treatment.[26]

In addition to employee assistance programs sponsored by individual employers, several industrywide programs have been established. The Federal Railroad Administration has been working cooperatively with management and labor in the railway industry on a voluntary educational effort, Operation Red Block, which is designed to reduce tolerance among nonusers of alcohol and drugs and to identify and refer employees with substance abuse problems to treatment before their problems pose threats to safety. Workers who suspect that a co-worker has an alcohol or drug problem can advise the union's local prevention team, which will then request that the individual suspected of having the problem meet with a counselor from the employee assistance program and, if appropriate,

23. Washington Post, May 5, 1986, at B8.

24. Daily Lab. Rep. (BNA), No. 68, at A–12 (Apr. 10, 1987).

25. *Railroad Drug Test*, Washington Post, Feb. 19, 1987.

26. BNA, EMPLOYEE ASSISTANCE PROGRAMS: BENEFITS, PROBLEMS AND PROSPECTS (1987).

enroll in a rehabilitation program. Operation Red Block was initiated by the Union Pacific Railroad and its labor groups in 1983 and has proven to be a great success. Nearly half the nation's major railroads have now instituted the program.[27]

A similar voluntary program, HIMS, which was developed in 1975, is used in the airline industry for cockpit crew members represented by ALPA. Based on a federally funded project entitled the Human Intervention and Motivation Study, the HIMS program relies on education, peer identification, treatment, and posttreatment monitoring by employees and employer representatives to encourage abstinence by alcoholic pilots. Under the program, pilots with substance abuse problems are identified by co-workers and encouraged to enter rehabilitation. Pilots who enter treatment are taken off active duty and placed on sick leave. Once rehabilitation has been completed, the pilots are returned to work and monitored for a minimum of two years. More than six hundred pilots have been identified, treated for alcoholism, and resumed flying under the program. ALPA claims a long-term success rate of 93 percent.[28]

Government Initiatives

In response to the increasingly visible problem of substance abuse in the workplace, the federal government has taken a proactive approach in addressing the problem. On February 1, 1986, regulations on alcohol and drug abuse covering the nation's 200,000 railroad employees were implemented by the Federal Railroad Administration.[29] These regulations, in addition to prohibiting on-duty alcohol and drug use, mandate preemployment drug screening and postaccident alcohol and drug testing for employees involved in major rail accidents. The regulations also authorize toxicological testing when there is reason to suspect impairment.[30]

---

27. *Proposed Drug-Testing Legislation (S. 356/362): Hearings Before the Senate Judiciary Comm.*, 100 Cong., 1st Sess. 9 (1987) (testimony of Elizabeth H. Dole).

28. *Id.* at 98 (testimony of Capt. Richard Stone, Executive Chairman for Aeromedical Research).

29. 49 C.F.R. pt. 219 & 212, 217, 219, & 225, as amended.

30. The Federal Railroad Administration's regulations have been challenged by four union groups in *Railway Labor Executives' Ass'n v. Dole*, No.

Although there is currently no comparable broad government regulation of the airlines regarding substance abuse, on April 9, 1986, the FAA amended its rules relating to the consumption of alcoholic beverages by crew members before or during flights.[31] These amendments require crew members to submit to blood alcohol tests requested by local law enforcement officials if there is a "reasonable basis" for believing that crew members may have unlawfully used alcohol. Failure to submit to the test is grounds for suspension, revocation of a certificate or rating, or civil penalty. Tests must be taken within four hours after acting or attempting to act in the capacity of a crew member. Current FAA rules on alcohol consumption prohibit any person from acting in the capacity of a crew member if (1) there is a blood alcohol level of .04 percent or higher by weight; (2) alcohol has been consumed within the previous eight hours; or (3) any drug has been used that negatively affects the crew member's faculties.[32]

In the fall of 1986, President Ronald Reagan and Congress joined together in a call for a "drug-free" America. On September 15, 1986, Reagan issued Executive Order 12564, entitled "Drug Free Federal Workplace," which announced a program of mandatory drug testing for federal employees in "sensitive" positions whose job responsi-

---

85-2891 (1986), which is currently pending before the Ninth Circuit Court of Appeals. Prior to this appeal, a temporary restraining order had been issued by the district court halting implementation of the regulations. On November 26, 1985, however, Judge Legge of the U.S. District Court for Northern California, granted the government's motion for summary judgment and dissolved the temporary restraining order. Characterizing the issue before him as one of individual rights versus the public interest in transportation and employee safety, Judge Legge found the Federal Railroad Administration's regulations to be a proper exercise of government authority to protect public and employee safety, and he construed applicable case law as allowing employee blood tests and warrantless searches of employees in such heavily regulated industries as the railroads. The regulations were set to take effect January 6, 1986, but the Ninth Circuit, on January 3, 1986, by a two-to-one vote, imposed a temporary stay pending its consideration of the union's appeal. Upon emergency request by the Reagan administration, the U.S. Supreme Court, on January 27, 1986, set aside the lower court's stay, thereby allowing the regulations to be placed into effect while their validity is being challenged before the Ninth Circuit. Daily Lab. Rep. (BNA) at A–8 (Nov. 27, 1985), A–7 (Jan. 8, 1986), A–4 (Jan. 28, 1986).
    31. 14 C.F.R. pts. 61, 63, & 91, as amended.
    32. 14 C.F.R. § 91.11.

bilities involve public safety, including personnel in law enforcement, public health and safety, and air traffic control.[33] Congress subsequently passed, and the president signed, the Anti-drug Abuse Act of 1986, which launched a major attack against substance abuse through increased law enforcement efforts and enhanced awareness programs.[34]

On December 4, 1986, the FAA published an Advance Notice of Proposed Rule Making (ANPRM),[35] which invited "comments on drug and alcohol abuse by personnel in the aviation industry and the options available for regulatory or other actions in the interest of aviation safety." In comments filed with the FAA by the Air Transport Association in response to the ANPRM, the Air Transport Association urged the enactment of regulations that would require each part 121 and part 135 carrier to develop a comprehensive written program designed to promote a drug- and alcohol-free workplace. Covered employees would include certificated and noncertificated crew members, mechanics, and any other employees whose duties affect the safety of aircraft operations.

On January 21, 1987, Secretary of Transportation Elizabeth Dole announced several key drug abuse initiatives she planned to undertake to "ensure the safe passage of the travelling public." Pursuant to existing statutes and Reagan's September 1986 executive order, Dole proposed a comprehensive drug-testing program for DOT employees in critical safety or security positions, which included railroad, truck, aviation, and highway inspectors and air traffic controllers. Tests would be given prior to employment, at random thereafter, and on the basis of reasonable suspicion, or following an accident or unsafe practices. Additionally, individuals whose jobs required periodic medical examinations would be routinely tested as part of the examination. All other DOT employees would be subject to testing following an accident or if there was reasonable suspicion of impairment from alcohol or drugs. Testing under this program began in September 1987.

---

33. On September 16, 1986, the day after Reagan issued Executive Order 12564, the National Treasury Employees Union filed suit against Reagan seeking an injunction halting the mandatory drug-testing plan for federal employees. The government moved to dismiss the action; however, the government's motion was denied. 651 F. Supp. 1199 (E.D. La. 1987).

34. Pub. L. No. 99–570 (Oct. 27, 1986).

35. 14 C.F.R. pt. 91 (Docket No. 25148, Notice No. 86–20, 1986).

For airline pilots and crew and other employees directly responsible for the safety of flight operations, Dole announced her intent to promulgate regulations that would require preemployment, postaccident, reasonable suspicion, and random drug testing. Dole's proposed regulations would also require airline pilots to submit to periodic testing during their annual physical examinations.

On the legislative front, Senator John Danforth (R-Missouri) and Representative E. Clay Shaw, Jr., (R-Florida) introduced identical bills (S. 356 and H.R. 693) into Congress in 1987 that would amend the Federal Aviation Act to require drug testing, including random testing, for airline employees and amend the Federal Railroad Safety Act to require random testing of all rail workers in positions affecting public safety. Senator Ernest Hollings (D-South Carolina) authored a similar drug-testing proposal (S. 362).

On March 12, 1987, the Senate Commerce Committee approved and sent to the Senate floor comprehensive drug-testing legislation co-sponsored by Senators Danforth and Hollings. This legislation, the Transportation Employee Safety and Rehabilitation Act of 1987, would provide for "testing for the use, without lawful authorization, of alcohol or controlled substances by the operators of aircraft, railroads and commercial motor vehicles, and for other purposes."

With respect to the airline industry, the Danforth-Hollings bill would require the secretary of transportation, within twelve months of the bill's enactment, to issue regulations mandating the establishment of testing programs providing for preemployment, periodic recurring, reasonable suspicion, random, and postaccident testing of pilots, crew members, airport security screening personnel, and other airline employees responsible for safety-sensitive functions.

On October 30, 1987, the Senate approved the Danforth-Hollings bill as part of the Passenger Protection Act. The comparable drug-testing bill in the House has not been passed. The Senate drug-testing bill is now scheduled to go to a joint House-Senate conference.

It is clear from the Senate and House committee hearings on the subject that industry employers are split on random testing. The Association of American Railroads and the ATA have expressed support for the principle, whereas the American Bus Association and the American Trucking Association have gone on record as opposing any legislation with a random testing component. Likewise, organized labor is, for the most part, opposed to random testing.

American's Approach

RULES AND POLICIES GOVERNING ALCOHOL AND DRUGS

American Airlines has, for many years, strictly enforced rules pertaining to alcohol and drugs. Under these rules, an employee is subject to discharge for the following:

> reporting to work showing the signs of the use of intoxicants or knowingly permitting another employee to do so; possessing or drinking any intoxicants on company premises at any time, or drinking intoxicants in public while in uniform; or possessing, dispensing, or using drugs, either on or off duty, except in accordance with medical authorization.[36]

There is no requirement that an employee be shown to be "under the influence" or "impaired" to be subject to discharge. Any evidence of intoxicant or drug use is proof of a violation.[37] Enforcement has

---

36. Rules proscribing off-duty use of drugs are coming under increased scrutiny as employees and their representatives claim that off-duty use of drugs is not within an employer's legitimate interest and that there is no reliable way to evaluate the effects of drugs on employees' work performance. Yet in a November 1985 study by the Veterans Administration in conjunction with the Stanford University School of Medicine, ten experienced airplane pilots were tested on a flight simulator both before and twenty-four hours after smoking one marijuana cigarette. The study showed significant carry-over effects of marijuana on all ten pilots' performance, including one instance in which a pilot completely missed the runway on approach even while feeling no effects of the marijuana. Yesavage, Leirir, Denari, & Hollister, *Carry-over Effects of Marijuana Intoxication on Aircraft Pilot Performance: A Preliminary Report*, 142 AM. J. PSYCHIATRY, Nov. 1985, at 11.

37. *See, e.g.*, American Airlines v. TWU Local 512, No. S–21–85 (Eaton, 1986) (urinalysis showing presence of drugs warranted discharge); American Airlines and TWU Local 512, No. M–476–80 (Luskin, 1980) (discharge upheld for drinking one-half can of beer); American Airlines and TWU Local 552, No. SS–45–74 (Stark, 1974) ("rule 26 means what it says and provides for no exceptions, either in terms of amount of alcohol consumed or the employee's prior record of service"); American Airlines and TWU Local 552, No. SS–44–75 (Turkus, 1975) (rule prohibiting the drinking of an intoxicant while on duty, regardless of the amount, is rationally related to carrier's obligation to safeguard the safety and well-being of passengers, crews, and aircraft; discharge upheld).

been accomplished through a variety of means, including alcohol and drug testing, and they have been upheld as reasonable by numerous arbitrators.

Pursuant to the testing policy, the company may direct urinalysis testing and offer blood testing whenever there is reasonable suspicion that an employee is violating American's rules on alcohol and drug use. Reasonable suspicion is based on the following:

> observations of the employee that indicate changed, unusual, or unexplained behavior or appearance, including involvement in an accident or injury that appeared to result from lack of attention or coordination, gross negligence, or otherwise inexplicable causes; any other circumstance supporting a basis for reasonable suspicion.

Should an employee refuse to obey a supervisor's directive to submit to urinalysis testing or to cooperate with an investigation, he or she will be subject to discharge on the basis of gross insubordination.

Once the investigation is completed, the employee will be discharged if the facts substantiate that the employee was in violation of the company's rules.

Admittedly, American's approach is tough.[38] It is intended to be. It is American's policy that the federal statutory mandate to ensure public safety dictates that American strictly enforce alcohol and drug use rules.[39] Additionally, American has concluded that one of the

---

38. American's policy on alcohol and drugs is also communicated to each of the airline's contractors and vendors in prospective purchase orders and in a contractor notification bulletin. Any variance with the company's policy by a contractor or vendor results in denial of access and, in the case of illegal drugs, notification of law enforcement authorities.

39. An airline's obligations to consider passenger safety are imposed by federal law. Congress has directed the administrator of the FAA to give full consideration to the duty of carriers to perform their services "with the highest degree of safety in the public interest." 49 U.S.C. § 1421(b) (Supp. 1987). The courts have recognized this duty. Air East v. NTSB, 512 F.2d 1227 (3d Cir.) *cert. denied*, 423 U.S. 863 (1975); United Air Lines v. Wiener, 355 F.2d 379 (9th Cir.) *cert. dismissed sub nom.* United Air Lines v. United States, 379 U.S. 951 (1964). Airline flight attendant crew members must meet rigorous safety qualifications and training established by the FAA. *See* 14 C.F.R. § 121.391 and 14 C.F.R. § 121.400, *et seq.* Failure of an airline to comply with the provisions of the FAA and regulations issued pursuant to

most powerful weapons in combating alcohol and drug use in its work force is to make it unequivocally clear that substance abuse will not be tolerated.[40]

EMPLOYEE ASSISTANCE PROGRAM

American's management embraces the philosophy that troubled employees should be retained and helped before their job performance or misconduct warrants discipline, their health and safety or the safety of others is affected, or their problem renders them unemployable. It is the company's belief that alcoholism and other forms of chemical dependency are treatable conditions and that early detection and treatment increase the probability of successful rehabilitation. To help employees seeking rehabilitation, American has instituted a comprehensive employee assistance program. All current employees and their dependents and all retired employees of American are eligible.

American's employee assistance program began in the early 1970s amid the heightened public awareness of drug and alcohol problems. In 1971, Marion Sadler, then chairman of the board at American, shocked the airline industry by saying it was time to "pull our heads out of the sand" and treat alcoholism as a disease.[41] That year American became the first major airline to establish a program for the treatment of alcoholism. By 1983, American's alcohol treatment program had rehabilitated more than one thousand employees.

In 1984, a full-scale employee assistance program was initiated with the enthusiastic support of American's senior management. The objectives of the program were to provide

confidential help to employees, retirees, and their dependents through specialists who possessed the experience to assist individuals with alcohol and drug problems;

---

the act can result in both administrative and civil penalties against the carrier. *See* Air East v. NTSB, *supra*, and In re Paris Air Crash, 399 F. Supp. 732, 747–48 (C.D. Cal. 1975).

40. The advantage of communicating a strong position on alcohol and drugs to employees is discussed by Sidney Cohen, M.D., a long-time worker in the field of substance abuse. *Drugs in the Workplace*, 45 J. CLINICAL PSYCHIATRY, Dec. 1984, at 4.

41. The success of American's early alcoholism program is analyzed in Sadler & Horst, *Company/Union Programs for Alcoholics*, 50 HARV. BUS. REV., Sept.–Oct. 1972, at 22.

protection to employees who voluntarily sought help through the program.

The program's evolution has included an increase in the number of full-time EAP professionals from five to seven and an emphasis on a "case management" role for the staff during follow-up and aftercare. There has also been an increased emphasis on educating supervisors to identify potential problems and to recommend the services of the program to employees.

The role of the network of union and nonunion volunteer employee coordinators has also been expanded. Employee volunteers are an important source of program referrals, but, equally important, they provide invaluable support to program participants during the aftercare phase of the program. Many of the volunteers have themselves undergone treatment for alcohol or drug dependency and know firsthand the difficulties of maintaining sobriety.

American has adopted the philosophy endorsed by many of the leaders in the field of alcohol and drug abuse treatment that a firm but empathetic approach should be taken with employees suffering from alcohol and drug dependencies. Borrowing from the experts, American has taken a stronger approach in several key areas.

First, in all cases of active chemical dependency or abuse, the recommendations of the EAP professionals must be followed. Should an employee elect not to follow those recommendations, the employee is placed on an unpaid medical leave of absence until the recommendations are followed. This approach not only promotes a safe airline operation but also provides the necessary incentive for the employee to seek treatment.

Second, employees are afforded only one external rehabilitation program per lifetime reimbursable under the company's health plan. The cap on paid treatment, which may be in-patient, out-patient, or a combination of the two, does not reduce access to the company-sponsored employee assistance program or prevent substance abusers from obtaining treatment more than once. Any treatment costs (except detoxification) incurred after the initial treatment, however, must be at the employee's expense.

Third, follow-up treatment must be a component of the employee's overall treatment plan. Moreover, in cases of drug dependency or abuse, a component of aftercare treatment must include periodic random drug screens conducted by the aftercare facility. The use of periodic drug screens as a component of aftercare provides assistance to the employee by providing an incentive to maintain sobriety.

COEXISTENCE OF DISCIPLINE AND REHABILITATION

From its inception, American's employee assistance program has been viewed as a strategy that is distinct from other approaches the airline uses, including discipline, in the fight to maintain a workplace free from alcohol and drugs. No one approach in isolation is the answer.

An employee's failure in or refusal to use the program is not cause for disciplinary action. Likewise, an employee's use of the program will not jeopardize job security or advancement opportunities. In addition, assistance is kept confidential. Should an employee's job performance continue to be unsatisfactory, however, the employee is subject to discipline for poor job performance or, if alcohol and drug rules have been violated, to immediate discharge. Participation in the employee assistance program does not provide a sanctuary from the disciplinary process.

CONDITIONAL REINSTATEMENT POLICY

The interplay between discipline and rehabilitation is most visible in American's conditional reinstatement policy. In the event that an employee is discharged for violating the rules on alcohol and drug use, the employee *may* be provided a second chance, provided that the employee enters and successfully completes an approved rehabilitation program, including any necessary aftercare treatment.

The conditional reinstatement policy has been in existence since 1983. Under the terms of the original policy, only employees discharged for alcohol violations were eligible for reinstatement. The philosophy was predicated on American's recognition that alcoholism was a treatable disease and that many alcoholic employees were unable or unwilling to admit to their dependency on alcohol until the loss of their job was imminent. American also recognized that providing a second chance to employees who were willing to undergo treatment was mutually beneficial.[42] The policy was expanded in 1985 to cover employees discharged for drug use or possession.

---

42. In general, an employer does not have a legal obligation to give

Discharged employees who wish to be considered for conditional reinstatement must meet a number of prerequisites prior to their return to work. Until then, their status remains that of terminated employees. Employees discharged for being dishonest, dispensing drugs, injuring employees or customers, or damaging company equipment or aircraft are not eligible for conditional reinstatement. Employees returned to work suffer no loss of seniority but do not receive back pay. The period from the date of termination until the commencement of work is treated as a disciplinary suspension.

An employee is not required to pursue conditional reinstatement. Once discharged, an employee has the option of leaving the discharge action unchallenged, challenging the discharge through the applicable grievance procedure, or electing to be considered for conditional reinstatement. All employees who wish to be considered, however, must agree to do the following:

(1) Enter an approved rehabilitation program within thirty days of the incident resulting in termination, successfully complete the program, and demonstrate that an effective aftercare program is being pursued.

(2) Sign the conditional reinstatement agreement within sixty days of termination, which includes signing an undated letter of resignation.

(3) Withdraw all grievances and claims against American relating to the termination.

(4) Participate in an approved aftercare program for up to two years following reinstatement.

(5) Maintain complete abstinence from alcohol or drugs except as authorized by the company's medical department.

(6) Agree to submit to any procedures necessary to confirm compliance with the conditional reinstatement agreement.

(7) Agree that American may implement the undated letter of res-

---

employees who are abusing alcohol or drugs a second chance unless there is a contractual commitment or established past practice of doing so. At least one state, California, requires private employers to permit employees to enter and participate voluntarily in alcohol rehabilitation programs, provided such accommodation does not impose undue hardship on the employer. CAL. LAB. CODE § 1025–28 (1984). This statute does not, however, prohibit an employer from refusing to hire or from discharging individuals whose alcohol use renders them incapable of performing their jobs.

ignation as a result of any failure to comply with any of the conditions set forth in the conditional reinstatement agreement either before or following reinstatement.

Between 1983, when the policy was instituted, and 1987, fifty-six employees have regained their positions. The conditional reinstatement policy appears to be working well, in that the vast majority of these employees have remained substance-free.

COST-BENEFIT ANALYSIS

The cost effectiveness of an employee assistance program "is not a return on investment that shows up on the annual financial report since the costs and returns, like employee productivity, are subjective and not easily quantifiable."[43] This is certainly true in the airline industry, where the costs of accidents are not known until they occur and the hard dollar costs associated with lost or reduced productivity on the job as a result of alcohol, drugs, or serious personal problems are speculative at best. Nevertheless, the cost benefits of an employee assistance program can be significant.

Through cost controls, American has seen the costs of its drug and alcohol rehabilitation program decrease nearly $1,700 per case between 1984 and 1987. The program has also contributed to reducing absenteeism. Absenteeism among program participants decreased 60 percent in the first year of the program and 37 percent in the second year. Savings related to lost time totaled nearly $500,000 for the initial two years of the program alone. In addition, it appears that the program has resulted in less turnover (and associated training costs) and improved job performance.

Equally important, more individuals and families are seeking help. In 1986 nearly 1,200 of American's employees, retirees, and dependents took advantage of the program, an increase of 42 percent over the previous year and an increase of 120 percent since the program began in 1984. Eighty percent of the employees referred to the program in 1984 for alcohol problems are still employed at American. This percentage for alcohol referrals increased to 84 percent in 1985 and to 92 percent in 1986. The retention rate for

---

43. J. SPICER & P. OWEN, FINDING THE BOTTOM LINE: THE COST IMPACT OF EMPLOYEE ASSISTANCE AND CHEMICAL DEPENDENCY TREATMENT PROGRAMS (Hazelden Research Reports, 1985).

employees referred for drug problems has also been very favorable. Eighty percent of those referred for drug problems in 1984 remain employed at the airline. This figure increased to 88 percent in 1985 and to 92 percent in 1986.

Conclusion

The problem of substance abuse in the workplace is a national problem of immense proportion. Although it goes without saying that the goal of every employer is to achieve a "drug-free" workplace, it is also self-evident that the problems of substance abuse will continue for some time. The determination to find an answer to the problem, however, is stronger than ever.

Despite the concerns raised by some that employers will adopt an "either/or" philosophy with respect to disciplinary and rehabilitative approaches, we believe that enlightened employers will not abandon rehabilitation in favor of a purely disciplinary approach. The benefits of rehabilitation for troubled employees are simply too well recognized.

While we believe the great majority of employers are committed to using both disciplinary and rehabilitative approaches, in the interest of public safety, employers must, in our view, retain the right to enforce company policies strictly. For those of us in the transportation industry, where safety is a paramount concern, an employer's right, and we would argue obligation, to enforce company policies in furtherance of the safety of the traveling public is critical.

A Pilot's Perspective on Substance Abuse

Kenneth B. Cooper

ALPA, which was established in 1931, represents more than forty thousand professional crew members flying for forty-three air carriers. ALPA functions not only as a labor organization but also as a professional association of airline pilots which engages in collective bargaining, the administration of labor agreements, and a host of activities related to aviation safety and the flying environment. Combating alcohol abuse among its members became a challenge in the early 1970s. Today, although there is no credible evidence of drug abuse by airline pilots, ALPA is facing up to the challenge presented by the current popular demand for ensuring a drug-free work force, particularly focusing on testing employees, such as airline pilots, in safety-related positions. While meeting this challenge, ALPA continues to defend vigorously those members who are the unfortunate victims of alcoholism and whose careers are jeopardized by disciplinary action resulting from their drinking.

Dealing with Alcoholism among Pilots

ALPA's PROGRAM

By the early 1970s, alcoholism treatment had become relatively straightforward throughout the United States. The techniques used were particularly successful when the workplace was an integral part of treatment. At that time, no systemwide method of providing assistance to pilots with alcohol problems had evolved. Although a few commercial carriers offered alcoholism treatment programs, few, if any, professional pilots availed themselves of their services. The public image problems faced by the pilots' union, the air carriers, and the FAA were powerful dampers in keeping alcoholism a hidden problem.

Although the existence of alcoholism among pilots was persistently denied,[1] alcoholism-related problems frequently surfaced, in the form of excessive absenteeism, declining proficiency, and violation of company rules prohibiting the consumption of alcoholic beverages within a specified period before reporting for duty. It was generally accepted that breach of the no-drinking rules constituted a cardinal offense, and such cases were treated in what has been described as the "straight-forward application of the traditional corrective discipline model."[2] Although some pilots were offered medical disability retirement rather than discharge, virtually all retirement and disability plans excluded benefits for pilots suffering from alcoholism, which was commonly lumped with the exclusion for "self-inflicted injury."

Birth of the HIMS. Against this background, in the fall of 1972, ALPA's aeromedical advisor reported to the union's biennial convention that alcoholism presented a serious medical problem for the organization's membership. Shortly thereafter, the Human Inter-

---

1. HUMAN INTERVENTION & MOTIVATION STUDY, AIR LINE PILOTS ASS'N, AN EMPLOYEE ASSISTANCE PROGRAM FOR PROFESSIONAL PILOTS (AN EIGHT YEAR REVIEW) (1982). This comprehensive report was produced under the direction of ALPA's aeromedical advisor, Richard L. Masters, M.D., and is a primary source for the information concerning the HIMS program in this chapter.

2. T.S. DENENBERG & R.V. DENENBERG, ALCOHOL AND DRUGS: IS-SUES IN THE WORKPLACE 3 (1983):

Employees are judged solely on the basis of their performance on the job without regard to clinical explanations of their shortcomings. Discharges even of those suffering from alcoholism are upheld so long as the employer has adhered to the disciplinary requirements of the collective bargaining agreement.

vention and Motivation Study, a euphemism for an occupationally oriented alcohol program, was launched.

Government assistance was seen as necessary in starting the program, not only to obtain funding but also to add an objective party to the task of bringing the FAA, air carriers, and ALPA together to work toward common goals. Initial funding was secured by a grant from the National Institute for Alcohol Abuse and Alcoholism (NIAAA) for a project intended to develop a model alcoholism program for airline pilots. Initially, a sample of three airlines representing about 10 percent of ALPA's membership was chosen to develop the program. Within a short time, however, the remaining members requested that the program be available at all airlines. What was originally planned as a short-term project expanded through continued NIAAA funding to a ten-year effort to develop strategies for recognition, intervention, evaluation, referral to treatment, rehabilitation, and FAA medical licensure.

The HIMS program followed the principles of intervention developed by the Johnson Institute of Minneapolis. These principles are detailed by Dr. Vernon E. Johnson in his book *I'll Quit Tomorrow* (1980) and in Dr. George A. Mann's book *Recovery of Reality— Overcoming Chemical Dependency* (1979). The concept of intervention is based on the premise that impaired judgment keeps an alcoholic or drug-dependent person locked into self-destructive patterns that keep him or her out of touch with reality. The five principles of intervention include concern, meaningful people, specific information, realistic alternatives, and follow-up. Use of these principles in an intervention format is almost always successful, particularly if a supervisor is involved.

A program specifically for pilots was developed based on the principles of intervention but in recognition that, for the following reasons, a traditional on-the-job supervisory identification system would not work: pilots are not generally subject to "supervisory scrutiny," and in many instances as many as several hundred pilots report to a single supervisor. It was assumed therefore that a pilot's ability to function effectively as a flight crew member was best observed by other pilots. Accordingly, a peer-identification and referral system was created.

Philosophy of the HIMS Program. The HIMS program was based on the principles that alcoholism is a treatable disease and that total abstinence is essential to successful rehabilitation. Education of the membership about alcoholism was to be the program's focus in changing drinking behavior.

ELEMENTS OF THE HIMS PROGRAM

Education. The HIMS staff and outside consultants provided training, primarily through extensive seminars, to selected pilots as well as representatives from management, other alcoholism treatment programs, and the FAA. The primary objective was to educate the pilots so that they could identify alcoholism among their peers and assist in an intervention program. Consequently, the training focused on the physiological, psychological, sociological, and interpersonal effects of alcoholism and the problems associated with denial; the principles of intervention; attitudes toward alcohol abusers; program development techniques; attitudes of the FAA toward alcoholism and other medical and behavioral problems; and the need for confidentiality. Trainees were cautioned not to act as diagnosticians or counselors but simply to express appropriate concern for their fellow pilots' health and careers.

Program Development. Policy statements, which emphasized cooperation among ALPA, the FAA, and airline management, were drafted and tested at six airlines. Cooperation between ALPA and management was especially important, in particular to dispel rumors about "witch hunts" and "big-brother" tactics.

Procedures were developed for self-referrals, the management of infractions of company or FAA rules, and the handling of peer reports of excessive drinking or problem behavior. ALPA and airline management agreed to handle self-referrals identically whether they were made first to ALPA or to the company. In either case, confidentiality was ensured.

Procedures involving the disposition of pilots who violated company or FAA rules varied widely, however. Some airlines terminated pilots immediately, either temporarily or permanently. Most airlines held disciplinary action in abeyance pending the outcome of evaluation, diagnosis, and treatment.

Interim Assistance Program. ALPA's intention initially was to provide alcoholic pilots with a staff of professionals who would offer interim help, including professional diagnosis, referral to treatment, and medical recertification by the FAA. The developers of the HIMS program believed this phase of ALPA's involvement would be brief and that these functions would be handled by the programs developed at each airline. This was not the case, however, and ALPA continued to be a primary resource throughout the eight years (1974–82) that the HIMS program elected to continue to receive funding from the NIAAA.

From the outset, the HIMS staff included highly trained professionals, including physicians who were experts in alcoholism and employee assistance programs. Although alternative private resources were available, the HIMS program was used the most often by pilots. The HIMS staff never provided treatment for alcoholism; however, it established liaison between the HIMS and treatment centers to ensure the best possible care and the availability of medical records for subsequent FAA review during the recertification process.

To maximize the gains of in-patient treatment, the HIMS staff favored long-term aftercare. Treatment centers have become more sensitive to this philosophy and have developed aftercare plans with consideration for HIMS and FAA certification needs. The FAA protocol requires submission of monthly written reports from airline and peer representatives, as well as results of quarterly clinical evaluations and semi-annual or annual psychiatric assessments. An unwritten requirement is that the pilot participate regularly in Alcoholics Anonymous activities. This reporting regimen is routinely required for a minimum of twenty-four months.

Acceptance of the HIMS Program. The HIMS program has found widespread support among the nation's airlines. Over the eight-year period of the program, sixteen airlines, which employed 90 percent of ALPA's members, developed formal employee assistance programs for helping alcoholic pilots. Seven of these airlines hired alcoholism experts to take charge of the programs. As a result of these cooperative efforts, more than nine hundred flight deck crew members have been rehabilitated and returned to work since 1972.

FAA POLICY ON RECERTIFYING REHABILITATED
ALCOHOLIC PILOTS

The Early, Punitive Approach. Each airline pilot must possess not only a valid certificate ("pilot license") but also a current medical certificate issued by the FAA's chief medical officer, the federal air surgeon. In 1959, the FAA adopted regulations that disqualified pilots with a medical history or clinical diagnosis of alcoholism from receiving a certificate from the federal air surgeon. This decision was based on the then-prevailing medical opinion, including that of the American Psychiatric Association, that alcoholism could not be cured and an individual who was or had been an alcoholic could never be trusted not to resume drinking.[3] The FAA's regulations did provide exemptions from the medical standards it had established. The agency adhered so strictly to its position, however, that between 1960 and 1971 only eight petitions for exemption were filed with the FAA by airline pilots, and none of these was granted.[4]

In 1972, the FAA's policy began to change and the agency started to grant exemptions from the alcoholism standard on a highly selective basis. By 1976, with the issuance of its watershed policy statement "Alcoholism and Airline Flight Crewmembers," the FAA increased the number of alcoholic airline pilots granted recertification through the exemption procedures, to the extent that by May 1, 1984, more than five hundred such pilots were made eligible to return to flight duty.

This change of position by the FAA occurred in part, as the 1976 FAA bulletin pointed out, because "adequate treatment and evaluation" of alcoholics had become medically feasible. In particular, in the "early nineteen-seventies . . . the FAA medical staff became aware that programs had been developed which were having considerable success in treating alcoholics, restoring their careers and ability to function, and maintaining abstinence on a long term basis."[5] The driving force behind the change in the FAA's position was not so much the improved medical techniques for treating alcoholism, however, as the desire to enhance air safety. The FAA came to recognize that the problems of denial associated with alcoholism tended to discourage the identification and treatment of alcoholic airline pilots, thus enabling them to fly in an impaired state.[6] Particularly in light

---

3. Affidavit of H.L. Reighard, M.D., Northwest Airlines v. FAA, 795 F.2d 195 (D.C. Cir. 1985). Dr. Reighard served as deputy federal air surgeon from 1963 to 1975 and as federal air surgeon from 1975 until 1984.

4. DEPARTMENT OF TRANSPORTATION, FAA, ALCOHOLISM AND AIRLINE FLIGHT CREWMEMBERS (1976).

5. Reighard affidavit, *supra* note 3.

6. Affidavit of Barton Pakull, M.D., Northwest Airlines v. FAA, *supra*

of the HIMS program, the FAA thus concluded that it could max-imize air safety by adopting a policy that would induce alcoholic pilots to come forward—or, more likely, to be pushed forward by fellow pilots, supervisory personnel, friends, or family—to reveal their illness and seek treatment.[7]

Regulatory Changes. In 1982, the FAA amended its regulations re-garding its medical standards relating to alcoholism. These amendments were prompted by the holdings in *Delta Airlines v. United States*[8] and *Jensen v. FAA.*[9] These cases held, respectively, that the FAA had improperly used the exemption procedure as a substitute for making rules and that the FAA's regulations con-flicted with the Comprehensive Alcohol Rehabilitation Act.[10] Un-der the amended regulations, a medical history or clinical diagnosis of alcoholism is no longer "absolutely disqualifying"; the applicant is entitled to a first-class medical certificate if "there is established clinical evidence, satisfactory to the Federal Air Sur-geon, of recovery, including sustained total abstinence from alco-hol for not less than the preceding two years."[11] In addition, the amended regulations provide for "special-issuance" medical certif-icates to be granted at the discretion of the federal air surgeon even if an applicant does not meet the specified medical stan-dards. For example, applicants with medical histories of alcohol-ism who seek recertification before the two-year period of abstinence is over, may be granted a special certificate if they can "show to the satisfaction of the Federal Air Surgeon that the du-ties authorized by the class of medical certificate applied for can be performed without endangering air commerce."[12] The regula-tions further provide that, in determining whether to issue a spe-cial medical certificate, the federal air surgeon "may consider . . . any medical facts that may affect the ability of the applicant to

---

note 3. Dr. Pakull has served in the FAA's Office of Aviation Medicine since 1971 and as the FAA's chief psychiatrist since 1977.

    7. Reighard affidavit, *supra* note 3.

    8. 490 F. Supp. 907 (N.D. Ga. 1980).

    9. 641 F.2d 797 (9th Cir. 1981), *vacated as moot*, 680 F.2d 593 (9th Cir. 1982).

    10. 42 U.S.C. § 290dd–1-(c)(1).

    11. 14 C.F.R. § 67.13(d)(1)(1)(i)(c).

    12. 14 C.F.R. § 67.19.

perform airmen duties including...[the] prognosis derived from professional consideration of all available information regarding the airman."[13]

Current Criteria for Medical Recertification. In 1985, the federal air surgeon modified the 1982 regulations and required pilots to do the following to qualify for a special-issuance medical certificate:

(1) Successfully complete a professionally run, high-quality rehabilitation program, which normally means at least four weeks of intensive treatment on an in-patient basis.

(2) Obtain a medical sponsor acceptable to the federal air surgeon. The sponsor must conclude, based on the medical evidence, that the pilot not only is abstinent and likely to remain so but also is otherwise physically and mentally fit for flight duty. Although the FAA normally accepts medical examinations from thousands of private physicians designated as aviation medical examiners (AMEs) and first-class medical certificates from approximately 1,200 AMEs, there are only about a dozen private physicians in the United States and a couple of dozen airline physicians whom the FAA deems qualified to act on a regular basis as medical sponsors for alcoholic pilots. The FAA has reason to believe, through close monitoring by its Office of Aviation Medicine, that these doctors will make reliable medical judgments.

(3) Undergo a complete psychological and psychiatric assessment to ascertain that their alcoholism has been successfully treated and that any related problems have been resolved as well. There are only about a dozen psychiatrists in the country whose experience and performance are deemed sufficient by the FAA for making such assessments.

(4) Participate in a high-quality, structured aftercare program. Such programs usually require that the pilots meet at least once a week with a therapist and other recovering alcoholics. The core requirement must be ongoing contact with a professional experienced in dealing with alcoholism.

(5) Agree to be monitored by both a fellow pilot, usually an ALPA

---

13. *Id.*

representative, and a representative of the employing carrier. The monitors must have more than casual contact with the pilots and submit monthly statements to the pilots' medical sponsor affirming the pilots' continued abstinence insofar as they are able to observe.

(6) Agree to continue seeing their medical sponsors at least semi-annually and to semi-annual or annual psychiatric evaluations.

The regulations also required that the FAA's Office of Aviation Medicine—specifically, the chief psychiatrist, the chief of certifications, and the federal air surgeon or deputy—must be satisfied based on their own independent assessment of all the evidence that the pilots may safely be returned to flying.

If the pilots have successfully observed the foregoing conditions for acquiring and maintaining their special-issuance medical certificate, they are eligible for an unconditional first-class medical certificate when the federal air surgeon is satisfied that the pilots have been abstinent for at least two years, have faithfully observed the terms of the conditional certification, and, based on the recommendation of the pilots' medical sponsors and psychiatrists, it is safe for the pilots to fly without monitoring.[14]

Arbitral Decisions Recognizing the "Alcoholism Defense"

Three cases from three different airlines illustrate the process of review of a pilot's discharge for violating company rules prohibiting consumption of alcoholic beverages. These cases represent the few examples of what has been called the "modification of the corrective discipline model," in which the arbitrator "allows for some opportunity for recovery while insisting that employees remain substantially accountable for their behavior."[15]

Air Wisconsin involved the discharge of a thirty-two-year-old first officer for his admitted violation of the carrier's rule prohibiting consumption of alcoholic beverages within "10 hours preceding the

---

14. Reighard affidavit, *supra* note 3; Pakull affidavit, *supra* note 6.
15. Denenberg & Denenberg, *supra* note 2.

beginning of duty time involving intended flight operations."[16] The undisputed facts showed that the grievant had left a tavern in a "smashed" condition at closing time (2:00 A.M.) on April 28, 1981, then reported late for duty but nevertheless operated a passenger-carrying flight that departed about five hours after he left the tavern. When reports of his condition and the time at which he "closed the bar" reached management, he was permitted to fly his scheduled trips for the next several days but was then terminated. A grievance was promptly filed, and in the course of processing, management agreed to hold the termination in abeyance pending the outcome of a clinical evaluation of the grievant's condition. The grievant was diagnosed as alcoholic and advised to seek prompt in-patient treatment. The manager responsible for the case, however, concluded that strict enforcement of the no-drinking rule was warranted in both the public's and the company's interests. He denied the grievance, and the case went to the system board of adjustment.

Following his termination, under the guidance of his ALPA representatives, the grievant entered into a program of alcoholism treatment and rehabilitation. He did well and was assured that, if he was reemployed so that requisite company monitoring of his sobriety could be conducted, the FAA would grant him medical recertification through the special-issuance procedures.

In the proceedings before the arbitrator, Jacob Seidenberg, the carrier urged that because of its unique responsibility to the traveling public, its judgment that a pilot failed to meet the applicable high standard of conduct must not be reversed unless that decision was proven to have been made in an arbitrary and capricious manner. The airline also argued that the grievant's alcoholism was no defense, that he was not being discharged for being an alcoholic but rather for violating significant rules of conduct, and that there was no justification for treating the alcoholic pilot differently from the non-alcoholic pilot with respect to the consequences of violating the no-drinking-before-flight rule.

The grievant's defense focused on the uncontroverted evidence that at the time he violated the no-drinking rule he was suffering from the disease of alcoholism and that his misconduct was a result of that illness rather than a lack of character or will. In addition, ALPA argued that the carrier's policies recognized that alcoholism

---

16. ALPA No. AW–8–81 (1983) (Seidenberg, Arb.) (unpublished).

was a treatable illness, that the grievant had been successfully treated and rehabilitated, and that he was committed to sobriety. ALPA also contended that the grievant was the victim of disparate treatment because another alcoholic pilot whose condition became known to management had been offered rehabilitation rather than termination. Finally, ALPA urged that the company lost its right to discharge the grievant when management allowed him to fly for several days after receiving reports of his drinking, condoning the misconduct.

Arbitrator Seidenberg resolved this dispute by granting the grievance and reinstating the grievant, without back pay, on a medical leave of absence. The reinstatement was conditioned on the grievant's maintaining total abstinence from alcohol while he was employed by the company, the parties' arranging for a reasonable monitoring system for one year following his reinstatement, and the grievant's successfully passing a company-administered medical examination.

The arbitrator distinguished this case from other cases upholding dismissal of alcoholic pilots by noting that the grievant was rehabilitated, whereas the pilots in the other cases were not. Seidenberg summarized as follows:

> In summary, we conclude that this case represents a situation of a pilot who finally recognized his illness, and for the past two years since his discharge, entered into and successfully participated in a comprehensive rehabilitative program that has arrested his disease of alcoholism and which has enabled him to abstain completely from drinking alcoholic beverages. The Grievant's recovery has been attested to by competent medical, psychiatric and psychological authorities, including the FAA Air Surgeon. The record also shows conclusively that the Grievant has changed his former life style drastically, and demonstrates his ability to be gainfully employed in a responsible position and lead an exemplary marital life.
>
> The record also shows that the Grievant has not gone unscathed for his past derelictions. He has been compelled to work at a reduced income as well as assume the not inconsiderable costs of his extensive rehabilitation program.

In the years since this decision, the grievant has been promoted and is now a captain. He remains abstinent and continues to be an excellent employee.

Northwest Airlines[17] involved the discharge of Larry Morrison who,

---

17. ALPA No. NWA–82–23 (1984) (Nicolau, Arb.) (unpublished).

on August 1, 1982, flew as first officer on a Northwest jet carrying passengers from Las Vegas to San Francisco. A company-ordered test administered shortly after his plane landed in San Francisco revealed that his blood alcohol content was 0.13 percent, high enough to constitute intoxication under California law. Until then, to outward appearances, Morrison's career had been stable and satisfactory. He had started as a pilot with Northwest in 1966 and for sixteen years had unblemished service, during which he logged about fourteen thousand pilot hours. His personal life also seemed to be stable and satisfactory. He was married to a former Northwest flight attendant, and the couple had three children. As a youth growing up in Wyoming, Morrison had been attracted to ranching, and he and his wife had owned and operated an Angus cattle ranch while he was employed as a pilot.

These outward trappings were deceiving, however, since Morrison was an alcoholic and probably had been for some time. He began as a social drinker in high school, continued that pattern through three years of military service, then began increasing his social drinking after joining the airline. Over the years he began drinking alone and heavily, especially on long layovers between flights. Consequently, marital problems developed between the Morrisons, his ranching business came to a virtual standstill, and he was unable to advance to B-747 aircraft because he could not satisfactorily complete the training. By August 1982, he had become a compulsive drinker whose tolerance for alcohol was such that he could gulp down a pint of vodka without displaying obvious signs of intoxication.

During his July 30–August 1, 1982, layover in Las Vegas, Morrison consumed a quart of vodka plus some wine and a beer; he finished the last of his second pint of vodka not quite three hours before the schedule departure of his flight to San Francisco. To the other members of the cockpit crew, the captain and second officer, Morrison's performance of his co-pilot's duties both before and during that flight seemed quite normal and gave no indication that he had been drinking. The company's station manager in Las Vegas became suspicious, however, although probably because he confused the effects of a severe stomach virus from which Morrison was then suffering, and for which he eventually obtained medical treatment, with the effects of alcohol. In any event, whether for the right or wrong reasons, the station manager alerted Northwest's general manager of flight operations, who then ordered the blood test that revealed Morrison's level of intoxication.

Five days later, after conducting a perfunctory investigation, Northwest discharged Morrison for violating "Company rules and regulations prohibiting the consumption of alcoholic beverages within 24 hours of flight duty," a violation aggravated by Morrison's serving as an operating crew member "under the influence of alcohol during the flight." ALPA, which represented Morrison in the investigation, suggested that he might be suffering from alcoholism and urged the carrier at least to "investigate . . . whether or not there [was] an underlying medical problem" before taking disciplinary action. Northwest rejected the suggestion, despite its policy that "alcoholism and other forms of chemical dependency are treatable conditions and that early detection and treatment may increase the likelihood of successful rehabilitation."

Pursuant to that policy, Northwest would consider returning to flight duty a pilot with a medical history or clinical diagnosis of alcoholism provided the pilot had not violated the company's "twenty-four-hour rule" and provided further that the pilot received FAA medical certification, "which is unconditional except to the extent continued professional counseling may be required for a reasonable period of time." In short, a nonrule-breaking alcoholic pilot who came forward voluntarily to seek treatment faced a minimum unpaid two-year leave of absence from Northwest (although the company did hold out the possibility of alternative employment). The company would not accept the FAA's special-issuance medical certificate, even though such a certificate was conditioned on monitoring the pilot. Northwest's consistent refusal to participate in a monitoring program had been sustained in a prior system board award.[18]

The company's twenty-four-hour rule was published in its manual for pilots and, in various letters to all pilots, the company had emphasized that harsh consequences—immediate dismissal—would follow if a pilot violated the rule. In contrast, the company's policy of returning the nonrule-breaking alcoholic pilot to duty after two years of abstinence was "not published even in outline form to the pilots until December 1982," four months after Morrison was discharged.

---

18. Northwest Airlines v. ALPA Nos. NWA 548–78 et al. (1979) (Bloch, Arb.) (unreported).

On August 7, 1982, at the urging of an ALPA staff member and a fellow pilot who was a member of the local HIMS committee, Morrison entered an alcoholism treatment program. His progress was good, and he was discharged from the program on September 4, 1982, with a diagnosis of "chemical addiction to alcohol" but with no other medical problems of any significance. His condition was stated as "improved" and his prognosis was "good."

Following release from the treatment facility, Morrison engaged in an extensive aftercare program and maintained abstinence and sobriety. He overcame the depression frequently associated with alcoholism, successfully resolved his marital problems, kept occupied with his ranch, and enjoyed a happy life with his family.

On January 10, 1984, the federal air surgeon declared Morrison eligible for special-issuance medical certification. His eligibility, however, was conditioned on certain criteria that were impossible for Morrison to meet unless he was reemployed: he could not provide the requisite monthly reports from company representatives attesting to his continued abstinence. Northwest's response to the FAA's notification of Morrison's eligibility for special-issuance medical certification was to request that the FAA revoke its decision. It made clear to the FAA that, in accordance with established company policy, it would not monitor Morrison or submit monthly reports regarding his continued abstinence. Indeed, Northwest brought an action in the United States Court of Appeals for the District of Columbia Circuit attacking the FAA's decision to recertify Morrison as a commercial airline pilot. ALPA and Morrison intervened on the FAA's behalf. The court rejected Northwest's contentions, holding that the carrier lacked standing to challenge the FAA's determination.[19]

Morrison had appealed his termination, and the dispute was submitted to the pilots system board of adjustment at Northwest. The company argued that all evidence regarding Morrison's alcoholism and his postdischarge treatment and rehabilitation was irrelevant and should be excluded. The board rejected that contention.

After reviewing the parties' contentions, the system board acknowledged that Morrison's misconduct (drinking within the twenty-four-hour period before his flight and flying while intoxicated) "must weigh heavily against him." In determining whether discharge was appropriate, however, the board said it was obliged to take into

---

19. Northwest Airlines v. FAA, 808 F.2d 76 (D.C. Cir. 1987).

account "all the facts and circumstances . . . includ[ing] Morrison's alcoholism and evidence of his rehabilitation, as well as his admitted rule violations and prior record" of lengthy service, which the board found to be good. Specifically, the board pointed out that "the unrebutted medical evidence" clearly established that Morrison was "an untreated alcoholic" when he flew as co-pilot on August 1, 1982, and that his "uncontrolled drinking and subsequent flying under the presumptive influence were medically related to and the result of his affliction." The opinion further stated that "the credible evidence is that the continuing treatment he has undertaken has resulted in his achieving rehabilitation, i.e., control over his behavior and abstinence from intoxicants." Further, the board observed a "consistent pattern of recovery over an extended period of time":

> Thus, we have an employee who after 16 years of service committed serious offenses, but offenses that were the unavoidable consequence of the illness of alcoholism, which illness has been arrested and successfully treated. Our weighing of these factors leads a majority of the Board to conclude that Morrison, despite the seriousness of the infractions, should be given an opportunity to demonstrate, as were the six diagnosed alcoholics [previously returned to duty by Northwest], that he can meet the Company's standards for flying.

The board emphasized that it was not promulgating any general rule "that the Company cannot, under its present policy terminate rule violators who are found to be alcoholics"; rather, "[t]hose alcoholics who do not come forward before breaking the rules are still subject upon a full review of the facts and their medical condition, to the severest of consequences, including termination." Accordingly, all that the board was holding "is that on the facts as presented, Morrison's reinstatement, subject to unconditional qualification by the Federal Air Surgeon, is justified" and that "[o]ther facts may dictate other results."

The board rejected the argument that reducing discharge to discipline (which, in effect, would constitute a suspension without pay or benefits subject to Morrison's securing unconditional FAA medical certification) would be contrary to public policy. Indeed, the board determined that it could distill no such public policy from prior court and arbitration cases. Instead, it found more persuasive the FAA's stated "policy of returning recovering alcoholics to the flight line when companies cooperate in monitoring and even returning recovered alcoholics to the flight line without monitoring after a minimum of two years of sobriety." Additionally, the board pointed out that

> [the] Award does not reinstate Mr. Morrison. The Award directs that he shall be offeɪ∪d reinstatement if and only if the Federal Air Surgeon determines that he meets the standards of Section 67.13(d)(1)(i)(c) of the Federal Air Regulations. Those standards are higher than the monitoring procedures, which the Company does not accept, and require "clinical evidence, satisfactory to the Federal Surgeon, of recovery...."
> As previously stated, these are the same high standards the Company itself has required for other airmen. Inasmuch as the Federal Air Surgeon has the statutory authority to make such determination and must do so with the highest regard for air safety,...the Award herein is consistent with public policy and within the Board's authority to make.

This determination was unacceptable to the carrier, and Northwest brought an action in the United States District Court for the District of Columbia seeking to set aside the award.

The case of *Delta Airlines*[20] concerned the discharge of a captain for violating company rules by consuming alcoholic beverages within twenty-four hours of his scheduled flight and then reporting for duty and operating a flight under the influence of alcohol on January 10, 1985. At the conclusion of the flight, a blood test revealed that the grievant's blood alcohol level was 65 mg percent.

In support of termination, the company emphasized that it was charged by law to provide "the highest possible degree of safety in the public interest" and that its "determination regarding a pilot's fitness and competency is not to be set aside unless it can be shown that the airline acted arbitrarily or in bad faith." The carrier pointed to its policy encompassing a "comprehensive set of incentives and deterrents to encourage pilots with alcohol problems to come forward and seek assistance prior to an incident of alcohol related job misconduct," including eligibility for participation in Delta's alcohol rehabilitation program, in which the costs of treatment, sick leave, and other benefits are paid for by Delta. The company also pointed to its "safety net of policies and practices...designed to maximize the opportunity for detection of impaired pilots prior to the point at which the safety of the traveling public is directly threatened" by

---

20. ALPA No. DAL 1–85 (1987) (Kahn, Arb.) (unpublished).

determining "that the period of detection of an impaired pilot without fear of automatic discharge should run to the point that a pilot reports to the aircraft." Thus, the company urged, fellow pilots would be encouraged to "intervene in a positive manner in the interest of safety without fear of reprisal for reporting a co-worker," thereby "break[ing] the conspiracy of silence among pilots to ensure that its safety net works so that no flight operates with a pilot under the influence of alcohol." The carrier argued that insofar as the grievant crossed the line and operated the aircraft as pilot in command while under the influence, his case was distinguishable from those of four other pilots who had violated the no-drinking rule and reported for duty but were intercepted before flying. Terminations of those pilots were eventually rescinded, either by management or by decision of the system board of adjustment.

Although the company conceded that at the time of his discharge the grievant was an undiagnosed alcoholic who had experienced blackouts, including one on the evening before the flight in question, it argued that his alcoholism could not excuse his violation of the company's safety rules. Further, Delta maintained that there was no contractual agreement between ALPA and Delta to submit safety matters to arbitration and that the system board of adjustment lacked jurisdiction to consider the grievant's alcoholism defense. "To do so would effectively place the System Board in the position of substituting its judgement for that of Delta's management in an area where the airline has substantial and exclusive responsibility for establishing and enforcing safety rules."

In defense, ALPA contended that the grievant's misconduct was "inextricably tied to his alcoholism" and that he was not aware of his impaired condition when he operated the aircraft on January 10, 1985, because of his blackout the previous night and because of the denial characteristic of alcoholism. ALPA contended that significant mitigating factors were present since the grievant had engaged in a successful rehabilitation effort and his prognosis for sustained recovery was excellent. Because his disease was in remission, his return to service would not compromise safety of the public and of the carrier's employees.

ALPA also contended that the grievant was the victim of disparate treatment since the other pilots whose discharges were rescinded had also reported for duty under the influence and would have flown but for unexpected intervention. Consequently, his case should not be singled out for sustained discharge merely because, through no fault of his own, no co-worker or supervisor intervened to prevent him from flying.

Arbitrator Mark Kahn swiftly disposed of the company's challenge to the jurisdictional authority of the system board in safety-related cases, affirming the ruling made during the course of the hearing:

> With regard to the Company's position on what we call the limits of the Board's jurisdiction, the simplest way to put it is: The Board does not accept that limitation on its jurisdiction.... In principle, the Board has the right to entertain, for example, an allegation or claim that a Company-formulated rule is unreasonable; or that in a particular application a reasonable rule has not been reasonably applied. Obviously, if a reasonable rule has been reasonably applied and appropriate action has been taken, then presumably the grievance should be denied; but these are all matters that fall within the Board's authority.

The arbitrator found that the specific rule at issue "says only that *reporting* for flight duty under the influence is cause for discharge" (emphasis in original) but that the rule had not been consistently applied since other pilots who had reported for duty under the influence were not discharged.

> Grievant appears to be the first example of a pilot who actually flew a trip under the influence of alcohol. Although this consequence of his alcoholism—and I am persuaded that grievant was indeed an alcoholic—was egregious, grievant's case is not logically distinguishable, from a disciplinary perspective, from that of the intoxicated pilot who reports for duty but is fortunately intercepted.

Taking into consideration the grievant's nineteen satisfactory years of service as a pilot, the board determined that he should have been offered the option of entering the company's alcohol rehabilitation program, and since he undertook a successful rehabilitation program on his own, the company was directed to reimburse him for the cost of that program as though he had not been discharged and had accepted rehabilitation as an option.

In closing, the neutral chairman stated:

> [I]t is my view that grievant is not otherwise entitled to be made whole for earnings and other benefits lost as a consequence of his misconduct on January 9–10, 1985. He did commit a dischargeable offense. If not for his long record of competent service and the Company's failure in

this instance to implement its own alcohol policy with rigor and equity, I might have found just cause for his termination. Accordingly, a make-whole remedy—apart from the cost of his rehabilitation—is not appropriate.

Delta filed a petition to vacate the award, and on September 30, 1987, Judge Orinda D. Evans of the United States District Court in Atlanta ruled in Delta's favor.[21] An appeal is pending in the United States Court of Appeals for the Eleventh Circuit.

The Public Policy Question

As noted above, Northwest petitioned the federal district court to vacate the system board award to reinstate Larry Morrison. ALPA responded by requesting that the court enforce the award. The court ruled in favor of Northwest on cross-motions for summary judgment. The court examined the Federal Aviation Act and determined that air carriers were obligated "to perform their services with the highest possible degree of safety in the public interest."[22] The court further observed that "Federal regulations promulgated pursuant to the Federal Aviation Act make clear that it is the carrier's responsibility to evaluate the competency of its pilots and detect defects in training" and "personal characteristics that could adversely affect safety."[23] In conflict with this federal policy of furthering safe air travel was a federal policy of resolving labor differences through arbitration. The court noted the limited grounds for setting aside an arbitration award, which are enumerated in the Railway Labor Act: "(1) failure of the board to comply with the provisions of the Railway Labor Act . . . ; (2) failure of the board to confine itself to matters within its jurisdiction; and (3) fraud or corruption." Noting well-established case law characterizing the scope of judicial review in RLA enforcement cases as "among the narrowest known to the law," the court recognized that

[o]nce the court determines that the board acted within the scope of its authority—that is, that the board conformed to the limits on its

---

21. Delta v. ALPA No. C87–239-A (N.D. Ga. decided Sept. 30, 1987) (unpublished).

22. 49 U.S.C. § 1421(b).

23. 14 C.F.R. § 121.413.(4)(i)(ii).

authority set forth in the labor agreement, and that the award draws its essence from the agreement—the court's task is finished. . . .

The Board's decision must be enforced unless the Award is "without foundation in reason or fact." . . . This test, in turn, hinges on "whether the remedy fashioned by the Board is rationally explainable as a logical means of furthering the aims of [the] contract."

The court thus refined the issue as "whether the balance between the two federal policies lies sufficiently in favor of air safety to rule that the arbitrator has exceeded his jurisdiction or 'acted contrary to public policy' in ordering Morrison's reinstatement."

In the district court's view, because application of the company's twenty-four-hour rule to Morrison's situation was "a matter about which the collective bargaining agreement is silent," involving only a grievance rather than interpretation of specific contract language, "[a]t best the subject matter of the dispute sits only on the outer perimeter of the arbitrator's jurisdiction." The board was faulted for denying Northwest the "right" to enforce its own safety rules, even though Northwest's rules on consumption of alcohol were not incorporated in the collective bargaining agreement. Indicating that "judicial review might well not be permissible" if safety rules were listed as a legitimate subject for arbitration, the court found there was "no specific agreement . . . to submit safety matters to arbitration" and therefore "the arbitration Board has exceeded its jurisdiction not because the Company retains *exclusive* jurisdiction over safety matters under the FAA, but because the Board's decision substantially interferes with air safety responsibilities entrusted to Northwest without encroaching unduly on concerns underlying federal arbitration policy."

ALPA appealed, and on January 6, 1987, Judge Harry Edwards rendered the unanimous decision of the Court of Appeals for the District of Columbia Circuit reversing the district court decision and remanding the case with instructions to enter judgment for ALPA.[24] The appellate court found that the district court "had no valid basis upon which to set aside the board's award" and that its decision was "plainly at odds with well-established Supreme Court precedent and with this court's recent de-

---

24. ALPA v. Northwest Airlines, 808 F.2d 76 (D.C. Cir. 1987), *petition for cert. filed*, 55 U.S.L.W. 3789 (U.S. Mar. 26, 1987) (No. 86–1548).

cision in *American Postal Workers Union v. United States Postal Service*, 789 F.2d 1 (D.C. Cir. 1986)."

The rationale of the court's decision was expressed succinctly as follows:

> Generally, a labor arbitration award must be enforced if the arbitrator acts within the confines of his jurisdiction and his award draws its essence from the parties' collective bargaining agreement; this is so even when a reviewing court disagrees with the arbitrator's judgement on the merits. In some limited circumstances, an arbitration award may be set aside if it is found to be violative of "public policy." However, as we made clear in *Postal Workers*, "judges have no license to impose their own brand of justice in determining applicable public policy; thus, the exception applies only when the public policy emanates from clear statutory or case law '*not from general considerations of supposed public interests.*'" *Id.*, at 8 (emphasis in original). There can be no doubt that the Board's award in the instant case does not require the invocation of a public policy exception; therefore, the district court had no authority to substitute its judgement for that of the parties' lawfully designated arbitration panel.[25]

After observing that the applicable collective bargaining agreement conferred jurisdiction on the system board of adjustment to hear and determine "an unresolved grievance claiming the absence of 'just cause' with respect to a disciplinary action taken against the pilot" and that the board's decision with respect to such dispute was bargained to "be final, binding and conclusive between the Company and the Association and anyone they may represent having an interest in the dispute," the court determined that "there is *nothing* in the parties' agreement that even suggests that a disciplinary action related to an alleged breach of a safety rule is excluded from arbitral review. . . . There is no conceivable way to construe the parties' agreement as removing from the Board's jurisdiction disciplinary actions related to alleged breaches of the twenty-four-hour rule."[26]

Thus finding that the question of just cause for Morrison's discharge was within the system board's jurisdiction, the court went on to examine whether the board's decision was somehow contrary to public policy and therefore unenforceable. Quoting from its decision in *Postal Workers*, the court described the "public policy exception"

---

25. 808 F.2d at 78.
26. *Id.* at 81–82.

as "narrow so as to limit potentially intrusive judicial review of arbitration awards"[27] and noted that the Supreme Court in *W.R. Grace*[28] "meant to say only that an arbitration award may not be enforced if it transgresses 'well defined' and 'dominant' laws and legal precedents."[29] Further, the court had said in *Postal Workers* that *W.R. Grace* makes it clear "that judges have no license to impose their own brand of justice in determining applicable public policy; thus, the exception applies only when the public policy emanates from clear statutory or case law, *not from general considerations of supposed public interests.*"[30]

Guided by these precepts, the court of appeals concluded that "the award plainly is not unlawful in its determination that Morrison's alcoholism was an illness that could not support a finding of 'just cause' for dismissal in this case."[31] Northwest petitioned for certiorari, but as of this writing the Supreme Court has not acted on that request.

Ensuring that a Cockpit Is Drug-Free

APPLICATION OF THE HIMS CONCEPT

As rare cases of drug use have surfaced over the years, usually in conjunction with alcohol disorders, the HIMS concept has proved flexible enough to encompass the management of these matters. There appears to be no significant reason why the HIMS concept cannot be applied to the management of drug problems, should they arise in pilots.[32] HIMS has developed a good track record; it has a

---

27. *Id.* at 83.

28. W.R. Grace & Co. v. United Rubber, Cork, Linoleum & Plastic Workers Local 759, 461 U.S. 757 (1983).

29. 808 F.2d at 83.

30. *Id.*

31. *Id.*

32. Source material for this section of the chapter is derived from R.B. STONE & R.L. MASTERS, DRUG TESTING AND THE AIRLINE PILOT (1986), a report to ALPA's board of directors, and from the series of articles *Drug Testing: The Dilemma*, AIR LINE PILOT, Feb. 1987. Captain Richard B. Stone is ALPA's executive chairman for aeromedical resources, and Dr. Richard L. Masters is the aeromedical advisor.

reputation for achieving results that benefit the ALPA membership and the airline industry as a whole. It is well known throughout the industry and has been recognized nationally as a model of rehabilitation programs for professionals.

As the HIMS alcoholism program progressed at various airlines, both pilots and supervisors gained experience in recognizing problems, and the overall effect often was salutary. The comfort level of peers and supervisors in dealing with alcohol problems increased, which made for smoother management of cases and earlier detection. That may not be the case with drug abuse and addiction cases, for a number of reasons. First, the number of cases is unlikely to be as high. Second, the symptoms of drug abuse are difficult for professionals to recognize, let alone for lay people. Third, the overall message to come out of alcohol rehabilitation programs, especially in the airline industry, is that rehabilitation is based on expectation of success. Unless the success rates with drug abusers and addicts improve dramatically, the small numbers of people affected, subtle symptoms, and poor prognosis may be expected to mitigate against the positive reinforcement seen with alcoholics.

Effective recognition of drug abuse will require that training programs be developed. Although some supervisors and pilots with experience in recognizing alcoholism may be able to transfer some of their knowledge, care must be taken to avoid the mistake of thinking that alcoholism and drug abuse are alike. As with alcoholism, education is a preventive tool that must be widely provided for all airline pilots. A specific formal training program has been implemented by ALPA covering a sufficient number of people to provide coverage for all carriers. The training does not make supervisors and peers into diagnosticians but gives them the information they need to recognize the problem and help afflicted individuals.

Because pilots are observed by their supervisors only infrequently, the recognition of drug abuse will depend on help from pilots themselves. As with alcoholism, acceptance of the HIMS concept requires a cooperative effort by unions and management to get the clear message out to all concerned that drug abuse is a medical condition that is treatable and dangerous and that from rehabilitation efforts can come the salvaging of careers. Only when pilots are convinced that this message is sincere and that companies are willing to provide assistance rather than automatic discipline or discharge will the program have a chance of success.

Case Management of Substance Abuse. The aim of intervention in substance abuse cases is to encourage the afflicted individual to accept the need for and follow the recommendations that arise from professional evaluation. In the HIMS program, practically the only time the intervention process has failed was when one or more of the five delineated steps were neglected.

As with alcoholism, substance abusers do not usually "get well" in treatment but following it. There is reason to believe that this is especially true for substance abusers and that the duration of aftercare, unlike the generally accepted two-year period for alcoholics, has to be longer. Effective treatment programs require long-term follow-up, including return visits to the treatment and aftercare facilities and usually periodic and random drug testing. Recovering substance abusers must be fully aware of the testing requirements and of the consequences of a confirmed positive test. It is anticipated that these requirements will come not only from the treatment center or aftercare facility but from management and the FAA.

As with the HIMS program, the substance abuse program should be formalized and include the protection due all pilots: that drug testing and treatment will not be used as punitive tools. The program should also be constructed to protect the rights of all, including the innocent, and to avoid the automatic presumption of guilt inherent in drug-screening programs that use random testing.

FAA Rules and Policies. The medical standards embodied in the Federal Aviation Regulations specify that an established medical history or clinical diagnosis of "drug dependence" is disqualifying for any class of medical certificate.[33] The regulations also prohibit a person from acting as a pilot "while using any drug that affects his faculties in any way contrary to safety" and prohibit a pilot from allowing a person "obviously under the influence of intoxicating liquors or drugs" (except a medical patient under proper care, or in case of emergency) to be carried on the aircraft.[34] Operation of an aircraft with knowledge that "narcotic drugs, marijuana, and depressant or stimulant drugs or substances" are on board is also prohibited by the regulations, except when authorized by federal or state law.

An indication of the FAA's attitude toward substance abuse may

---

33. 14 C.F.R. § 67.13, .15, .17.(d)(1)(d).
34. 14 C.F.R. § 91.11.

be garnered from an "action message" issued on August 14, 1985. This "Agency Policy on Substance Abuse" spells out standards for on-duty and off-duty conduct of FAA employees who have direct safety-related positions in aviation or whose duties could affect the safety of people or property. Basically, any involvement in growing, processing, manufacturing, selling, or transporting illicit drugs is cause for loss of a federal aviation job. Using, possessing, purchasing, or being under the influence of drugs or alcohol on duty is also prohibited. Further, the policy authorizes a drug-screening program. In 1987, in a complex injunction proceeding, the federal district court in Alaska upheld the FAA's policy requiring certain employees in safety-related positions to submit to drug testing as part of their required periodic medical examinations.[35]

Medical Recertification. Since the diagnosis or history of drug abuse disqualifies an individual from working as an airline pilot under FAA medical standards, recertification following treatment for the problem is mandatory. The special-issuance provisions set forth in part 67.19 of the Federal Aviation Regulations applicable to recertification following treatment for alcoholism also apply to recertification after treatment for drug abuse. Thus we can anticipate that those few medical sponsors who are recognized by the FAA, after demonstrating competence or receiving training, will bear the responsibility for preparing special-issuance certification cases for submission to the FAA. Each case will require the same thorough documentation that alcoholism-related cases do.

Drug Testing. Although there have been occasional, shocking revelations about alleged drug abuse by pilots, it is not a significant problem. Preemployment urinalysis tests of prospective applicants at American in 1985 "showed less than 1 percent of the pilot applicants tested positive for both prescribed and illegal drugs, 20–25 percent of the other applicants tested positive."[36] The hearsay, hyberbole, and hysteria associated with the drug-testing issue far surpass the reality of the problem. Nevertheless, a survey conducted in

---

35. National Ass'n of Air Traffic Specialists v. Dole, No. A-87073 (D. Alaska Feb. 1987).

36. Moorman, *Keeping the Cockpit Clean,* Air Line Pilot, Feb. 1987, at 9.

1986 showed that 88 percent of the people polled felt that airline pilots should submit to mandatory drug testing.[37] The pressure to test airline pilots appears to be coming from a general feeling that drug problems are pervasive in society and therefore threaten public safety. It seems fruitless to point out that there is no record of drug-related aircraft accidents involving United States air carriers.

The sensitivity of the industry and unyielding high standards that the public expects from airline pilots will likely overcome the argument against testing. On December 4, 1986, the FAA published an Advance Notice of Proposed Rule Making (ANPRM) (86–20), "Control of Drug and Alcohol Use for Personnel Engaged in Commercial and General Aviation Activities." The ANPRM invited comments from interested individuals and organizations regarding "drug and alcohol abuse by personnel in the aviation industry and the options available for regulatory or other actions in the interest of aviation safety." The document stated that the FAA was interested in gathering "information on the extent to which abuse of drugs or alcohol is impairing the performance of personnel in the aviation industry . . . and on the costs and effectiveness of various drug and alcohol countermeasures." Included was a suggestion that mandatory random testing of pilots might be forthcoming, because, as the ANPRM stated, "random testing has had the greatest impact on reducing the incidence of drug use," apparently by encouraging total abstinence.

The FAA asked those responding to focus on major categories of inquiry, including the following: How does drug and alcohol abuse affect aviation safety? What is the extent and nature of drug and alcohol abuse in aviation by occupational categories? What kind of mandatory drug- and alcohol-testing programs should be required, if any? Who should be included in such programs? Under what circumstances should reasonable suspicion be the basis for drug and alcohol testing? How can the FAA best implement a program to achieve a drug-free and alcohol abuse–free environment throughout the airline industry?

In May 1986, the Air Transport Association (ATA) submitted a proposal regarding drug testing and other issues to the FAA. The proposal called for the adoption of new federal aviation regulations

---

37. *Id.* at 8.

that would preempt all state or local laws dealing with the control of alcohol and drug abuse which were inconsistent with the new regulations. There would thus be a uniform industrywide approach for dealing with the problem. Carriers would be required to establish programs to reduce employee drug abuse, including drug testing during preemployment screening, after an accident or incident (unless airline management found that alcohol or drug abuse could not have been a contributing factor), and when there was "reasonable suspicion." The proposal defined "reasonable suspicion" as including but not limited to "a supervisor's personal observation of an employee's appearance, behavior, or speech or the body odors of the employee."

Although it suggested that all drug programs for airline employees should include the opportunity for rehabilitation, the ATA proposal stated that such rehabilitation should be available only to the employee who "admits voluntarily (whether directly or through an employee referral group) to being drug or alcohol dependent prior to the occurrence of an identifying event," such as an accident, incident, or case of "reasonable suspicion." Further, according to the ATA proposal, the employee must be found to be actually suffering from alcoholism or drug dependence; not be under active investigation; and not have a grievance pending regarding a violation of the airline's drug or alcohol rules that might lead to disciplinary action or discharge. Thus the ATA's recommendations maintained the old distinction between the addict who voluntarily comes forward seeking help and the addict who surfaces through a crisis involving breach of his or her employer's rules of conduct.

ALPA's proposed drug abuse program incorporates many of the elements of the HIMS program, namely, the focus on a multidimensional approach to drug treatment, including problem recognition, professional diagnosis and evaluation, treatment, rehabilitation, medical recertification and return to work, monitoring, and aftercare.

ALPA believes that only four conditions justify drug testing: (1) preemployment screening of job applicants; (2) probable cause; (3) an accident or incident; and (4) rehabilitation monitoring. Random testing should be permitted only for the last situation. ALPA is adamantly opposed to random drug testing other than for limited therapeutic purposes in connection with monitoring during rehabilitation. In his "President's Forum" column in the February 1987 issue of the *Air Line Pilot* magazine, the president of ALPA, Captain Henry A. Duffy, stated:

> Let me be clear on one point, under no circumstances will we accept random testing. Aside from the question of Constitutional rights, random testing would expose our members to the possibility of career-ending actions based on false-positive test results. That's the type of extreme we want to stay away from.

In ALPA's view, the minimum requirements for any drug-testing program are a combined management-ALPA steering committee, written agreements and policy statements, provisions for careful testing (including tests to double-check positive results), professional guidance of testing programs, and an opportunity for individuals with problems to be evaluated, treated, rehabilitated, and returned to work, as has been the case with ALPA's HIMS program since 1974.

On March 14, 1988, the FAA published a Notice of Proposed Rule Making titled "Anti-Drug Program for Personnel Engaged in Specified Aviation Activities,"[38] which advocates amending the Federal Aviation Regulations to incorporate mandatory periodic and random drug testing of pilots, flight attendants, and other employees who perform sensitive safety- and security-related functions, while requiring their employers to establish and maintain employee assistance programs that meet certain minimum specifications. With regard to the method by which the stated goal of meeting the public expectation of a "drug-free environment in those aviation activities that involved that personal safety"[39] might be achieved, the NPRM proposes that aviation employers establish anti-drug programs that require testing covered employees in five circumstances: (1) preemployment; (2) periodically (during required physical examinations); (3) randomly (as by selection, using a random number table); (4) postaccident; and (5) based on reasonable cause (based on a reasonable and articulable belief that a covered employee is using drugs). With regard to the circumstances under which an employee would be given an opportunity to seek rehabilitation, the NPRM proposes three options. Under the first option, an employee who comes for-

---

38. 53 Fed. Reg. 8368–88.
39. *Id.* at 8639.

ward voluntarily or tests positive for drugs for the first time would be eligible for rehabilitation rather than be discharged. Nonemployees given a preemployment drug test need not be given an opportunity for rehabilitation. Once rehabilitated, the employee would be reinstated into his or her prior position. The second option would provide rehabilitation rights to employees who come forward voluntarily or who are identified as drug users during periodic or random tests but would not require that the same opportunity be afforded to drug users identified in postaccident or reasonable cause tests; those not afforded the right to rehabilitation could be discharged. In the third option, only volunteers could claim rehabilitation rights. Anyone testing positive for drugs (regardless of the circumstances, e.g., random, periodic, postaccident, reasonable cause) could be fired immediately. In all cases, employers would be free to offer more rehabilitation options than the mimimum proposed. Thus, for example, an employer could voluntarily offer two chances at rehabilitation rather than one.[40]

The proposed amendments would also prohibit covered employees from using the services of any employee who failed a required drug test unless the employee has successfully completed an approved rehabilitation program and has been recommended for return to duty as a result of the program. Finally, the NPRM proposes to make refusal to submit to a drug test grounds for denial of an application for requisite FAA certification as well as grounds for revoking or suspending an employee's current FAA certification.[41]

Comments on the NPRM are due June 13, 1988, and the FAA has indicated its intention to hold a public hearing on the proposal.[42]

Conclusion

In an editorial in the *Journal of the American Medical Association*, Dr. George Lundberg of the University of Southern California School of Medicine stated:

> The drug abuse epidemic continues to be a major phenomenon of our time. The number of abusers waxes and wanes and the drugs change

---

40. *Id.* at 8377.
41. *Id.* at 8380.
42. *Id.* at 8368.

but the problems remain, seemingly recalcitrant to whatever efforts we put forth. Psychoactive drugs continue to be widely available at relatively low cost and are widely used. People continue to die every day of both legal and illegal drugs, but much more legal than illegal.[43]

Despite the current hysteria regarding abuse of illegal drugs, alcohol continues to be the most abused drug of choice of most Americans. Clinical research points to a genetic predisposition toward alcoholism.[44] As more about this illness is learned, and as the airlines come to accept the concept that alcoholism and other forms of chemical dependency are largely physiological conditions, it is hoped that arbitrators will deal with the pilots who are its victims in a more compassionate and realistic fashion than has been seen to date.

---

43. Lundberg, *Mandatory Unindicated Urine Drug Screening: Still Chemical McCarthyism*, 256 J. AM. MED. A. 3003 (1986).

44. *See, e.g.,* D. GOODWIN, IS ALCOHOLISM HEREDITARY? (1976); S.E. HYMAN & N.H. CASSEM, 2 MEDICINE (1987).

A Union President's View of Drug Testing

Victoria L. Frankovich

The zealousness with which drug problems are being handled at the workplace, including mandatory random testing, has been called "chemical McCarthyism."[1] Such testing is insidious because it rests on the premise that unless people have something to hide, they should not oppose it, however intrusive or embarrassing it may be. To oppose random drug testing is not to approve illegal drug use. We, as Americans, do not permit random mandatory searches of our homes to prove we have nothing to hide; nor do we allow such intrusions into every house on a block purely on the premise that one person may be hiding something illegal. As a court found in *Capua v. City of Plainfield* in overturning urine testing of fire fighters without individual cause: "If we choose to violate the rights of the innocent in order to discover and act against the guilty then we will have transformed our country into a police state and abandoned one of the fundamental tenets of our free society."[2]

In December 1986, the Department of Transportation issued an Advance Notice of Proposed Rule Making (ANPRM) inviting comments on proposed regulations that would require mandatory random drug testing of various aviation industry employees without evidence of job impairment or probable cause. Of the 681 responses

---

1. Lundberg, *Mandatory Unindicated Urine Drug Screening: Still Chemical McCarthyism*, 256 J. AM. MED. A. 3003 (1986).
2. 643 F. Supp. 1507 (D. N.J. 1986).

filed by the public with the FAA, 624 were against the proposed rule making and only 36 were in favor. Two days before the deadline for public comment on the notice and without waiting to review the public sentiment on the issue, Secretary of Transportation Elizabeth Dole announced her decision to promote random drug testing in the aviation industry. On the same day, two proposed pieces of legislation were introduced into the United States Senate that would require mandatory random drug testing in the railroad and airline industries. On March 3, 1988, in spite of the negative response to the ANPRM, James Burnley, the new secretary of transportation, issued a Notice of Proposed Rule Making and announced that it was the intention of the DOT to proceed to the rule-making stage. These actions appear to be the result of political pressure generated by the Reagan administration's drive to create a "drug-free society." They are quite obviously not the result of drug- or alcohol-related safety problems in the industry since the FAA cited none in its filing and in fact admitted: "There have not been any fatal accidents involving commercial airline pilots where drug or alcohol were shown to be factors."[3] The same is true for flight attendants.

The aviation industry bears a heavy burden of responsibility to protect the safety of passengers. Both the government and the airlines are therefore legitimately concerned about achieving a work environment free of alcohol and drug abuse. The question is, How is this best accomplished, and to what extent will the rights of employees be compromised to achieve this goal? The issues are serious, for they involve not only the principle of individual freedoms but also the potential destruction of careers and lives through false-positive test results.

Problems with Drug Testing

The most commonly used drug-testing procedure is a urinalysis test called EMIT (Enzyme Multiplied Immunoassay Technique). This is the test proposed in the NPRM to be used to test airline employees. EMIT tests do not test for a drug; rather, they detect only the

---

3. 14 C.F.R. pt. 91 (proposed Dec. 4, 1986).

presence in the urine of a metabolite (byproduct) of the active ingredient of certain drugs.[4]

In addition to false-positive results, the test can yield false negatives (failing to find a drug that is there) and "misidentification" (finding a drug but misidentifying it.[5] False-positive reports may result when prescription or over-the-counter drugs cross-react with food or other substances, including enzymes produced by the body. Drugs such as Advil, Motrin, and Nuprin, for example, sometimes test positively for marijuana. Certain over-the-counter cold preparations (e.g., Nyquil, Contact) and diet pills that are closely related in chemical composition to amphetamines will test positive for amphetamines. The immunoassay test also cannot distinguish between codeine (a legal drug) and heroin (an illegal drug), both of which are opiates.[6]

Immunoassay tests are highly unreliable, concludes toxicologist Arthur McBay:

> It is, therefore, virtually impossible, in practice, to standardize immunoassays so that results are comparable when urine is analyzed by two different immunoassays or even the same immunoassay using different batches of antibody. Thus, a single urine specimen can be positive by one immunoassay and negative by another.[7]

The scope of such unreliable findings is immense. The *American Medical News* reported on July 27, 1984, that the Army mishandled 52,000 urine samples tested for marijuana.[8] A May 5, 1986, *Newsweek* article cited a study at Northwestern University that concluded that "25 percent of EMIT tests that came up positive were really 'false positives.' "[9] Various reports indicate that false positives may be as high as 5 to 25 percent[10] in some drug tests, 30 to 60 percent in

---

4. NATIONAL INSTITUTE ON DRUG ABUSE, URINE TESTING FOR DRUGS OF ABUSE 85 (1986).

5. *See* Lundberg, *supra* note 1, at 3004.

6. Comments by Lloyd B. Egenes (O'Gara, Friedman, Egenes, & Burke) in response to the ANPRM before the FAA (Jan. 27, 1987). Analysis from affidavit of Arthur J. McBay, a toxicologist with a doctorate in pharmaceutical chemistry. *See also supra* note 1 & JESSIM, *Employment Drug Test*, in PRIVILEGED INFORMATION 6 (ACLU 1987).

7. McBay, *Letter*, 249 J. AM. MED. A. 881 (1983).

8. Am. Med. News, July 27, 1984.

9. Remtzer, *Can You Pass the Job Test?* NEWSWEEK, May 5, 1986, at 50.

10. *Id.*

others, and 20 to 70 percent in still others.[11] James Woodford, a forensic chemist in Atlanta and consultant to the United States Public Health Service, has said that urinalysis tests may be racially biased: "[Blacks have a] high concentration of the pigment melanin, which has an ion identical to THC," the active ingredient in marijuana; melanin may also produce metabolites similar to THC.[12]

TESTS CANNOT DETERMINE JOB IMPAIRMENT

Perhaps the most significant drawback to these tests is that at best they can only suggest that a drug was ingested; they cannot determine when the drug was ingested, the amount ingested, or the degree of impairment. Because the primary object of drug testing is to ensure that employees are capable of performing their jobs, impairment should be the central focus. A test showing that a person may have ingested a substance one to two days, or even weeks, earlier fails to determine ability to perform the job.[13]

Gas chromatography and mass spectrometry (GC/MS) is a more sophisticated and therefore more expensive technique. Literature by the Syva Company, which manufactures EMIT, indicates that the GC/MS test does not measure the psychoactivity of drugs. A marijuana "high" lasts only about two hours. Urine testing merely shows

---

11. *See supra* note 1. See also FREQUENTLY ASKED QUESTIONS ABOUT SYVA AND DRUG ABUSE TESTING (Syva 1982) (the Syva Company, which manufactures EMIT, acknowledges an error rate of 5 percent for its immunoassay); Zeese, *Marijuana Urinalysis Test*, DRUG LAW REP., May-June 1983 (discusses a 1982 study by the Department of Defense and the Army that found EMIT had 11.1 percent false positives); Morgan, *Problems of Mass Screening for Misused Drugs*, 305 J. PSYCHOACTIVE DRUGS (1984) (cites error rates of 20 to 70 percent and quotes one authority that "the performance of even the 'best' toxicology laboratories on urine drug screens is grossly defective, with frequent false-positives . . . and misidentifications").

12. See Remtzer, *supra* note 9, at 50.

13. Centers for Disease Control, *Urine Testing for Detection of Marijuana: An Advisory*, 32 MORBIDITY & MORTALITY WEEKLY REP. 469 (1982). Literature provided by test manufacturers and testing laboratories (e.g., CompuChem Laboratories 1986 literature) concurs with this conclusion. The *Newsweek* article, *supra* note 9, indicates that marijuana, for example, can leave traces in the urine for three to five weeks although the psychoactive impact of the drug is long gone. Cocaine can leave traces for three days.

(if valid) that the individual ingested some amount of the target drug, at some time.[14]

EFFECT OF LIQUIDS

Test results of body fluids may be skewed by the intake of liquids, which change the concentration of drug metabolites as the metabolites are secreted from the body. This can result in a higher drug concentration in the morning than in the afternoon.[15] Someone who has taken a drug the previous day will therefore test negative the following afternoon.

CHAIN OF CUSTODY

Another problem starts the moment the urine is collected, the first step in the "chain of custody." If the urinalysis is not performed under "direct, informed observation of urine flow from the urethra to the container," specimen identification is impossible. Further, "without large numbers of diligent and devoted micturition observers, the entire mandatory urine drug screening system becomes a travesty and is certain to fail."[16] One wonders when the president of the United States agreed, on a one-time basis, to have his urine analyzed (to set an example to federal employees whom he was calling on the FAA to test) whether or not he agreed to the embarrassment of "positive specimen identification under direct observation." It is doubtful. In any event, agreeing on a one-time basis to submit urine for testing is not at all the same as being subjected (at the demand of the government or one's employer) to recurrent random testing.

OTHER PROBLEMS

Beyond the problems of false-positive test results, there is always the possibility of faulty laboratory work. Because of such drawbacks,

---

14. BNA, ALCOHOL AND DRUGS IN THE WORKPLACE 29 (1986). *See also* FREQUENTLY ASKED QUESTIONS ABOUT SYVA AND DRUG ABUSE TESTING, *supra* note 11.

15. AMALGAMATED TRANSPORTATION UNION, MARIJUANA TESTING IN TRANSIT: USES AND ABUSES OF THE EMIT TEST (1986).

16. *See supra* note 1.

immunoassays are being recommended for screening only; alternate methods would be used for confirmation of results. The manufacturer of GC/MS claims it is "state-of-the-art." But this method can also produce erroneous results. As toxicologist McBay has stated:

> All drug testing procedures result in false positives. The reliability of all drug determinations, whether by immunoassay or GC/MS, depends on such factors as the certainty of specimen identification; specimen storage, handling and preparation; preparation and storage of test reagents; proper cleaning and calibration of testing instruments and hardware; and qualification and training of laboratory personnel performing the test and interpreting the results. The danger of carelessness in test performance and/or inadequately trained personnel may be a particular problem with immunoassays, which are popular for low-cost, large-scale screening of many specimens with readily available equipment and minimum personnel training. The problem nonetheless is also present when GC/MS is utilized.[17]

Although confirmation tests may help minimize the chance of error, even advocates of drug testing admit that errors still occur. Notes Robert Angorala, "No matter how accurate a testing method is, there will always be a certain small number of incorrect test results.... False results are not only caused by problems with the urinalysis itself. They also occur if specimens are accidentally switched at the collection point or in the laboratory, or if the sample is tampered with. Errors in reporting results may also occur."[18]

The relative ease with which the tests can be performed encourages their use by nontechnical personnel. This results in untrained individuals performing the tests in nonlaboratory settings and thereby invalid results being used to justify discipline and discharge.

An additional area of uncertainty is that of "passive inhalation." It is possible for an individual to test positive after being around someone who has been smoking drugs.

Impact on Labor Relations

The posting of the Notice of Proposed Rule Making regarding drugs and alcohol in itself had an impact on the industry. Some carriers,

---

17. *See supra* note 6.

18. R. Angorala, *The Legal Issues of Urine Testing*, in Urine Testing in the Workplace 21 (American Council for Drug Testing 1985).

for example, have implemented new drug-testing programs. For instance, in 1987, TWA announced a new drug and alcohol policy that contrasted sharply with its previous policy. Notable changes included:

(1) Employees who use, distribute, or possess unlawful drugs or controlled substances while *on or off duty* will be subject to discharge.
(2) Employees undergoing medical treatment with drugs or controlled substances must, as standard practice, submit documentation regarding medication, dosage, frequency, and related information to a supervisor. This applies even to employees showing no evidence of job impairment.
(3) Mandatory drug testing may be undertaken on a reasonable suspicion that an employee is under the influence of, or impaired by, alcohol, controlled substances, or other drugs.
(4) "Reasonable suspicion" includes mandatory testing after any on-duty accident or incident that resulted in personal injury or property damage. Visible impairment (such as slurred speech or out-of-focus eyes) is not necessary for a finding of reasonable suspicion.
(5) Insubordination for refusal to submit to tests may result in firing.
(6) Confirmed positive tests shall be grounds for discharge even without evidence of impairment.

This program was introduced unilaterally: the airline unions were not permitted to negotiate on the issue. At the same time, TWA continues to refuse to allow employees to use the employee assistance program (Special Health Services) when job impairment becomes obvious and an employee is in jeopardy of losing his or her job. TWA explained its policy by saying, "The Department of Transportation asked for comments for proposed rule making to control drug and alcohol use in the airline industry. Drug and alcohol abuse is an industry-wide concern." Neither TWA nor the FAA claims any drug-related incident or evidence of a problem that would justify such extreme measures.

Employees should not be exempt from constitutional principles. These principles include the right to privacy and the right not to be subjected, as Geoffry Stone, professor of constitutional law at the

University of Chicago, puts it, to "invasive activities without justification."[19]

Unionized employees are entitled to due process and fundamental rights under collective bargaining agreements creating industrial self-government, in much the way that citizens enjoy similar protections under the constitution. Private employers may not be subject to the same constitutional restrictions as the federal government, because, unlike the government, private employers do not have any legitimate authority over the personal habits, life-styles, or conduct of employees away from the workplace. Nor do they have any business enforcing real or imagined societal values. The employer is not a law enforcement agent.

EXISTING LABOR POLICIES

A number of well-established principles of industrial jurisprudence will undoubtedly be the subject of court cases regarding drug testing. Some of the major issues include whether an employer may

> control the off-duty conduct of employees when it has no adverse impact on job performance;
>
> charge an employee with insubordination for failure to agree to mandatory testing;
>
> fire on the basis of test results (in the absence of impaired job performance);
>
> accept a lesser burden than "probable cause" as a reason to compromise an employee's right to privacy (reasonable suspicion is a far lesser burden than to require random testing only if probable cause exists);
>
> accept less than "beyond a reasonable doubt" burden of proof for termination when potential criminal conduct may be charged (acceptance of drug test results without regard for other factors cannot possibly meet the burden of proof beyond reasonable doubt).

---

19. Remtzer, *supra* note 9, at 47.

Discipline regarding Employees' Off-Duty Conduct

It is well established in labor relations that employers have no disciplinary authority over employees' conduct (even potentially criminal conduct) off the job. For example, in an arbitration proceeding concerning the termination of a laborer who pleaded guilty to contributing to the delinquency of a minor, arbitrator Clair Duff ruled: "If the employee commits no misconduct in the plant or during working hours he is not subject to disciplinary penalty, though he may beat his wife, spend his money foolishly, or otherwise behave like an undesirable citizen."[20] A similar decision was reached in a case involving an employee who was terminated after being convicted of possessing narcotics and giving narcotics to a minor. The arbitrator, Joseph McMahon, decided to reinstate the employee and stated:

> [W]hat an employee does on his own time and off the employer's premises, unless related to or having an adverse effect on the employer's business, is not a proper basis for criminal law and having charges filed against him or even being convicted of a criminal offense for acts committed outside of working hours and while off employer's premises, does not necessarily constitute a proper basis for disciplinary action unless there is an adverse effect upon the employer-employee relationship, or the employer's business is adversely affected.[21]

Another case involved soldiers who had taken drugs off base. In *Merritt v. Department of Justice*, it was decided that the employer had to be able to show a nexus between the employee's conduct and employment relationships:

> The fact that appellate's misconduct may have been unlawful did not relieve the agency of its burden to establish the requisite nexus, particularly in view of limitations upon the power of government to intrude unnecessarily upon the discreet conduct of citizens, including federal employees, in the privacy of their homes.[22]

---

20. Babcock & Wilcox, 43 Lab. Arb. (BNA) 242–43 (1965).
21. Movie Lab, Inc., 50 Lab. Arb. (BNA) 632–33 (1968).
22. Merritt v. Department of Justice, 6 M.S.P.B. 653 (1981).

In an arbitration involving the off-duty use of marijuana by Grey-hound mechanics, it was decided that "[w]orkers in our society are free men and women, with the fundamental right to live their lives as they choose when away from the workplace and not performing employment duties, so long as their off-duty doesn't affect their job performance."[23]

Similar decisions have overturned terminations for off-duty drug use for police officers, fire fighters, pilots, and other workers involved with public safety. When an Eastern pilot smoked marijuana, stabbed his supplier, served time in jail, and was discharged for the off-duty offense, the arbitrator, Hubert Wykoff, reinstated the pilot because none of the conduct occurred at or affected his work.[24] In an arbitration concerning a truck driver terminated after he pleaded guilty to a second-degree felony charge of theft committed while off duty, arbitrator Charles La Cugna ruled:

> Collective bargaining agreements, essentially employment contracts, necessarily, by their very terms, limit the Employer's right to discipline employees to on-duty hours: an employee cedes his freedom and subjects himself to discipline only during the stipulated "hours of employment." It is inconceivable that a Union would, or in fact could, bind its members to any employment contract where reach would extend beyond the stipulated duty hours. If an Employer would discipline or discharge an Employee for off-duty conduct, the employer would become a continuing Employer and a moralizing agent, an ever-present moral judge of an employee's total conduct not only during on duty hours, but also during off duty hours.[25]

INSUBORDINATION FOR REFUSING TO BE TESTED

Arbitrators have ruled that, in the absence of probable cause, employees should not be forced to undergo mandatory drug tests. In a case involving an employer that packages and distributes hazardous chemicals, the arbitrator Marian Warns found drug testing unenforceable because it required employees

> to submit to a test and place their medical situation on record with the constant possibility of incriminating themselves in terms of illegal drugs

---

23. *Experts Warn Companies: Don't Get High on Drug Tests*, LUPA NEWS-LINE (UAW), Jan. 1987.

24. Eastern Airlines, 64 Lab. Arb. (BNA) 828 (1975).

25. Maust Transfer Co., 78 Lab. Arb. (BNA) 780 (1984).

without probable cause on the job to suspect that any of the individuals are in fact taking drugs. Lacking such probable cause to suspect a particular individual and forcing them to take such a test is an invasion of privacy and unwarranted requirement to furnish such confidential information. In essence, it is requiring an employee to incriminate himself without probable cause. It is also requiring the test as a condition of continued employment when no reason exists in the performance of the individual to place such a condition upon him.[26]

IMPAIRED JOB PERFORMANCE

FAA regulations proscribe the consumption of alcohol by pilots for eight hours preceding flights. The use of any drug that "affects the individual's faculties contrary to safety" is also prohibited. The critical question is, What causes job impairment? The practical reality is that no drug test can determine job impairment.[27]

To get around this complication, employers are inclined simply to establish policies that prohibit the use of drugs on the employees' off-duty time as well as on the job. This leads to the unacceptable interjection of the employer into the private affairs of employees. Moreover, it leads to an inconsistent handling of alcohol versus drugs. An employee who smokes marijuana on Friday night and is tested at work on Saturday afternoon may still have the metabolite THC in the urine but suffer no job impairment. This is because the psychoactive effect of the drug lasts only a few hours but the residue of the drug may remain in the system for days.[28] A second employee who drinks an excessive amount of alcohol on Friday night and reports to work the following day may suffer a hangover and job impairment but have insufficient levels of alcohol in his urine to be classified as intoxicated.

RANDOM TESTING

Even when arbitrators have felt that "reasonable suspicion" rather than "probable cause" may suffice as a reason for drug testing, the facts in a given case had to be convincing. In looking at this question at the Three Mile Island nuclear generating facility, arbitrator Jonas

---

26. Gem City Chemicals, 86 Lab. Arb. (BNA) 1023 (1983).
27. Centers for Disease Control, *supra* note 13.
28. *Id.*

Aaron included the following comments in his decision to overturn this policy:

> [T]here should be some reasonable grounds or suspicions or bases for an employer action of investigating or interrogating or testing employees to find misconduct. The alternative of permitting broad employer action I believe, strips the employees of basic rights, which are incorporated in the concept of "proper cause." The concept of an employer having proper cause before acting to discipline or investigate or test an employee to determine whether there has been misconduct and thus go on to the actual act of discipline has to incorporate some types of, at the very least, minimal due process rights. Even given the nature of the facility involved here—and I am not ignorant of the recent history of the volatility of such sites and the public concern of these events, still, to my mind, there is something inherently offensive about the type of testing sought to be imposed.[29]

Another arbitrator, Robert Ables, overturned a random testing program for employees at a plant that manufactured missile propellants, citing that "the custom of a 'cause' is standard in unionized industries."[30]

Considering a similar case with school bus drivers, a court decided that "even public safety considerations connected with a school bus driver do not outweigh the employee's privacy rights where there is no probable cause."[31]

Proof beyond a Reasonable Doubt

When an offense involves possible criminal conduct or contains an element of moral turpitude, arbitrators frequently require proof beyond a reasonable doubt. Any reasonable doubt should be resolved in favor of the employee.[32] After reviewing more than eighty arbitration awards involving drug abuse, arbitrator Edward Levin wrote: "Because of the difficulty of getting other jobs, if an employee is discharged for drug abuse, arbitrators usually insist upon an unusually strict standard of proof."[33]

---

29. Metropolitan Edison (Aaron, Arb.) (unpublished).

30. Hercules (Ables, Arb.) (1986) (unpublished).

31. Jones v. McKenzie, 628 F. Supp. 1500 (D. D.C. 1986).

32. 4 F. Elkouri & E. Elkouri, How Arbitration Works 661–63 (1985).

33. Levin & Denenberg, *How Arbitrators View Drug Abuse*, 97 Arb. J. 98 (1976).

CONCLUSION

Public and private employers are increasingly instituting random drug testing. The number of Fortune 500 companies testing employees or job applicants for drug use jumped from 3 percent in 1982 to 30 percent in 1985.[34] As a result, manufacturers of drug tests are seeing their business double and triple. In 1986, for example, the FAA awarded a contract of just under one million dollars to CompuChem Laboratories to conduct systematic mandatory urinalysis tests of twenty-four thousand FAA employees.[35] Yet, the Centers for Disease Control in Atlanta has found that 25 to 66 percent of urinalysis tests are inaccurate.[36] It is almost as though once a product or service is invented, a way must be found to use it.

EDUCATION AND SUPPORT ARE THE ANSWER

Everyone has an interest in eliminating the abuse of drugs and alcohol in the workplace. This is particularly true for safety-related jobs in the airline industry. The first step toward this goal is to recognize that alcohol and drug abuse is an illness. Testing will not eliminate the problem. It may be a step toward ensuring that drug users are unemployed, but it will not solve their addiction. It is very likely that the addicted user or drug abuser will find a way to outmaneuver the tests, and the innocent will instead be inadvertently caught in the net.

Furthermore, the emphasis on ridding the airline industry of alcohol and drug abuse has distracted attention from a potentially greater problem: prescribed drugs. The FAA's *Guide to Drug Hazards in Aviation Medicine* (1962) lists a large number of substances that should not be taken by pilots within twelve to twenty-four hours of flying. These include commonly prescribed diuretics, antihistamines, antibiotics, tranquilizers, antiprotozoal agents, and narcotic pain killers. Few airline pilots, flight attendants, or policy makers at airlines are likely to have seen this book. The FAA should consider updating this publication to include a list of safe alternative medications that

---

34. *Drop Drug Testing—SEIU Says Tests Are Illegal—and Often Wrong.* SERVICE EMPLOYEES INT'L UNION NEWSLETTER, Jan. 1986.

35. Stanfield, *Drug Testing of Safety Employees,* AIRLINE EXECUTIVE, Oct. 1986, at 4.

36. *See Drop Drug Testing, supra* note 34.

will not jeopardize employees or the public. Such a publication should be distributed widely to airline employees and management.

EMPLOYEE ASSISTANCE PROGRAMS (EAPS)

The few comments filed with the FAA in support of random drug testing came primarily from airline management. Further, only management objected to the portion of the FAA's proposal that recommended establishment of EAPs to address alcohol and drug abuse problems.

Job impairment resulting from alcohol or drug abuse should not be handled by terminating the affected employees but by referring them to an EAP program. Too many airlines fear that employees will "hide behind" EAPs and thus never give the programs a chance.

Eliminating substance abuse problems requires that the airlines make a commitment to rehabilitation and education—not punishment. Money that is being invested in "big brother" drug testing would be much better spent on aggressive educational campaigns.

Part 8
The Future of Airline Labor Relations

In Defense of
Deregulation

Alfred E. Kahn

The historic rationale for economic regulation of the airline industry was that unregulated competition might degrade the high quality, continuity, and even safety of airline service and result in discrimination among localities and passengers. This argument was not illogical. But as it was practiced in the forty-year life of the CAB, regulation entailed a thoroughgoing suppression of competition. During the 1960s and the 1970s, a consensus emerged among disinterested observers (a group that did not, of course, include members of the industry itself) that regulation had inflated prices, denied the public the variety of price and service offerings that competition typically offers, sheltered inefficiency, and encouraged the wage-price spiral that was at the heart of our national stagflation problem.

That consensus eventually spanned the whole spectrum of political orientations. The coalition actively supporting deregulation included Ralph Nader's Public Citizen, the National Association of Manufacturers, Common Cause, Sears Roebuck, the Consumer Federation of America, and the National Federation of Independent Businesses. Liberals and conservatives alike agreed that it was time to eliminate the comprehensive cartelization of the industry.

Whatever the problems to which deregulation has given rise (and there have been many) and whatever the surprises, deregulation has also done most of what its supporters expected it to do. It has certainly brought travelers the benefits of price competition. In 1986, 90 percent of passengers traveled at discount prices, with an average discount of 60 percent below the coach price. Between 1976 (the last year before the CAB began to permit widespread discounting) and 1986, the average yield per passenger mile—that is, the average price passengers actually paid—declined by about 28.5 percent in real terms. Competition has also, as expected, resulted in a wider range of price and service options, from the "maxsavers" on the one side to the increased variety of business-class and first-class options on the other. It has certainly forced the airlines to improve their efficiency and, by permitting them to restructure their routes and schedules, freed them to do so. And it has exerted very healthy downward pressure on grossly inflated wages.

Clearly, despite the progressive oligopolization of the industry, the airlines are more effectively and intensely competitive today than they ever were under regulation. But the change has been far from costless. The newly introduced and intensified competition has imposed far more severe strains on labor-management relations than any of us predicted, mainly because, of course, some part of the benefits that travelers have received in the form of lower fares have come out of those inflated wages.

From the standpoint of the general public, the most obvious costs have been the increased congestion, delays, apparent threats to safety, and the general deterioration in the quality and civility of air travel. There are several points to be made about these developments. First, increased congestion and inconvenience are not in themselves a sign that deregulation has failed. The competition deregulation unleashed has in fact resulted in very low fares, albeit with correspondingly less convenient or comfortable service—having to stay over a weekend, face cancellation penalties, make reservations thirty days in advance, sit in narrower seats on more crowded planes, or wait in longer lines at counters. The overwhelming majority of travelers have apparently considered these concessions worth it.

Second, this deterioration in service has emphatically not shown up in accident rates. On the contrary, the annual averages for total number of accidents, fatal accidents, and fatalities on a per million flight basis have been dramatically lower since deregulation than in the five- or ten-year period immediately preceding.

Nor, third, has service to small communities deteriorated. Not a single community that enjoyed certificated, that is to say regulated, service under regulation has lost it. This is, in part, because commuter airlines have moved in and in part because of the subsidized

Essential Air Service program. Small towns as a group have experienced on the order of a 15 to 20 percent increase in the number of weekly departures.

It is widely contended that the margin of safety has narrowed. The number of "near misses" has apparently increased, and carriers may well be cutting corners on safety precautions. If so, the responsibility rests with government, particularly the federal government. The FAA criticizes the airlines for scheduling too many flights at times of congestion. It has the wrong culprit. The airlines have been doing what we expected them to do under the pressure of competition—giving passengers the flights they want, when and where they want them. The result is the simplest of all economic problems: demand at certain times and places exceeds supply. That is the reason planes line up for an hour or two waiting for the privilege of taking off. It does not take a doctorate in economics to understand that this calls for two kinds of remedy: one on the supply side and the other on the demand side.

As for the supply side, passengers pay an 8 percent tax on all the tickets they buy, the proceeds from which are supposed to be used primarily to expand airport capacity. In fact, instead, the proceeds have been permitted to accumulate, to the tune of $5.7 billion in 1987, in the Airports and Airways Trust Fund. This does not mean that airline passengers have on balance been helping to reduce the federal budget deficit: total federal outlays in support of aviation have regularly exceeded revenues from these taxes. It does mean, however, that the capacity of airports and airways has been expanded far less than travelers have been paying for or, more important, would be willing to pay for under a rational system of user fees for services rendered.

It is the responsibility of the federal government to ensure that staffing of the FAA is adequate to monitor airline safety practices and to maintain the air traffic control system. The FAA has until very recently claimed it did not need to rehire any of the air traffic controllers who struck back in 1981 and have been locked out since. Yet mysteriously, in 1987, as public and congressional outrage over traffic delays mounted, the FAA suddenly discovered it needed 955 more controllers.

Equally crying out for reform are the relations between the traffic controllers and management, which a panel of consultants told the DOT years ago were worse than in any other industry in their experience. Working conditions for traffic controllers are also deplorable. If ever a union was needed, it is here.

Returning to elementary economic principles, the other reason there is excess demand for takeoff and landing slots and excessive congestion at certain times and airports is that these facilities are underpriced. The obvious solution is to auction off those valuable rights, or raise landing fees to whatever extent necessary to limit demand to the available supply. The landing fee for private planes at Washington National Airport ranges from $3 to $10, depending on the weight of the plane. Under a free market, those fees would be set at thousands of dollars, which might translate into, say, $50 increases in ticket prices. Then travelers to whom it was very important to take off and land at peak times and places would be able to get the delay-free service they paid for. The millions of dollars of additional airport revenues could be used to expand capacity and to subsidize negative landing fees at off-peak times or at feeder airports. Price-conscious travelers would thus be induced voluntarily to travel at off-peak times to take advantage of the bargains this would make available to them.

These are not the only ways in which government derelictions bear a heavy responsibility for the problems that beset air travelers these days. When we deregulated the industry, our notion was that protection of the traveling public (apart from safety) could be entrusted to competition; this meant we expected airlines to be treated like other competitive industries. That meant, among other things, that the industry would be fully subject to antitrust laws. Instead, approval or disapproval of mergers was transferred to the DOT. In three major cases the DOT, overriding objections by the Antitrust Division of the Department of Justice, approved mergers—United's acquisition of the transpacific assets of Pan Am, Northwest-Republic, and TWA-Ozark—that, whatever else might be said about them, clearly involved significant suppressions of competition.

Finally, and similarly, we certainly never intended the federal government to get out of the business of protecting consumers from deception, violations of implied contracts, and the like, such as the Federal Trade Commission is supposed to administer in industry generally. When a person is denied a reserved seat because an airline has overbooked, taking his or her reservation is a deception and bumping a violation of a contract. That is why the CAB under my chairmanship, while in the process of deregulating, nevertheless instituted the bumping rules that require airlines to find volunteers to give up their seats on overbooked flights. Similarly, it is, or should be, a violation of contract to cancel a flight for economic reasons or lose a passenger's baggage. If the Reagan administration believed in consumer protections or the antitrust laws, a great deal of the basis for the consumer complaints would disappear.

Nothing is going to discredit a free market, or deregulation, or competition more quickly than failure on the part of the government to fulfill its proper responsibilities. These include, in this case, providing adequate airport and traffic control capacity, adequate enforcement of safety, correct pricing of airport slots, enforcement of the antitrust laws, and consumer protection.

Airline deregulation has been a great success. The solution to most of the problems that have accompanied it is not to reregulate but for the government to fulfill the responsibilities we never intended it to abandon.

The Airlines: On Track or Off Course?

Robert L. Crandall

Finding new ways for labor, management, and government to work together creatively is the single most pressing challenge facing the airline industry. Indeed, it may well be the most pressing economic challenge facing the country. It is hard to think of any industry in the United States whose leaders—management and labor alike—have not expressed concern about competitiveness, productivity, and job security. In every corner of the country, concern is mounting about America's ongoing ability to provide good jobs and a rising standard of living in an ever-tougher world marketplace. Has our nation lost the ability to produce good products, high-quality services, and secure jobs? My answer is no. But to meet the economic challenges before us requires the best efforts of all those involved—labor, management, and government. Above all, it requires a new spirit of active cooperation and a willingness to change old ways of thinking.

After forty years on a carefully regulated course, the airline industry is in unexplored territory in which the charts and compass headings of the past are no longer adequate, especially with regard to labor-management relations. We have heard a lot about the changes deregulation has caused—the hub-and-spoke system, the volatile price structures, the frequent-flyer programs, the distribution upheavals, the computerized reservations systems. Unfortunately, we have heard far too little about the most profound change of all: the impact of deregulation on the *people* who work for our nation's airlines and on whom the public depends for the high service standards that have been the hallmark of America's commercial aviation industry.

During the years of regulation, the pay and benefits of airline employees were essentially the same at all carriers. Fares, routes, and economic opportunities were controlled; thus there was little incentive for any carrier to risk a costly strike by defying union demands and equally little incentive for union leadership to experiment with more cost-effective contracts. Meanwhile, the government showed little interest in rising labor costs and allowed them to be recovered through higher and higher fares. As a result, the industry simply did not focus on labor productivity. As new fuel-efficient aircraft replaced older models, the industry had the benefit of an automatic cost-control mechanism, which made it seem unnecessary for airline managements to think very hard about how to use their *human* resources more efficiently and thereby maximize productivity and minimize costs. Organized labor likewise ignored the danger that lurked in such an attitude. Like shoppers blithely running up huge credit card bills, both labor and management put off the day of reckoning. Meanwhile, air travel became less attractive to consumers, who increasingly used their discretionary dollars on purchases such as campers, automobile trips, and electronic gadgetry.

Then came deregulation. The delusions of regulation—that neither rising costs nor declining productivity were subjects about which airline management or labor should be concerned—were shattered once and for all.

New and reborn low-cost carriers raised the banner of "friend of the consumer" and, sheltered by the cost advantages airlines such as American had given them, started taking away customers. From the standpoint of cost, deregulation certainly has been pro-consumer. The quality of service has clearly suffered, however, and deregulation has proved to be far more anti-labor—anti-people—than most of its advocates had anticipated. A disturbing trade off occurred. Passengers won low fares, but a substantial part of their gain came at the expense of airline employees.

There was—and is—nothing evil about controlling costs. Indeed, *not* doing so during the years of regulation was a grave mistake. But after deregulation removed the old restraints on competition, some airlines went far beyond the bounds of cost control. They tried to make up for a range of corporate ills, including those attributable to poor management decisions, such as bad route selections, unwise choices in aircraft, ill-advised acquisitions, and shortsighted deferrals of pension plan contributions. Cost control was often little more than a scam, a way to justify slashing ticket prices and jumping to the head of the line, all under the "pro-consumer" banner. The result was, and continues to be, anything *but* "pro-consumer." Today, an industry long known for excellent service is the subject of daily headlines criticizing its service for failing.

Need for Labor-Management Cooperation

What can be done? To begin with, those who deplore the state of the airline industry—management and labor alike—must recognize one another's essential interests and work together to build cost-effective competitors without imposing undue hardship on either stockholders or employees. Samuel Gompers stated it well when he said that "the worst crime against working people is a company that fails to operate at a profit." Gompers would have understood that in a capital-intensive business such as the airlines, employees' individual opportunities depend on their company's ability to grow and be profitable. Without profitability and growth, there simply cannot be promotions, raises, or job stability for employees or, for that matter, high-quality service for customers.

Management, for its part, must recognize that labor has a powerful interest in maintaining income, benefits, and job security. Managers must understand that the periodic layoffs of days past are no longer acceptable and that substantial cuts in either income or benefits simply cannot be tolerated by employees who have built life-styles and undertaken obligations on the basis of their current salaries. Management must also recognize that the active participation and full commitment of every employee is essential for success in a service industry. Finally, management must acknowledge that, in return for commitment and participation, employees are entitled to a share of any earnings in excess of what is needed to provide an adequate return on capital. Maximizing profits goes hand in hand with maximizing commitment.

Labor, for its part, must recognize that an industry dominated by fierce competition cannot afford wasteful, job-creating work rules, above-market pay levels, and extraordinary benefits. Labor must recognize that it cannot thwart the marketplace and that its interests, like those of management, can be served only by a company in which everyone works together to create a more positive work environment *and* steadily growing profitability. A Wall Street saying applies here to management and labor in the airlines: "There's room for bulls and room for bears, but there's no room for pigs." In today's competitive airline industry neither management nor labor is likely to satisfy all its desires. Each must see that a problem facing the company threatens both.

At American, a growth plan was developed in 1984 to bring costs gradually down to more competitive levels without adversely affecting the airline's employees. As American's operations have expanded, the airline's unit costs have declined, largely as a result of the addition of fuel-efficient aircraft and the hiring of thousands of new employees at market rates.

American's starting wage rates are lower than what the airline paid during the years of regulation and may appear at first glance to be similar to those of the low-cost carriers. When the total wage and benefit package is considered, however, it compares very favorably with those of companies in other industries and is far better than those of the truly low-cost carriers.

American's growth plan could never have been launched without the cooperation of the airline's employees and unions. Employees were promised there would be no layoffs, no wage reductions, and no benefit cuts. A large proportion of the employees were given lifetime job security, and a corporationwide profit-sharing plan was established. In return, they agreed to the hiring of new employees at market rates and to broad improvements in productivity. Time has proven the wisdom of these agreements. The market-rate approach has been far better for everyone—management and labor alike—than the cutbacks, freezes, bankruptcies, and disruptive mergers so common in the industry. Still, a few union officials have not been able to resist taking potshots at what they insist on calling the "two-tier" pay scale. It is not "two tier" at all but simply a system in which entry-level employees are hired at market rates and work their way through a longer seniority ladder than existed in the past. The alternative would be to cut everyone's wages and benefits to a single competitive level.

Unless the operating costs of competitive carriers are forced up by the marketplace, including the forces of unionism, airlines such as American will have no choice but to reduce their costs to competitive levels. Companies like American could get by temporarily with superior service and top-notch marketing, but in the long run, cost parity—or near parity—is essential.

Need for Government Involvement

As labor and management learn to cooperate, another change, an external one, has to occur. The airlines must focus the attention of government and other third-party policy makers on the reality of airline labor relationships and on the hardships some employees have suffered. Bad decisions by the federal government have permitted a range of unsavory labor tactics. Examples include the following:

■ Today's largest airline, Texas Air, began its ascension by taking advantage of a loosely written bankruptcy law. During a single weekend, Texas Air slashed the pay and benefits of its employees by 50 percent.

■ For several years, the DOT's primary determinant in awarding carriers new international routes has been a carrier's willingness to promise low fares. That is how Continental persuaded the government to reassign the Texas-to-Calgary route from American to itself. But when fuel prices subsequently fell, ticket prices on the route did not. In fact, fares rose by 70 percent! Moreover, Continental failed to deliver the service to Edmonton it had promised as part of its plan for the route. Government policy thus took jobs away from American's employees and handed them over to a low-cost carrier paying submarket wages while simultaneously denying consumers American's superior service. In 1987, the DOT's public counsel and an administrative law judge recommended taking a Seattle–Tokyo route away from United and giving it to Continental, based in part on the promise of low fares. The quality of the service to be provided by the recommended carrier was not discussed at all.

■ The NMB has been unwilling to enforce the single-employer rule that the Railway Labor Act clearly mandates. Hence, when Texas

Air was about to take over Eastern in 1987, it told Eastern's employees that it would transfer Eastern's assets to another operating company unless the employees accepted enormous wage and benefit reductions.

The government should stop awarding international routes purely on the basis of an airline's promise of low fares. Such decisions should be made instead on the basis of a carrier's ability to use a route to contribute to the country's balance of payments, on conformance with generally accepted standards of labor relations, and on the total price/quality composite of each applicant's service.

Furthermore, government should wake up to the terrible inequities in benefit programs for airline employees. Medical costs in the United States are escalating, and protection from the risk of medical catastrophe—one of the primary benefits most companies provide for their employees—has become an enormous financial obligation. In 1987, for example, American spent around $1,666 on medical benefits per employee (excluding retirees), a total of more than $80 million. Employers across the country are very concerned about medical costs, and unless some mandatory coverage is required, it is likely that an increasing percentage of workers in the United States, including airline workers, will end up with substantially less medical coverage than they have today—or, in some cases, with none at all.

Medical coverage for retirees is potentially an even more serious problem. In 1986, American spent $16 million to provide medical benefits for retired employees. By 1996, we expect that figure to exceed $100 million annually. Yet Continental provides no medical benefits for retirees and little medical coverage for its active employees. Hence Continental enjoys a substantial cost advantage over American and most other carriers, and that advantage will grow as more and more of the employees at companies such as American retire.

Either all airlines must offer medical coverage approximating the industry norm, or, eventually, carriers such as American, which offers far more coverage than its low-cost competitors, will have no choice but to withdraw it. American does not want to withdraw it and therefore supports the idea that every business should offer at least a minimum level of health insurance to workers and dependents.

To cite another example, the Pension Benefit Guaranty Corporation, a government agency, requires that every corporate pension sponsor, including American, pay substantial premiums (in American's case, a million dollars annually) to cover the employees of companies that fail to fund their pension plans adequately. A far better solution would be to require adequate funding for all. Moreover, the fact that companies such as Continental, which offer *no* pension plans, are not required to participate is outrageous.

All these issues are examples of matters on which labor and management need to work together to protect their essential interests. Labor backs higher insurance premiums to cover the liabilities of underfunded pension plans. But in so doing it is jeopardizing its own interests. By bringing pressure on responsible companies to pay insurance premiums to cover irresponsible ones, labor creates a strong incentive for responsible companies to discontinue pension plans altogether.

It is hard to understand how pension plans become underfunded in the first place. Pension programs are covered by the Employee Retirement Income Security Act (ERISA), administered by the Internal Revenue Service (IRS). In effect, no company can fail to make required contributions unless it gets a waiver from the IRS. Yet, a few years ago, the IRS granted Braniff just such a waiver despite protests from many of its competitors, including American. The waiver did not save Braniff, it simply deprived Braniff's employees of the protection they thought they had. A company that cannot fund its pension plans is *already* broke, and it is a delusion to pretend otherwise. It is a disservice to the investing public, to labor, and to competitive corporations to expect others to fund the shortfall. As a matter of public policy, it is shortsighted, as well as just plain wrong, for government to allow or encourage a company to sacrifice its employees' financial security for competitive advantage.

Companies that behave irresponsibly are playing a risky game. There is clear evidence that employees perform in direct response to the way they are treated. During the first three months of 1987, for example, Continental experienced eight times more complaints per hundred thousand customers than American. But even the risk of losing business will not dissuade some companies; they will still act irresponsibly. Hence, it is time for labor, management, and government to join forces in making it clear that our society will no longer tolerate an airline, or, for that matter, any company, abusing its employees as a way of beating the competition. Government cannot be expected to mandate wage rates or dictate the fine details of employee benefits. But it should be expected to fashion a basic set of ground rules—including rules covering medical plans, pensions, and labor practices—within which management and labor can negotiate wage and benefit packages tailored to each company's needs and capabilities.

Labor and management must become more effective educators and lobbyists because certain problems can be solved only with government help, even in a deregulated environment. They must also become more willing to take risks, to be innovative, and to avoid the conflicts of the past. Finally, they must become more creative in solving our mutual problems.

Are Cooperative Labor Relations Possible? An Industry Perspective

Bruce R. LeMar

My perspective on labor relations in the airline industry has been shaped by some nine years at carriers formed considerably before deregulation, but also by some two years at the original new-entrant carrier, Midway. Midway was the first carrier ever formed as an all-jet carrier and the first certificated part 121 passenger carrier to begin operations following the enactment of the Airline Deregulation Act. The airline began service in November 1979 and currently flies thirty-four DC–9 and 737 aircraft in a route structure that goes as far south as St. Thomas and St. Croix, as far north as Minneapolis, as far east as Boston, and as far west as Las Vegas. Its hub is Chicago's Midway Airport.

At the end of 1986, Midway Airlines had more than $260 million in business and more than $9 million in profit, with a forecast of 25 percent growth for 1987. Part of that growth stemmed from Midway's acquisition of certain assets and employees from the bankruptcy estate of Air Florida Systems.

By 1985, Midway was operating two separate systems: Midway Airlines, Inc., where the pilots were represented by ALPA, and Midway Express, which was operated by Air Florida employees under a contract with the bankruptcy estate of Air Florida. There was considerable suspicion and hostility between the two employee groups of both carriers and apprehension among the former Air Florida employees about what would happen in July 1985 when Midway acquired the assets of Air Florida and brought the employees in as members of the Midway organization. That July, with the formation of a wholly owned subsidiary called Midway Airlines (1984), Inc., feelings that had been talked about privately by employees became topics of open discussion between employees and management.

Having witnessed the bitterness of seniority integration between the pilot groups at National and Pan Am during their merger in 1979 and at Texas International and Continental in 1983, I suggested to the other members of upper management at Midway that the two pilot groups should become actively involved in establishing the seniority list. Beginning in late August 1985, Midway began what many airlines would deem to be a foolhardy approach. Unlike most mergers in the airline industry, in which management has effectively said to employees, "We will agree to any seniority arrangement provided that it does not create an undue economic impact on the organization," Midway's management opted to get right in the middle. For the next six months I served as moderator and mediator for the two pilot groups, who recognized that they might be able to do as good a job as an arbitrator in coming up with a single seniority list for Midway's three hundred pilots.

The agreement that was ultimately negotiated was satisfactory to both pilot groups and ensured the continued growth of Midway at a level the company could afford. As part of that agreement, Midway pilots were ensured expedited negotiations for a single working agreement that would pertain to all pilots as long as the corporation continued to hold an airline subsidiary. The agreement also contained a provision for a standing committee composed of pilots and management for the express purpose of saving Midway $100,000 annually.

Midway's relationship with its pilots and ALPA is as cooperative as any in the industry. The mutual efforts of labor and management have permitted everyone to focus on competing with other airlines instead of fighting each other.

There is no certain formula for cooperative labor relations under deregulation, nor is there a single carrier that can be held out as a role model. There are, however, numerous examples of cooperative relationships. To the extent that cooperation implies mutual respect and common interests, however, several airlines—Piedmont, Delta, USAir, and Midway, among them—have such relationships of long standing.

Essential Elements of a Cooperative Relationship

Airlines that have cooperative labor-management relationships share certain common elements. First, there is honesty in the relationship. There are no excuses for surreptitious behavior or hesitation to share accurate information and intent, even when the news is bad.

Second, there is a willingness to communicate not only with the labor representatives of the employees but with the employees themselves. Too often, communication occurs only in times of crisis. Communication of bad news occurs only when management is indulging in concession bargaining and when management perceives that the only way to gain employees' cooperation is by creating an atmosphere of hysteria. Management needs to communicate on a steady basis, whether the news is good or bad.

Third, there is a recognition that the labor-management relationship is a long-term one that cannot be managed for the short term. Too often, one party, if not both, fails to remember that each side pays in negotiations for any inadequacies in the administration of the contract and that if contracts are administered in an adversarial climate, cooperative negotiations will be impossible.

There is nothing to suggest that the airline industry will be any less turbulent or competitive in the future than it is today. Those who have experience in managing an airline like a business and not a utility have already discovered that the alliance of employee and management interests is a very potent combination for success.

Are Cooperative Labor Relations Possible? A Union Perspective

Susan Bianchi-Sand

Deregulation of any industry has proven to be an acid test for labor-management relations. The stress from deregulation in the airline industry is evident whether one is a CEO, a flight attendant, or a passenger. Deregulation was supposed to provide a free marketplace for the airlines, competitive prices, and better service for the flying public. The actual results have been a volatile marketplace, job loss and lower wages for all airline employees, a decline in passenger safety and service, and jittery airline executives waiting for the ax to fall. Are cooperative labor-management relations possible in such a chaotic atmosphere? Only if management is prepared to take labor concerns seriously instead of engaging in power bargaining, and only if this cooperation is not regarded as capitulation.

The Imbalance of Power

As Flying Tiger and Midway illustrate, one of the labor problems deregulation has created is an imbalance of power in the industry. In 1986, during negotiations with ALPA and AFA, the Board of Directors of Flying Tiger decided to cease operations and liquidate the company's assets. The company was losing money, and a great deal of the blame was put on high labor costs. Because AFA wanted to save the flight attendants' jobs at Flying Tiger, it agreed to conces-

361

sions in both pay and work rules, which prevented the airline from shutting down.

At Midway, there are two separate operations, each with different labor conditions and each pitted against the other. Midway, Northern Division, was the original airline. Later, Air Florida was purchased and became Midway, Southern Division, which is the airline AFA represents. In 1987, the nonunionized Northern Division flight attendants were given bonuses that AFA members in the Southern Division were not offered. Furthermore, during training class for flight attendants in the Southern Division, it was pointed out that the union wages negotiated by AFA's predecessor (Air Florida Independent Flight Attendants Association) were lower than those paid at the nonunionized counterpart. (The Northern Division flight attendants missed voting in AFA by six votes in 1986.) Moreover, flight attendants in the Northern Division were threatened with loss of seniority if they demonstrated support for a union.

Management sets the tone for all collective bargaining in the airlines by contending that the competitive marketplace forces them to cut wages and benefits and to demand that hard-won work rules go by the wayside. Deregulation has given management the power to win many of its demands. Union concessions may temporarily create a profit for the owners, but they do not build a healthy company or a healthy airline industry for the nation. To do that requires well-maintained aircraft, well-trained and experienced personnel, and adequate management support.

The system of power bargaining that the airlines foster is one AFA and other flight attendants' unions will fight with all their energy, and one they will successfully resist. As the following examples illustrate, one way this power bargaining is used is to treat groups of employees unequitably. At American, flight attendants are working without a contract, and at Continental, flight attendants are on a four-year pay scale and cannot earn more than approximately $18,000 a year no matter how long they work for the company. At the same two airlines, however, pilots have received raises or pay incentives because of the pilot shortage. This disparity of treatment underscores that it is easier to hire flight attendants than pilots. It says to the flight attendants that they are dispensable and unimportant. Such a policy does not build cooperative labor relations.

The same forces are at work in determining whether employees will share in the management or ownership of the airline. So far only airlines in serious financial difficulty have been interested in having employees on the boards of directors or in their voting stock. When the airlines begin making money again, they quickly try to jettison the excess baggage. At Western, the union members have been removed from the board since Western's merger with Delta in 1987, and at Republic, employees were bought out of their voting shares the same year.

Elements of a Cooperative Labor-Management Relationship

Some airlines do run counter to this trend. These carriers are still operating with preregulation values. At Hawaiian and USAir, for example, AFA contract negotiations went without a hitch in 1987 because both airlines recognized the dignity of the flight attendants and their need to establish themselves as experienced, essential members of the flying team. Further, cooperative negotiations occurred at Hawaiian even though the airline had been on the verge of financial failure and had even shut down operations for a day. These airlines also recognized the relationship between employees' and passengers' satisfaction. A look at the list of airlines with the fewest complaints discloses that Hawaiian and USAir are at the top. Conversely, the airlines with the most passenger complaints are the ones troubled with poor labor relations and poor airline service.

AFA members have long demonstrated that if airline management wants a stable industry based on reasonable fares and an experienced work force, they can get the job done. When management agrees that a unionized work force may result in higher wages but also a more productive and experienced work force, cooperative labor relations can begin. Whenever AFA is at the bargaining table, it does what it can to help maintain an airline's stability and growth. AFA has consistently been a knowledgeable and reasonable union. In return, it expects similar support from management, including respect for seniority issues when a merger occurs; jobs for those who want to work until retirement age; and respect for the union as the spokesperson for all employees, not just as a special-interest group. There is no easy way to achieve cooperative labor-management relations, but the first step is to look at the areas in which both groups' interests coincide.

What Lies Ahead for Labor?

William W. Winpisinger

When legislation to deregulate the air transport industry was before Congress, the International Association of Machinists and Aerospace Workers led the opposition to it. It did so for a number of reasons.

Safety Concerns

The IAM maintained that deregulation would lead to increased safety hazards and problems, and it has. In 1987, there were 30 percent more aircraft to service than in preregulation days. The number of flights during the 1980–84 heyday of deregulation skyrocketed. Yet money spent by carriers for maintenance in that same period declined from 8.85 percent to 7.6 percent of the carriers' budgets. Reorganization into the hub-and-spoke system has meant fewer mechanics and less servicing for more planes, under tighter scheduling. The hub-and-spoke system has also meant little or no maintenance or repairs at away-from-hub bases. Yet the FAA, eager to show its faith in the deregulated system, reduced its inspection force on the notion that carriers would police themselves.

As a result, the number of aircraft fires increased; the number of accidents caused by metal fatigue and corrosion increased by 17.3 percent that year as flight time doubled before safety inspections were made. Between 1974 and 1978, only 16.6 percent of aircraft involved in accidents caused by metal fatigue had more than thirty thousand hours flying time. In the five years that followed, after deregulation, 66.7 percent had more than thirty thousand hours flying time. That is significant because 25 percent of the prederegulation accidents (1974–78) involved aircraft with more than thirty thousand hours flying time, whereas five years after deregulation 41.9 percent of the aircraft involved in accidents had more than thirty thousand hours.

Before deregulation, inadequate maintenance and inspections were cited as a contributing cause in only 28.5 percent of accidents. After deregulation, inadequate maintenance and inspections were cited as a contributing cause in 35.6 percent.

The total safety picture, including the dangers from the chaotic air traffic control system, gives Congress ample reason to legislate inspection, maintenance, and other safety measures. Without such measures, air passengers will be seriously at risk.

IAM mechanics and service people can resist pressures by carriers to speed up or neglect maintenance and safety checks because they have collective bargaining contracts that protect them from unreasonable demands and harassment. Nonunion maintenance and service personnel, however, are vulnerable to such job pressures. If they want to resist demands to short-circuit safety, they have no recourse but to quit.

Loss of Service

When deregulation was still in the discussion stage, the IAM predicted it would result in loss of service to medium, rural, and small communities. That is exactly what has happened. By the end of 1986, 465 cities had lost service in weekly departures or available seats. Some 150 communities have lost service altogether.

Senate Majority Leader Robert Byrd (D-West Virginia) has felt firsthand the drastic curtailment of service in his own state. He told the *Los Angeles Times* in a 1986 interview, "Now [after deregulation] if you want to go to West Virginia . . . you have to give two days [for such a trip]."[1]

The IAM also predicted that there would be a marked decline in

---

1. Dallos & May, *Debate Still Rages over Deregulation*, L.A. Times, Nov. 2, 1986, at 1.

the quality of airline service. No one disputes that today. During the first six months of 1986, an average of 1,050 daily delays were recorded nationally, compared with an average of 914 daily delays during the first six months of 1985.

Not surprisingly, most consumer complaints are lodged against those carriers with Rambo-style chief executives and managers. Continental, Eastern, and TWA ranked first, second, and third, respectively, in complaints per passenger miles in May 1987. Compared with May 1986, the number of complaints increased sevenfold against Continental (from 3 to 21 per 100,000 passengers); fivefold against Eastern (from 2.5 to 10 complaints per 100,000 passengers); and twofold against TWA. No wonder Representative Guy Molinari (R-New York) said that passengers on upstart and no-frill airlines are "treated like a herd of cattle."[2]

In 1987, Continental was fined $250,000 for violating consumer protections. That is the first enforcement of consumer rights since the CAB was eliminated. Not surprisingly, the Aviation Consumer Action Project says that Continental is "head and shoulders" ahead of other carriers in passenger complaints.

Nowhere is there evidence of the improved service that was promised by deregulation enthusiasts. Quite the opposite. The IAM warned that air fares would be lower only temporarily and that service would be compromised to achieve them.

In 1987, TWA and Texas Air made that prophecy come true by announcing "fuel surcharge" rate increases. It is ludicrous to think that TWA and Texas Air were not already recovering their fuel costs. Hence the term "surcharge": a charge on top of a charge.

If the entire airline industry were to adopt the TWA–Texas Air rate increases, it would cost air passengers an additional $2.6 billion over a year's time. The TWA–Texas Air increases would mean a 20 percent increase in fares from Los Angeles to New York; a 10 percent increase in fares from New York to Chicago; a 53 percent increase in fares from San Francisco to Los Angeles; a 56 percent increase in fares from Houston to Chicago; and a 43 percent increase in fares from New York to Miami.[3]

---

2. *It's Your Business: Air Travel Mess—Temporary or Permanent* (U.S. Chamber of Commerce television broadcast, Jan. 31, 1987) (transcript at 6).

3. Thomas, *Summer Climb: Texas Air Fuels Latest Round of Fare Increases*, Wall St. J., June 9, 1987, at 37.

Neither TWA nor Texas Air has decided if it is going to level with the public and tell the truth about those "surcharges," or even whether they will announce them in their published fares. Even without the "surcharge," full-fare levels increased 153 percent from 1980 to 1987, whereas the inflation rate rose only 67 percent. So much for "competitive fares."

Greater Monopoly

In 1977, the IAM said deregulation would result in greater monopoly, not greater competition. After all the bankruptcies, mergers, route swaps, greenmail, and hostile takeovers since deregulation, six mega-carriers have a lock on nearly 90 percent of the passenger business. At fifteen of the nation's hub airports, either half the passenger traffic is dominated by one airline or two share more than 70 percent.[4]

Is the deregulation party over? It is for Air Florida, Frontier, New York Air, Ozark, People Express, Republic, and Western, not to mention a score of others that began overnight. They bought a couple of pieces of old and used equipment and got a route approved by the DOT, but they could never get a slot or a gate in the main terminal.

Demoralizing Effect on Employees

Finally, the IAM predicted that the impact of deregulation on air transport workers would be predatory and demoralizing. It was right about that too, but it underestimated the severity. Some twenty-seven thousand IAM members have had their lives and jobs disrupted by mergers, acquisitions, route transfers, bankruptcies, and cost-cutting drives. Some eight thousand airline employees are currently on the streets looking for work. Several thousand more retirees are suffering the anxiety of losing their pensions or having them suspended until their rights are determined in the legal jungle of corporate law.

What lies ahead for labor, management, and the airline industry? The IAM agrees with Robert L. Crandall, chairman and president of American Airlines, who said: "I think it's time for all of us—labor, management, and government—to join forces to make it clear that our

---

4. Kilman, *Growing Giants*, Wall St. J., July 20, 1987, at 1.

society will no longer tolerate an airline—or, for that matter, *any* company—abusing its employees in order to beat the competition."[5]

A sacrificial policy regarding employees is not only bad social policy, it is bad trade union policy. There are certain realities peculiar to each employer, however, that must be faced in each bargaining agreement and contractual relationship. To meet those peculiarities and deviations from industrywide norms, the IAM has had to adopt a flexible attitude. This approach is applied case by case, rather than uniformly across the industry.

IAM's Wage-Investment Policy

One of the most innovative and practical tools the IAM has developed is a wage-investment policy. It is predicated on three principles. First, the employer must really need help and open the company's books to prove it. Second, IAM members must get something of value in return for their wage investment. This entails compensation plus future return on investment, which is negotiable. Although the IAM recognizes the long-term convergence of our members' financial interests with those of shareholders, it is determined not to use its members' jobs and incomes to subsidize the short-term interests of management or of any other investor, employee, or group. All the IAM asks is that its wage-investment policy be a fair quid pro quo for any burdens its members shoulder to keep the carrier flying. Third, the wage investment will be negotiated by the IAM and implemented through the collective bargaining process. When the IAM invokes this policy, it does not want to run the airline, it just wants the airline to run.

There are three notable cases in which the IAM implemented a flexible wage-investment plan. In 1983, Republic came to the IAM with a financial and operating-cost problem, and the IAM negotiated a wage-investment program that involved the IAM giving up some short-term wages in exchange for stock purchases for about 2,500 IAM members and other Republic employees. When Republic and Northwest merged in 1986, the IAM's Republic members shared $33 million, giving them a healthy return on their initial wage investment. The Republic case had a happy landing.

---

5. R.L. Crandall, Chairman and President, American Airlines, Remarks at the Air Transport Labor Relations Conference (June 17, 1987).

The second wage-investment case involved TWA. In April 1985, Carl Icahn, who had just greenmailed his way into the TWA corporate cockpit, asked the IAM for concessions. The IAM offered, and he accepted, a wage-investment package that cost each IAM member $2 per hour, and the IAM gave up TWA's contribution to its supplemental pension plan for three years. The IAM thought it would establish a solid partnership with that good-faith cooperation and flexibility. Alas, all the IAM received in return was confrontation, not cooperation.

The third wage-investment case involved Eastern. Between 1976 and 1986, Eastern employees contributed some $921 million to the carrier. Then in 1986, Texas Air purchased Eastern for $660 million, $260 million *less* than Eastern employees had invested in the company over the previous ten years! In effect, the employees were bilked out of $260,000. For almost any other class of investor, that sale would have been illegal. Wall Street brokers are going to prison for exactly that sort of offense. Needless to say, Eastern employees tried to stop the sale but were unable to do so.

Continental, which is also owned by Texas Air, is now embarking on a union-busting strategy that permits the airline to whipsaw its nonunion employees against the IAM's members at Eastern. This whipsawing tactic is also known as the "single-employer" strategy. It is similar to the double-breasting tactic used by employers in the building and construction trades and should be outlawed. Substandard, substandard, subscale Continental employees are being pitted against the IAM's unionized members at Eastern to force down Eastern employees' wages, hours, and work standards. If this practice spreads throughout the industry, the least common denominator will become the norm.

The lesson to be learned from these three experiences is that when the IAM has worked with good-faith managements, its flexible wage-investment plan has been successful. When management acted in bad faith, there was no way the IAM could cooperate. As one enlightened airline executive noted, "An airline's future should not depend on its ability to take advantage of its employees."[6] The IAM could not agree more.

---

6. C.A. Pasciuto, Vice President, Employee Relations, American Airlines, What's Ahead in the Airline Industry from Management's Viewpoint, Remarks at the NMB Staff Conference (Apr. 28, 1987).

Restoring Excellence to the Airline Industry

Captain Henry A. Duffy

Advocates of deregulation predicted a variety of consumer benefits, including lower fares and improved service. The Air Line Pilots Association, however, correctly predicted some of the costs. In 1976, ALPA outlined many of the negative effects, including the threat of bankruptcy and less secure jobs for airline employees. In a presentation to the National Democratic Platform Committee in 1976, an ALPA representative stated, "Sooner or later the weaker companies will be unable to compete, and will be forced to withdraw from the market, leaving it to the domination of the few."[1]

A Look Back

What has deregulation actually wrought? Economists such as Alfred Kahn, architect of deregulation and former head of the CAB, would say a more efficient airline industry. Kahn measures efficiency in terms of lower fares, improved route systems, innovative marketing strategies, and lower costs. But these so-called efficiencies come at a cost to employees—a great cost: lower salaries, poorer work rules, terminated and underfunded pension plans, low starting pay, and lost jobs. The traveling public has paid the price in reduced safety,

---

1. ALPA, Presentation to the National Democratic Platform Committee, Kansas City, Mo. (Apr. 24, 1976).

lower-quality service (including delays, last-minute cancellations of reservations, and lost luggage), and, in the wake of airline bankruptcies, disrupted travel plans. These costs have more than offset the efficiencies touted by advocates of deregulation.

The industry's turmoil began with poor management decisions to expand unrealistically fast and disastrous fare wars spawned by the new low-cost, low-fare airlines. This situation was compounded by escalating fuel prices, the PATCO strike, and a recession. Although some airlines were able to maintain their profitability, a greater number became mired in red ink. A significant price was paid by the industry as a whole: losses of nearly $1.3 billion between 1981 and 1983. Some airlines paid even greater prices; twenty-four declared bankruptcy during those three years, most notably Braniff and Continental.

Clearly, management in the airline industry was not ready for deregulation. It did not know how to compete, and the consequences were predictable. Employees at airlines with financial problems lost jobs or took pay cuts to keep their airlines viable. During the 1981–82 period, pilots at ten major and national airlines agreed to pay cuts ranging from 6 to 25 percent, with little or no payback. This downward adjustment in wages was accepted by unions to preserve jobs, but adjustment turned to abuse when Continental filed for Chapter 11 and used its bankruptcy to abrogate union contracts. This move produced an instant low-cost airline, as Continental implemented wages on a par with the new entrants. Congress recognized this abuse and corrected the bankruptcy law, but it was too late for Continental employees.

As the economy strengthened and incumbent airlines improved their ability to compete, new entrants began to struggle. Financially healthy airlines embraced the strategy of internal expansion. Again, employees were asked to subsidize these efforts through the adoption of two-tier wage scales. The bitter lessons of the previous few years helped ALPA recognize the importance of more centralized negotiations, and in 1984 it solidified its collective bargaining policies. The B-scale issue became the first major test of these strategies. American ambushed ALPA in 1983 by instituting a *nonmerging* lower tier for determining pilots' pay. Fortunately, the pilot strike at United was successful in reducing the scope of B-scales, and on a national level ALPA has been successful in negotiating agreements that bring B-scale pay to parity within five years.

Current Trends

Industry trends during the late 1980s have blurred what were supposed to be the benefits of deregulation emphasized by Kahn and other advocates. The most glaring example is the trend toward mergers, which has reduced the industry to a handful of mega-carriers. Dominant airlines have used their market power to eliminate most new entrants and seriously inhibit further entry. Many airlines have developed holding companies, some of which have either placed less emphasis on the airline subsidiary or have spun off profitable divisions such as reservations systems, reducing the airline's profitability.

Despite improvements in the financial condition of the industry during the late 1980s, the human costs of deregulation are still evident in lower pay, less job security, and lost jobs. Some airline industry experts have argued that there are *more* jobs for pilots now than ever before as new airlines start up and a few of the largest, most financially secure airlines prosper and grow. This is a callous abuse of statistics. The quantity of jobs *has* increased, the quality of jobs has not.

Most newly hired pilots are on substandard B-scales for their first few years with an airline; they generally are paid less than the industry norm and have fewer fringe benefits. At many established carriers, pensions for pilots are underfunded. At Eastern, working conditions are so poor that pilots with as much as fifteen years of service are going to other airlines to start over—at the bottom of the seniority list.

The human costs of deregulation are also evident in the lower quality of service. Although free-market advocates predicted improved quality, recent events indicate that this has not been achieved.

Another cost of deregulation has been safety. The authors of deregulation did not have the foresight to regulate the industry to prevent unscrupulous managers from compromising airline safety. Airline pilots in particular believe safety has been adversely affected by deregulation. Their concerns are echoed in reports made in 1987 by the General Accounting Office and by the National Transportation Safety Board.

The Future

What about the future? As a union, ALPA expects change to occur primarily in three areas of the industry: capacity, consolidation, and collective bargaining. The capacity of the industry is expected to grow at a steady rate for the foreseeable future. Major and national airlines have a total of 450 aircraft on order for delivery in 1987 and 1988 (nearly 500 were ordered during the previous two years) and more than 900 aircraft on order or option beginning in 1989. The industry's ability to purchase aircraft is meaningless, however, if the problem of airport and airway overcrowding is not addressed by the federal authorities.

As mentioned earlier, one consequence of industry growth is an increased demand for pilots. Expansion since 1984 has pushed the number of pilots who have been hired to record levels. In 1985, major, national, and regional jet airlines hired more than 7,800 pilots, a 43 percent increase over the previous year. In 1986, the market for pilots remained strong; more than 6,300 were hired. The combination of an increase in the number of aircraft deliveries and in the number of pilots who are retiring—expected to rise from less than four hundred in 1987 to more than one thousand in 1992— will require jet airlines to add between four thousand and six thousand pilots to the work force each year through the early 1990s.

Industry expansion and the increased demand for qualified personnel has benefited airline employees, particularly pilots, by reducing the disparity between A- and B-scales. At American alone, the rates of compensation for new hires increased by more than 50 percent from 1983 to 1987. As airlines continue to compete for qualified pilots, rates of compensation for all pilots are likely to increase at a steady pace. ALPA's goals are to eliminate all B-scales and to bring the pay, benefits, and working conditions of all pilots up to the industry standard. Toward these goals, ALPA plans to negotiate more agreements like the one between Pan Am and Pan Am Express, which establishes a rate at which pilots with regional carriers can fill vacancies at the major airline. This approach is likely to become widespread and will thus create a pool of qualified pilots and reduce turnover, as well as training costs, at the regional airlines.

Consolidation has redefined the industry. The number of certificated airlines, which rose from 36 to 123 in the first six years of deregulation, will decline to 73 after all proposed mergers are completed. If intra-Alaskan, intra-Hawaiian, and intra-Caribbean carriers are excluded, the number of airlines operating within the continental United States will decline to thirty-seven. Any further consolidation will focus on the acquisition of code-sharing regionals and, to a lesser degree, smaller national airlines. Major airlines will continue to increase their financial ties to regionals to guarantee a high volume of flights into their hubs. More than 80 percent of regional airlines provide service to major and national airlines under code-sharing agreements. It is likely that eventually most regionals will be partially or fully owned subsidiaries of the majors.

ALPA is seeing the visible benefits of consolidation in greater job stability as well as improved compensation for its pilots. The majority of the airlines surviving this wave of mergers are those that have experienced financial success since deregulation and whose employees have avoided the salary-cutting tactics prevalent at other airlines. Moreover, the merging of operations will increase the pay of employees at the acquired airlines. In six of the seven current airline mergers involving a major airline, pilots at the acquired airline will experience increases in pay averaging more than 30 percent.

Aided by the recent consolidation trend, ALPA is continuing to move toward a more centralized approach to collective bargaining. It will also develop negotiating strategies to limit the ability of management to engage in whipsaw bargaining. In addition, ALPA is continuing to emphasize the importance of organizing pilot groups at all levels. Since deregulation, ALPA has organized twenty-six new carriers into ALPA and plans to organize all commercial pilots, including night package operators and those flying for regionals involved in code-sharing agreements with ALPA airlines.

In response to an increase in anti-union business strategies, ALPA has developed stronger ties with Wall Street investment bankers to avoid bankruptcies and to pursue alternatives such as employee ownership to preserve job security. In 1985, employees at TWA accepted pay and productivity concessions to help TWA president Carl Icahn win the battle against Frank Lorenzo of Texas Air for control of TWA. Currently the employees at United are attempting to purchase the airline to reverse the effects of corporate diversification. In this vein, I predict that airline employees will become more involved in all actions and business decisions that affect their careers.

ALPA is also pressing for labor legislation that would guarantee labor protective provisions for workers who find themselves trapped in a merger. This legislation, which is now in conference, will restore the balance of power between labor and management in collective bargaining.

One of ALPA's greatest concerns is that foreign airlines may be allowed to serve domestic American routes. Alfred Kahn has suggested this as a way to reduce the oligopoly spawned by deregulation. How can United States airlines compete with foreign airlines that are subsidized by their governments? This concept is so abhorrent to the airline pilots of this country that if it is ever adopted, the ultimate protest—a nationwide suspension of service—will be waged.

Profits alone may provide the incentive for airlines to restore high quality and cooperative labor relations. Delta and USAir, two of the industry's most profitable airlines, rank first and second in compensation per employee. Both have conducted tough but fair negotiations with their pilots. Both voluntarily offered their employees LPPs during their 1987 merger, and both were ranked near the bottom in consumer complaints in that year. Coupled with this, American, the airline that introduced the B-scale in 1983 to lower labor costs, in 1987 publicly called for an employee bill of rights to ensure that its employees would be fairly treated. American and a few other airlines are beginning to recognize that motivated employees are the most critical component in a successful operation and that to be successful they must treat their employees fairly.

The airline industry is at a crossroads. The public, the administration, the Congress, and the people within the industry will determine which road is selected. Down one road is deregulation and a continued emphasis on windfall profits at the expense of employees and passengers. Down the other road are continued but more stable profits, cooperative labor-management relations, restored excellence in service and safety, and, essential to any successful operation, employee pride.

Contributors

John B. Adams is the vice president of human resources for Eastern Air Lines. He joined Eastern in 1986 from Continental Airlines, where he was the vice president of personnel. He has also held senior positions at Trans World and Texas International.

Susan Bianchi-Sand is president of the Association of Flight Attendants, which represents twenty-three thousand flight attendants at twelve carriers. She took office in 1987, after serving as its vice president since 1979. She began her career as a flight attendant with United Airlines in 1969 and shortly thereafter became involved in union work.

Michael H. Campbell is an attorney in the Atlanta firm of Ford & Harrison, where he specializes in representing airline management in employment and labor matters.

Peter Cappelli is the Joseph Wharton Associate Professor of Management at the Wharton School. He has written and published widely on labor relations in United States industries, especially the airlines.

James E. Conway is a partner on leave from the law firm of Akin, Gump, Strauss, Hauer & Feld, in Washington, D.C. He is currently the assistant executive director and general counsel of the National Football League Management Council.

Kenneth B. Cooper is the assistant director of the representation department of the Air Line Pilots Association. He was the legal advisor to the ALPA Alcohol Program from 1974 to 1982 and an attorney with the National Labor Relations Board from 1968 to 1972.

Stephen E. Crable is a private attorney and impartial arbitrator and mediator who practices in the Washington, D.C., area. From 1978 to 1987, he worked for the Association of Flight Attendants as an attorney and director of collective bargaining and before that taught and worked as an attorney in Chicago.

Robert L. Crandall is the chairman and chief executive officer of the AMR Corporation and of American Airlines. He joined American in 1973 as senior vice president, finance; became senior vice president, marketing, in 1974; and became president in 1980. He was named chairman and CEO in March 1985.

William J. Curtin is a senior partner and chairman of the Labor and Employment Law Section of Morgan, Lewis & Bockius in Washington, D.C. He has served as the chairman of the American Bar Association's Special Committee on National Strikes in Transportation (1967–70) and of the Labor Relations Committee (1967–82) of the ABA's Public Utility Law Section.

Henry A. Duffy represents forty thousand commercial pilots at forty-three carriers as the president of the Air Line Pilots Association, a position he has held since 1982. A pilot for twenty years with Delta Air Lines, he has been involved in numerous ALPA activities, including negotiating every Delta-ALPA contract from 1970 to 1982.

Terry M. Erskine is the vice president of law and labor relations at Northwest Airlines. He is the chief collective bargaining spokesman for Northwest with unions representing thirty-four thousand employees.

Victoria L. Frankovich is the president of the Independent Federation of Flight Attendants, a position she has held since 1984. She was hired in 1969 by TWA as a "cabin attendant and service manager" and has been active in union work since 1971.

John J. Gallagher is an attorney with Akin, Gump, Strauss, Hauer & Feld, in Washington, D.C., where he is principally involved in labor law and litigation, including representation of clients subject to the Railway Labor Act.

C. Raymond Grebey, Jr., is vice president of human resources for Texas Air. Before joining Texas Air, he was the senior vice president of industrial relations at Pan American World Airways.

Marvin L. Griswold is a principal officer of Local 2707 of the Teamsters Airline, Aerospace and Allied Employees and the director of the Airline Division of the Western Conference of Teamsters. A negotiator for the International Brotherhood of Teamsters Airline Division for twenty-five years, he is also an executive board member of the Joint Council of Teamsters, No. 42.

Joseph Guerrieri, Jr., is a partner in the law firm of Guerrieri Edmond & James. He was the co-chairman from 1982 to 1985 of the Railway and Airline Labor Committee of the Labor and Employment Law Section of the American Bar Association. His firm represents unions in the railway and airline industries.

William N. Hiers, Jr., is an attorney in the Atlanta firm of Ford & Harrison, where he represents airline management in employment and labor matters.

Jalmer D. Johnson is the chief economist and manager of the Economic and Financial Analysis Department of the Air Line Pilots Association. He is responsible for all economic and financial analysis for negotiations, litigation, legislative issues, and ALPA planning.

Alfred E. Kahn is a professor of economics at Cornell University. He was the chairman of the New York Public Service Commission from 1974 to 1977 and chairman of the Civil Aeronautics Board from 1977 to 1978.

Mark L. Kahn is an arbitrator who specializes in airline cases and an emeritus professor at Wayne State University. From 1986 to 1987, he was the president of the Society of Professionals in Dispute Resolution and from 1983 to 1984 the president of the National Academy of Arbitrators.

Wesley Kennedy is an attorney and partner with Cotton, Watt, Jones & King, in Chicago, where his specializations include the representation of airline employees. He has been involved in several airline seniority integration proceedings.

Bruce R. LeMar is the vice president in charge of personnel and administration for Midway Airlines, a position he has held since 1985. From 1978 to 1985, he held various labor and employee relations positions with Texas International and Continental Airlines and before that was a labor relations attorney with Northwest.

William Lurye is an attorney with Gardner, Robein & Henry, in Metairie, Louisiana, representing labor organizations. He served as an attorney with Baptiste & Wilder, P.C., in Washington, D.C., from 1986 to 1987, also representing labor organizations, and earlier as an attorney in the NLRB's Office of General Counsel both in Washington and New Orleans.

Jean T. McKelvey is an emeritus professor in the New York State School of Industrial and Labor Relations at Cornell University and coordinator of off-campus graduate credit programs. A widely recognized authority on labor relations, she is an arbitrator for many airlines and serves on the Federal Service Impasses Panel and the Public Review Board of the United Automobile Workers.

Thomas R. Miller is the managing director of employee relations for American Airlines in Dallas–Ft. Worth. Before joining American in 1980, he was a labor relations attorney for National Airlines in Miami.

Robert H. Nichols is an attorney and partner with Cotton, Watt, Jones & King, in Chicago, where his specializations include the representation of airline employees and serving as general counsel for the Air Line Employees' Association. He has been involved in many airline seniority integration proceedings.

Susan M. Oliver is employee relations counsel for American Airlines in Dallas–Ft. Worth. Before joining American in 1986, she was assistant counsel for Wien Airlines in Anchorage. Before that she was in private practice with the labor law firm of Stettner, Miller & Cohen in Denver.

Charles M. Rehmus is an arbitrator who specializes in airline cases. He was the dean of the New York State School of Industrial and Labor Relations at Cornell University from 1980 to 1985 and the chairman of the Michigan Employment Relations Commission from 1976 to 1980. He is the author of many books and articles, including *The Railway Labor Act at Fifty*.

Seth D. Rosen is the director of representation for the Air Line Pilots Association. Before joining ALPA in 1971, Rosen was on the staff of the National Labor Relations Board (1966–71). His current responsibilities include overseeing negotiations, FAA matters, arbitration, research, and organizing for ALPA.

William L. Scheri is the airline coordinator for the International Association of Machinists and Aerospace Workers, a position he has held since 1980. Previously, he held various IAM positions, including assistant airline coordinator and general chairman for District Lodges 141 and 147.

Asher W. Schwartz is a partner with O'Donnell & Schwartz, where he is the general counsel to the Transport Workers Union of America, the American Postal Workers Union, the Flight Engineers International Association, and various local unions.

Martin C. Seham is a partner in Seham, Klein & Zelman, where he specializes in labor relations law. He is general counsel to the Allied Pilots Association and labor counsel to seven foreign air carriers.

Bonnie Singer is the director of labor relations, in-flight services, for Pan American World Airways. She has been with Pan Am since 1975. Her experience includes advocacy representing management before system and field boards with several unions.

Roland P. Wilder, Jr., is a senior member of Baptiste & Wilder, P.C., in Washington, D.C., representing labor organizations. He served as associate general counsel of the International Brotherhood of Teamsters from 1975 to 1985 and before that as a supervising attorney in the NLRB's Office of General Counsel.

William W. Winpisinger is the international president of the International Association of Machinists and Aerospace Workers, a position he has held since 1977. He has risen within the international organization, with jurisdiction over rail and air, since 1967.

General Index

Cases Cited